Chiefdoms and Chieftaincy in the Americas

Chiefdoms and Chieftaincy in the Americas

Edited by Elsa M. Redmond

Foreword by Neil L. Whitehead

University Press of Florida

Gainesville · Tallahassee · Tampa · Boca Raton

Pensacola · Orlando · Miami · Jacksonville

03 02 01 00 99 98 6 5 4 3 2 1

Library of Congress Cataloging-in-Publication Data

Chiefdoms and chieftaincy in the Americas / edited by Elsa M.
Redmond: foreword by Neil L. Whitehead.
p. cm.
This volume is largely derived from the symposium of the International Congress of Americanists.
Includes bibliographical references and index.
ISBN 0-8130-1620-7 (alk. paper)
1. Indians—Kings and rulers. 2. Chiefdoms—America—History.
3. Indians—Politics and government. 4. America—Antiquities.
I. Redmond, Elsa M. II. International Congress of Americanists.
E59.K56C47 1998
970.01—dc21   98-8522

The University Press of Florida is the scholarly publishing agency
for the State University System of Florida, comprising Florida
A&M University, Florida Atlantic University, Florida International
University, Florida State University, University of Central Florida,
University of Florida, University of North Florida, University of
South Florida, and University of West Florida.

University Press of Florida
15 Northwest 15th Street
Gainesville, FL 32611
http://nersp.nerdc.ufl.edu/~upf

CONTENTS

List of Figures and Tables   vii

Foreword by Neil L. Whitehead   ix

Preface by Elsa M. Redmond   xi

Introduction: The Dynamics of Chieftaincy and the Development of
      Chiefdoms   1
      Elsa M. Redmond

1 What Happened at the Flashpoint? Conjectures on Chiefdom
      Formation at the Very Moment of Conception   18
      Robert L. Carneiro

2 Less than Meets the Eye: Evidence for Protohistoric Chiefdoms in
      Northern New Mexico   43
      Winifred Creamer and Jonathan Haas

3 In War and Peace: Alternative Paths to Centralized Leadership   68
      Elsa M. Redmond

4 Investigating the Development of Venezuelan Chiefdoms   104
      Charles S. Spencer

5 Tupinambá Chiefdoms?   138
      William C. Sturtevant

6 Colonial Chieftains of the Lower Orinoco and Guayana Coast   150
      Neil L. Whitehead

7 War and Theocracy   164
      Pita Kelekna

8 The Muisca: Chiefdoms in Transition   189
      Doris Kurella

9   Social Foundations of Taino *Caciques*   217
    William Keegan, Morgan Maclachlan, and Bryan Byrne

10 Native Chiefdoms and the Exercise of Complexity in Sixteenth-
    Century Florida   245
    Jerald T. Milanich

11 The Evolution of the Powhatan Paramount Chiefdom
    in Virginia   265
    Helen C. Rountree and E. Randolph Turner III

Contributors   297

Index   299

FIGURES AND TABLES

Figures

3.1 Intertribal exchange networks in the Jivaroan area 88

3.2 Hierarchies of Jivaroan shamans 93

3.3 Waiwai village-level administrative hierarchy (after Fock 1963) 98

4.1 Map of Venezuela, showing locations mentioned in the text 111

4.2 Bar graph of settlement sizes, Corozal I phase, Parmana region 112

4.3 Bar graph of settlement sizes, Corozal II phase, Parmana region 112

4.4 Bar graph of settlement sizes, Corozal III phase, Parmana region 113

4.5 Bar graph of settlement sizes, Camoruco I phase, Parmana region 113

4.6 Bar graph of settlement sizes, Camoruco II phase, Parmana region 113

4.7 Bar graph of settlement sizes, Camoruco III phase, Parmana region 113

4.8 Location of the 1983–88 Barinas Project in the western llanos of Venezuela 114

4.9 Settlement patterns for Early Gaván (high llanos) and Early Curbatí (piedmont) phases, A.D. 300–550 117

4.10 Bar graph of site sizes, Early Gaván phase 117

4.11 Settlement patterns of Late Gaván (high llanos) and Late Curbatí (piedmont) phases, A.D. 550–1000 118

4.12 Bar graph of site sizes, Late Gaván phase 118

4.13 Map of the Gaván site (B12) 120

4.14 Area B excavation on the encircling earthwork at the Gaván site 122

4.15 Area A housefloor, Gaván site 123

4.16 Area D housefloor, Gaván site 124

4.17 The Gaván locality 126

8.1 Groups and chiefdoms of the northern Andean region at the time of the Spanish Conquest   190
8.2 Long-distance trade relations of the groups and chiefdoms at conquest   191
8.3 The chiefdoms of the Muisca and their neighboring groups at conquest   193
8.4 Levels of social organization in Muisca society   195
8.5 Muisca ceramic figurine of a cacique   197
8.6 Trade relations of the Muisca   203
9.1 Map of native West Indian peoples in 1492   219
9.2 Matrilineal kinship   224
9.3 Map of the Taino provinces and their caciques on Hispaniola   234
10.1 Florida chiefdoms mentioned in text   251
11.1 The Powhatan chiefdom in 1607   267
11.2 Downstream limits   276
11.3 Indian towns and warrior counts in 1607–8   277
11.4 Core areas of major Late Woodland ceramic types in the Powhatan area   280

Tables

4.1 Late Gaván site sizes   119
4.2 Distribution of *manos* and *metates* in excavation operations at the Gaván site (B12)   121
4.3 Distribution of figurine heads and burned daub at five excavated Late Gaván sites   122

FOREWORD

The original impulse for the symposium of the International Congress of Americanists, from which this volume largely derived, started with conversations between Robert Carneiro and Neil Whitehead as to how the "problem of chiefdoms" might be theoretically advanced. Although we were in agreement as to the importance of several factors in the discussion of this topic, including warfare, colonial invasions, and the utility of the chiefdom concept itself, it was also clear to us that any theoretical refinement had to begin with an integration of archaeological, ethnohistorical, and ethnographic paradigms.

The topic of chiefdoms had been broached before in a symposium of the ICA (see Drennan and Uribe 1987) but from an exclusively archaeological point of view. Building on that symposium, the theoretical work of Carneiro (1981, 1990), and the emergence of detailed ethnohistorical studies in South America, it was proposed to extend the discussion of chiefdoms by the inclusion of data from history and ethnography. We anticipated that the main advantage of this procedure would be to allow discussion of the dynamics of *chieftaincy* as well as the forms and characteristics of chiefdoms. This distinction between chieftaincy and chiefdoms therefore recalls the "structure and agency" debate in anthropology more generally.

The importance of such theoretical distinctions for understanding political evolution is considerable, for there are important differences among the criteria used to identify chiefdoms from archaeological, ethnohistoric, and ethnographic situations. Thus what counts as a chiefdom in the archaeological sense may well exclude from consideration those cases where physical remains are inadequate for, or irrelevant to, the use of this description. However, it is easily demonstrable from the historic or ethnographic record that well-documented or directly observed chieftains do not always leave the kind of physical remains that would induce archaeologists to ascribe chiefdom-level organization.

This contrast may be partly resolved by a more careful consideration of the relation of physical remains to documentary evidence but perhaps also by the recognition of the theoretical distinction between chieftaincy and chiefdoms, as discussed at the symposium. In this way, chieftaincy may be considered a political stratagem that is open to be exercised in many situations (from tribes to states) but that only successfully endures in those situations we call chiefdoms. In order to explain how the ever present ability of individuals to exercise chieftaincy over their fellows is converted into the relatively stable situations that produced archaeological chiefdoms, it will be necessary to consider external factors such as trade, warfare, and physical settings; that is, the nature of circumscription (after Carneiro). At the same time, by focusing on the processual aspects of chieftaincy and not just on the static contexts of chiefdoms, we hope that the vital question of the transition between political forms is made clearer analytically.

The necessity for such a theoretical advance is shown by the continuing controversy over the analytical status of the chiefdom. Is it or is it not a "stage" through which all proto-states must pass? Can chiefdoms be meaningfully distinguished from "colonial tribes" or kingdoms? Do they display structural commonalities as well as evolutionary ones? In sum, the concept of a chiefdom as it has been developed archaeologically benefits from the long time span during which political behaviors are examined; but at the same time the detailed political dynamics described by history and ethnography suggest that there should be either greater discrimination within the general category of chiefdom or a recognition that the archaeological contexts are illustrative and not definitional of the exercise of chieftaincy, both now and in the past.

It was with such perplexities in mind that the original discussion began and to these that the symposium members enthusiastically responded. The results of those discussions, the addition of some new material, and the marvelous efforts of the editor, Elsa Redmond, thus constitute this volume.

Neil L. Whitehead

References

Carneiro, Robert L.
1981 The chiefdom: Precursor of the state. In *The Transition to Statehood in the New World*, edited by G. D. Jones and R. R. Kautz, 37–79. Cambridge: Cambridge University Press.
Drennan, Robert O., and Carlos A. Uribe, eds.
1987 *Chiefdoms in the Americas*. Lanham, Md.: University Press of America.

PREFACE

This volume stems from a symposium that Robert Carneiro and Neil Whitehead organized for the 47th International Congress of Americanists, held at Tulane University in New Orleans in July 1991. Entitled "Chiefdoms and Chieftaincy: An Integration of Archaeological, Ethnohistorical, and Ethnographic Paradigms," the symposium focused on the development of chiefdoms in the Americas by calling for papers from archaeologists and ethnohistorians who have examined these societies as they evolved in pre-Columbian times, and as they were documented by Europeans during the early colonial period. Ethnographic cases of tribal chieftaincies contributed new ground for understanding how the exercise of chieftaincy on the part of achieved leaders among autonomous village societies might relate to—and, under certain favorable conditions, might lay the groundplan for—the institutionalization of permanent, centralized, regional leadership by hereditary chiefs. The participants included Bryan Byrne, Robert Carneiro, Winifred Creamer, Jonathan Haas, Charles Hudson, William Keegan, Pita Kelekna, Morgan Maclachlan, Jerald Milanich, Elsa Redmond, Helen Rountree, Charles Spencer, William Sturtevant, Randolph Turner, and Neil Whitehead.

On the basis of the quality of the symposium papers and the enthusiastic response of the participants and participating members of the audience, Robert Carneiro and Neil Whitehead decided to edit a volume devoted to the dynamics of leadership exhibited by tribal chieftaincies and to the development of chiefdoms. All symposium participants save Charles Hudson contributed final versions of their papers, with additional data and after further reflection on the internal dynamics and external factors affecting a range of South American, circum-Caribbean, and North American societies in pre- and postcontact times. With the intention of sampling further the variability of leadership development among chiefdoms in the

Americas, Robert Carneiro invited Doris Kurella to prepare a paper on the Muisca, whom many consider to have been on the threshold of statehood at the time of European contact.

As the editor of this volume, I wish to thank Robert Carneiro and Neil Whitehead for the opportunity to undertake this responsibility and above all for the enjoyable moments spent spearheading the volume. I also wish to thank Charles Spencer for his help at various stages of the editing process, which was completed in May 1997.

Elsa M. Redmond

The Dynamics of Chieftaincy and the Development of Chiefdoms

Elsa M. Redmond

Chiefdoms are regional polities made up of subordinate villages under the permanent control of a paramount chief. This definition of chiefdoms, according to Robert Carneiro (1981, 45), focuses on the permanent political unification of villages in a region under the centralized leadership of a paramount chief. The paramount chief occupies a formal office at the top of a regional administrative hierarchy of local village chiefs, in a decision-making hierarchy that Gregory Johnson (1982, 396) has termed a "simultaneous hierarchy." Most leadership functions are centralized in that institutionalized, hereditary office of the chief, which exists apart from the individual who occupies it for life, and which in theory will be acceded to by succeeding generations of chiefly officeholders (Flannery 1972, 403). Johnson (1978, 101) has suggested that in order to reduce potential sources of disruption in the intergenerational transfer of chiefly authority, the development of chiefly control-hierarchies is usually accompanied by the development of institutionalized social ranking and status differentiation. Not only do such ascribed status differences legitimize and enhance the chief's effectiveness as the overall decision maker, but they also expedite the recruitment and training of future chiefs, thereby serving to perpetuate the chiefdom (Spencer 1987, 371). Accordingly, "chiefdoms are profoundly inegalitarian" (Service 1971, 140).

Since 1981, when Robert Carneiro (1981, 71) called for the study of chiefdoms from all parts of the world and at all levels of development, an enormous amount of information about chiefdoms—principally ethnohistorical and archaeological—has been collected and made available (Drennan and Uribe 1987, vii). Conferences and symposia have been held to discuss the evolution of chiefdoms (e.g., Earle 1991), the cycling of chiefdoms (e.g., Anderson 1994; Scarry 1996), and their accompanying social inequality (Price and Feinman, 1995). Archaeological investigations of specific prehistoric chiefly political economies (e.g., Blitz 1993; Pauketat 1994; Welch 1991) and ideologies (e.g., Helms 1995) have, just as Carneiro expected, allowed the chiefdom to emerge from the penumbra into the full light.

A number of prehistoric and historic trajectories are examined in this volume devoted to the origins and development of complex chiefly societies in the Americas. The contributors see the utility of considering independent data sets—ethnographic, ethnohistorical, archaeological—as they refine current models of the dynamic processes underlying the emergence of chiefdoms, their growth, and their perpetuation (Spencer, chap. 4; Keegan, Maclachlan, and Byrne, chap. 9; Milanich, chap. 10; Rountree and Turner, chap. 11). Steering away from a reliance upon the evolutionary typologies that have previously dominated most discussions of complex societies, and particularly any discussion of the development of these middle-range societies called chiefdoms, the contributors seek instead to weigh the available and often complementary archaeological, historical, and ethnographic data bearing on the *conditions* favoring the evolution of centralized leadership, the *mechanism* or mechanisms of sociopolitical transformation and reproduction, and the specific *parameters* of these dynamic chiefly systems (Whitehead, chap. 6).

The examination of multiple data sets underscores the growing concern for considering the variability in the structure and extent of leadership development and, in some ethnohistorical cases, specifying the individual agents of change. The fifteenth-, sixteenth-, and seventeenth-century chiefdoms of the lower Orinoco River and Guayana coast (Whitehead, chap. 6), the Altiplano of Bogotá (Kurella, chap. 8), and the temperate coastal plain of Virginia (Rountree and Turner, chap. 11) happen to be ethnohistorically rich but meager from the standpoint of archaeological preservation and recovery. The expansionistic Muisca of Bogotá and the Powhatan paramountcy of Virginia, with its thirty districts, are among the most complex chiefdoms to have emerged in the Americas, yet like the chiefdoms of the lower Orinoco and the Guayana coast, they are incommensurately represented in the archaeological record. Neil Whitehead rightly suggests that neither historical nor archaeological evidence should claim any interpretive priority in our developmental schemes, since they represent only different types of information, not different realities revealed by that information. This point is also raised by William Sturtevant (chap. 5) in his examination of the exceptionally well documented Tupinambá of coastal Brazil in the sixteenth and seventeenth centuries and by Doris Kurella (chap. 8), who critically evaluates the abundant ethnohistorical data pertaining to the paramount chiefdom of Bogotá. In his contribution, Charles Spencer proposes that on the whole, refinements in our models of chiefdom development will require the careful linking of ethnohistoric and ethnographic data concerning chiefdoms with long-term prehistoric trajectories in as many regions as possible (e.g., Drennan 1991; Braun 1990, 72).

The Chieftaincy

This volume addresses the theoretical distinction between the short-term chieftaincy exercised by achieved leaders in autonomous village societies and the permanent regional leadership wielded by the hereditary chief. The chieftaincy is centralized political leadership that operates from time to time among autonomous village societies but that is generally short-lived. An aspiring leader or big man who exercises such leadership can also be called a *chieftain*. Although some may wonder why yet another term must be introduced into the anthropological literature on leadership when we already have the terms *big man* and *headman,* among others, to refer to such achieved leaders in autonomous village societies, *chieftain* designates explicitly the form of centralized leadership that is generally associated with permanent, hereditary chiefs. Also, although the term *chieftain* can be considered synonymous with big man, it is not culture bound in the way that the Melanesian big man is (Strathern 1991, 1). Finally, the term *chieftain* has the advantage of being gender neutral, which is significant inasmuch as it is increasingly being recognized that women can achieve positions of leadership in autonomous village societies (e.g., Howell 1995, 126, 141–45).

The chieftain not only heads his household and leads his faction in a village but in time might also preside over the other factions and member households comprising the village as a whole. Especially in intervillage relations, he might act as the sole village headman or "chief."[1] Through his intervillage alliances, the chieftain can extend his ties beyond the village and achieve considerable prominence in the region, if not outright authority over other villages.

The chieftaincy is a situational hierarchy occurring from time to time among nonhierarchical, uncentralized tribal societies, which, like other small-scale egalitarian societies, exhibit a nested arrangement of consensual decision making that Johnson (1982, 402–3) has designated a "sequential" hierarchy. Consensus is achieved sequentially by the members of households, the heads of households, the heads of lineages, the heads of factions, council of elders, village headmen, and so forth, in ever larger inclusive units, in a protracted, circuitous manner. The centralized and hierarchical structure of the chieftaincy, wherein the chieftain actually wields authority and makes decisions for the entire village and sometimes for other allied villages as well, mimics the simultaneous hierarchy of the chiefdom. Thus, the chieftaincy represents an emergent simultaneous hierarchy in which an achieved leader exercises hierarchically differentiated decision-making functions, albeit on a temporary basis (Johnson 1982, 403–4). Under certain conditions, which are outlined later, the limitations of consensus-based decision making are experienced by autonomous village societies and give way to an emergent simultaneous hierarchy—the chieftaincy.

There are many aspiring leaders in Amazonian societies such as the Akwẽ-Shavante of central Brazil, all vying for *prestige,* or the ability to influence others (Maybury-Lewis 1974, 198). Prestige is acquired through one's success at hunting, prowess as an athlete, talents as an orator, curing and bewitching skills as a shaman, access to trade goods, or exploits in warfare, among many other personal qualities, including charisma. According to David Maybury-Lewis, "a man cannot aspire to the chieftaincy unless he has prestige and once he has achieved that status he can only function as a chief through the exercise of prestige" (Maybury-Lewis 1974, 198). Once he has achieved the status of a big man, headman, or chieftain, he can actually wield *power,* which Maybury-Lewis suggests is based on the support of the followers of his faction but which can emanate from other sources as well (Redmond 1994, 124–25; Carneiro 1981, 61, 63; 1993, 5). As headman or chieftain, then, he has prestige that verges on the power of centralized leadership; or, as Marie Reay characterized power in the case of New Guinea Kuma leadership, he has the "power to make acceptable decisions which either commit the group to certain action in relation to other groups or resolve some conflict within the group itself" (Reay 1959, 113).

Generally the leader wields power in the context of a men's council, at which consensus decisions are reached; he may be overruled in most matters, as in suggesting when the group should move and where or in making ceremonial arrangements, but in matters of life and death that affect the entire community, he often gets his way. Figuratively, the Akwẽ-Shavante leader or chieftain is considered the "father" and "watcher" of the community; he watches over the community, directs people's activities, and looks after their interests (Maybury-Lewis 1974, 190–91).

Not only are there many aspiring leaders, but there is also considerable variability in the forms and extent of achieved leadership in these autonomous village societies. Marshall Sahlins (1963) reduced some of this variability to two sectors or fields of leadership among Melanesian societies: (1) the internal or local, in-group leader of a faction made up of relatives and other followers, designated the "center-man"; and (2) the external "man of renown" whose leadership extends across a broader "tribal galaxy consisting of many similar constellations" (Sahlins 1963, 285, 289–90). Aspiring leaders depend initially on the support of their followers, the members of their faction, but their careers involve widening their field of leadership, amassing a network of additional followers beyond their faction and community, and, in short, "creating supralocal organization" (Sahlins 1963, 292). Accordingly, Spencer (1994, 32–33) has noted that leadership variability ranges from a village where the leaders of several factions compete but none emerges as truly dominant over the others to circumstances in which the leader of the dominant faction assumes centralized authority over the entire village—and sometimes beyond the village, albeit for a short duration. The latter end of the political spectrum is the chieftaincy, which resembles the centralized authority structure of a regional-scale chiefdom but, since it is not institutionalized and made permanent, will eventually dissipate and be supplanted by the ascendancy of another aspiring leader. Spencer proposes that the successful transformation of a temporary chieftaincy into a permanent hereditary chiefdom requires the expansion and regular coordination or articulation of both the internal and external fields of centralized leadership achieved by aspiring leaders among autonomous village societies. The linking of these complementary dimensions of centralized authority involves simply "the regularization of behaviors that occasionally appear within the range of variation exhibited by uncentralized societies" (Spencer 1994, 35).

David Braun has directed our discussion of such leadership variation in nonhierarchical societies by suggesting that we need to distinguish the processes that generate such variation from those that may shape change (Braun 1990, 64). It is from the existing pool of leadership variability, of course, that future generations will adopt their forms of leadership and act upon them. Change comes about when different social practices (namely, forms of leadership) vary in their replicative success under particular socioenvironmental conditions—such as population growth, increasing group size, scalar stress, social and environmental circumscription—or in the face of particular historical circumstances. The form of leadership that offers the greatest selective advantages in terms of material and reproductive benefits to its members will be replicated successfully and will persist

(Braun 1990, 79–80). The hierarchically differentiated decision-making organization characteristic of a chieftaincy emerging from time to time among nonhierarchical societies increases the efficiency and speed with which decisions are made, especially in situations that call for sorting *quickly* through a great quantity and diversity of information. Resolution of conflicts, coordination of tasks, and negotiation of intervillage or external affairs can be expedited by such hierarchical, centralized leadership (Braun 1990, 70).

If the chieftaincy mode of organization confers selective advantages upon its ambitious leader and his followers in the community and the region at large, a chieftaincy will probably experience greater replicative success than will other forms of leadership in spite of the relative loss of freedom of action on the part of followers. If it persists, the chieftaincy might well be poised for permanent institutionalization as a hereditary chiefdom. For the temporary chieftaincy to persist and become a permanent hereditary chiefdom, the benefits of this centralized, hierarchical leadership must greatly outweigh the loss of political autonomy among followers, who in most egalitarian societies resist change and, above all, any social, political, and economic subordination (Braun 1990, 70; Upham 1990, 10). Consequently, in the historical trajectories of egalitarian societies, such "accidents of social change" will not happen very often (Braun 1990, 84–85). We need, then, to determine these historical instances or accidents of social change that allow the chieftaincy to persist. The contributors to this volume address the conditions under which the chieftaincy emerges and consider how this form of centralized leadership exercised episodically by an aspiring tribal leader over a community and sometimes over a region might be transformed and established permanently as a hereditary chiefdom.

The Dynamics of Chieftaincy

Aside from lowland South America and Melanesia, the egalitarian societies of the American Southwest have for long been investigated by ethnographers, ethnohistorians, and archaeologists. The remarkable degree of archaeological preservation in the Southwest and the fine-grained chronological sequences established there by archaeologists are two of the reasons it is possible to investigate the sociopolitical dynamics of its small-scale village societies and to evaluate whether chieftaincies emerged there in prehistoric times (Creamer and Haas, chap. 2; Johnson 1989, 383, 386). To do this, Stephen Plog (1995, 192) has suggested that we need to develop more comprehensive models of the full spectrum of variability apparent in the leadership dynamics of prehistoric Pueblo societies. We need also to expand upon the types of archaeological evidence that have traditionally been used to evaluate models of sociopolitical complexity in the Southwest. Lynne Sebastian's (1991) assessment of the centralized leadership—probably a case of chieftaincy—that emerged in Chaco Canyon in the eleventh century is a good example of what Plog has in mind, in terms of asking the right questions, building a holistic, processual model, and examining multiple data sets. Following Kent Lightfoot's (1984, 22) focus on the conditions that stimulate the initial development of leadership positions and the dynamics of leader-follower relationships in the subsequent expansion of centralized decision-making organizations, Sebastian argues that we can monitor this process archaeologically by examining different kinds of evidence "of *leadership*—evidence of a level of planning and organization and a potential for quick decision making that is beyond the capacity of acephalous societies" (Sebastian 1991, 115).

Accordingly, the investigation of leadership in the archaeological record not only entails the search for "leaders" in mortuary data (e.g., Howell 1995, 1996) but also requires the examination of regional and community-level settlement patterns; of the distribution of utilitarian versus exotic imported material goods therein; and of public works, including the construction of great houses and great kivas, mounds, earthworks, roads, and water-control facilities, which reflect the ability to mobilize and direct massive labor projects (Sebastian 1991, 115–19; Plog 1995, 192–202; see also Hayden 1995, 49–51). However, the very occurrence of such archaeological evidence of a centralized leadership structure, in spite of the selective advantages that its decision-making organization and accompanying social differentiation might offer, does not explain why or how such a structure arises among prehistoric autonomous village societies. As Sebastian points out, "the presence of a leadership structure could have yielded many benefits: subsistence assistance in times of individual domestic failures of production, resolution of disputes, protection from aggression, opportunities to form a wide network of useful alliances, access to a wide range of imported goods. But none of these benefits from an in-place functioning leadership structure can be offered as an explanation of the *origins* of that political phenomenon. Societies do not 'get complex' in order to do any of these things" (Sebastian 1991, 124).

To explain the emergence of chieftaincies, and of fully institutionalized chiefdoms for that matter, we must examine the conditions that favor the development of such centralized leadership and that shape its persistence and change over time. We must also determine the actual mechanisms responsible for this sociopolitical transformation among autonomous village societies. The contributors to this volume present an array of ethnographic, ethnohistorical, and prehistoric examples to this end. Carneiro (chap. 1) maintains that conditions of resource concentration and environmental circumscription promote population pressure, from which chiefdoms evolve from chieftaincies through warfare.[2] Spencer demonstrates that chiefdom development in Venezuela occurred under conditions of environmental and social circumscription, which evidently spurred extensive warfare. William Keegan, Morgan Maclachlan, and Bryan Byrne view the development of ranked avunculocal Taino chiefdoms as a "political machine" that was capable of spurring population growth and higher levels of productivity within the context of resource concentration and environmental and social circumscription. A number of contributors emphasize the importance of external relationships of warfare and trade in the dynamics of chieftaincies (Creamer and Haas, Redmond, Milanich) and in the development of paramount chiefdoms (Kurella, Rountree and Turner). Although some have argued that the arrival of Europeans was responsible for the development of chieftaincies and hereditary chiefdoms in the Americas, Rountree and Turner note that one of the last of America's paramount chiefdoms seems to have arisen in the late sixteenth century largely uninfluenced by the arrival of Europeans. Finally, Sturtevant, Whitehead, and Milanich examine certain historical circumstances, namely warfare and interaction with European colonial powers, that prompted the emergence of chieftaincies, as a response to military threats or to opportunities presented by those historical encounters.

When it comes to elucidating the mechanisms of sociopolitical transformation and change in our models of the dynamics of chieftaincies and the development of chiefdoms, ethnographic data are most useful. With ethnographic data from some twenty New Guinea Highlands societies, Pierre Lemonnier (1990, 144–48, table 3; 1991, 20–27, fig. 1.1) has proposed a hypothetical sequence of leadership forms: from the multiple, achieved leadership roles of great men, who distinguish themselves as great warriors or great shamans or great hunters (Godelier 1986, 80, 96–97, 103–30), to the emergent simultaneous hierarchies of big men, who are in the process of concentrating both the internal and external dimensions of centralized leadership through their competitive feasting and ceremonial exchanges in postpacification times.[3] Big men assume multiple leadership functions in diverse activities—exchanges, warfare, promoting spirit cults, and presiding over diverse ritual activities (Strathern 1970, 571–72, 578, 582). A Kuma "strong man" (big man) who is a leader in any of these spheres of action is a leader in practically every other. Their duties as "first" or "authorized" leaders include giving commands and maintaining law and order in the community, with the help of an assistant. And as leaders to be reckoned with, they are listened to and obeyed by their followers—their "children" (Reay 1959, 113–14, 117). Just as Spencer (1994, 35) has argued, these big men are attempting to preside over most leadership functions, both local community decision making and in the region at large. Moreover, not only is there a concentration of leadership functions in a single "authorized" leader, but in about 64 percent of the cases, his eldest son will succeed him (Reay 1959, 114).

The ascendancy of a big man is quite an achievement, in view of the fact that in Kuma society, for example, three-fifths of the mature men between thirty-five and fifty-five years of age are leaders, who dominate the remaining two-fifths of their own generation and all the younger men (Reay 1959, 116). The competition for followers is intense, and those who succeed as truly big men are few; in 1954 there was only one man, according to Reay (1959, 130), who had achieved such regional renown and leadership.

In the process of assuming multiple leadership functions and expanding their networks of followers, these chieftains participate in and often preside over ritual activities. They acquire esoteric knowledge and begin to wield ritual power. Mark Aldenderfer has argued that the wielders of ritual power in small-scale societies have a competitive edge in extending their control of a ritually defined hierarchy to control other domains, especially under conditions of social circumscription and historical contact (Aldenderfer 1993, 15–16, 30–33). The wielders of ritual power have the necessary sanctity and moral authority to convince their followers that the extension of their control over other leadership functions will be beneficial and to the common good; their ritual sanctity enables them to preside over an emergent simultaneous hierarchy, which as we have seen is generally associated with more permanent regional leadership. They also begin to promote their ancestors as powerful intermediaries with the supernatural world, and they oversee the construction of ancestral shrines that embody the power and presence of their ancestors (Hayden 1995, 56–57). In her examination of the force of ideology in the evolution of Amerindian hierarchical political systems, beginning with the chieftaincy, Pita Kelekna (chap. 7) notes that the *arutam* power sought by Jivaroan war leaders stems from their first ancestors, who were great warriors. Ritual power can be a dynamic force, "pathway" (Aldenderfer 1993, 29, 35), or mechanism in the expansion and institutionalization of a chieftaincy.

Accordingly, Elsa Redmond considers how aspiring Yanomamö and

Jivaroan leaders achieve supravillage renown, increasingly today, through intervillage exchange and the acquisition of shamanic power, which present alternative paths to permanent centralized leadership. Kelekna demonstrates how the very pursuit of warfare, far from being motivated by secular considerations, can be a sacred undertaking. Ideology and ritual both promote militarism and legitimize the emergent political and social hierarchy.

Short-Term Chieftaincy and Development
of the Permanent Hereditary Chiefdom

In order for the periodic chieftaincy to outlive the chieftain and to persist and become institutionalized in the form of a permanent hereditary chiefdom, then, the socioenvironmental *conditions* that favor this kind of centralized, hierarchical leadership must be present: e.g., resource concentration, environmental and social circumscription, population growth, increasing group size, scalar stress, warfare, and other intersocietal relations. Moreover, the following *mechanisms* are pivotal in this sociopolitical transformation: (1) successful recruitment of followers; (2) expansion and articulation of both internal and external dimensions of centralized leadership; (3) ritual sanctification of centralized leadership; and (4) institutionalization of centralized leadership through hereditary succession. We must consider the third and fourth mechanisms, both of which are concerned with the legitimation of centralized leadership.

Actually, the origins of the practice of hereditary succession to leadership positions are to be found in chieftaincies. We have seen how Kuma big men are frequently succeeded by their eldest sons. The practice of inherited leadership is even more prevalent among Melpa big men, 75 percent of whom are sons of big men (Strathern 1971, 209; Lemonnier 1990, 43). Sons of these Melanesian big men receive sows and gardens but, most important, they receive wives from their fathers, whereupon they enter into their fathers' exchange networks. Sons of big men, and especially eldest sons, have an advantage as they take up some of their fathers' important exchange partnerships and effectively assume their fathers' leadership roles (Strathern 1971, 195–97, 211–13; Lemonnier 1990, 45).

The sons of Amazonian war leaders are destined to become war leaders as well through the pursuit of warfare, and today the sons of traders and sons of shamans are assuming their fathers' leadership roles under conditions of relative peace and contact with the outside world (Redmond). The sons of Massim leaders on Goodenough Island, and ideally the eldest sons, stand to inherit their fathers' leadership roles (Young 1971, 77, 95–109). Eldest sons are taught their fathers' ritual property—the garden magic, sorcery, and spells—upon which their own ritual leadership and supravillage renown will depend. When properly trained and endowed with his father's ritual property, the son of a ritual leader will already have substituted for his father on ritual occasions and will literally have taken his place before the father's death, making for a relatively smooth succession to leadership (Young 1971, 38, 95–96, 101, 108–9).

The sons of chieftains are poised to inherit their fathers' chieftaincies, by their birthright and formal training but also by their own abilities and successful pursuits. Their birthright, together with their well-honed leadership skills and their privileged access to resources and esoteric knowledge, are sought after and selected by their followers in succeeding generations, thereby paving the way for institutionalized hereditary succession to positions of leadership. The sons of chieftains, with direct genealogical ties to their fathers' fund of power and network of alliances, become members of a privileged, "submerged" social rank (Young 1971, 63) in these otherwise egalitarian societies. The deceased fathers become ancestors—mythical founding ancestors (Strathern 1971, 211) and functioning ancestors at that (Helms 1995, 107–8; n.d., 8–10)—who can channel their supernatural power directly through their still-living counterparts, their sons and successors, for the benefit of their followers (Hayden 1995, 56). Hence chieftains and sons of chieftains possess this indisputable link with their influential ancestors that can catapult them into leadership roles and through which they become identified as "living ancestors" (Helms n.d., 8).

Mary Helms demonstrates how successful political legitimation of the centralized leadership achieved by chieftains rests on the privileged access that sons of chieftains can claim to their sacred ancestors and creators of their cosmos: "Association with, and knowledge about, times and conditions of cosmological and/or cultural origins and creations is a major preoccupation of political and religious authorities in traditional societies because association with origins, with beginnings, both legitimizes authority and creates personal political ability" (Helms 1995, 106–7). And of course eldest sons, as firstborn, can rightfully claim the most powerful association with their founding ancestors and cosmological origins.

As living ancestors, Massim leaders make ritual appeals to their functioning ancestors at various stages of the gardening cycle. These leaders are revered for their knowledge of garden magic and their ritual ability to make the rain come, make the garden fertile, make the yams grow, make the sun right, and prevent theft (Young 1971, 148–55). Massim leaders can literally "chase away" drought and famine (Young 1971, 63, 81). At the same time, however, they are feared for their ritual ability to "chase away" the food supply by magically summoning crop pests or excessive rain, wind, or sun. For their ritual powers and the life or death sanctions associated with their leadership they are both revered and feared (Young 1971, 82–85, 177, 185). Accordingly, their emergent hereditary, supravillage leadership is ritually sanctified and legitimized.

At the same time that chieftains acquire the legitimacy to succeed to their fathers' leadership roles and to hold office as living ancestors, they assume a social rank that is separate from others (Helms, n.d., 8). We have seen how certain hereditary leaders from a single Massim clan, whose myths were being adopted by the larger community of villagers whom they served as "guardians," were recognized as members of a privileged social rank (Young 1971, 62–63). A fundamental cleavage in society occurs whereby chieftains inheriting leadership roles, who have privileged access to knowledge and who exercise heightened authority that may include supernatural powers, become members of an elite sector of society. Ordinary people who cannot claim such birthright and succession to leadership roles make up the remainder of society—"the rest of them" in the Taíno social order (Redmond and Spencer 1994, 193, table 10.1). Over time the social distance widens between the privileged hereditary leaders who make up the elite sector of society and the commoners who make up the nonelite sector. Moreover, this difference is formalized and exploited by the emergent hereditary chiefly elite. Keegan, Maclachlan, and Byrne demonstrate how the emergent Taíno chiefdoms headed by semidivine chiefs established the rules of succession and forged marriage alliances with other members of this elite sector.

Under the "right" (Rountree and Turner) or favorable conditions, permanent centralized leadership in the form of the hereditary chiefdom thus becomes institutionalized. The complex Taino chiefdoms that arose in the Greater Antilles under conditions of circumscription, and of competitive raiding and trading, sought to localize males from matrilineages through avunculocal residence and matrilineal descent, for the purposes of securing labor and intensifying production, maintaining a military force ready, and conducting long-distance exchange. Above all, Keegan, Maclachlan, and Byrne point out that the emergence of avunculocal chiefdoms created a power base of related males and ensured their orderly succession to political office.

In sum, from that pool of leadership variability present in the multiple leadership roles achieved by highly competent tribal war leaders, shamans, hunters, traders, and headmen, the centralized, regional-scale chieftaincy emerges from time to time, usually in response to external factors and intersocietal relations. The leadership dynamics of the chieftaincy can reach a point at which the benefits of centralized leadership in a region outweigh the loss of political autonomy on the part of the subordinate villagers. At this "flashpoint" (Carneiro), concern for the perpetuation of centralized authority will be realized in the institutionalization of the chiefdom under the permanent control of a hereditary paramount chief.

Notes

1. This is why so many ethnographers studying autonomous village societies have often dubbed village headmen "chiefs," yet with reservations about doing so (e.g., Maybury-Lewis 1974, 196–97; Carneiro 1993, 4, 8; Kracke 1993, 9). Lévi-Strauss (1944, 21–23, 28–31) used the term to characterize the leaders of Nambikuara groups. In describing Yaruro chiefs, Anthony Leeds admitted that the very word seemed inappropriate but that it was convenient for describing this heightened status achieved by certain individuals. More important, Leeds asked what ecological and/or historical conditions might have been responsible for creating and maintaining chieftaincies (Leeds 1969, 377–80).

2. Robert Carneiro has brought to my attention the case of one such "predatory chieftain," the Scottish highlander Rob Roy, who would be immortalized in the novel by Sir Walter Scott. In the introduction to *Rob Roy* (1817), Scott distinguished "*Chieftains*, which, in the Highland acceptation, signifies the head of a particular branch of a tribe, in opposition to *Chief*, who is the leader and commander of the whole name" (Scott 1950, lvi, xxiii).

3. Their likely precursors prior to contact, however, were great warrior-leaders, who emerged as leaders through their successful conduct of warfare and the attendant compensation exchanges they oversaw, and whose burgeoning authority was overwhelmingly sanctioned by their community (Lemonnier 1990, 125–26; see also Carneiro, this volume). Through their warring and peacemaking abilities, these great warrior-leaders successfully recruited followers and acquired multiple wives and unprecedented wealth in an expanding network of exchanges.

References

Aldenderfer, Mark
1993   Ritual, hierarchy, and change in foraging societies. *Journal of Anthropological Archaeology* 12(1):1–40.
Anderson, David G.
1994   *The Savannah River Chiefdoms: Political Change in the Late Prehistoric Southeast.* Tuscaloosa: University of Alabama Press.

Blitz, John H.

1993 *Ancient Chiefdoms of the Tombigbee*. Tuscaloosa: University of Alabama Press.

Braun, David P.

1990 Selection and evolution in nonhierarchical organization. In *The Evolution of Political Systems: Sociopolitics in Small-Scale Sedentary Societies*, edited by S. Upham, 62–86. School of American Research. Cambridge: Cambridge University Press.

Carneiro, Robert L.

1981 The chiefdom: Precursor of the state. In *The Transition to Statehood in the New World*, edited by G. D. Jones and R. R. Kautz, 37–79. Cambridge: Cambridge University Press.

1993 Factors favoring the development of political leadership in Amazonia. In *Leadership in Lowland South America*, edited by W. H. Kracke, 4–8. South American Indian Studies no. 1. Bennington, Vt.: Bennington College.

Drennan, Robert D.

1991 Pre-Hispanic chiefdom trajectories in Mesoamerica, Central America, and northern South America. In *Chiefdoms: Power, Economy, and Ideology*, edited by T. Earle, 263–87. School of American Research. Cambridge: Cambridge University Press.

Drennan, Robert D., and Carlos A. Uribe

1987 Introduction. In *Chiefdoms in the Americas*, edited by R. D. Drennan and C. A. Uribe, vii–xii. Lanham, Md.: University Press of America.

Earle, Timothy

1991 The evolution of chiefdoms. In *Chiefdoms: Power, Economy, and Ideology*, edited by T. Earle, 1–15. School of American Research. Cambridge: Cambridge University Press.

Flannery, Kent V.

1972 The cultural evolution of civilizations. *Annual Review of Ecology and Systematics* 3:399–426.

Godelier, Maurice

1986 *The Making of Great Men: Male Domination and Power Among the New Guinea Baruya*. Cambridge: Cambridge University Press.

Hayden, Brian

1995 Pathways to power: Principles for creating socioeconomic inequalities. In *Foundations of Social Inequality*, edited by T. D. Price and G. M. Feinman, 15–86. New York: Plenum Press.

Helms, Mary

1995 *Creations of the Rainbow Serpent*. Albuquerque: University of New Mexico Press.

n.d. Observations on the complexity of societies in the tropics—and elsewhere. In *Complex Polities in the Ancient Tropical World*, edited by E. A. Bacus and L. Lucero. Archaeological Papers of the American Anthropological Association, no. 9. Forthcoming.

Howell, Todd L.

1995 Tracking Zuni gender and leadership roles across the contact period. *Journal of Anthropological Research* 51:125–47.

1996 Identifying leaders at Hawikku. *Kiva* 62(1):61–82.

Johnson, Gregory A.

1978 Information sources and the development of decision-making organizations. In *Social Archeology: Beyond Subsistence and Dating*, edited by C. L. Redman et al., 87–112. New York: Academic Press.

1982 Organizational structure and scalar stress. In *Theory and Explanation in Archaeology: The Southampton Conference*, edited by C. Renfrew, M. J. Rowlands, and B. A. Segraves, 389–421. New York: Academic Press.

1989 Dynamics of southwestern prehistory: Far outside—looking in. In *Dynamics of Southwest Prehistory*, edited by L. S. Cordell and G. J. Gumerman, 371–89. School of American Research. Washington, D.C.: Smithsonian Institution Press.

Kracke, Waud H.

1993 Kagwahiv headmanship in peace and war. In *Leadership in Lowland South America*, edited by W. H. Kracke, 9–18. South American Indian Studies no. 1. Bennington, Vt.: Bennington College.

Leeds, Anthony

1969 Ecological determinants of chieftainship among the Yaruro Indians of Venezuela. In *Environment and Cultural Behavior*, edited by A. P. Vayda, 377–94. Garden City, N.Y.: Natural History Press.

Lemonnier, Pierre

1990 *Guerres et Festins: Paix, Echanges et Compétition dans les Highlands de Nouvelle-Guinée.* Paris: Editions de la Maison des Sciences de l'Homme.

1991 From great men to big men: Peace, substitution and competition in the Highlands of New Guinea. In *Big Men and Great Men: Personifications of Power in Melanesia*, edited by M. Godelier and M. Strathern, 7–27. Cambridge: Cambridge University Press.

Lévi-Strauss, Claude

1944 The social and psychological aspect of chieftainship in a primitive tribe: The Nambikuara of Northwestern Mato Grosso. *Transactions of the New York Academy of Sciences*, Series II, 7(1):16–32.

Lightfoot, Kent G.

1984 *Prehistoric Political Dynamics: A Case Study from the American Southwest.* DeKalb: Northern Illinois University Press.

Maybury-Lewis, David

1974 *Akwē-Shavante Society.* New York: Oxford University Press.

Pauketat, Timothy R.

1994 *The Ascent of Chiefs: Cahokia and Mississippian Politics in Native North America.* Tuscaloosa: University of Alabama Press.

Plog, Stephen

1995 Equality and hierarchy: Holistic approaches to understanding social dynamics in the Pueblo Southwest. In *Foundations of Social Inequality,* edited by T. D. Price and G. M. Feinman, 189–206. New York: Plenum Press.

Price, T. Douglas, and Gary M. Feinman, eds.

1995 *Foundations of Social Inequality.* New York: Plenum Press.

Reay, Marie

1959 *The Kuma: Freedom and Conformity in the New Guinea Highlands.* Melbourne: Melbourne University Press.

Redmond, Elsa M.

1994 *Tribal and Chiefly Warfare in South America.* University of Michigan Museum of Anthropology, Memoirs, no. 28. Ann Arbor.

Redmond, Elsa M., and Charles S. Spencer

1994 The *cacicazgo:* An indigenous design. In *Caciques and Their People: A Volume in Honor of Ronald Spores,* edited by J. Marcus and J. F. Zeitlin, 189–225. University of Michigan Museum of Anthropology, Anthropological Papers, no. 89. Ann Arbor.

Sahlins, Marshall D.

1963 Poor man, rich man, big man, chief: Political types in Melanesia and Polynesia. *Comparative Studies in Society and History* 5:285–303.

Scarry, John F.

1996 Stability and change in the Apalachee chiefdom. In *Political Structure and Change in the Prehistoric Southeastern United States,* edited by J. F. Scarry, 192–227. Gainesville: University Press of Florida.

Scott, Sir Walter

1950 *Rob Roy.* London: Thomas Nelson and Sons.

Sebastian, Lynne

1991 Sociopolitical complexity and the Chaco system. In *Chaco and Hohokam: Prehistoric Regional Systems in the American Southwest,* edited by P. L. Crown and W. J. Judge, 109–34. Santa Fe: School of American Research Press.

Service, Elman R.

1971 *Primitive Social Organization: An Evolutionary Perspective.* 2nd edition. New York: Random House.

Spencer, Charles S.

1987 Rethinking the chiefdom. In *Chiefdoms in the Americas,* edited by R. D. Drennan and C. A. Uribe, 369–89. Lanham, Md.: University Press of America.

1994 Factional ascendance, dimensions of leadership, and the development of centralized authority. In *Factional Competition and Political Development in the New World,* edited by E. M. Brumfiel and J. W. Fox, 31–43. Cambridge: Cambridge University Press.

Strathern, Andrew

1970 The female and male spirit cults in Mount Hagen. *Man* 5(4):571–85.

1971 *The Rope of Moka: Big-men and Ceremonial Exchange in Mount Hagen, New Guinea.* Cambridge: Cambridge University Press.

Strathern, Marilyn

1991   Introduction. In *Big Men and Great Men: Personifications of Power in Melanesia*, edited by M. Godelier and M. Strathern, 1–4. Cambridge: Cambridge University Press.

Upham, Steadman

1990   Decoupling the processes of political evolution. In *The Evolution of Political Systems: Sociopolitics in Small-Scale Sedentary Societies*, edited by S. Upham, 1–17. School of American Research. Cambridge: Cambridge University Press.

Welch, Paul D.

1991   *Moundville's Economy.* Tuscaloosa: University of Alabama Press.

Young, Michael W.

1971   *Fighting with Food: Leadership, Values and Social Control in a Massim Society.* Cambridge: Cambridge University Press.

CHAPTER 1

What Happened at the Flashpoint?

Conjectures on Chiefdom Formation
at the Very Moment of Conception

ROBERT L. CARNEIRO

When, following A.D. 1500, Europeans began to explore lands that lay beyond their shores, they encountered literally hundreds of chiefdoms. These were by no means limited to a single area of the world. They occurred over parts of the Americas, Africa, Asia, and the Pacific. And as many chiefdoms as were then in existence, there had once been even more. Those the Europeans found were merely the ones that had survived. Many more had existed but had either evolved into states themselves or been swallowed up by states already in existence. For centuries before the arrival of Europeans, then, chiefdoms had been a conspicuous feature of the political landscape.

Viewed against the entire sweep of human history, though, chiefdoms were a relatively late development. No evidence suggests that they existed anywhere in the world before the Neolithic. And even with the coming of agriculture, it still took several millennia for the first chiefdoms to arise. Kent Flannery (1972, 403) once assigned a date of 5500 B.C. to the earliest Mesopotamian chiefdom, and I know of none any earlier. However, within a few millennia of their inception, chiefdoms began to proliferate. The fact that so many arose in so many different parts of the world, and that they did so in a relatively short time, supports the idea of there having been some common and pervasive causes vigorously at work. Nothing fortuitous or idiosyncratic marked the rise of chiefdoms. They were the determinate result of a regular and recurring process.

That chiefdoms arose independently in areas varying widely in cultural tradition and environment is most instructive. It points to the fact that many details of clime and culture that accompanied the emergence of individual chiefdoms were nevertheless *irrelevant* to their rise. On the contrary, the widespread occurrence of chiefdoms strongly suggests that only *a few basic factors* were required to bring them about.

To be sure, the specific conditions attending the rise of each individual chiefdom contributed to its peculiarities.[1] After all, no two chiefdoms were exactly alike. But what should be stressed is that only a limited number of factors were needed to set the process in motion. Wherever these factors were present, and given enough time for them to operate, chiefdoms eventually, and almost irresistibly, arose.

Now, if my contention is correct, then in order to account for the emergence of chiefdoms we need not conduct an exhaustive search for a multiplicity of causes. We do not need one set of causes to account for the rise of chiefdoms on Fiji, and an entirely different set to account for their emergence in the Cauca Valley. Instead, we seek a unitary theory combining in one tight package those few causal elements that can account for the chiefdom anywhere.

This is, of course, a high presumption. While it is clearly a desideratum, as is any unifying principle in science, it cannot be claimed as an established fact. Indeed, it flies in the face of what many anthropologists are ready to assert. Nonetheless, my aim here is to ferret out that small cluster of factors I believe to be responsible for chiefdoms and to unite them into a simple theory that will explain their rise.

The Concept of the Chiefdom

Before proceeding, we need to have a clear and common understanding of just what a chiefdom is. There are, after all, various notions of the chiefdom, which are often at odds with one another. The concept of the chiefdom was first formally advanced by Kalervo Oberg in 1955,[2] and the core of it was simply that a chiefdom is an aggregate of villages under the centralized rule of a paramount political leader (Oberg 1955, 484). This is the basic structural nature of a chiefdom. Its evolutionary significance lies in the fact that it represented, for the first time in human history, the transcending of village autonomy and the establishment of a supravillage polity.

This central element of the chiefdom is often lost sight of, however. Thus Elman Service, in his *Primitive Social Organization* (1962), the first book to give wide currency to the idea of the chiefdom as a major evolutionary *stage* (and not just a type of political structure, as Oberg had done), virtually ignored its multivillage aspect. Instead, Service focused on ranking as its most conspicuous feature. Morton Fried, discussing the chiefdom in *The Evolution of Political Society* (1967), also put the emphasis on ranking. Indeed, he preferred the term *ranked society* to *chiefdom* in labeling the type of polity standing between the egalitarian tribe and the stratified state (Fried 1967, 109–29).

The emphasis on ranking strikes me as misplaced. To take ranking as the essence of a chiefdom is like defining an elephant by its tail instead of by its trunk. To be sure, ranking is an all-but-universal feature of the chiefdom—that is, where it has not yet given way to distinct social stratification. But I would argue that ranking is an epiphenomenon of the chiefdom, and not its central core. Ranking is merely the series of intergrading status differences that develops in emerging chiefdoms as certain individuals come to be rewarded disproportionately in terms of the social standing accorded them.

Initially, these differential statuses reflect the respective roles individuals have played in creating the chiefdom. But while based in the first instance on personal achievement, rank soon tends to become hereditary. One's social position comes to depend more on birth than on deeds. In more formal terms, statuses become ascribed instead of achieved. And with the sharpening and hardening of these categories, distinct social classes come into being.

A much more fruitful approach in characterizing a chiefdom is to look at its component units—a multiplicity of villages—and at the political means by which these villages are organized and integrated. Thus, closely following Oberg's original conception, I would define a chiefdom as *an autonomous political unit comprising a number of villages under the permanent control of a paramount chief* (Carneiro 1981, 45). This definition focuses attention where it belongs: on the fact that chiefdoms are *political* entities, brought into being by the surmounting of village autonomy and held together as unified multivillage wholes by a powerful chief.

This way of defining a chiefdom, incidentally, seems to be gaining ground. Once it was common for Northwest Coast tribes to be routinely called chiefdoms, with little regard for the fact that while individual village chiefs in this region were ceremonially ranked in relation to one another, their villages remained politically autonomous. The chief of the highest ranking Kwakiutl village, for example, could not issue orders to persons of the village ranked lowest in the scale. But, as indicated, things appear to be changing. Thus when Bruce Miller and Daniel Boxberger (1994) examine the question of whether the tribes of Puget Sound were once chiefdoms, they take it for granted that in order to qualify as such, the various villages had to have been under the permanent political control of a single chief.

Transcending the long-standing autonomy of individual villages, then, was the key to the rise of the chiefdom. It was this critical and decisive step that had to be taken before chiefdoms could emerge. And it is the manner in which this was done that we now need to consider.

Theories of the Origin of Chiefdoms

Broadly speaking, there are two ways in which village autonomy could have been surmounted: voluntarily or by force. I have long held that autonomous political units, whatever their size, never willingly give up their sovereignty. They surrender it only through coercion—either by intimidation ("voluntarily") or by outright conquest. Nor is this simply an article of faith on my part. Years of searching have failed to turn up any genuine exceptions to this rule. Autonomous political units simply do not relinquish their sovereignty without being compelled to do so.

When we look at chiefdoms reported in the ethnohistorical record, we find that, with almost no exceptions, they were headed by men who stood out as both military and political leaders. Not only were they the titular commanders in chief of their armies; they actually led their men into battle.[3] Indeed, the association between paramount chiefs and military power is so strong and so consistent as to be incontestable. Redmond (1994, 118) was thus entirely correct when she observed that "chiefly authority . . . was closely linked to the conduct and consequences of warfare." Moreover, what we find to be true synchronically—that is, as we study individual chiefdoms at a single moment in time—also has important implications diachronically. It points unmistakably to the fact that war and military leadership lay at the very root of the chiefdom.[4]

Nevertheless, the quest for the precise mechanism by which military leadership gave rise to chiefdoms still needs to be worked out. It could have happened in more than one way. That is to say, more than one series of military circumstances could have led to the surmounting of village autonomy. Until recently (e.g., Carneiro 1992a, 198), my assumption had been that chiefdoms had emerged when an especially effective war leader, initially the chief of a single village, had defeated, one by one, several neighboring villages and had incorporated them into his expanding domain. Over the past few years, however, I have come to reconsider this view. A somewhat different path to the chiefdom now seems to me more likely. I here explore this alternate route to see if it can be supported with argument and evidence.

That there should still be so much uncertainty as to how such a fundamental step in human history was actually taken is a measure of how little deep research and hard thinking has gone toward the solution of this problem. A good deal of excogitation has been done, but much of it lies in the realm of fantasy, conveniently divorced from a close study of the facts.

The Alternate Scenario

In proposing a pathway for the formation of chiefdoms different from the one I originally envisioned, I begin by looking at warfare as waged at lower levels of political organization. At the outset, we must recognize the fact that while human societies were still at the autonomous village stage, warfare was already extremely widespread. We need only look at the recent history of Amazonia and New Guinea, the two largest areas of the world where autonomous villages continue to flourish, to verify this.

Wherever autonomous villages are frequently at war, they tend to form military alliances with neighboring villages. Of the Yanomamö, widely known for their belligerence, Chagnon writes: "Because of the ever-present risk of being driven from one's garden, no Yanomamö village can continue to exist as a sovereign entity without establishing alliances with other groups.... Thus, the military threat creates a situation in which intervillage alliance is desirable" (1983, 147). Before Western contact had damped down indigenous warfare in Amazonia, military alliances among tribal villages were more the rule than the exception.

At simple levels of political organization, such alliances usually involve little in the way of centralized leadership. The Yanomamö again typify this stage. If two or three Yanomamö villages unite to carry out a raid, the warriors of each village are generally led by their own chief. No one takes full command of the joint forces.

At a somewhat higher level of military engagement, the procedure begins to change. When going into battle, the warriors of allied villages often subordinate themselves to the orders of a single leader. This leader may be formally elected or informally recognized. Either way, as commander of the combined forces of several villages, he assumes powers well beyond those he held before. And as warfare becomes even more frequent and intense, this subordination to his authority becomes increasingly common and rigid. Among the Caribs of northern South America, for example, it was reported that "in time of peace [they] ... admitted of no supremacy but that of nature ... [but] in war, experience had taught them that subordination was as requisite as courage; they therefore elected their captains in their general assemblies with great solemnity" (Edwards 1801–19, 1:49; quoted in Spencer 1967, 33).

The same was true of a number of other South American tribes. Among the Catío of northern Colombia, for instance, several autonomous villages would come together and elect an ad hoc war leader whenever hostilities with neighboring tribes threatened. But while election as war leader bestowed on a Catío chief far more power than he normally possessed, this power was of short duration, lapsing once hostilities had ceased (Carneiro 1991, 179). Much the same was true of the Quijos of what is now Ecuador. Writing in 1577, Diego de Ortegón said of them: "They do not form a great state or an organized nation: each section is governed by itself; and, when they go to war, they elect for leader the most valiant and courageous among the caciques, and his command lasts the duration of the war, no longer" (quoted in Stirling 1938, 47). Among the Kagwahiv of south-central Brazil, war leaders were likewise endowed with special but only temporary powers (Kracke 1993, 13). And the same could be said of many other Amazonian tribes.

It was not unusual, moreover, for the powers temporarily assumed by a war chief to include the greatest of them all—the power of life and death. I offer the following example. The naturalist Karl Philip von Martius was once walking through the rain forest of the northwest Amazon region with a Miranha chief when they came upon a skeleton tied to a tree. The chief explained to von Martius that the bones were those of one of his own men, whom he had ordered shot to death with arrows for failing to summon allies when ordered to do so in the face of an impending attack by the Omagua (Tylor 1916, 431).

Conferring this ultimate power on an ad hoc war leader seems, indeed, to have been a common practice, not only in Amazonia but wherever in the world warfare was zealously pursued. For example, Julius Caesar reported of the ancient Germans that "when a tribe is attacked or intends to attack another, officers are chosen to conduct the campaign and invested with powers of life and death" (Caesar 1982, 144).

As I have said, such extraordinary powers were generally short-lived. To cite one more example of this limitation, after describing the wartime powers assumed by a Tupinambá chief of the coast of Brazil, Gabriel Soares de Sousa noted, by way of contrast, that "in peacetime each person does what his appetite commands" (quoted in Fernandes 1963, 329).

Nonetheless, while the powers of a war leader diminished sharply once the fighting had stopped, if he had distinguished himself in war, he continued to enjoy great respect and acclaim. Such sixteenth-century Tupinambá chiefs as Abati-Poçanga and Japí-açu, each of whom had successfully led the combined forces of several villages, had gained renown that extended far beyond the limits of their own village (Fernandes 1963, 328, 330).

Instances such as these suggest the possibility that chiefdoms may not have emerged through a powerful village chief having successively conquered and incorporated the villages immediately surrounding his. For one thing, I have yet to find in the ethnohistorical literature an instance of this sort of piecemeal conquest. Instead, then, let us consider the following alternate route to supravillage integration.

It seems safe to assume that a military leader who had already proven himself successful in previous wars would be called upon again by allied villages to lead them in any new engagement. Not just his own village but members of all other villages in the alliance would thus be accustomed to having him issue orders and to carrying them out. And it stands to reason that the greater the military triumphs accruing to these villages while obeying his commands, the more likely they would be to turn to him again and seek his leadership whenever the situation called for it. The villages of the alliance would thus become progressively readier to subordinate themselves to him. As Redmond (1994, 130) has noted: "Those distinguished war leaders who have built up a large network of supravillage alliances and obligations, who can mobilize large fighting forces on short notice, will be poised for positions of permanent leadership." Moreover, the war leader, grown more and more accustomed to exercising the power of his office as well as to enjoying its many fruits, would become increasingly reluctant to relinquish this power once hostilities ended.

There is a further factor to consider here. The war chief normally developed a cadre of able and disciplined warriors, men who were his special adherents and could be counted on to be devoted to his cause. These men were used to carrying out his orders with alacrity and to benefiting materially from his successes. Since their prestige and prosperity were so closely linked to his, their tendency would be to remain loyal and subordinate to him in times of peace as well as of war. Such a group of warriors would form a solid core of supporters whose allegiance would be to their leader rather than to their village. It seems entirely likely, then, that they would be ready to uphold a war leader's assertion of power during peacetime, once he decided to take that bold step. A successful ad hoc war leader would thus have more than just his own ability and charisma to bring to bear against a reluctant populace, should his retention of power during peacetime be resisted.

Wherever this state of affairs existed, it would not be surprising for a strong war leader, riding the crest of his successes, to attempt to hold onto his extraordinary powers beyond the point at which he would normally surrender them. And the day he was able to do so successfully would signal the end of village autonomy in that region. With one decisive stroke, the flashpoint of chiefdom formation would have been reached. If a war chief's assumption of permanent power were not later reversed, so that the subordination of several villages to a single leader continued in effect during peacetime, a de facto chiefdom would thus have been established.

Ethnographic Evidence for the Hypothesis

Sketched here somewhat hypothetically, these conditions and events seem not to have been uncommon among warlike societies.[5] Let me offer some concrete evidence drawn from the Caribs of the Guianas, Venezuela, and the Lesser Antilles as well as from the Tupinambá of the coast of Brazil, evidence that tends to substantiate this reconstruction. These areas encompassed societies that lay on either side of the great divide: some appear to have been on the brink of becoming chiefdoms, while others had already crossed that threshold.

I begin by quoting from Neil Whitehead's (1988) recent ethnohistorical study of the Guiana Caribs. War raids were common among them, and when a raid was to be carried out, several villages joined forces. "Knotted cords or an arrow would be sent out to neighbouring villages and the warriors assembled. Among these there seems to have been a definite group of war-chiefs, from among whom the leader of the expedition would be chosen" (Whitehead 1988, 60–61). At these assemblies of warriors, "The leadership of . . . raiding expeditions seems to have been decided either by common assent of those gathered for the purpose or by deferment to the individual who had initiated the enterprise, though clearly any such individual would have had to have demonstrated prowess in war and the taking of captives even to be considered for such a role" (Whitehead 1988, 60). When a party of raiders set out to engage the enemy, "the war-chief has a special position of precedence [over the peace chief] in the pirogue [canoe]" (Whitehead 1988, 62).

The Guiana Caribs thus show us some early steps toward the formation of chiefdoms. In time of war—but then only temporarily—one man was empowered to exert authority over the men of several villages beyond his own.

When we come to the Caribs of the Venezuelan coast, we find political evolution to have advanced a step further. Among such groups as the Palenque, Cumaná, and Paria, true chiefdoms with strong paramount leaders had emerged. Of the Palenque paramount chief, Guaramental, for example, the Spanish chronicler Fernández de Oviedo wrote that he was "a very virile man and obeyed for more than twenty leagues around and very respected and feared by his vassals, and even by [other] surrounding groups" (quoted in Saignes 1946, 32; my translation).

However, several groups on the Venezuelan coast—the Caracas being an example—were still at the autonomous village stage (Saignes 1946, 24).[6] Thus what we find here is a *mosaic* of autonomous villages interspersed with chiefdoms. From the mixed distribution of political entities that occurred in this region of Venezuela, we can reasonably infer that chiefdom formation was actively taking place here. And it seems safe to assert this even if no Spanish chronicler happened to have caught this transformation in the act.

In the Lesser Antilles a similar situation prevailed, although chiefdom formation seems to have gone somewhat further. Aided by the environmental circumscription that small islands naturally afford, powerful Kallinago war chiefs had succeeded in establishing permanent hegemony over all the villages of an island. And the authority they were able to exert was evidently quite substantial since, according to Father Rochefort, "in the presence of the island cacique no man speaks if he do not ask or command him to do it" (quoted in Roth 1924, 568).[7]

On certain occasions, the scope of a war chief's political control extended beyond a single island. When planning a large-scale military expedition, the inhabitants of several islands might join forces and send off an immense flotilla of war canoes to attack their enemy. To lead such a fleet, one of the various island war chiefs was chosen as supreme commander. However, the power he thus assumed lasted only for the duration of the raid. Multi-island chiefdoms had thus not yet emerged.[8] Nonetheless, while noting that after such an expedition a Kallinago *ouboutou,* or principal cacique, "hath no authority but only on his own island," Father Rochefort added, "true it is that if he hath behaved himself gallantly in his enterprise he is ever after highly respected in all the islands" (quoted in Roth 1924, 573).

In summary, we can say that certain parts of the coast of Venezuela and the Lesser Antilles had already witnessed the emergence of chiefdoms. In the latter, it is apparent that they were the direct result of a war leader having retained political control over all the villages of his island. That much the same had also occurred on the coast of Venezuela seems no less likely.

Turning to the Tupinambá of the Brazilian coast, the picture is again a mixed one. Over most of the area, villages seem to have remained autonomous except in times of war, when they subordinated themselves to a military leader. However, along certain parts of the coast, multivillage chiefdoms had emerged. That this had actually occurred was recognized by Alfred Métraux at least as early as 1948. In his article on the Tupinambá in the *Handbook of South American Indians,* Métraux (1948, 113) clearly noted that "some chiefs extended their power over a whole district and commanded a great many villages."

More recently, evidence for the existence of Tupinambá chiefdoms has been put forward by William Balée in his ecological reinterpretation of Tupinambá warfare. Here Balée writes, "Among the Tupi-speaking Tamoios of Rio de Janeiro, the Capuchin chronicler Ives d'Évreux declared that 'each habitation [i.e., house, of which a village had four] has its chief. These four chiefs are under the orders of the village chief, who jointly with those of many villages obeys the great chief of the province'"(Balée 1984, 255).

Describing the same chiefdom and its leader, the Franciscan friar André Thevet wrote: "The populations of this region are more bellicose than any other in America . . . compelled to live in continual war. Their king is Quoniambebe, and he is by their peculiar martial and warlike instincts, the most feared chief in the land. . . . His village, with its surrounding territory, is vast, fortified all around by bastions and platforms of earth" (quoted in Balée 1984, 255).

As among the Caribs of northern South America, then, the Tupinambá showed regional differences in their degree of political development. Even if all or most Tupinambá groups had not evolved into chiefdoms, it is clear that some of them had. And just as among the northern Caribs, it is evident that what had prompted supravillage aggregation among the Tupinambá was warfare. Virtually all Carib and Tupinambá groups in both areas, whether they were autonomous villages or chiefdoms, were continually at war. At lower levels of organization, temporary military alliances between autonomous villages were led by ad hoc war chiefs. And again, among those groups in both areas that had crossed the threshold and become chiefdoms, paramount chiefs were, first and foremost, leaders in war (see Redmond 1994, 117).

Insofar as the Carib and Tupinambá evidence can be taken as representing the general process of chiefdom formation, then, there can be little doubt as to how paramount chiefs had come to establish permanent control over multiple villages. One can hardly escape the conclusion that it was the ability of a successful war leader to continue to maintain control over subordinate villages, instead of relinquishing it during peacetime, that constituted the most likely avenue for the emergence of the chiefdom.

The War Leader Examined Close Up

Having decided that a temporary military leader's extension of his wartime power was the way chiefdoms arose, let us take a closer look at the individuals who might have been expected to take this bold step.

To begin with, it should be noted that the qualities required of a war leader differ markedly from those expected of an ordinary village chief. By and large, the latter's role is to maintain order and promote harmony within the group. A war leader, on the other hand, plays the opposite role. Instead of quieting his fellows, his job is to incite them. When the occasion demands, he must be able to stir them up, get them ready to fight, and lead them successfully into battle. He must thus be ready to command rather than conciliate. And to command effectively, he has to be assertive and aggressive.

Instead of merely listing the attributes of such a person, though, let us look at a few individuals who in their personalities and their exploits exemplified this way of being. Given the appropriate circumstances, the men I am about to describe were ones who might readily have taken the forceful and decisive steps needed to forge a chiefdom out of a number of disparate villages.

Möawa, chief of the Yanomamö village of Mishimishimaböwei-teri, was such a man. Through his aggressiveness and strength of character, he was able to keep together—for a time at least—a village of 281 persons, the largest Yanomamö village ever reported (Chagnon 1974, 130). He was feared not only in his own village but also by surrounding villages. Here is how Napoleon Chagnon described him:

> Möawa . . . was fierce, a man of great personal courage and renown, strong, an excellent marksman, and forceful to the point of awesome-

ness. He took what he wanted when he wanted it, and scorned those who would pretend to impose their will on him. People feared him because he was capable of great violence and expressed it unhesitatingly. But people also looked up to him, if they were not his competitors, and did what he demanded of them. He was a man of his word, and when he spoke or commanded, people listened and obeyed. When he threatened, everyone knew he meant what he said. Because of his forceful bearing and abilities, he was able to attract a large following and hold it together. (Chagnon 1974, 166)

Yet, due to circumstances we shall explore a little later, Möawa's effective control was limited in scope. As we saw earlier, while Yanomamö villages often form wartime alliances, they never select a single individual to lead their joint forces. Thus, even in wartime, Möawa's power did not become regional. He never succeeded in extending his authority much beyond the confines of his own village.

Chagnon regarded Möawa as representing "the archetypical expression of his culture's . . . political ideals" (1974, 166). Another Amazonian society in which aggressive leaders played a similarly conspicuous and culturally recognized role are the Jivaroan-speaking Shuar and Achuar of eastern Ecuador and northern Peru. Settlements of these groups are basically autonomous, but for the purpose of raiding they sometimes form alliances with other settlements. Moreover, if hostilities escalate to an especially high level, several settlements may combine their forces under a powerful military leader known as a *kakáram* or "strong man." This role, well-defined though it is, is not hereditary. Every young warrior aspires to bravery in war, but only the individual who has demonstrated his fearlessness and leadership in years of hard fighting achieves the distinction of kakáram.

Starting in boyhood, by regularly undergoing ordeals of endurance and by consuming the hallucinogen *Datura* to induce supernatural visions, an individual gradually attains the sacred *arutam* strength that ensures military prowess. Beyond that, however, the increase in power needed to become a kakáram depends on the warrior's ambition and military exploits. As Pita Kelekna (n.d.b, 18) tells us, "a man who has killed many times is believed to have extraordinary spiritual strength." And once he has thus accumulated sufficient arutam, an Achuar kakáram "is considered invincible in war" (Kelekna n.d.b, 18).

Certain war leaders acquire great reputations for ferocity and are widely feared. One such kakáram, "Ujukam," has been described by Kelekna. By repeated raiding along both banks of the Pastaza River, Ujukam played a conspicuous role in repelling Shuar invasions of Achuar territory and was likewise able to intimidate his Achuar rivals. In fact, being a kakáram of extraordinary vigor and aggressiveness, "Over a thirty-year period, Ujukam dominated a broad area between two major rivers, expelling from the zone eight major settlements" (Kelekna n.d.a, 11).[9]

Of kakáram in general, Kelekna (n.d.b, 18–19) notes that "as an outstanding warrior's fame spreads, he is invited by men of distant locations to lead war expeditions in their areas," and this was the case with Ujukam. But although he successfully led a military alliance of settlements located far from his own, Ujukam was never able to create a cohesive, integrated, and enduring political unit. Thus, despite his qualities of leadership, he fell short of giving rise to a chiefdom. Moreover, being the personal achievement of one man, and depending entirely on his military exploits, Ujukam's "domain" did not survive him.[10]

Möawa and Ujukam afford examples of men with the requisite initiative, aggressiveness, and ruthlessness to have hammered together a multivillage polity. But it never happened. Conditions simply did not favor their expanding and solidifying their power beyond a certain point. Why it was that even when led by such formidable men the Yanomamö and Achuar were unable to evolve to the level of the chiefdom, we shall consider shortly.

First, though, turning from Amazonia to Melanesia, let us look for a moment at the New Guinea "big man." Big men are commonly thought of as economic entrepreneurs, this being the portrait of them painted by Marshall Sahlins in his well-known "Poor Man, Rich Man, Big-Man, Chief" (1963) and repeated in *Stone Age Economics* (1972, 135–39). But this was by no means the whole story. Before colonial authorities sharply curtailed the incidence of war, the New Guinea big man was often a feared and formidable warrior, at least in certain parts of the island. Thus, according to D. K. Feil, "'Bigmen' in the eastern highlands are, more often than not, aggressive warriors and killers rather than manipulators and transactors of wealth" (Feil 1987, 65). Like Ujukam, these New Guinea big men intimidated not only their own village but surrounding ones as well. Such a big man was Matoto, a Tairora of the Eastern Highlands, as described by James B. Watson (1973, 244): "Matoto was so powerful he would intervene between warring factions, give solid assurance to distressed refugees, scatter his enemies, and in general have his way with friend or foe. It is the sheer force and power of the man from which people apparently think all else flowed. No one points to any astuteness of Matoto's, only to his ability to do uncommon favours for his supporters, great harm to his opponents. He is overwhelming as a fighter, frightening as a man."

But Matoto lived and died without so much as uniting another village to his own. Given his nature and his exploits, however, Matoto was clearly an individual around whom a chiefdom might have crystalized. Under more favorable conditions he might first have successfully led the combined warriors of a dozen villages and, with this as a springboard, might then have taken the critical next step of imposing himself as permanent leader of them all. But for all his military prowess and the fear he instilled in those around him, he never came close to doing so.

Why not? Why did Matoto, Ujukam, and Möawa proceed no further? One reason, perhaps, was that their skills ran too heavily toward sheer intimidation. For this they showed great aptitude, but for welding disparate communities together into a cohesive and enduring whole, less so. If ever they dreamed such grandiose dreams—and we have no evidence that they did—they were never able to implement them. Summing up their careers, we might say that the net effect of their ferocity was more to terrorize than to organize.

Yet this analysis is superficial and incomplete. I would argue that deeper reasons than simply personal shortcomings kept Matoto, Ujukam, and Möawa from establishing chiefdoms. Certain specifiable conditions that greatly favor the rise of chiefdoms were lacking in the areas where they lived. Most important of these was the absence of environmental circumscription, which made it more difficult for population pressure to develop and to exert its effects (Carneiro 1970). While such pressure heightens the incidence of war and magnifies its consequences, if natural barriers are absent, and escape becomes readily feasible, population pressure can be relieved before it reaches a critical level. Defeated groups have the simple expedient of moving away.

Thus, where environmental circumscription is lacking, no amount of military skill or personal prowess on the part of a war chief may suffice to establish a chiefdom. Had the regions where Möawa and Ujukam and Matoto lived been more sharply bounded, allowing population pressure to build, producing a concomitant increase in the level of fighting, it would have been easier for each to overcome village autonomy and parlay his military skills into a multivillage chiefdom (Carneiro 1970).

Nor am I alone in this assessment. Karl Schwerin, for example, in discussing chiefdoms in the Americas, recognized the same effect: "Conditions [for the formation of chiefdoms] were not so favorable in the Amazonian lowlands, but to the north in the Circum-Caribbean proper . . . a greater geographical circumscription stimulated a rapid emergence of cacicazgos" (Schwerin 1973, 9).[11] Thus in areas like the small islands of the Lesser Antilles and the long, narrow Paria peninsula on the coast of Venezuela, where environmental circumscription did occur, chiefdoms in fact arose.

Somewhat similar conditions prevailed along the Atlantic coast of Brazil, the region inhabited by the Tupinambá. While environmental circumscription was not as sharp here as along the coast of Venezuela and in the Lesser Antilles, a certain measure of it did exist. Along some stretches of the coast, mountains came within a few miles of the sea, serving to hem in the populations that had settled there.

But the really important ecological factor at work in this region, and which contributed to the rise of the chiefdom, was resource concentration (Carneiro 1970, 736–37; 1987). Its effect was to attract indigenous groups to settle within a relatively narrow coastal strip. While the lands running back from the coast were by no means barren, they ran a poor second in terms of subsistence possibilities to those that bordered the sea. Villages located along the coast had at their disposal a wealth of marine food resources. As Balée (1984, 244) notes, "The seacoast proved rich in aquatic fauna, often absent in the hinterlands." And he quotes from the sixteenth-century chronicler Gabriel Soares de Sousa to the effect that "the Tupinambá of the seacoast ate manatee, which breed in the brackish waters of coastal river mouths," adding that "the seashore offered a cornucopia of shrimp, lobster, crabs, oysters, and other species of fish" as well (1984, 244).

A century earlier, the Tupinambá had displaced the Gê-speaking Tapuya from this rich habitat, but in the years that followed, they had been forced to ward off the latter's efforts to regain their lost "cornucopia." Moreover, the Tupinambá themselves, with larger and more powerful villages than the Tapuya, also warred with each other, often over the choicest coastal zones. The intense competition thus engendered, focused as it was on a narrow littoral of great desirability, was hence instrumental in giving rise to chiefdoms. The most powerful of these seems to have been that headed by Cunhambebe (Quoniambebe), whom we mentioned earlier.

To the distinctly limited and sharply contested margins of the Caribbean and Atlantic coasts, the immense and boundless forests of Achuar and Yanomamö habitats offered a marked contrast. These uninterrupted stretches of *selva* made possible a relatively easy dispersal of weaker villages threatened by more powerful neighbors, and thus, by preventing great population pressure from building up, militated against the formation of chiefdoms.

But we should not lose sight of the fact that the kinds of individuals who could spearhead the formation of a chiefdom, wherever the appropriate conditions were found, already existed. They were waiting in the wings, so to speak, ready to begin welding together a multivillage polity whenever the circumstances proved favorable.

Selecting a Worthy Chief

That warlike societies actively sought out military leaders of indomitable courage and fortitude is well attested to in the ethnographic record. Often such societies had formal means for ensuring the selection of a man who exhibited these qualities in the highest degree. Among the Caribs of Venezuela and the Guianas, for instance, candidates for the office of chief underwent a series of rigorous trials. As described by Richard Schomburgk:

> If a new chief had to be chosen, the candidate for the honour must submit beforehand to the most gruesome and cruellest ordeals to put his courage, his endurance, and his steadfastness to the test. Such trials were a long, extremely stringent fast which ended with the famished individual having to drink to the bottom a large calabashful of a strong decoction of peppers without pulling the slightest face. Were this successfully accomplished he would be placed in a hammock filled with large ants, which would be tied tightly above him so as to prevent the tormentors getting away, and here without a groan, without a movement, he had to bear for hours the attacks of the excited and irritated insects. If he bore all these ordeals with equanimity he would be acknowledged chief with cheers: his will was thenceforth that of the whole company. (Schomburgk 1923, 2:344)

Tests conducted by other tribes of the region were even more severe. Relentless flogging, the drinking of a bowl of tobacco juice, and a slow roasting over a low fire were features of some of these trials (Gumilla 1963, 337–40; Whitehead 1988, 60–63). It was through ordeals such as these that a village could assure itself of an intrepid leader capable of achieving military successes against the staunchest foe. And it is not hard to imagine that under favorable conditions, such a leader might seek to crown his military triumphs with a corresponding political one.

The Chiefdom Becomes an Institution

Returning to the chiefdom itself, which we left barely arisen and still in an inchoate form, let us see if we can set it on its course toward greater things.[12] If we accept the sequence of events presented so far, the question still remains: How did societies evolve from a de facto aggregate of villages, owing its unity to the iron hand of a single dominant figure, to the permanent, even consensual *institution* of a chiefdom? In other words, how was a war-born clustering of villages transformed into an enduring political structure? Let me suggest an answer to this question.

In discussing succession to political office, Herbert Spencer distinguished between what we might call the principle of ability and the principle of stability: "While succession by efficiency gives plasticity to social organization, succession by inheritance gives it stability. No settled arrangement can arise in a primitive community so long as the function of each unit [that is, each individual] is determined exclusively by his fitness, since, at his death, the arrangement, in so far as he was a part of it, must be recommenced. Only when his place is forthwith filled by one whose claim is admitted does there begin a differentiation which survives through successive generations" (Spencer 1967, 116–17).

When fully operative, the principle of ability ensures that someone of unquestioned competence will be chosen to fill a vacant office. The principle of stability, on the other hand, acts to assure that the mantle of authority will pass from one person to another with the minimum of disruption and uncertainty. When a chiefdom first emerges in a region of unmitigated warfare, selecting a leader of established military prowess is the foremost concern. Even at this stage, though, both considerations may come into play. For example, speaking of a Guiana Carib group, W. H. Brett observed: "They had no strictly hereditary sovereigns:—if the son of a great leader equalled his father in bravery and skill, he might succeed to his power;—if not, they would choose another to head them in any warlike undertaking" (1868, 130).

Once a chiefdom becomes more than a transitory aggregate of villages, increasing regard is given to stability. And here heredity provides the most convenient mechanism. Understandably, a ruling paramount chief normally wants to be succeeded by his son (or, in a matrilineal society, his sister's son). With this in mind, the chief generally sees to it that from childhood on, his son receives special training in the martial arts. Even among the Achuar, still far removed from a chiefdom, Kelekna tells us that the sons of a kakáram "are subject to rigorous discipline, ordeals of endurance, and systematic instruction in military techniques" (n.d.a, 8). In this manner, when the time arrives, it may well be that by both training and inclination the son of a chief will turn out to be a worthy successor to his father. And so gradually it becomes recognized as an established rule that the son of a paramount chief succeeds him.

Heredity, which furnishes a ready means for the succession to the chief- tainship, is also the avenue for the entrenchment of a noble class. Beginning as a small core of close supporters of the war-leader-turned-paramount- chief, men who were initially distinguished only by rank based on their personal exploits in battle eventually find their positions formalized and consolidated into distinct social classes.[13] This stage is clearly signaled when nobles are able to transmit their status to their descendants through inheritance.

When fully crystalized as a social class, nobles are sharply distinguish- able from commoners. And commoners for their part are sharply distin- guishable from war prisoners who, no longer sacrificed or cannibalized, are now incorporated into the society as slaves. Thus arise the three con- spicuous social classes so typical of more advanced chiefdoms and all but universal among established states.

We might also note here that in addition to his coterie of nobles, a para- mount chief begins to surround himself with personal servants and retain- ers, all of whom together form an incipient court. At the same time, chiefs are demanding and acquiring certain privileges and distinctions: they are received with obeisances, are carried in litters, are addressed deferentially, have distinct titles, wear special insignia of their office, obtain numerous wives and concubines, etc. And of course, they periodically collect tribute and taxes, exactions which enable them to accumulate wealth far beyond that of any of their subjects.

The details of how a paramount chief increases his power, wealth, and privilege are beyond our proper scope here. My main objective has been to ascertain what happened at the flashpoint—that is, to lay bare the series of steps by which autonomous villages gave way to a higher polity. Of the many issues surrounding the chiefdom, this one remains the most crucial.

Final Considerations

Elman Service (1962, 145) has stated that "no one has observed the actual origin of a chiefdom." While we may yet find exceptions to this rule, such cases will be, at best, exceedingly rare. Thus we may never be able to tell from direct observation just how this momentous step took place. If our aim is to reconstruct how it occurred, we must be ready to make liberal use of inference. In the aforegoing discussion, this is precisely what I have done. And although I am confident of the proposed scenario, I cannot claim to have established it as an absolute fact. I believe, though, that the ring of uncertainty has been closed perceptibly, and if there still remains a gap for the spark of understanding to have to jump, it is surely a narrow one.

Of one thing we can be sure, however. There *was* a flashpoint. At some moment in history, there came a time in many regions of the world when village autonomy was transcended. This step necessarily involved the subordination of previously independent villages and their incorporation into a single overarching political structure.

From this point on, chiefdoms grew rapidly in number. Repeatedly and in many areas of the world, conditions began to emerge that led autonomous villages to fuse into larger political units. Central to this process was warfare. We can be certain of this because the ethnographic record shows warfare to have been extremely frequent and recurring among societies just before the flashpoint, and to have become even more frequent and intense immediately after it (see Carneiro 1990). Why, then, should anyone suppose that war, as an active agent in the formation of chiefdoms, was somehow suspended at the very moment of conception?

That warfare and chiefdoms were, from the start, intimately linked, we can take as securely established. But exactly how warfare contributed to the rise of the chiefdom has been an open question. Contrary to the view I once held, I now believe that the first chiefdoms did not arise by the outright conquest of one village after another by the strongest among them. Instead, as I have argued, it was more likely to have happened by a temporary war leader continuing to exercise his extraordinary powers over allied villages beyond the time he normally gave them up.

Of course, it is possible that chiefdoms arose in both ways, depending on the circumstances. My inclination, though, is always to look for unitary theories of cultural causation. Thus I incline to the belief that the route here proposed as leading to the chiefdom was the one followed—if not in every case, at least in a substantial preponderance of them. Once a chiefdom was established, though, the doors were open for it to grow by the successive conquest and incorporation of surrounding villages and other chiefdoms. Indeed, it was by such serial conquests, followed by an elaboration of the internal structure now required to consolidate and integrate the growing polity, that the state ultimately emerged.

Despite my convictions in this matter, I readily admit that much about the origin of the chiefdom remains in doubt. And I believe this uncertainty should serve as a stimulus for students to scrutinize the ethnohistorical record more closely, searching for further evidence in this regard. We should look particularly at those societies which, when first observed, if not at the very flashpoint of the process, were at least either just below or just above it. Clearly, it is these cases that have the most to tell us.

Unfortunately, although a great deal of written evidence exists on the subject of chiefdoms, it is widely scattered and has been largely neglected by current theorists. As noted, anthropologists often prefer to excogitate how chiefdoms arose than to ascertain it by immersing themselves in the facts. Once a more thorough search of the ethnohistorical sources has been made, though, we should be much closer to elucidating the process. And we should count this as a major triumph. After all, the rise of the chiefdom may well have been the single most important step ever taken in political evolution. It certainly took the longest to achieve. And it marked a crossing of the Rubicon. Before it, village autonomy represented a severe and impassable barrier to cultural development. But once multivillage polities became established, human societies were poised to burst through this barrier. And indeed, close on the heels of the first chiefdoms came a rapid series of developments leading inexorably, in but a few millennia, to the state. Once the state was in existence, all restrictions were off, and cultural evolution, on an ever widening front and at an accelerating pace, gave rise to the enormous societal complexity that surrounds and engulfs us today.

Notes

1. For example, we can distinguish *impacted* chiefdoms like those tightly wedged into the Cauca Valley of Colombia; *dispersed* chiefdoms, like those distributed throughout much of the southeastern United States, with large tracts of no-man's-land between them; *riparian* chiefdoms, like those strung in linear fashion along the Amazon River; and *insular* chiefdoms, which arose within the sharply bounded confines of an island. But there are also other typologies of chiefdoms, such as *minimal, typical,* and *maximal* (Carneiro 1981, 47), and *simple, compound,* and *consolidated* (Carneiro 1992b, 36–37), representing not adaptations to varying local conditions but rather stages in a single evolutionary process.

2. I should point out, however, that the term *chiefdom* was used at least as early as 1940 by Audrey Richards in her description of the political structure of the Bemba of southern Africa (Richards 1940, 92); no doubt it can be found in still earlier writings. But to highlight the confusion that the lack of a formal concept of the chiefdom has entailed, Richards, in the title of her article on the Bemba, referred to them as a "tribe"!

3. At more advanced levels of the chiefdom, it sometimes happens that the paramount chief designates someone else to march at the head of his warriors. Among Guaca and Popayán in the Cauca Valley, for instance, it was the brother of the paramount chief who fulfilled this role (Carneiro 1991, 179), while among the Palenque of Venezuela the war chief was someone named by the paramount chief (Saignes 1946, 52).

4. The few instances of chiefdoms that appear to have been peaceful when first observed by outsiders occurred largely on small and isolated islands in the Pacific, where, once established islandwide, they no longer had anyone to fight against.

5. For example, the medievalist Sidney Painter notes that "from very early times the various Germanic peoples had been accustomed to choose chieftains to lead them in war. When the state of war was prolonged, these chieftains tended to become permanent" (Painter 1951, 1).

6. It is not always easy to tell from the accounts of the Spanish chroniclers what level of political organization was being described. In general, though, when the chroniclers described a people as being "divididos en numerosos pueblos," they meant autonomous villages, and when they referred to them as living in "provincias," they were referring to chiefdoms.

7. There is a common misconception that the paramount chief of a chiefdom is a benign figure, readily accountable to his fellows. Thus, for example, Schwerin (1973, 6) says of a paramount chief that his authority "depends wholly on the common consent of the other members of the society." But the facts tell a different story. A more realistic appraisal of the matter is found in Hermann Trimborn's statement that "in fact, the rulers of the Cauca Valley, like the Cueva chiefs [of Panama], exercised a despotic rule, which especially in warfare, or rather, as a consequence of the continual state of war, grew to an unbounded power" (quoted in Redmond 1994, 118, 148).

8. However, some islands in the Pacific, such as Tongatapu and Hawaii, after the political consolidation of the island had been achieved, saw their paramount chiefs begin efforts to conquer neighboring islands.

9. "Ujukam" (a fictitious name given him by Kelekna) is known to have killed many enemies during his military career, and this is not uncommon among kakáram. The Shuar war leader Tukup', whose fascinating life history is recounted in detail by Janet Hendricks, was known to have killed some twenty men (Hendricks 1993, 19).

10. Writing in the 1930s, Matthew Stirling (1938, 39) said of the Shuar: "Often . . . a weak curaka, fearing that his group would not be able to successfully defend themselves against an attack from enemies, will voluntarily place himself and his group under the influence of the strong curaka [that is, a kakáram] in a loose sort of alliance. In this way the strong group tends to grow and to become even stronger until one curaka may have 8 or 10 lesser curakas more or less under his control. This state of affairs is usually not very permanent. Owing to the loose organization and lack of any real power on the part of the head curaka, the large group becomes

unwieldy or develops diverse interests and it tends to split up again into the independent units."

11. Indeed, volume 4 of the *Handbook of South American Indians* was entitled *The Circum-Caribbean Tribes*, and its contents were separated from volume 3, *The Tropical Forest Tribes*, in recognition of the fact that the societies in the circum-Caribbean area, as far as their sociopolitical structure was concerned, represented a distinct advance over those of Amazonia (see Carneiro 1981, 38–40).

12. To be sure, not all chiefdoms, having once emerged, evolved into larger and more firmly consolidated political units. It was not unknown for an incipient chiefdom to fragment back into its constituent units of autonomous villages.

13. "Andagoya and Oviedo y Valdés reported that [among the Panamanian chiefdoms] common warriors who committed great feats on the battlefield . . . were rewarded with the noble title of *cabra* [military captain]. A chief further rewarded these distinguished warriors with women, territory, and subjects to command. War was thus a vehicle for aspiring commoners to enter the elite sector of society" (Redmond 1994, 128).

References

Balée, William
1984   The ecology of ancient Tupi warfare. In *Warfare, Culture, and Environment*, edited by R. B. Ferguson, 241–65. Orlando: Academic Press.
Brett, Rev. W. H.
1868   *The Indian Tribes of Guiana*. London: Bell and Daldy.
Caesar, Julius
1982   *The Conquest of Gaul*. Translated by S. A. Handford, revised by J. F. Gardner. Harmondsworth, England: Penguin Books.
Carneiro, Robert L.
1970   A theory of the origin of the state. *Science* 169: 733–38.
1981   The chiefdom: Precursor of the state. In *The Transition to Statehood in the New World*, edited by G. D. Jones and R. R. Kautz, 37–79. Cambridge: Cambridge University Press.
1987   Further reflections on resource concentration and its role in the rise of the state. In *Studies in the Neolithic and Urban Revolutions: The V. Gordon Childe Colloquium, Mexico, 1986*, edited by L. Manzanilla, 245–60. BAR (British Archaeological Reports) International Series, no. 349. Oxford.
1990   Chiefdom-level warfare as exemplified in Fiji and the Cauca Valley. In *The Anthropology of War*, edited by J. Haas, 190–211. School of American Research. Cambridge: Cambridge University Press.
1991   The nature of the chiefdom as revealed by evidence from the Cauca Valley of Colombia. In *Profiles in Cultural Evolution*, edited by A. T. Rambo and K. Gillogly, 167–90. University of Michigan Museum of Anthropology, Anthropological Papers, no. 85. Ann Arbor.

1992a Point counterpoint: Ecology and ideology in the development of New World civilizations. In *Ideology and Pre-Columbian Civilizations,* edited by A. A. Demarest and G. W. Conrad, 175–203. Santa Fe: School of American Research Press.

1992b The Calusa and the Powhatan, native chiefdoms of North America. *Reviews in Anthropology* 21:27–38.

1993 Factors favoring the development of political leadership in Amazonia. In *South American Indian Studies,* no. 1, *Leadership in Lowland South America,* edited by W. H. Kracke, 4–8. Bennington, Vt.: Bennington College.

Chagnon, Napoleon A.

1974 *Studying the Yanomamö.* New York: Holt, Rinehart and Winston.

1983 *Yanomamö: The Fierce People.* 3rd edition. New York: Holt, Rinehart and Winston.

Edwards, Bryan

1801–19 *History of the British Colonies in the West Indies.* 5 vols. London: G. and W. B. Whittaker.

Feil, D. K.

1987 *The Evolution of Highland Papua New Guinea Societies.* Cambridge: Cambridge University Press.

Fernandes, Florestan

1963 *Organização Social dos Tupinambá* (1949). 2nd edition. São Paulo: Difusão Européia do Livro.

Flannery, Kent V.

1972 The cultural evolution of civilizations. *Annual Review of Ecology and Systematics* 3:399–426.

Fried, Morton H.

1967 *The Evolution of Political Society.* New York: Random House.

Gumilla, P. José

1963 *El Orinoco Ilustrado y Defendido* (1745). Biblioteca de la Academia Nacional de la Historia, no. 68. Fuentes para la Historia Colonial de Venezuela. Caracas: Italgráfica, C.A.

Hendricks, Janet Wall

1993 *To Drink of Death: The Narrative of a Shuar Warrior.* Tucson: University of Arizona Press.

Kelekna, Pita

n.d.a Kashintiu kakaram: Strongman, hierarchy, and alliance among the Jivaroan Achuar. Unpublished Ms.

n.d.b Achuar political atomism: Personal strategies of power. Unpublished Ms.

Kracke, Waud H.

1993 Kagwahiv headmanship in peace and war. In *South American Indian Studies,* no. 1, *Leadership in Lowland South America,* edited by W. H. Kracke, 9–18. Bennington, Vt.: Bennington College.

Métraux, Alfred
1948   The Tupinamba. In *The Handbook of South American Indians*, vol. 3, *The Tropical Forest Tribes*, edited by J. H. Steward, 95–133. Bureau of American Ethnology Bulletin 143. Washington, D.C.: Smithsonian Institution.

Miller, Bruce G., and Daniel L. Boxberger
1994   Creating chiefdoms: The Puget Sound case. *Ethnohistory* 41(2):267–93.

Oberg, Kalervo
1955   Types of social structure among the lowland tribes of South and Central America. *American Anthropologist* 57(3):472–87.

Painter, Sidney
1951   *The Rise of the Feudal Monarchies*. Ithaca, N.Y.: Cornell University Press.

Redmond, Elsa M.
1994   *Tribal and Chiefly Warfare in South America*. University of Michigan Museum of Anthropology, Memoirs, no. 28. Ann Arbor.

Richards, Audrey I.
1940   The political system of the Bemba tribe—North-Eastern Rhodesia. In *African Political Systems*, edited by M. Fortes and E. E. Evans-Pritchard, 83–120. London: Oxford University Press.

Roth, Walter E.
1924   *An Introductory Study of the Arts, Crafts, and Customs of the Guiana Indians*. Bureau of American Ethnology, 38th Annual Report, 1916–17. Washington, D.C.: Smithsonian Institution.

Sahlins, Marshall D.
1963   Poor man, rich man, big-man, chief: Political types in Melanesia and Polynesia. *Comparative Studies in Society and History* 5(3):285–303.

1972   *Stone Age Economics*. Chicago: Aldine-Atherton.

Saignes, Miguel Acosta
1946   *Los Caribes de la Costa Venezolana*. México: Acta Antropológica.

Schomburgk, Richard
1923   *Travels in British Guiana during the Years 1840–1844*. Translated and edited by W. E. Roth. 2 vols. Georgetown, British Guiana: Daily Chronicle Office.

Schwerin, Karl H.
1973   The anthropological antecedents: Caciques, cacicazgos and caciquismo. In *The Caciques*, edited by R. Kern, 5–17. Albuquerque: University of New Mexico Press.

Service, Elman R.
1962   *Primitive Social Organization*. New York: Random House.

Spencer, Herbert
1967   *The Evolution of Society: Selections from Herbert Spencer's Principles of Sociology*. Edited and with an introduction by R. L. Carneiro. Chicago: University of Chicago Press.

Stirling, Matthew W.
1938   *Historical and Ethnographical Material on the Jivaro Indians.* Bureau of American
       Ethnology Bulletin 117. Washington, D.C.: Smithsonian Institution.
Tylor, Edward B.
1916   *Anthropology.* New York: D. Appleton and Company.
Watson, James B.
1973   Tairora: The politics of despotism in a small society. In *Politics in New Guinea,*
       edited by R. M. Berndt and P. Lawrence, 224–75. Seattle: University of Wash-
       ington Press.
Whitehead, Neil L.
1988   *Lords of the Tiger Spirit: A History of the Caribs in Colonial Venezuela and Guyana,*
       1498–1820. Dordrecht: Foris Publications.

CHAPTER 2

Less than Meets the Eye

Evidence for Protohistoric Chiefdoms in Northern New Mexico

WINIFRED CREAMER AND JONATHAN HAAS

For more than a century, the native peoples of the southwestern United States have provided insights into general issues about the evolution of political systems across time and cultural boundaries. Geographically, the Southwest was on the periphery of the complex evolution of state societies in Mesoamerica to the south. Indeed, many of the environmental, economic and demographic conditions that drove state evolution in parts of Mesoamerica, particularly in such places as central Mexico and Oaxaca, look similar to the conditions found in much of the Southwest.

The occasional bursts of political development in the Southwest, such as those found at Chaco Canyon (Sebastian 1991) or in the development of the Hohokam regional system in southern Arizona (Crown and Judge 1991; Doyel 1987), may represent examples of temporary chieftaincy. Development of chiefdoms having hereditary leaders did not follow, however. In each case, these systems collapsed and did not lead to or stimulate the increased complexity and centralization of a state level of organization.

The question of the political trajectory of the Southwest is an interesting one in terms of evolutionary models. Was this region on the track of evolving toward a state level of organization but at a slower pace than in Mesoamerica? Or, alternatively, had the different cultural groups of the Southwest gone off on a different evolutionary trajectory by developing egalitarian solutions to the challenges of the material conditions of their lives? Although the evolution of Southwest societies was significantly altered by the arrival of the Spaniards in the sixteenth century, we can gain some insight into the nature and trajectory of aboriginal political organization by looking at the years immediately before and after the first European contact.

To begin addressing the question of the nature of aboriginal political organization in the Southwest and the precolonial trajectory of the political systems, in this paper we employ archaeological and ethnohistoric data on the Rio Grande pueblos of the Protohistoric period, taken here to be A.D. 1450–1680. We specifically want to address the question of whether the precolonial Pueblo people had developed centralized and hierarchical forms of chieftancy in the years just before and after the arrival of the first Europeans. There is evidence from earlier prehistoric periods that Puebloan people were organized in relatively simple and decentralized, "tribal" forms of society which were found earlier in prehistory (Haas and Creamer 1993), and this tends to be the classic interpretation made of the modern ethnographic record. On the other hand, it has been specifically proposed that just prior to the arrival of Europeans, the Pueblos of the Southwest had developed chieftancy, if not formal chiefdoms (see, for example, Upham 1989), and this evolutionary development was then adumbrated by European colonialism. Both of these views are based primarily on the ethnographic record and need to be examined in light of archaeology and ethnohistory.

Models of Chiefdom Organization

In a recent discussion of the evolution of chiefdoms, Earle "loosely defined" the concept of chiefdom as "a polity that organizes centrally a regional population in the thousands. Some degree of heritable social ranking and economic stratification is characteristically associated" (Earle 1991, 1). Fried (1967) earlier defined ranking as unequal access to *positions of status*, and stratification as unequal access to the *basic resources* that sustain life. Elsewhere (1985) we have discussed the expected material characteristics of chiefdoms, including differences in size and quality of residences, site-size hierarchy, communal labor projects at the regional level, surplus food production, specialized craft production, extensive exchange of subsistence and sumptuary goods, and intensified warfare (see also Peebles and Kus 1977). This model has been applied to the archaeological evidence from Chaco Canyon in northwest New Mexico; Akins (1986) concluded that the Chaco system at its height had a centralized hierarchy with at least three levels of social ranking. However, the Chacoan political system, collapsing in the twelfth century, is anomalous in the Southwest, and archaeologists have yet to be able to establish solid evolutionary connections with any of the Puebloan groups that were extant at the time of the arrival of the first Spaniards in the sixteenth century.

Elsewhere around the Southwest, there is considerable debate as to whether chiefdoms emerged prior to the arrival of the first Europeans. The question specifically is whether there were polities beyond the level of the individual village that organized centrally a regional population in the thousands. Were there elite rulers or "chiefs" who had some differential access to basic resources and were able to exercise effective power over their respective populations through control of resources and/or the means of production? Our research in the northern Rio Grande region has been organized to address this question, and we here begin to look at the available archaeological and ethnohistoric evidence of precontact stratification and chiefdoms.

There is a general consensus that there was some kind of ranking in the precolonial Southwest, as status differences are manifested in some residential differences and in differential burial treatment and funerary objects (Clark 1969; Crotty 1983; Lightfoot and Feinman 1982; Upham 1982; Upham and Plog 1986; Upham, Lightfoot, and Feinman 1981, 824; but see Whittlesey 1978, 1984). True stratification, however, with differential access to basic resources, is a different matter—and more to the point in the debate over Southwest political organization. Differential access to basic resources implies a power differential within the population. Some people eat better and generally live better because of enhanced control over the means of producing or acquiring certain basic resources within that political economic system (Haas 1982). Generally, routes to stratification include either control of large-scale trade, warfare and conquest, or control over a centralized mode of production, such as irrigation.

In support of the chiefdom model is the evidence of extensive precontact trade ranging from northern New Mexico to Mexico and to the Gulf of California on the Pacific (Snow 1981) and extensive trade between the Plains and Puebloan groups (Habicht-Mauche 1995; Spielmann 1983, 1989). There is also historic evidence for specialization in trade goods from one settlement to another (Ford 1972). Although overall population figures are very much open to question (Creamer and Haas 1993), individual settlements in the period just before and after contact ranged from several hundred to several thousand people (Palkovich 1985; Schroeder 1979; Zubrow 1974). It has been argued that shifting alliances bound together groups of these villages for mutual protection (cf. Habicht-Mauche 1988; Plog

1983; Upham and Reed 1989). An examination of site distributions has also shown that the large villages were gathered together in discrete clusters in the northern Rio Grande region (P. Reed 1990). The levels of trade and evidence of alliance and clustering all correspond to patterns that can be expected to occur (though not necessarily exclusively) in chiefdom societies.

On the other side of the debate, complex chiefdoms seem unlikely to have developed in the context of the general low population density of the American Southwest as a whole, despite the size of some settlements. Though it should be pointed out that in the northern Rio Grande region the information on demographics is scanty and indirect, it is at least possible that there were population densities in the area equal to those found in historic chiefdoms in Hawaii, South America, and Africa (Creamer and Haas 1993; Upham and Reed 1989). The extensive residential architecture tends to be highly uniform, with no marked differences in size or quality to identify the home or residential complex of a chief or chiefly lineage (Habicht-Mauche and Creamer 1989). However, it has been suggested that kivas and plazas were used as public spaces by political leaders in efforts to exercise social and political control (Adams 1991; Lekson 1988). Perhaps the most influential line of reasoning employed in arguing against formal political organization in the Southwest is the use of the direct historic method to interpret aspects of life in the area before the arrival of Europeans. Those who believe that ethnography collected at the turn of the twentieth century depicts the substance of Pueblo life of the preceding centuries point out that in the ethnographic record of the Southwest, there are no chiefdoms extending beyond the boundaries of any individual village (Dozier 1970a, 1970b; Eggan 1950).

At present, there is simply not enough evidence to reach a conclusion about whether there were classic, multivillage chiefdoms as loosely defined by Earle. However, there are data that point to complex forms of political organization without regional centralization.

Political Organization without Centralization

The limited data that are available point to a form of village-oriented political organization without evidence of any kind of "paramount" chief or a centrally organized, large labor force beyond the village (as proposed by Johnson and Earle for chiefdoms [1987, 207]). There are communal labor projects, such as great kivas, at the village level, but across the region there are no exceptional examples of large-scale construction beyond the capacity of the local village. Warfare, while present, does not seem to be a vehicle to transcend village autonomy in that there are no indications in either the archaeological or ethnohistoric record of one village conquering another. Nor is there evidence of individual political leaders controlling trade or production as a means of exercising power over their respective villages, though a single village may have controlled a specific resource, such as lead or turquoise.

At the same time, the Pueblos of northern New Mexico were clearly not egalitarian societies. There is evidence for social and economic specialization, hierarchies, and differentiation at both the household and the village level (Ford 1972; Snow 1981; Wilcox 1981). There was also some form of centralized decision making, either by a village council or by a local chief or headman (Smith 1983; Wilcox 1991), though more restricted decision-making groups have been suggested (Brandt 1977, 1994). A number of authors have examined alternatives to centralized political organization that may provide frameworks appropriate for testing (Habicht-Mauche et al. 1987).

In a recent analysis of land productivity data for the northern Southwest, Kohler and Van West (1994) identify specific conditions of soil fertility, moisture, and variability in crop yield that led to food sharing in their study area. The authors see food sharing and other cooperative behavior as fundamental to the development of more complex forms of political organization. They suggest that a large resource surplus does not have to be accumulated before food sharing begins; nor, in their scenario, does a village necessarily have to have an individual leader for food sharing or other cooperative activities among households to take place (Kohler and Van West 1994). Their study focuses on the period prior to A.D. 1300, however, and does not address subsequent developments.

A model from Asia also suggests that cooperative activities such as trade and food sharing and other extensive networks can develop without individual leaders and large-scale organization. Along the north coast of New Guinea, among people who speak many distinctive languages, widely shared elements of material culture are reflected both in museum collections and in archaeological data (Welsch et al. 1992). Ethnographic study indicates that a system of inherited "friendships" has created a flexible institution of economic and political organization that "might even be called a polity without (in pre-European times) an overarching political authority or governmental central place" (Terrell and Welsch 1990).

From archaeological data at the toe of the North American continent, Sheets (1992, 36) has suggested that Central America is another area in which the general processes of state formation did not proceed beyond the chiefdom level and depicts this situation as intentional: "Two of the most important internally generated characteristics of the Intermediate Area are the early establishment and the remarkable persistence of the village tradition." Sheets concludes (1992, 37): "Egalitarian villages and simple ranked societies (small chiefdoms) were the rule, as the state level of development was largely avoided." The conditions that supported long-term village organization included the dispersed nature of resources and reliance on wild, "nonintensifiable" subsistence resources. The dispersed resource base resulted in "pressures . . . to control populations and maintain adaptive efficiencies (high production per unit *effort*) more than in areas where agriculture was burgeoning" (Sheets 1992, 37; emphasis in original). These conditions sustained villages as the enduring form of social and political organization.

Spencer (1993) has used the concept of biased transmission in discussing the development of chiefly authority. Indirectly biased transmission "results from choosing a behavioral model to emulate on the basis of certain features, called indicator traits by Boyd and Richerson, after which other features (called the indirectly biased traits) also exhibited by the models are accepted by individuals as a package without further evaluation" (1993, 47).[1] He suggests that permanent centralized authority is most likely to develop where there are individuals in competition for leadership roles as a result of factionalism or economic competition. This must be in a context where speedy sharing of information (about resources, climate, or potential conflict, for example) is widely important. However, a single individual must be able to best the competition, coordinate information sharing, and sustain both intravillage and supravillage political relationships. For archaeological examples in Mexico and Venezuela, Spencer argues that this appears to have taken place, with biased transmission among the mechanisms that made centralized authority acceptable. This model may be tested in the northern Rio Grande, though it is possible that the necessary conditions were not met, suggesting that individual human agency may prevent change as often as it promotes change.

Models such as these complement the work of Gregory Johnson, who introduced the concept of sequential hierarchy, a decision-making structure invoked as needed rather than requiring specialized bureaucrat/decision maker/leader positions to be permanently filled (Johnson 1978, 1982, 1989).

That such an on-demand system may have existed is hinted at by reports of the early Spanish explorers in New Mexico. Castaño de Sosa, for example, referred to regions or districts that have long been interpreted as language groups (Ford et al. 1972) but that may in fact have been multi-village political and economic systems.

These models share a common perspective in assuming that coordination of activities beyond the level of a kin group can occur without either individual leadership or mobilization of resources or labor. While Kohler and Van West examined relations that span households, others consider supravillage relations. The recent emergence of models of decentralized political organization also reflects shifts in analytical priorities away from understanding the shared patterns of social and political organization of early evolutionary anthropology toward a focus on understanding the range of variability in the configuration of political organization (Johnson and Earle 1987).

Archaeological and ethnohistoric data from the northern Rio Grande can be used to assess the extent to which differences in rank and in access to resources existed during the Protohistoric period. We also obtained information on the nature of suprafamily political relations. Taking these data together, it is possible to establish a clearer picture of which models are our highest priorities for further testing.

Archaeological Data from the Northern Rio Grande Valley

Archaeological evidence of Puebloan political organization, warfare, and trade comes from nearly a century of research, including our own recent excavations at pueblo sites in the northern Rio Grande Valley. While data from existing survey and excavation outline the nature of settlement, with ample evidence for trade, there is much less information on warfare and on the organization of economic production, topics which do not always lend themselves to interpretation from material remains without specifically targeted original research.

The evidence we have concerning the protohistoric settlement pattern, site sizes, and the internal composition of settlements shows some evidence of ranking but does not indicate significant stratification. Archaeological survey from northern New Mexico indicates that during the Protohistoric period, a majority of the population lived in large, aggregated villages of several hundred to 3,000 rooms. Our search of the survey records for the northern Rio Grande Valley indicates there were between 60 and 65 villages of 300 to 3,000 rooms, which appear to have been occupied sometime during the period from A.D. 1450 to 1680. Few people lived in smaller hamlets during the Protohistoric period (Cordell 1978; Stuart and

Gauthier 1981). This archaeological pattern is confirmed by chronicler Pedro de Castañeda, who in 1540 commented that "all combined [the pueblos] must contain about 20,000 men. This can be easily estimated by the population of the pueblos, *for between them there are no villages or houses,* but, on the contrary, the land is all uninhabited" (Hammond and Rey 1940, 259; emphasis added).

Although there is variation in the maximum size of sites seen in the archaeological record, the largest sites may not have been fully occupied at any one time. Analysis of surface and subsurface collections made at two of the largest sites, San Marcos Pueblo and Pueblo Blanco, revealed that both sites are composed of three or more distinct groups of contemporaneous roomblocks, which were occupied at different times (Creamer n.d.; Nelson 1997). Room counts at large sites thus are not a useful indicator of occupation size, as all the rooms at any given site were not in use at any given time. This pattern also contributes to there being no clear evidence for a site-size hierarchy in the northern Rio Grande region in the time immediately before or after European contact.

Within individual sites, the architecture of the sixteenth century was homogeneous, with modest variation in room size (Creamer 1993; Habicht-Mauche and Creamer 1989; Hamlen n.d.). There is no indication of differential quality of housing provided to any individuals based on rank or authority. However, the number of interconnected rooms in a living unit varied greatly within sites (Creamer 1993, 125) and could have been based on rank and differential access to resources. At the same time, it is also possible that differences in the number of rooms per household may have been a factor of family size rather than of status. Rooms can be grouped in relatively few categories—primarily storage rooms and living rooms, though grinding and ceremonial rooms have been identified (Creamer 1993; Creamer et al. 1993). Specialized rooms for tool making, weaving, pottery making, working hides, or any other clearly defined activities have not been identified, suggesting that if there was any specialization in production, it would have been at the household level only.

Burials are among the key areas where evidence of social stratification is found in other regions, but there is little differentiation among burial accompaniments in the northern Rio Grande Valley on the basis of age, sex, or social status (Palkovich 1980; Stodder 1990). The only individuals standing out in terms of funerary objects are accompanied by items indicating that they were shamans or medicine men of some kind (Palkovich 1980, 17). Differences in health that might reflect restricted access to specific foods by one class of people have not been reported for any of the human skeletal samples available from the region (Kahl 1993; Palkovich 1980; Stodder and Martin 1992).

Trade

Extensive trade is represented archaeologically by widespread distribution of glaze-painted ceramics and biscuit wares in sites outside their region of manufacture (Beal 1987; Elliott 1982; Mera 1934). Small amounts of polychrome ceramics, such as Heshataouthla, St. Johns, Zuni, Zia, and Acoma polychromes, and of Hopi yellow wares were apparently traded into the northern Rio Grande from their source area in the Little Colorado drainage (Kidder and Shepard 1936).

There is a major source of turquoise in the Cerrillos Hills outside Santa Fe, and turquoise from this source has been recovered from archaeological sites throughout the Southwest (Snow 1973; Warren and Mathien 1985; Weigand et al. 1977). Trade in this turquoise is believed by some to have been controlled by the residents of San Marcos Pueblo, located several kilometers south of the source. Our own recent excavations at San Marcos revealed numerous fragments of turquoise throughout the site in much higher densities than at any other site in the region. There was, however, no indication that turquoise was either restricted to or concentrated in only certain parts of the site. Rather, it occurs prominently all over the surface and in subsurface units, suggesting household-based production (Snow 1981).

There was some trade in obsidian from the area of the Jémez Mountains, and obsidian from Jémez sources has been found at Plains sites (Baugh and Nelson 1987). The nature and extent of trade in obsidian across the northern Rio Grande region, however, have not been clearly defined (Cordell 1989).

Cotton, although described by the chroniclers as a significant resource in the northern Rio Grande region, has been recovered only rarely in archaeological context (Harlow 1965; Lang 1986) and is not present in the available pollen analyses (Bohrer 1986). In Nelson's excavations at large Protohistoric period sites in the Galisteo Basin (Nelson 1914), however, he did recover an abundance of bone tools apparently used for sewing and weaving. As with the distribution of turquoise mentioned earlier, these objects were found throughout the site rather than restricted to one area or group of rooms. (These tools have never been written up in a published report; the information is derived from an examination of the Nelson collections at the American Museum of Natural History.) In general, archaeological sites in the Rio Grande Valley have not yielded evidence for stockpiling of trade items that might indicate centralized distribution of goods, yet the possibility that members of a single pueblo may have controlled the turquoise trade suggests limited access to that commodity and arguably some degree of political centralization for mining, processing, and trade.

Warfare

Evidence for warfare during the early sixteenth century is limited but present. Furthermore, all of the excavated large pueblos have been found to have been constructed defensively, with limited access to enclosed plazas and ground floor rooms accessible only from rooftop entries (see Creamer 1993). Sites were often located in elevated places with good views, which made them relatively easy to defend. Skeletal remains indicate an increase in cranial trauma among adults during the Protohistoric period (Stodder and Martin 1992, 61), possibly correlated with an increase in conflict within the region. Overall, there is evidence for relatively low level endemic warfare in the northern Rio Grande region during the Protohistoric period but little evidence for large-scale warfare that might have resulted in the conquest and subjugation of one village by another.

Organization of Production

The organization of production has been most thoroughly studied from the perspective of pottery making. Shepard (1942) was the first to suggest that the glaze-painted pottery of the Rio Grande Valley indicated centralized production. After examining the glaze wares from Pecos Pueblo, Shepard noted close similarity in temper in some groups of sherds, which she suggested indicated a group of ceramics from one place of origin (Shepard 1942).

Warren's study of ceramic temper from Tonque Pueblo and in the Cochiti area have led her to believe that most glaze-ware types were produced at the site of Tonque, which she proposed as a regional center for glaze-decorated ceramic production during the period A.D. 1450–1600. San Marcos Pueblo was proposed as a center for the production of glaze-decorated vessels slightly earlier, during the fifteenth century (Warren 1969, 190). However, there is an active debate over whether the ceramics of this period were being made in only a few locations by craft specialists; a recent, detailed chemical analysis of ceramics points to the localized production of glaze wares at individual sites throughout the Protohistoric period (L. Reed 1990).

Ethnohistoric Data from the Northern Rio Grande Valley

The first European explorers entered the northern Rio Grande Valley in 1540. Led by Francisco Vázquez de Coronado, the group hoped to encounter mineral deposits, a large population of native people who could be used as laborers, and tracts of fertile land that could be awarded to each of the participants in the expedition. They were disappointed on every count, withdrew from New Mexico in 1541, and returned to Mexico. Other explorations followed, however, including expeditions led by Francisco Sánchez Chamuscado in 1581, Antonio de Espejo in 1582, Gaspar Castaño de Sosa in 1591, and Juan de Oñate in 1598. Other explorers and colonists entered New Mexico during the seventeenth century as well, but we focus on the first half-century of contact for the present.

Each of the expeditions mentioned is documented in the form of accounts or letters reporting to Spanish and colonial authorities (Hammond and Rey 1940, 1953, 1966). The present discussion utilizes reports from the first 60 years of European contact to focus on the period when we expect the least disturbance of traditional Pueblo life. By the end of Oñate's colonizing efforts in 1628, there was already considerable disruption of the indigenous tradition (Gutiérrez 1991; Simmons 1991).

Perhaps the most notable aspect of the documentary material available on the sixteenth-century exploration of New Mexico is how little the indigenous people of the region were mentioned despite the extent of the accounts. Pedro de Castañeda, for example, noted, "All these pueblos have, in general, the same ceremonies and customs, although some have practices among them not observed elsewhere" (Hammond and Rey 1940, 253–54). Such brief remarks are characteristic of the European reports.

Political Organization

Description of Pueblo political organization is equally brief—somewhat surprising, considering that the Europeans wished to gain political control over the territory they explored. For the period of the Coronado expedition (1540–41), Castañeda noted that "they have no rulers as in New Spain, but are governed by the counsel of their oldest men" (Hammond and Rey 1940, 253). He also described the role of village leaders in dealing with the Europeans' requests for supplies: "ill feeling [among the people of Tiguex] was aggravated by the general's desire to gather some clothing to distribute among the soldiers. For this purpose he sent for an Indian chief of Tiguex with whom we were already acquainted and with whom we were on good terms [Juan Alemán].... The general spoke with him, asking him to furnish

300 or more pieces of clothing which he needed to distribute to his men. He replied that it was not in his power to do this, but in that of the governors; that they had to discuss the matter among the pueblos; and that the Spaniards had to ask this individually from each pueblo" (Hammond and Rey 1940, 224).

Hernán Gallegos, reporting on the later Chamuscado-Rodríguez explorations, made no comments on political organization beyond assuming there were leaders: "Then we asked twenty or thirty Indians who appeared on the roofs and who seemed to be the chief men of the pueblo—the cacique among them—to give us either the horses or the culprits who had killed them" (Hammond and Rey 1966, 97). *Cacique* in the context of early Spanish explorers could best be translated as something like a village chief or group leader.

Writing of the Espejo expedition (1582), Pérez de Luxán noted, "These people are governed by caciques, as they do not have any ruler who has authority beyond his own pueblo" (Hammond and Rey 1966, 179). Espejo himself remarked: "All the pueblos [Piro according to the footnote] have caciques, allotted according to the number of inhabitants. Thus there are the principal caciques, who in turn have other caciques under them, that is to say, their *tequitatos,* who then proclaim the order aloud throughout the pueblo concerned and in a very short time all bring what they have been asked to provide" (Hammond and Rey 1966, 220).

After this point in his narrative, Espejo often noted, "They are governed like the people of the provinces already mentioned" (Hammond and Rey 1966, 222), without noting any differences among the various Puebloan groups he visited in the Rio Grande Valley.

By the time Castaño de Sosa entered the northern Rio Grande region in 1591, it seems to have been assumed that each village had a headman. Castaño de Sosa and his followers appear to have been utterly indifferent to the indigenous way of life, and they made a practice of entering a village, gathering the people present, and making a speech about allegiance to the king of Spain, a ceremony followed by their appointing village leaders. Typically it was noted, "In the pueblo that I am now describing, we followed the same practice as in the others, appointing a governor, an alcalde, and an alguacil" (Hammond and Rey 1966, 283). Unfortunately, no mention is made of any of these officials either before or after their appointment.

While the historic records are somewhat ambivalent about the role of village leaders, they certainly give no hint of organization or leadership extending beyond the limits of the individual village.

Trade

Trade among indigenous people was rarely reported by the Spaniards even though archaeological evidence indicates that trade was extensive. As early as 1521, Cabeza de Vaca and his companions, survivors of a shipwreck off the coast of Texas, heard of people living to the north who grew cotton, possibly the Rio Grande Pueblos. Castañeda noted, "Throughout these provinces one finds pottery glazed with alcohol, and jugs of such elaborate designs and shapes that it was surprising" (Hammond and Rey 1940, 256). Elsewhere Castañeda saw "many ollas filled with a select shiny metal with which the Indians glazed their pottery" (Hammond and Rey 1940, 244)—apparently lead ore used to make glaze-painted pottery that was widely traded.

Trade with non-Pueblo groups from the plains may be indicated by Castañeda's reference to "dealings" between Plains groups and the people of Pecos, discussed later. Castaño de Sosa observed that "all agreed to camp for the night at some huts a long harquebus shot from the pueblo [possibly San Juan], where there were people from other places who had come to trade with this settlement" (Hammond and Rey 1966, 284). There are no direct references to the magnitude or nature of this "trade," but it does not appear (either in the historic or in archaeological records) to have been a large-scale exchange of resources between the Plains and Pueblo groups.

Exchange of goods among the Rio Grande settlements, a practice that was of both economic and social importance throughout the nineteenth century and perhaps earlier (Ford 1972), is not mentioned specifically in the early Spanish accounts. However, the absence of such mention may not be particularly significant as the early written accounts of Spanish chroniclers lacked attention to detail and operated under the general assumption already noted, that all the Puebloan groups were similar.

Warfare

Despite little evidence of interest in trade apart from identifying resources that could be commandeered, there was consistent reporting on inter-Pueblo hostilities. Perhaps owing to the military background of most of the participants in expeditions of exploration, more attention was paid to evidence of indigenous warfare than to trade. Both warfare and trade took Pueblo people beyond the confines of their home villages and suggest that there was organization of some activities on a larger scale.

Available documents from the period when the first Spaniards arrived do not indicate significant battles with any of the Pueblo groups in the Rio

Grande Valley, as was often the case elsewhere in North America (Blakely and Mathews 1990). The early Spanish chroniclers did, however, describe reports of interpueblo and Plains-Pueblo conflict (Hammond and Rey 1940; Spielmann 1991).

From Coronado's expedition onward, European chroniclers noted fortification of some villages, the abandonment of others, and the use of refuge sites in the mountains. Castañeda recorded that Coronado "came to a pueblo called Acuco [Acoma], built on a rock. It contained some two hundred warriors-robbers who were feared throughout the land" (quoted in Hammond and Rey 1940, 218). In the Rio Grande Valley, Castañeda noted mountain refuge sites: "Those of Yuque-Yunque abandoned two very beautiful pueblos which were on opposite sides of the river, while the army was establishing camp, and went to the sierra where they had four very strong pueblos which could not be reached by the horses because of the craggy land" (Hammond and Rey 1940, 244).

At Pecos Pueblo, Castañeda observed the reception of Plains people: "The Teyas often go to the latter's pueblos to spend the winter, finding shelter under the eaves, as the inhabitants do not dare to allow them inside. Evidently they do not trust them, although they accept them as friends and have dealings with them. At night the visitors do not stay in the pueblo, but outside under the eaves. The pueblos keep watch at night with bugles and calls, as in the fortresses in Spain" (Hammond and Rey 1940, 258).

By the time of Espejo's observations in 1582, warfare among the Pueblos was still common: "[We] came to the pueblo of Jumea [Galisteo?], in the province of the Atamues [Tanos], a people more bellicose than those of the other provinces. They possess well-built houses, as is characteristic of people astute in war, and the flat roofs have drainage troughs. The houses are three and four stories high, with movable ladders, so that when these are raised the inhabitants cannot go up" (Hammond and Rey 1966, 206).

Villages were routinely fortified in some way, as Espejo describes: "From this pueblo we went two leagues farther for provisions, to the very large pueblo of Pocos [San Cristobal?] of this province. It must have over fifteen hundred warriors armed with bows and arrows. The houses are of four and five terraces, with wooden palisades in front of them as a defense in case of war" (Hammond and Rey 1940, 206).

Castaño de Sosa noted similar defensive fortifications in 1591. "The lieutenant governor [Castaño] called to the Indians in sign language, but none would leave his dwelling or come out from behind the barricades, trenches, or ramparts which the pueblo maintained for its defense at the most vital points" (Hammond and Rey 1940, 270). At Pecos, Castaño reported that "the houses in this pueblo are built like military barracks, back to back, with doors opening out all around; and they are four or five stories high. There are no doors opening into the streets on the ground floors; the houses are entered from above by means of portable hand ladders and trap doors" (Hammond and Rey 1940, 277).

While it is possible that Castaño de Sosa and his group were unduly concerned with the supposedly fierce Puebloans, his account repeatedly observes the defensive posture of the people, "the pueblo was very strong in people and supplies, and the houses were seven or eight stories high. The terraces were topped by a breastwork the height of a man behind which the Indians could shield themselves" (Hammond and Rey 1966, 284). Castaño de Sosa also observed the consequences of Puebloan warfare. "As they went along [from Santo Domingo], taking possession of various settlements, they crossed some mountains where they found two pueblos that had been deserted only a few days earlier on account of wars with other pueblos. . . . This was the explanation given by the Indians who accompanied us, and we ourselves could see plainly that it was true, because there were signs of many having been killed" (Hammond and Rey 1966, 291–92).[2]

While there is extensive mention of fortifications and conflict among Pueblo groups, and between Pueblo and other groups, little detail is provided about how groups were organized or led. It is also difficult to identify how much of what the Spaniards witnessed was actually a reaction to the Spaniards themselves and to their aggressive stance toward the native peoples. For example, when they first moved into the Rio Grande region, Castañeda gives an account of the preliminary events that preceded the arrival of the main Coronado party: "From here they went to Tiguex [near present day Albuquerque] where they were well received and lodged. . . . Our men had already burned a pueblo the day before the army arrived and were returning to their quarters" (Hammond and Rey 1940, 223).

Castañeda goes on to discuss in some detail the immediate disruption of some aspects of Pueblo life by the very first European expedition. Referring again to the Tiguex pueblos, he wrote in 1541, "However, the twelve pueblos of Tiguex were never resettled as long as the army remained in the region, no matter what assurances were given them" (Hammond and Rey 1940, 233–34). This observation of the Tiguex province remained applicable in 1591, when Castaño de Sosa visited the region, noting, "From this point, 14 other settlements could be seen along the river. The Indians said that most of them had been abandoned by the inhabitants due to fear and that they had sought refuge in the mountains or in other pueblos" (Hammond and Rey 1966, 292–93).

Summary

The existing archaeological and ethnohistoric data for stratification, political and economic centralization, and chiefdoms are highly ambiguous. In the northern Rio Grande region, there were concentrations of people living in large villages and engaged in a variety of horticultural practices and long-distance trade. The few written records indicate that the operative governing body at the village level was either a council or an individual who seems to have had undefined or perhaps temporary chiefly authority. There are signs of status differences, suggesting that an individual chieftain could have been in place. However, there are no signs of centralized control of acquisition or production of basic resources and no manifestations of the clear exercise of power by any kind of centralized authority. Paramount chiefdoms with hereditary rulers had not formed. There is evidence of warfare both within the region and with Plains people to the east, but there are no indications of the kind of intervillage conquest or subordination that has been suggested by Carneiro for the transition from tribe to chiefdom (Carneiro 1978, 1981, 1990). In the ethnohistoric record, there is no mention anywhere of a paramount chief beyond the borders of a particular village. As is typical of colonial interaction at many other times and places, the Spaniards themselves were responsible for appointing a single "governor" and imposing the concept of individual leadership and control.

Conclusions

Archaeological data indicate the existence of clusters of Protohistoric period sites within the northern Rio Grande region (P. Reed 1990). Each group of sites included independent villages economically organized by household. Evidence of trade and reports of warfare strongly indicate the existence of networks of organization at the village and supravillage level. Documentary reports indicate only that village governance was in the form of councils and/or village chiefs, and that the pueblos were in contact with each other and coordinated their actions but acted individually.

The northern Rio Grande region was probably composed of a number of small interaction spheres, clusters of cooperating villages. While we believe that trade and warfare were the activities that held highest priority for group action, the scanty documentary reports do not identify a source of coercive power behind group consensus. The documents are similarly mute about the vehicle for cooperative action. As historic reports are also silent about the role of native religion in society at the time of European arrival, it seems clear that there is a need to examine the possibility that leaders were members of the religious organization and that this connection was overlooked by the Europeans. If religious leaders were also civil leaders, a common situation in tribal and chiefdom societies, the fact that such leaders had permanent, known positions in the religious structure may explain how such leaders would be able to act only as necessary. Their status and primacy was built into the system through periodic religious ritual, and maintenance of civil activity manifested as "trade partnerships" or "inherited friendships." Repression of religious ritual and replacement of council leadership with individual leaders by the European explorers resulted in the survival today of only the ritual portion of the system, which was hidden early in colonial times and still relies heavily on secrecy (Brandt 1994).

Short-term, periodic chieftaincy as described by Redmond (see introduction to this volume) appears to be the maximum level of complexity manifested during the Protohistoric period by groups occupying the northern Rio Grande. Further, there is evidence of large villages and relatively high population densities in some areas, which suggests that there must have been significant restrictions on individual action and close coordination of community actions by village leaders. For specific villages and possibly for the region as a whole, individual leaders or village chiefs may have been in positions of authority over some aspects of social life, especially ceremonial activities that reinforced achieved leadership status. Individual authority did not appear to extend to economic production, centralized trade, or coordinated warfare, however. The northern Rio Grande may have been a chieftaincy in encompassing a large territory, united by long-term relationships demonstrated through religious ritual, trade, and constant conflict to maintain the whole. What is absent from the Rio Grande is any evidence of accumulating personal wealth or of a trend toward the formation of enduring chiefdoms or the institutionalization of chiefdoms through labor mobilization for monument construction. The harshness of the climate made stockpiling of basic economic resources extremely difficult, and without a means to acquire an economic power base, the key to long-term maintenance of an extensive, collaborative system is lacking.

Continued search of the historic records and study of Pueblo oral history is needed to understand better the politics of the Pueblos in response to the arrival of Europeans. Archaeological research needs to examine the role of religion and ritual in communication and control within the region. The benefits will include a better ability to appreciate the contribution of the Pueblo people to principles of social control and the function of complex systems of economic production in the absence of centralized leadership.

Notes

1. Spencer (1993, 47) gives the following example of indirect bias: "A person in our own culture who has built a successful business (the indicator trait) may be regarded by others as an attractive model for other attributes, such as dress, diet, manner of speech, political ideology, and leisure time activities, which might then be widely adopted as indirectly biased traits in the Boyd-Richerson terminology."

2. Marjorie Lambert (1954) sees these as Paako and San Antonio, with the destruction carried out by Plains Indians.

References

Adams, E. Charles
1991   *The Origin and Development of the Pueblo Katsina Cult.* Tucson: University of Arizona Press.
Akins, Nancy J.
1986   *A Biocultural Approach to Human Burials from Chaco Canyon, New Mexico.* Reports of the Chaco Center, no. 9. Santa Fe: Branch of Cultural Research, U.S. Department of the Interior, National Park Service.
Baugh, Timothy G., and Fred W. Nelson Jr.
1987   New Mexico obsidian sources and exchange on the Southern Plains. *Journal of Field Archaeology* 14:313–29.
Beal, John D.
1987   Foundations of the Rio Grande Classic: The Lower Chama River A.D. 1300–1500. Prepared for Office of Cultural Affairs, Historic Preservation Division, Project No. 35–84–8617.07, Southwest Project No. 137. Santa Fe.
Blakeley, Robert L., and David S. Mathews
1990   Bioarchaeological evidence for a Spanish–Native American conflict in the sixteenth-century Southeast. *American Antiquity* 55(4):718–44.
Bohrer, Vorsila
1986   The ethnobotanical pollen record at Arroyo Hondo Pueblo. In *Food, Diet and Population at Prehistoric Arroyo Hondo Pueblo, New Mexico,* edited by W. Wetterstrom, 187–250. Santa Fe: School of American Research Press.
Brandt, Elizabeth
1977   The role of secrecy in a Pueblo society. In *Flowers in the Wind: Papers on the*

Ritual, Myth and Symbolism in California and the Southwest, edited by T. C. Blackburn, 11–28. Ballena Press Anthropological Papers, no. 8. Socorro, N.M.: Ballena Press.

1994   Egalitarianism, hierarchy, and centralization in the Pueblos. In *The Ancient Southwest Community,* edited by W. H. Wills and R. D. Leonard, 9–23. Albuquerque: University of New Mexico Press.

Carneiro, Robert L.

1978   Political expansion as an expression of the principle of competitive exclusion. In *Origins of the State: The Anthropology of Political Evolution,* edited by R. Cohen and E. R. Service, 205–24. Philadelphia: Institute for the Study of Human Issues.

1981   The chiefdom: Precursor of the state. In *The Transition to Statehood in the New World,* edited by G. D. Jones and R. R. Kautz, 37–79. Cambridge: Cambridge University Press.

1990   Chiefdom-level warfare as exemplified in Fiji and the Cauca Valley. In *The Anthropology of War,* edited by J. Haas, 190–211. School of American Research. Cambridge: Cambridge University Press.

Clark, Geoffrey

1969   A preliminary analysis of burial clusters at the Grasshopper site, east-central Arizona. *Kiva* 35(2):57–86.

Cordell, Linda S.

1978   A Cultural Resources overview of the Middle Rio Grande Valley, New Mexico. Report for the USDA Forest Service, Southwestern Region, Albuquerque, and the Bureau of Land Management, New Mexico State Office, Santa Fe.

1989   Northern and central Rio Grande. In *Dynamics of Southwest Prehistory,* edited by L. S. Cordell and G. J. Gumerman, 293–336. School of American Research. Washington, D.C.: Smithsonian Institution Press.

Creamer, Winifred

1993   *The Architecture of Arroyo Hondo Pueblo, New Mexico.* Arroyo Hondo Archaeological Series. Santa Fe: School of American Research Press.

n.d.   Demography from disparate data: Sixteenth-century documents and archaeological excavations in northern New Mexico. Manuscript in preparation.

Creamer, Winifred, and Jonathan Haas

1985   Tribe and chiefdom in lower Central America. *American Antiquity* 50(4):738–54.

1993   Demography of the Protohistoric Pueblos of the northern Rio Grande, A.D. 1450–1680. In *Current Research on the Late Prehistory and Early History of New Mexico,* edited by B. J. Vierra, 21–28. Albuquerque: New Mexico Archaeological Council.

Creamer, Winifred, Janna Brown, Thomas Durkin, and Michael Taylor

1993   Salvage Excavations and Surface Collections at the Site of Pueblo Blanco (LA 40), Galisteo Basin, New Mexico. Report submitted to the State of New Mexico Historic Preservation Division.

Crotty, Helen K.
1983　*Honoring the Dead: Anasazi Ceramics from the Rainbow Bridge–Monument Valley Expedition.* Museum of Cultural History, University of California at Los Angeles Monograph Series, no. 22.
Crown, Patricia L., and W. James Judge, eds.
1991　*Chaco and Hohokam: Prehistoric Regional Systems in the American Southwest.* Santa Fe: School of American Research Press.
Doyel, David E., ed.
1987　*The Hohokam Village: Site Structure and Organization.* Glenwood Springs, Colo.: Southwestern and Rocky Mountain Division of the American Association for the Advancement of Science.
Dozier, Edward P.
1970a　*The Pueblo Indians of North America.* New York: Holt, Rinehart and Winston.
1970b　Making inferences from the present to the past. In *Reconstructing Prehistoric Pueblo Societies,* edited by W. A. Longacre, 202–13. Albuquerque: University of New Mexico Press.
Earle, Timothy
1991　The evolution of chiefdoms. In *Chiefdoms: Power, Economy, and Ideology,* edited by T. Earle, 1–15. School of American Research. Cambridge: Cambridge University Press.
Eggan, Fred
1950　*Social Organization of the Western Pueblos.* Chicago: University of Chicago Press.
Elliott, Michael L.
1982　Large Pueblo sites near Jemez Springs, New Mexico. Santa Fe National Forest Cultural Resources Report 3.
Ford, Richard I.
1972　Barter, gift, or violence: An analysis of Tewa inter-tribal exchange. In *Social Exchange and Interaction,* edited by E. N. Wilmsen, 21–45. University of Michigan Museum of Anthropology, Anthropological Papers, no. 46. Ann Arbor.
Ford, Richard I., Albert H. Schroeder, and Stewart L. Peckham
1972　Three perspectives on Puebloan prehistory. In *New Perspectives on the Pueblos,* edited by A. A. Ortiz, 22–40. Albuquerque: University of New Mexico Press.
Fried, Morton H.
1967　*The Evolution of Political Society.* New York: Random House.
Gutiérrez, Ramón A.
1991　*When Jesus Came, the Corn Mothers Went Away: Marriage, Sexuality, and Power in New Mexico, 1500–1846.* Stanford: Stanford University Press.
Haas, Jonathan
1982　*The Evolution of the Prehistoric State.* New York: Columbia University Press.
Haas, Jonathan, and Winifred Creamer
1993　*Stress and Warfare among the Kayenta Anasazi of the Thirteenth Century A.D.* Fieldiana: Anthropology n.s., no. 21. Chicago: Field Museum of Natural History.

Habicht-Mauche, Judith A.
1988   Town and province: Regional integration among the Classic period Rio Grande Pueblos. Paper presented at the 53rd annual meeting of the Society for American Archaeology, Phoenix.
1995   Changing patterns of pottery manufacture and trade in the northern Rio Grande region. In *Ceramic Production in the American Southwest,* edited by B. J. Mills and P. L. Crown, 167–99. Tucson: University of Arizona Press.

Habicht-Mauche, Judith A., and Winifred Creamer
1989   Analysis of room use and residence units at Arroyo Hondo. Paper presented at the 54th annual meeting of the Society for American Archaeology, Atlanta.

Habicht-Mauche, Judith A., John Hoopes, and Michael Geselowit
1987   Where's the chief?: The archaeology of complex tribes. Paper presented at the 52nd annual meeting of the Society for American Archaeology, Toronto, Canada.

Hagstrum, Melissa
1985   Measuring prehistoric ceramic craft specialization: A test case in the American Southwest. *Journal of Field Archaeology* 12:65–75.

Hamlen, Patricia
n.d.   Room size at Pueblo Blanco (LA 40) using Nelson's notes. Unpublished manuscript on file at Northern Illinois University.

Hammond, George P., and Agapito Rey
1940   *Narratives of the Coronado Expedition, 1540–1542.* Albuquerque: University of New Mexico Press.
1953   *Don Juan de Oñate, Colonizer of New Mexico, 1595–1628.* 2 vols. Albuquerque: University of New Mexico Press.
1966   *The Rediscovery of New Mexico, 1580–1594: The Explorations of Chamuscado, Espejo, Castaño de Sosa, Morlete, Leyva de Bonilla and Humaña.* Albuquerque: University of New Mexico Press.

Harlow, Francis
1965   Recent finds of Pajaritan pottery. *El Palacio* 72(2): 27–33.

Hunter-Anderson, Rosalind L.
1979   Explaining residential aggregation in the northern Rio Grande: A competition-reduction model. In *Archaeological Investigations in Cochiti Reservoir, New Mexico,* vol. 4, *Adaptive Changes in the Northern Rio Grande Valley,* edited by J. Biella and R. Chapman, 169–75. Office of Contract Archaeology, University of New Mexico.

Johnson, Allen, and Timothy Earle
1987   *The Evolution of Human Societies: From Foraging Group to Agrarian State.* Stanford: Stanford University Press.

Johnson, Gregory A.
1978   Information sources and the development of decision-making organizations. In *Social Archaeology: Beyond Subsistence and Dating,* edited by C. L. Redman et al., 87–112. New York: Academic Press.

1982 Organizational structure and scalar stress. In *Theory and Explanation in Archaeology: The Southampton Conference,* edited by C. Renfrew, M. J. Rowlands, and B. A. Segraves, 389–421. New York: Academic Press.

1989 Far outside—looking in. In *Dynamics of Southwest Prehistory,* edited by L. S. Cordell and G. J. Gumerman, 371–90. School of American Research. Washington, D.C.: Smithsonian Institution Press.

Kahl, Kirsten

1993 Incidence of osteoporosis in skeletal remains from the Cochiti Reservoir Salvage Project. Master's thesis, Department of Anthropology, Northern Illinois University.

Kidder, Alfred V., and Anna O. Shepard

1936 *The Pottery of Pecos: The Technology of Pecos Pottery.* New Haven: Yale University Press.

Kohler, Timothy A., and Carla R. Van West

1994 The calculus of self interest in the development of cooperation: Sociopolitical development and risk among the Northern Anasazi. In *Resource Stress, Economic Uncertainty, and Human Response in the Prehistoric Southwest,* edited by J. Tainter, 1–30. Santa Fe Institute Studies in the Sciences of Complexity. Reading, Mass.: Addison Wesley.

Lambert, Marjorie

1954 Paa-ko: Archaeological Chronicle of an Indian Village in North Central New Mexico. Monograph no. 19, pts. 1–5. Santa Fe: School of American Research.

Lang, Richard W.

1986 Artifacts of woody materials from Arroyo Hondo Pueblo. In *Food, Diet and Population at Prehistoric Arroyo Hondo Pueblo, New Mexico,* edited by W. Wetterstrom, 251–76. Santa Fe: School of American Research Press.

Lekson, Stephen H.

1988 The idea of the kiva in Anasazi archaeology. *Kiva* 53:213–34.

Lightfoot, Kent G., and Gary M. Feinman

1982 Social differentiation and leadership development in early pithouse villages in the Mogollon region of the American Southwest. *American Antiquity* 47(1):64–86.

Mera, H. P.

1934 *A Survey of the Biscuit Ware Area in Northern New Mexico.* Laboratory of Anthropology Technical Series Bulletin, no. 6. Santa Fe.

Nelson, Kit

1997 Pottery and chronology: Determining the sequence of occupation at the site of Pueblo Blanco, New Mexico, using the site-use model. Master's thesis, Department of Anthropology, Northern Illinois University.

Nelson, Nels C.

1914 *Pueblo Ruins of the Galisteo Basin, New Mexico.* Anthropological Papers of the

American Museum of Natural History no. 15, pt. 1. New York: American Museum of Natural History.

Palkovich, Ann M.

1980   *The Arroyo Hondo Skeletal and Mortuary Remains.* Santa Fe: School of American Research Press.

1985   Historic population of the eastern Pueblos: 1540–1911. *Journal of Anthropological Research* 41 (4):401–26.

Peebles, Christopher S., and Susan M. Kus

1977   Some archaeological correlates of ranked societies. *American Antiquity* 42(3):421–48.

Plog, Fred

1983   Political and economic alliances on the Colorado Plateaus, A.D. 400–1450. In *Advances in World Archaeology,* vol. 2, edited by F. Wendorf and A. Close, 289–330. New York: Academic Press.

Reed, Lori S.

1990   X-ray diffraction analysis of glaze-painted ceramics from the northern Rio Grande region, New Mexico: Implications of glazeware production and exchange. In *Economy and Polity in Late Rio Grande Prehistory,* edited by S. Upham and B. D. Staley, 90–149. New Mexico State University Occasional Papers, no. 16. Las Cruces.

Reed, Paul F.

1990   A spatial analysis of the northern Rio Grande region, New Mexico: Implications for sociopolitical and economic processes from A.D. 1325–1540. In *Economy and Polity in Late Rio Grande Prehistory,* edited by S. Upham and B. D. Staley, 1–89. New Mexico State University Occasional Papers, no. 16. Las Cruces.

Schroeder, Albert H.

1979   Pueblos abandoned in historic times. In *Handbook of North American Indians,* vol. 9, edited by A. Ortiz, 236–54. Washington, D.C.: Smithsonian Institution.

Sebastian, Lynne

1991   *The Chaco Anasazi: Sociopolitical Evolution in the Prehistoric Southwest.* Cambridge: Cambridge University Press.

Sheets, Payson

1992   The pervasive pejorative in Intermediate Area studies. In *Wealth and Hierarchy in the Intermediate Area,* edited by F. W. Lange, 15–41. Washington, D.C.: Dumbarton Oaks, Trustees for Harvard University.

Shepard, Anna O.

1942   *Rio Grande Glaze Paint Ware: A Study Illustrating the Place of Ceramic Technological Analysis in Archaeological Research.* Carnegie Institution of Washington Publications, no. 528, Contributions to American Anthropology and History, no. 39. Washington, D.C.

Simmons, Marc
1991   *The Last Conquistador: Juan de Oñate and the Settling of the Far Southwest.* Norman: University of Oklahoma Press.
Smith, M. E.
1983   Pueblo councils: An example of stratified egalitarianism. In *The Development of Political Organization in Native North America,* edited by E. Tooker, 32–44. Washington, D.C.: American Ethnological Society.
Snow, David H.
1973   Prehistoric southwestern turquoise industry. *El Palacio* 79(1):33–51.
1981   Protohistoric Rio Grande Pueblo economics: A review of trends. In *The Protohistoric Period in the North American Southwest, A.D. 1450–1700* edited by D. R. Wilcox and W. B. Masse, 354–77. Anthropological Research Papers, no. 24. Tempe: Arizona State University.
Spencer, Charles S.
1993   Human agency, biased transmission, and the cultural evolution of chiefly authority. *Journal of Anthropological Archaeology* 12:41–74.
Spielmann, Katherine A.
1983   Late prehistoric exchange between the Southwest and southern plains. *Plains Anthropologist* 28(102):257–72.
1989   Colonists, hunters, and farmers: Plains-Pueblo interaction in the seventeenth century. In *Columbian Consequences,* vol.1, edited by D. H. Thomas, 101–13. Washington, D.C.: Smithsonian Institution Press.
Spielmann, Katherine A., ed.
1991   *Farmers, Hunters, and Colonists.* Tucson: University of Arizona Press.
Stodder, Ann L. W.
1990   Paleoepidemiology of eastern and western Pueblo communities in Protohistoric New Mexico. Ph.D. dissertation, University of Colorado.
Stodder, Ann L. W., and Debra L. Martin
1992   Health and disease in the Southwest before and after Spanish contact. In *Disease and Demography in the Americas,* edited by J. W. Verano and D. H. Ubelaker, 55–74. Washington, D.C.: Smithsonian Institution Press.
Stuart, David, and Rory P. Gauthier
1981   *Prehistoric New Mexico: Background for Survey.* Albuquerque: University of New Mexico Press.
Terrell, John E., and Robert L. Welsch
1990   Trade networks, areal integration, and diversity along the north coast of New Guinea. *Asian Perspectives* 29:156–65.
Upham, Steadman
1982   *Polities and Power: An Economic and Political History of the Western Pueblo.* New York: Academic Press.
1989   East meets west: Hierarchy and elites in Pueblo society. In *The Sociopolitical Structure of Prehistoric Southwestern Societies,* edited by S. Upham, K. Lightfoot, and R. Jewett, 77–102. Boulder: Westview Press.

Upham, Steadman, and Fred Plog
1986   The interpretation of prehistoric political complexity in the central and Northern Southwest: Toward a mending of the models. *Journal of Field Archaeology* 13:223–38.

Upham, Steadman, and Lori S. Reed
1989   Regional systems in the central and northern Southwest: Demography, economy, and sociopolitics preceding contact. In *Columbian Consequences,* vol. 1, edited by D. H. Thomas, 57–76. Washington, D.C. : Smithsonian Institution Press.

Upham, Steadman, Kent G. Lightfoot, and Gary M. Feinman
1981   Explaining socially determined ceramic distributions in the prehistoric Plateau Southwest. *American Antiquity* 46(4):822–32.

Warren, A. Helene
1969   Tonque: One pueblo's glaze pottery industry dominated middle Rio Grande commerce. *El Palacio* 76:36–42.

Warren, A. Helene, and Frances Joan Mathien
1985   Prehistoric and historic turquoise mining in the Cerrillos District: Time and place. In *Southwestern Culture History: Collected Papers in Honor of Albert H. Schroeder,* edited by C. H. Lange, 93–127. Santa Fe: Ancient City Press.

Weigand, Phil C., Garman Harbottle, and Edward V. Sayre
1977   Turquoise sources and source analysis: Mesoamerica and the southwestern U.S. In *Exchange Systems in Prehistory,* edited by T. K. Earle and J. Ericson, 15–34. New York: Academic Press.

Welsch, Robert L., John Terrell, and John A. Nadolski
1992   Language and culture on the north coast of New Guinea. *American Anthropologist* 94(3): 568–600.

Whittlesey, Stephanie M.
1978   Status and Death at Grasshopper Pueblo. Ph.D. dissertation, University of Arizona, Tucson.
1984   Uses and abuses of Mogollon mortuary data. In *Recent Research in Mogollon Archaeology,* edited by S. Upham, F. Plog, D. Batcho, and B. Kauffman, 276–84. New Mexico State University Occasional Papers, no. 10. Las Cruces.

Wilcox, David R.
1981   Changing perspectives on the protohistoric Pueblos, A.D. 1450–1700. In *The Protohistoric Period in the North American Southwest, A.D. 1450–1700,* edited by D. R. Wilcox and W. B. Masse, 354–77. Anthropological Research Papers, no. 24. Tempe: Arizona State University.
1991   Changing contexts of Pueblo adaptations, A.D. 1250–1600. In *Farmers, Hunters, and Colonists,* edited by K. A. Spielmann, 128–54. Tucson: University of Arizona Press.

Zubrow, Ezra B. W.
1974   *Population, Contact, and Climate in the New Mexico Pueblos.* Anthropological Papers of the University of Arizona, no. 24. Tucson.

CHAPTER 3

In War and Peace

Alternative Paths to Centralized Leadership

ELSA M. REDMOND

The Yanomamö have no word for peace, and strictly speaking, no word for war either. "Shooting arrows at each other" (*niyayou*, with its reciprocal suffix *yo*) is how the Yanomamö express the state of fighting or being at war (Lizot 1991, 70; Valero 1984, 506). War and peace are not considered antithetical relationships by the Yanomamö, suggests Lizot; rather, they are just two forms of exchange and reciprocity (Lizot 1991, 70). In view of the continuous presence of war and peace in the intervillage relations of South American tribesmen like the Yanomamö (Sahlins 1972, 182), I would like to explore some of the alternative paths to permanent, centralized leadership on the regional level among the autonomous villages that comprise these tribal societies.

There are many potential male candidates for leaders (or big men) of these villages, who are influential due to prowess in hunting, supernatural powers as shamans, success in warfare, effective oratory, and diplomatic acuity. But the authority of these big men is generally limited and episodic in nature because most decisions affecting the village as a whole are reached by consensus of adult males in these autonomous village societies. Village headmen or big men endeavor to reach the consensus they need on a matter of importance, yet even after a decision has been made, as Father John Cooper remarked, "one word from the chief and everyone does whatever they want" (cited by Gregor 1990, 113). They lead by example and by influence, as first among equals (Fock 1963, 203; Smole 1976, 70), in the absence of any institutionalized, centralized authority.

Given these constraints on the authority of tribal leaders, how can we explain the emergence of centralized chiefly societies, like the chiefdoms encountered by the first European explorers to journey across South America in the late fifteenth and early sixteenth centuries? In such chiefdoms, a paramount chief exercises permanent centralized authority over the subordinate villages in his region (Carneiro 1981, 45). I begin by examining some of the ways in which the leaders of war parties among the traditionally militant Yanomamö and Jivaroan groups that remain in the upper Orinoco and Amazon River basins actually wield authority beyond their villages and begin to act like emerging paramount chiefs. Their leadership in warfare can promote the political unification of previously autonomous villages under the permanent hereditary leadership of paramount chiefs. Since these tribal societies have traditionally oscillated between war and peace, however, and in the face of their evident pacification and acculturation by missionaries and governmental agencies today, I consider other ways in which tribal leaders consolidate their renown beyond their villages in times of relative peace.

Walking the Path of War

In his narrative (1982), the great Jivaroan Shuar war leader Tukup' referred to going to war as "carrying the lance" or "walking the path" (Hendricks 1993, 150–51, 164–65, 199, 210, 277–78, 284–85). Tribal war leaders like Tukup' are often village headmen as well as renowned warriors and/or great shamans. They propose a revenge raid or agree to lead a raid against an enemy or an enemy village, and they recruit warriors, sometimes from allied villages, for the raid. In their role as host of the prewar rituals and as leader of the raiding party they assume an unmistakable level of authority over the other warriors, in what is considered to be the most highly organized, all-male task force to leave a village (Kelekna 1981, 212–13). Theoretically, a war leader's command during a raid is unquestioned by his men; he organizes the warriors into their positions of encirclement; he signals the moment of the attack, oversees the seizing of women and other booty, including the heads of victims, and leads the retreat (Redmond 1994).

In addition to the palpable authority that war leaders gain from organizing and commanding allied raiding parties, they obtain experience and intelligence from traveling into distant enemy territory and observing the trails, gardens, settlements, and customs of their enemies. The authority and body of information that warriors gain through their participation in long-distance raids is cumulative as they become recognized as killers and distinguished warriors, and eventually as they are sought out as the leaders of war parties. Through warfare and killing, war leaders acquire considerable personal power (*kakárma,* to use the Jivaroan term) and become a *kakáram* or "strong man"; in time they may be recognized as a "very powerful one" or *ti kakáram* (Harner 1972, 115; Hendricks 1993, 6–7). Similarly distinguished Yanomamö warriors are recognized as being "fierce" or *waiteri* (Chagnon 1983, 6). So powerful do they become in the eyes of others that they can deter counterraids by their enemies and they can offer protection to kinsmen and allies (Chagnon 1988, 986; Ritchie 1996, 104).

Tribal war leaders gain material forms of wealth and power too. Not only do they obtain the usual loot seized from the villages they raid, but they are also promised rewards for leading war parties for other villages, in the form of *machetes,* axes, ammunition, and women (Ritchie 1996, 98; Ross 1984, 105; Stirling 1938, 39; Valero 1984, 398, 485, 532). With these material rewards successful war leaders begin to build a network of alliances and obligations beyond their villages, through exchange, through marriage, and through their willingness to lead revenge raids for other villages. They begin to gain renown in the region. In the process of leading raids for other villages and their allies, taking additional wives, and enlarging their kinship network of reciprocal obligations still farther, the leaders of allied war parties achieve a degree of centralized authority on the regional level.[1] It is significant that the Jivaroan Shuar have adopted the Quechua administrative term *curaca,* used by the Inka to refer to local hereditary native rulers, or chiefs, as one of their designations for these regional war leaders (Lowie 1949, 341; Stirling 1938, 39; González Holguín 1989, 55; Salomon 1986, 14, 45).

The regional authority of war leaders varies in geographical extent. When the Shuar gather to plan an allied raid, they elect a war leader or common chief, a curaca (Karsten 1935, 282). A curaca generally heads several neighboring villages along five or six miles of a small river. In times of war, however, some curacas can gain such renown and attract such a following that other curacas will turn to them and submit to their authority. By agreeing to conduct war parties for other, weaker curacas, a strong curaca may become head curaca over eight or ten lesser curacas, thereby becoming the leader over many villages in the region and sometimes beyond (Stirling 1938, 39; Cotlow 1953, 116). In this way, one such Shuar war leader, Tuki, emerged as a strong curaca on the Upano River in the late 1920s and headed a territory stretching from Macas on the Upano to Méndez on the Paute River in southeastern Ecuador, a distance of over 55 kilometers (Stirling 1938, 40). The curaca of an intertribal allied raid extends his reputed authority over a larger territory still, the largest known alliance being the one mounted in 1599 against the Spaniards by Quirruba, the great Shuar war leader of the Morona River. Under Quirruba's command, an allied fighting force of 20,000 warriors from the Morona, Paute, Upano, and Santiago rivers attacked the Spanish settlements of Logroño and Sevilla del Oro, spaced some 137 kilometers apart on the Upano and Paute rivers (Velasco 1842, 154–57).

In peacetime the alliances among a group of neighboring villages along a river have no common name other than the river on which they live, as in the case of *Kapawi shuar*, or "people of the Capahuari river" (Descola 1981, 626). In times of war, however, the Jivaroan Shuar and Achuar designate their war alliances by the name of the war leader or by the name of the river on which he resides. Because the chosen war leader represents the unity of his group of allied villages, often the territory of that leader's group will be named after him, as in the Achuar's reference to *Mashient nunkari*, "the land of Mashient" (Descola 1981, 627; Taylor 1985, 163). Indeed, Siverts has proposed that some of the tribal names recognized by the Jivaroans may have originated from such designations for war alliances under a strong curaca's leadership; thus "the Antipa may well have been an Aguaruna group distinguished from other Jívaro on account of a powerful leader by the name of Antipa" (Siverts 1975, 667).

While a curaca's centralized authority may be recognized on a regional scale, and as we have seen may sometimes assume supraregional dimensions, it generally lasts for a relatively short period of time. A tribal war leader's authority is born and enhanced in times of war, and while his influence over the members of his wartime alliance carries over into peacetime as well, a war leader's authority will inevitably be challenged by other warriors acquiring power and gaining renown through warfare. Generally, "in as little as 2 or 3 years' time, the original head curaka may find that one or more of his former lieutenants are now stronger than he" (Stirling 1938, 39).

But there are recorded cases of longer-lasting renown by some Jivaroan war leaders that resembles a more permanent, chiefly leadership. The biographies of several distinguished Shuar and Achuar war leaders—Tuki, Anguasha, Kashíjint, Utitiája, and Tukup'—document the trajectory of their leadership.

Tuki

Four or five years prior to Matthew Stirling's fieldwork in the Santiago River drainage of southeastern Ecuador in 1930–31, that is to say in about 1925, Tuki was the head curaca of a region the length of the Upano and Paute rivers; all the other curacas along these rivers recognized his overall authority. He was already getting older by this time, as Stirling noted (1938, 40), which agreed with his Spanish name, José Grande (for "big," "old," or *uunt*), a status that is generally accorded to men over forty years of age (Kelekna 1981, 97). When Tuki and three other curacas of the Upano River visited a curaca on the upper Yaup' River in 1931, he was third in line to greet the host ceremoniously, after Ambusha and Utita, and before Tsamagashi, who was an old man (Stirling 1938, 96–98). A final reference to Tuki came in 1945, when he was sought out for his powers as a shaman by the curaca Peruche on the Paute River (Cotlow 1953, 149–52). Tuki's term as head curaca of the Upano-Paute region, which he achieved when he was already a mature adult of *uunt* status, seems then to have lasted for at least three to five years.

Anguasha

Anguasha was curaca of the upper Yaup' River in 1925. He allied himself with Cucusha, the curaca of the tributary Canga River. Together they waged intensive warfare for a period of 10 or 15 years against "all of the tribes in the district and some quite distant, until they became the terror of the region" (Stirling 1938, 40). When Cucusha died in 1929, his eldest son, Asapa, went to Anguasha to ask him to become the head curaca for both the Yaup' and the Canga river groups, which then became consolidated under Anguasha's authority. Anguasha commanded warriors from a territory that extended over more than 45 kilometers of river courses in length. Stirling met Anguasha in 1931 and obtained information about raiding and headhunting from this great warrior, whose tally of heads stood at more than 50; the photograph of Anguasha in Stirling's report reveals that he was in his middle age (Stirling 1938, 50, 72, 75, plate 4d). Recognized as one of the greatest warriors and headhunters by Kashíjint and Tukup', who at times fought against him (Hendricks 1993, 231–32, 249–50, 254), Anguasha was still having his war exploits avenged by his enemies in 1945, when Cotlow visited curaca Peruche's settlement on the Paute River. Cotlow overheard Peruche's son, Juanga, instructing his son one morning on how he must someday seek revenge and kill Anguasha, whom Juanga referred to as a shaman, or *uwíshin* (Cotlow 1953, 130). Sometime after 1945, but before 1964 (when the Shuar Federation was founded), Anguasha participated in his final raid, upholding the Jivaroan saying "I was born to die fighting" (Harner 1972, 170). Anguasha was an elder or uunt at the time of his death, and he was participating in an allied raid led by other, younger war leaders, when he was killed by an Achuar, who later boasted of killing this great warrior (Hendricks 1993, 233, 253–54). Anguasha's chieftaincy over a territory that reached beyond the Yaup' river drainage lasted for perhaps 15 to 20 years, but his renown persisted until his death.

Kashíjint

The great Achuar warrior and war leader (kakáram) Kashíjint was already an uunt at the time of Anguasha's death, for he was sought out as the leader of an allied revenge raid that was planned to avenge Anguasha's death, sometime after Cotlow's second trip in 1945 (Hendricks 1993, 252, 258, 261; Cotlow 1953, 130). Kashíjint lived at Pumpuentsa, east of the Makuma River. He was considered the greatest and strongest of all Achuar warriors in the 1950s and for some time thereafter as well. The missionaries Frank and Marie Drown recorded ongoing hostilities between Kashíjint's group and neighboring Tsantiacu's group in the Makuma River area in 1959 (Drown and Drown 1961, 214–29, 249). Kashíjint led allied raids on several recorded occasions with Tukup' of Yaasnunka, also on the Makuma River drainage. In Tukup's narrative, he mentioned that Kashíjint had taught him how to fight, and he described at least three allied raids in which he walked the path with Kashíjint, two of which raids were commanded by Kashíjint (Hendricks 1993, 213, 227, 258). These events occurred when Kashíjint was an older and distinguished warrior and Tukup' a young, ambitious warrior, just prior to Tukup's emergence as a kakáram. Indeed, Tukup' alluded to the possibility that after the third raid, he may have supplanted Kashíjint in the eyes of others (Hendricks 1993, 276). Tukup' referred to Kashíjint as his late elder (*uuntmir*), making it clear that Kashíjint died prior to 1982 (Hendricks 1993, 79, 261–62, 265, 267, 270, 279).

Utitiája

Utitiája was fifty-six or fifty-seven when Lewis Cotlow met him at curaca Nayapi's settlement on the Seipa River, a tributary of the Upano River, in 1949. Utitiája had agreed to participate in the filming of a mock postwar *tsantsa* dance, together with three other Shuar groups along the Upano. Utitiája and his 25 warriors came from his settlement at the confluence of the Chupientsa and Upano rivers, some seven hours' walk away. It was immediately evident to Cotlow that Utitiája was the strongest curaca present, feared by most of the 70 warriors assembled there; "every pair of eyes followed him, and many of the eyes were filled with fear. I knew that there might well be a dozen young men in the clearing who had been told almost daily from boyhood that this was their greatest enemy" (Cotlow 1953, 229). Afterward, Utitiája told Cotlow his life story by way of a Shuar translator.

Utitiája was ten years old when he accompanied his father on a raid. He did not participate in the attack, but after his father killed the enemy, he had Utitiája thrust his lance into the enemy's body. Utitiája's father was killed when the boy was thirteen years old. Four "long" years later (at seventeen years of age), as Utitiája put it, he participated in his first raid and was finally able to avenge his father's death by killing his father's killer with a lance through the back and taking the man's head (Cotlow 1953, 238–41).

By 1930, when Utitiája would have been approximately thirty-five years old, he had become a curaca along the Chupientsa River, under the regional war leadership of Tuki, the head curaca of the Upano River. When Tuki's power as a regional war leader waned, however, Utitiája became a head curaca himself, and drew other war leaders along the Upano River to his following (Stirling 1938, 40). By 1945, Cotlow learned from the great curaca on the Paute River, Peruche, who had taken five heads the previous year, that Utitiája was the greatest warrior of all; in Peruche's words, "all Indians have heard of Utitiaja" (Cotlow 1953, 128). We know that Utitiája fought against Tukup', after Tukup' killed Utitiája's brother-in-law, Saantu, which precipitated a period of intense warfare between these two great war leaders and their many allies (Hendricks 1993, 279–80). By January of 1949, when filmmakers Miroslav Zikmund and Jirí Hanzelka met Utitiája at Chupientsa, Utitiája was considered the most greatly feared Shuar for miles around and the terror of the whole region; it was said that he had killed 52 persons, his most recent victim having been a member of the Tutanangosa group whose head he had taken in 1948 (Zikmund and Hanzelka 1963, 181). The filmmakers were impressed by the size of Utitiája's house, which they estimated measured 20–25 meters in length and 10 meters in width; "Inside it was like standing in a roofed rotunda, the bamboo beds and *kutungas* [stools] were practically lost in that huge space" (Zikmund and Hanzelka 1963, 188). The surrounding fields of tubers and manioc were also unusually large and well tended.

Later in 1949, an article by a Salesian missionary in a Quito newspaper reported a recent increase in the number of revenge raids along the Upano River. The missionary claimed that one of the principal factors responsible for the increasing warfare was "a chief named Utitiája, who was said to have taken fifty-eight heads. He was the most feared warrior the Jivaros had produced in many years" (Cotlow 1953, 212). Just a week or two later, Cotlow was able to meet and interview the great curaca and "chief" Utitiája himself, on the occasion of the four groups gathering at Nayapi's settlement for Cotlow's filming of the tsantsa dance. When Utitiája' entered the clearing, there was no question in Cotlow's mind that he was anything less than a leader:

> I had imagined a man big and strong and fierce-looking. Instead he was a trifle shorter than the average Jivaro, and of rather slight build, though compact and effortless in his movements. Most striking, however, was his face—mild, placid, and even somewhat gentle. No lines marked his forehead or cheeks and there was not the slightest suggestion of fierceness or cruelty in his expression. His simple *itípi* [loincloth] did not even have the human-hair belt so loved by most Jivaros. He did not wear a necklace of jaguar's teeth, but a simple one of plain white beads. Nevertheless, despite his mild appearance and his simplicity, he moved with authority, with an inner assurance and dignity that marked him unmistakably as the leader. (Cotlow 1953, 227)

Flanked by his son-in-law and his shaman, Utitiája sat down with Cotlow and negotiated with him, before greeting any of the other curacas. In an accompanying photograph of this moment, Utitiája appears wearing a magnificent headdress of light-colored feathers topped by tall dark-colored plumes. His fierce-looking son-in-law would play the role of the victor in Cotlow's film.

At that first meeting and the next evening, Utitiája told Cotlow that he had taken the heads of 58 enemies. Utitiája indicated that at times the warfare had been so intensive that he had been too busy fighting to celebrate the victory feasts. He attributed part of his success as a warrior to his revered father, who had trained him well. Like Tukup' (Hendricks 1993, 164–65, 290), Utitiája emphasized the importance of "seeing," of seeking the counsel of the "old ones" by drinking *natém* (*Banisteriopsis* sp.) or *maikiua* (*Datura arborea*) before participating in a raid (Cotlow 1953, 242–43).

As of 1949, Utitiája's chieftaincy had lasted for almost 20 years. Although he was in the process of adopting Western ways by this point, his interest in seeking revenge for the recent killing of another son-in-law and the abduction of his daughter was keen. Indeed, Utitiája was certain that the killer was one of the warriors who had gathered for Cotlow's film. That his career as a regional war leader persisted for at least a while longer Cotlow learned two months after his return to New York, when he received a newspaper clipping from Quito that reported Utitiája's killing of a member of the Tutanangosa group—his fifty-ninth head (Cotlow 1953, 244–45).

Tukup'

Tukup' was probably in his sixties or early seventies in 1982, when he recounted his life story to Janet Hendricks (1993, 19). Born in Yaasnunka on the upper Makuma River around 1918, he began fighting at about the age of nineteen, to avenge the killing of his father, a renowned warrior. It was a time of heightened warfare in the Makuma River drainage. Through his participation in raids, he gained the experience and the knowledge of a warrior and became an adult (Hendricks 1993, 122, 148–51). As a young warrior, Tukup' participated in an allied raid organized by his uncle together with the great Huambisa warrior Asap (who may be the same war leader as the Asapi encountered by Cotlow in 1945), against the Achuar at Maki, on the border with Peru (Hendricks 1993, 155–57; Cotlow 1953, 142–49).

Following his uncle's death in a treacherous attack, Tukup' took up the lance and embarked on a campaign of revenge raids against the Achuar, including some allied raids with the Achuar war leader Kashíjint and Shuar allies from Taisha. Tukup' referred to this period of escalating warfare as a time "when I was to drink of death, of war" (Hendricks 1993, 221), although he was still a young warrior. It was during the retreat from one of these raids that the great Shuar curaca Anguasha was killed by the Achuar, sometime after Cotlow's visit to the Paute River in 1945 (Hendricks 1993, 233). A series of retaliatory raids by Tukup' and his allies, in which Tukup' killed the elder Tsamaráint (father of Anguasha's killer) and the powerful Shuar shaman Saantu, culminated in his becoming a true warrior or kakáram (Hendricks 1993, 78–79, 278–79).

His killing of the great shaman Saantu drew Tukup' into a widening web of raids against both Achuar and Shuar communities, including that of Utitiája, who was the most powerful curaca along the Upano River in the 1940s. The wars escalated or "opened," to use Tukup's term (Hendricks 1993, 279), and "he is said to have fought throughout the Jivaroan territories, from west of the Kutukú Mountains to deep in the lowland forest, on both sides of the border between Ecuador and Peru, and as far north as the Pastaza River" (Hendricks 1993, 19). In 1948 the December 23 issue of the Quito newspaper *El Comercio* reported a surge in fighting among the Jivaroan groups on the Pastaza River during the preceding months (Zikmund and Hanzelka 1963, 133). Tukup' narrated a lengthy litany of "indeed because he killed again, indeed I killed again" between his enemies and his people, as he put it, to the point where "we finished each other" (Hendricks 1993, 280–81). He may have begun to supplant the older Kashíjint as war chieftain of the Makuma region at this time too (Hendricks 1993, 276).

Even after moving downstream on the Makuma River to where he was living in 1982, yet before the building of his *centro* there sometime in the mid-1960s, after the establishment of the Shuar Federation in 1964, Tukup' continued to lead allied revenge raids to avenge the deaths of his kinsmen. He was credited with killing as many as 100 men during his career as a kakáram across Shuar and Achuar territories (Hendricks 1993, 19). It was only after Tukup' had avenged the death of his younger brother Piruchkun that he stopped going to war—"I ended it" (Hendricks 1993, 285).

It seems that Tukup' then began acquiring shamanic knowledge, and he was still in the process of becoming a shaman in 1971 (Hendricks 1993, 20). Significantly, however, he admitted that becoming a shaman was the only way of knowing who one's enemies were, and that if at any moment his enemies began a war, he would walk the path and fight again (Hendricks 1993, 290). In 1982, Tukup' was the headman of his centro as well as an elder of uunt status, a much-sought-after shaman, and a kakáram warrior of legendary renown (Hendricks 1993, 4, 19). Hendricks learned of his rout of an Ecuadorian army patrol near the Peruvian border, as well as his confrontation with the president of the Shuar Federation, when he strode into Sucúa and stood before the federation headquarters armed with a shotgun and clad in Jivaroan dress, wearing face paint, ornaments, and an exceptionally fine feather headdress (Hendricks 1993, 20). Hendricks's first impression of Tukup' upon her arrival at his centro in 1982 was that "there was never any question as to who the headman was, for he spoke with an authority that denied his diminutive size and his advancing age. I was struck immediately by the power of his voice and his attitude of complete self-confidence" (Hendricks 1993, 2). Tukup's career as a regional war leader across both Achuar and Shuar territories lasted for almost 20 years, I estimate, and his renown persists today.

These piecemeal biographies of Jivaroan curacas reveal the extent and longevity of certain war leaders' authority. Their alliances extended across supraregional and even intertribal territories, and their chieftaincies prevailed for up to 20 years, especially under conditions of heightened warfare. Although there were some indications that the supraregional authority of Tuki, Anguasha, and Kashíjint as war chieftains was supplanted by that of younger, ambitious war leaders on the rise, their authority as regional war leaders persisted. What we know of their multiple wives, many offspring, many affines, their big houses and gardens, their acquired knowledge, and their commanding presence, even in their old age, attests to their ability to wield power beyond their villages, in the manner of chiefs.

How then, can these tribal war chieftains who are wielding power on the regional level institutionalize that authority, and become true hereditary paramount chiefs, following from Carneiro's (1981, 45) definition of a chiefdom as an autonomous political unit comprising a number of villages under the *permanent* control of a paramount chief? Actually, the seeds of hereditary succession are already sown in these warring South American tribal societies. Stirling, who obtained much of his information about Jivaroan warfare from the great curaca Anguasha, learned that in theory the eldest son of a curaca inherits his father's chieftaincy (Stirling 1938, 40, 50). Both Stirling and Rafael Karsten pointed out, however, that the hereditary succession to a curaca's chieftaincy by his eldest son occurred in times of war (Karsten 1935, 267). Therefore, it is under conditions of escalating or intensive warfare that this form of hereditary leadership is called for. That fund of knowledge, organization, and experience possessed by war leaders, together with the vast network of alliances they acquire through their command of allied raiding parties, is what is needed in times of war and what is sought after when such a chieftain dies.

Moreover, Stirling and Karsten also made clear that a curaca's eldest son inherits his father's chieftaincy only if he too distinguishes himself in warfare. Theoretically, the eldest son inherits his father's position as regional war leader "because he is, as it were, a direct continuation of his father, has received a careful education for the deeds of war, and has always had the good example of his great father before his eyes" (Karsten 1935, 267). Should the eldest son of a curaca prove not to be an able warrior, then another son, a son-in-law, or another aspiring warrior succeeds to the position of war leader. This was how Anguasha became the head curaca of both the Yaup' and the Canga River groups; when Cucusha, the curaca of the Canga River, died in 1929, his son Asapa, who was sickly and not able to go to war, went to Anguasha and asked him to become the curaca of both groups (Stirling 1938, 40–41). Similarly, it was not by being the eldest son that an Aguaruna by the name of Antún Tsamahén, who was the headman of Yupikús on the upper Marañón River in Peru when Henning Siverts conducted fieldwork there in 1970, inherited his father's position of leadership in the larger neighborhood. Antún had several older brothers but distinguished himself as a brave warrior, a killer, and as a war leader, and thereby achieved his father's position of leadership in the region (Siverts 1972, 17).

Given these two preconditions, so to speak, for the succession of war chieftaincies, Jivaroan groups show tremendous concern for nurturing future war leaders. Kelekna (1981, 157) learned that 75 percent of Achuar fathers preferred having sons; sons were considered more important, more useful in work and in warfare. To that end, boys begin their instruction in the ways of war at six years of age. Every morning they sit on stools in the men's section of the house and listen to their father recite the history of hostilities and killings of their ancestors, admonishing the boys to honor their sacred duty by becoming brave warriors and seeking blood revenge. Boys are taken along on raids after about six to eight years of age. They do not yet take an active part in the fighting. They go along simply to observe warfare, to overcome their fear, and to learn raiding tactics, although their fathers might have them practice thrusting a lance into a dead enemy's body (Cotlow 1953, 130–31, 238–39; Kelekna 1981, 93, 135).

At puberty, they begin their initiation rituals, which include fasting, ritual bathing, drinking green tobacco water, and eventually periods of seclusion in the forest, complete with the taking of maikiua to experience visionary ordeals and to encounter the supernatural world of the "old ones." The initiates' training for warfare includes the killing of a tree sloth, the taking of its head, and the celebration of mock victory feasts. We have seen how two renowned war leaders became full-fledged warriors at approximately seventeen and nineteen years of age, when they participated in their first raids and killed and beheaded an enemy (Cotlow 1953, 239–41; Harner 1972, 90–93; Hendricks 1993, 148–49, 152–53; Karsten 1935, 238–42; Kelekna 1981, 125–27).

But it is only through subsequent raids and killings that the son of a curaca gains the renown necessary for becoming a distinguished warrior and eventually the leader of war parties himself, thereby being in a natural position to inherit his father's chieftainship. When renowned war leaders are elders (uunt), they often serve as masters of ceremonies and direct their sons or sons-in-law to assume their role in war rituals. They also designate their sons to undertake their leadership of raiding parties. As they approach death, some great war leaders inform their sons of their desire to pass on their accrued power to the sons, by means of special posthumous funerary rituals (Cotlow 1953, 124–25, 229; Harner 1972, 116, 168–69; Stirling 1938, 53; Zikmund and Hanzelka 1963, 271). Although technically the succeeding war chieftain is elected by the warriors who assemble to plan future raids, or is sought by natém-taking shamans (Karsten 1935, 282; Cotlow 1953, 47), when the son of the previous war leader has gained power and renown as a warrior, killer, and leader of war parties, he will be favored to succeed his father.

The Jivaroans' concern for training their sons for war and empowering them as great warriors and war leaders helps to ensure their preparedness and success in warfare. Young warriors are imbued with the responsibility of honoring their fathers' wishes to seek blood revenge and of fulfilling their obligations. They eagerly aspire to become distinguished warriors and ultimately the leaders of war parties. In times of war these positions of military distinction and leadership become critical to the protection and survival of their kinsmen, fellow villagers, and even allied villagers. Villagers and allies turn to successful war leaders for their readiness, their ability to recruit warriors from a large network of allied villages, their successful leadership of allied raiding parties, and their proven invincibility. Renowned war leaders like Tuki, Anguasha, Kashíjint, Utitiája, and Tukup' are sought out again and again by the member villages of their regional chieftainship, and their authority extends beyond their villages to become truly regional in scale. Allied villages that previously valued their own sovereignty and that considered any form of submission contrary to their moral code (Chagnon 1968, 112; Lizot 1989, 33) seek the protective hegemony of such war leaders and submit to their centralized authority. Moreover, the centralized regional authority of such war leaders does not lapse with the evident cessation of hostilities but persists for their lifetimes, to be inherited by their designated, groomed successors, in the manner of hereditary chiefs. That is the path toward centralized leadership that might be taken in times of war, from which a lineage of war chiefs emerges to rule over the many villages in a region.

Burying the Lance

South American tribesmen do not experience perpetual warfare, however. Raids may be spaced weeks apart but are usually months apart; most raids are conducted during the dry season, when intervillage travel is easier. Moreover, times of war can be interspersed with periods of relative peace, when Jivaroan groups might go so far as to "bury the lance" with their enemy and initiate peaceful relations. Stirling learned that the shaman of each warring group ventures alone into the forest at night and buries the lance in a secret place, therein laying hostility to rest. All too soon, however, some detonator causes the lance to be officially disinterred and carried to war once again (Stirling 1938, 51–52, 98).

At any given moment, a Yanomamö village might be engaging in a full spectrum of relationships with other villages, ranging from red-hot hostilities with enemy villages to the intimate exchange of daughters with allied villages. Chagnon has outlined the gradation of relationships that a Yanomamö village maintains with other villages: enemy villages against whom revenge raids are targeted, villages with whom sporadic exchange occurs but which are still liable to revenge raids, and allied villages with whom feasting and exchange occur regularly, culminating in the reciprocal exchange of women. By hosting sumptuous feasts and delivering copious gifts in exchange, which will be reciprocated later, Yanomamö villages cultivate alliances with other villages over a period of months and sometimes years and enjoy relatively peaceful relations (Chagnon 1983, 147; Chagnon 1992b, 186). Chagnon characterizes the relative peace achieved:

> The Yanomamö tend not to attack villages with which they trade and feast, unless a specific incident, like the abduction of a woman, provokes them. Allies linked by trade and feasting, for example, will rarely accuse each other of practicing harmful magic, often the trigger for war. . . .
>
> . . . Rarely do relations reach the stage at which women are actually exchanged, particularly if the two villages are approximately equal in military strength. Fights and arguments break out over women, food, etiquette, generosity, status, and the like, and the principals may withdraw on semihostile terms, perhaps attempting a rapprochement later on. (Chagnon 1992b, 183–85)

Kenneth Good illustrates how difficult it is for the Yanomamö to maintain peaceful relationships through feasting and exchange:

> This is the typical pattern, the delayed trade, which underlies the relationships among communities. Commonly, the visitors will be given a pot, a machete, and an ax or some equivalents. In return they will promise a dog that is about to be born in their village—to be given at a later date when the visit is reciprocated. This kind of arrangement leads to repeated visits and an ongoing relationship. But it can also result in trouble, and it often does. When the return visit is made, the puppy may have died or may have been given to someone else. Or even worse, perhaps the owner just doesn't want to let it go. That's

when problems develop. The original hosts are angered. They gave the pot, machete, and ax—the others reneged. It can be the occasion for a raid and the beginning of years of hostility. (Good 1991, 97)

Tribal villages oscillate between raiding and trading with other villages, perhaps because exchanges are peacefully resolved wars and wars are the outcome of unsuccessful transactions (Lévi-Strauss 1943, 136). Peaceful relations are sought and maintained through intervillage exchange. But the resulting intervillage alliances that are born and bred of such exchanges can then be counted on for mobilizing allied raiding parties in times of war and, under the direst of wartime circumstances, for seeking refuge. It is through the "long and difficult road of feasting and trading" (Chagnon 1983, 148) that the Yanomamö establish political and military alliances with other villages. War and peace are continuously present in the building of intervillage alliances, which embody the sociopolitical dynamics of autonomous tribal villages in South America (Lévi-Strauss 1943, 139; Mauss 1954, 79–80; Sahlins 1972, 182).

Lizot sees the oscillation between war and peace in the intervillage relations of the Yanomamö as the simple transformation from one reciprocal form of exchange to another, wherein a relationship of reciprocal exchange of goods, women, and information in times of relative peace is replaced by a tit-for-tat exchange of poisoned arrows in the raids and counterraids of war. Neutral intervillage relations do not exist among the Yanomamö; "either they are peaceful and involve commercial and matrimonial exchanges, or else it is war" (Lizot 1985, 184, 1991, 69).

One form of peaceful reciprocity that acts as a monitor of intervillage relationships among the Yanomamö—and that assumes a pivotal role in the transformation of peaceful to hostile relations or the change from warring to peaceful relations—occurs during the nocturnal ceremonial dialogue (*wayamou*), which is celebrated only with visitors from distant villages (Lizot 1991, 57; Rivière 1971, 304–5). Male visitors from a distant village who arrive at a village for a feast may enter only when summoned by the headman. As they enter they perform an arrival dance, displaying their feather ornaments, their body-paint decorations, and their weapons. They assemble in the center of the village clearing and stand still with their heads held high and their bows and arrows held directly in front of their faces. At a signal from the headman, the hosts invite the visitors to their houses to rest in their hammocks and then to consume troughs of plantain soup. All the while, few looks or words are exchanged between the hosts and visitors (Chagnon 1992b, 202–3). At nightfall, the ceremonial dialogue is initiated by one of the visitors, who stands or squats in the village clearing, clutching his bow and arrows or his machete or ax. He is joined by one of the hosts, and the visitor-host pair face each other and begin the highly ritualized, energetic chant, with vocalizations that range from shouts to whispers, repeated staccato phrases, and body movements. Usually the dialogue begins with the visitor's request for exchange items, including women. These requests are conveyed in metaphorical expressions, as in the following dialogue recorded by Good: "'Give me a white woman,'" said one, though what he meant was a machete. 'No, she's too modest,' came the answer, meaning that the machete chose not to show itself" (Good 1991, 97). After an hour or more, another visitor-host pair takes over, and in this way the wayamou dialogue lasts throughout the night until shortly before dawn (Chagnon 1992b, 203–5; Cocco 1972, 326–28; Good 1991, 96–97, 128; Lizot 1991, 58; Valero 1984, 60, 435).

The nocturnal ceremonial dialogue, with its distinctly stylized, esoteric, and sometimes argumentative language, serves as the conduit for the exchange of a tremendous range of information between distant villages, communities which may or may not be on good terms and between which contact is infrequent. Although demands for exchange goods dominate the dialogue, much news about other villages and their changing alliances is exchanged in metaphorical terms, including information about recent thefts, abductions, or killings and about the consequent revenge raids being planned for which the visitors seek a war leader or allied warriors (Cocco 1972, 326–28; Lizot 1991, 62; Valero 1984, 226, 284, 433, 469, 486). Invitations to feasts are issued—which are often intended as a defensive strategy by the visitors, who are expecting a raid by their enemies—as are proposals of marriage, which serve to strengthen the existing relationship between the visitors' and the hosts' villages (Valero 1984, 404, 486). Actually, the topics that can be discussed during the ceremonial dialogue are limited only by each participant's knowledge and his mastery of the art of metaphorical discourse. As the night proceeds, pairs of older men, *los grandes* or big men (Valero 1984, 231), take their turn at the wayamou: "their mastery is greater and the tone changes; they are able to improvise and may slip a message into their discourse, or a bit of [secret] information, or a request" (Lizot 1985, 184). The samples of recorded wayamou include confrontations about the killing of kinsmen, demonstrations of personal bravery, and discussions about wars, exchange, geography, distant places, tribes, and foreigners. This information is often couched in discussions about hunting, body painting, gender relations, harmful magic, myths, cosmology, and supernatural beings (Lizot 1991, 61–62, 73–80).

After a rest and a meal, the actual exchange takes place, just before the visitors depart. Through its stylized rituals and metaphorical language, the ceremonial dialogue monitors the delicate relationship between distant villages. The wayamou can solidify existing alliances through expressions of solidarity and subsequent peaceful exchanges. Disputes can be raised and aired, thereby allowing for their peaceful mediation and, if need be, through the scheduling of duels that can still be considered alternatives to war (Lizot 1991, 58, 78–79; Rivière 1971, 306; Urban 1986, 380; Valero 1984, 232, 319–22, 484). The ceremonial dialogue is in the end a highly competitive endeavor, steeped in ritual, that can transform intervillage relationships. Should the participants' bluffing overstep the prescribed threshold of tolerance, or should the actual trade not meet the terms agreed upon during the wayamou, the visitors depart angrily and threaten to avenge the transgression. Finally, there are the occasional treacherous attacks that are planned and carried out during the wayamou ritual itself, or during the morning-after exchange, when the visitors are caught off guard in a squatting position and are clubbed over the head and killed. Attacks like these obviously catapult the participating villages into a state of war (Chagnon 1992b, 206–12; Valero 1984, 226–34).

In sum, the peaceful exchanges and warfare pursued by autonomous tribal villages in lowland South America can then be viewed as alternative forms of competition, through which villages maintain their autonomy and solidify their intervillage alliances. This point has been made by Pierre Lemonnier (1991, 9–10)[2] in his examination of the emergence of big men in certain traditional Western Highlands village societies of Papua New Guinea, among whom peaceful ceremonial exchanges alternated with warfare. Great warriors and war leaders in several Highlands societies also organized ceremonial exchanges, by means of which they expanded their network of supravillage alliances and began to wield the power of big men, who are simultaneously war leaders and peacemakers (Lemonnier 1990, 96–98). It was only after the imposition of colonial rule by the Australians in the late 1950s and the forced pacification of these societies (Godelier 1986, 194; Feil 1987, 273) that big men turned their attention exclusively to organizing large-scale ceremonial exchanges. Only after the cessation of war did this peaceful form of competition actually replace war (Lemonnier 1991, 23).

Catching Fire

The South American tribesmen examined here have pursued their raiding and trading relationships well into the second half of the twentieth century. It seems that their relative geographical isolation in remote, mountainous, forested areas of the Amazon Basin, together with their hallowed fierceness, slowed the impact of Western encroachment on their societies. Although headhunting raids among Jivaroan groups were last reported in the 1950s, the Achuar were still conducting occasional large-scale raids in the 1960s, and retaliatory assassinations continue to be carried out among Jivaroan groups at the present time (Harner 1972, 204; Kelekna 1985, 221). The Yanomamö still raid enemy villages, albeit less frequently than the raids spaced months or even weeks apart that were recorded in the 1940s, the 1960s, and as recently as 1970 (Valero 1984, 342, 419–20; Chagnon 1983, 71, 180; Smole 1976, xiv, 49). The simmering hostilities between Bisaasi-teri and Tayari-teri, which can be traced back to 1977 (and stemmed ultimately from a treacherous feast in 1951), escalated to war in 1980. The Bisaasi-teri recruited an allied fighting force of some 300 warriors, who traveled in canoes outfitted with motors and launched a double attack against Tayari-teri with bows and arrows and shotguns. They succeeded in killing men, women, and children, looting the village, and setting it on fire with gasoline. The revenge raids and counterraids resulting from this war were still being conducted and planned by the participating villages and their allies a decade later. Like the retaliatory assassinations of the Jivaroans, however, shotgun killings are on the rise among the Yanomamö and true intervillage warfare is diminishing (Chagnon 1990, 100–101; Chagnon 1992a, 219–20; Chagnon 1992b, 258–60; Ferguson 1995, 337–39; Ritchie 1996, 214, 217).

For the Yanomamö and Jivaroan groups, some of whom conceive of the trappings of civilized life in Shuar Federation centros as "catching fire" (Hendricks 1988, 226), the decline in intervillage warfare has resulted in the intensified pursuit of exchange relationships. Ambitious Yanomamö and Jivaroan men, who previously would have sought renown through warfare, are actively pursuing a variety of external relations in peacetime, much like Highland New Guinea big men, who are busy organizing large-scale ceremonial pig feasts (Feil 1987, 111–22; Strathern 1971). By handing over their pigs, shells, and feathers, New Guinea big men strive to give more than they have received, thereby "doing battle by means of gifts and countergifts" (Godelier 1986, 177) and winning. Through their participation in intervillage and intertribal relations, these tribesmen are building alliances and extending their network of obligations on a regional and even an interregional scale, thus enhancing their renown, amassing power, and creating alternative paths to centralized hereditary leadership. In spite of the peaceful context of these exchanges, Godelier rightly characterizes them as "war carried on by other means," or "as the peaceful extension of war" (Godelier 1986, 170).

Doing Battle by Means of Gifts

The Jivaroans and Yanomamö pursue exchange relationships literally with a vengeance. Although Yanomamö villages can be considered economically self-sufficient, each village produces special items for exchange: *curare* poison, hallucinogenic drugs, tobacco, cotton, arrowpoints, shafts, bows, hammocks, baskets, ceramic pots, ornaments, and dogs. This means that should a source for a desired trade item dry up due to warfare and to consequently shifting alliances, Yanomamö villagers might begin to produce and trade that hallucinogenic plant or that ceramic pot themselves (Chagnon 1992a, 55, 163). Western manufactured goods are also sought through exchange with other villages, principal items being steel machetes, axes, knives, fishhooks, nylon fishing line, aluminum pots, and matches (Chagnon 1992a, 64, 162; Ferguson 1995, 24; Lizot 1988, 512; Valero 1984, 226, 247, 284).

The Yanomamö enthusiasm for exchange is so great that anything is worthy of being exchanged. As Lizot points out, the ashes of the deceased are transferred and consumed by kinsmen and allies during formal mourning ceremonies or are distributed in small gourds. Esoteric information is exchanged, such as words, myths, or songs, and the farther its source, the more valuable it is deemed. Each item exchanged bears a history, including the imprint of its donor, which is transferred at the moment of its exchange; this is why after their guests left a Namowei-teri feast, laden with gifts, the Namowei-teri assembled in the village clearing and began to shout, to prevent the spirits of their gifts from departing (Lizot 1991, 64, 68–69; Mauss 1954, 8–9; Valero 1984, 277–78, 282–84, 358). Nevertheless, the Yanomamö honor the principle of obligatory generosity in exchange, and have traditionally abhorred avarice and hoarding. The headman of Namowei-teri could boast of his generosity and claim that he had never been stingy, that he had always given everything demanded of him, and that he had never asked for anything in return. Accordingly, the obligation to be generous in exchange limits an individual's ability to amass goods (Cocco 1972, 379; Lizot 1984, 230; 1985, 184; Valero 1984, 143, 317).

In addition to the exchange taking place in the context of a feast and its nocturnal wayamou, there is exchange between individuals, which can lead to the development of trade partnerships between them. These trade partnerships, which are solidified by the exchange of women, are growing in importance among the Yanomamö, some think as a response to the introduction of steel tools and other Western manufactured goods (Cocco 1972, 377; Ferguson 1995, 29–32). The exchange of native and Western goods through these trade partnerships between neighboring villages and allies follows a village-to-village pattern (Good 1984, cited by Ferguson 1995, 30, map 2; Smole 1976, 102). The partnerships adhere to the principles of extreme generosity and delayed reciprocity, wherein each exchange calls for its repayment in the future. Indeed, two individuals who have maintained a long-lasting trade partnership are said to own each other's arm (*poko thapoyou*, with the reciprocal suffix *yo*) (Lizot 1991, 68).

Jivaroans began to intensify their trade partnerships at the end of the rubber boom (1914–15), in order to obtain both native products from interior groups like the Achuar and Western manufactured goods from groups like the Shuar, who were closer to the sources of these goods at the outposts of white settlers (Harner 1972, 126–27, 200). These trading partnerships are formal exchange relationships between two men or "friends" (*amikri*), who generally live one to two days' walk apart and who visit each other three or four times a year in order to exchange. These traders are often energetic and ambitious men who strive to establish trade partnerships far outside their community and who build networks of trading obligations through time, much travel, and the obsequious behavior associated with delayed reciprocity. Their efforts have produced a chain of trading partners (fig. 3.1), facilitating the down-the-line exchange of native and Western trade goods across intertribal Jivaroan territories (Harner 1972, 132; Kelekna 1985, 230).

Since these trading partnerships foster economic interdependence between the participants, Jivaroan groups have instituted certain practices to ensure the perpetuation of this exchange. The amikri formalize their relationship with an Achuar ritual in which they kneel on a cloth, exchange several large baskets of trade goods desired by the other, and embrace. Thereafter, they address each other by the diminutive *amichi*, "little friend." The trade partners are honor bound to guarantee each other's protection and safe conduct in their respective territories; the host partner conceals the visitor's identity by simply referring to his visitor as his amikri, and he acts as a bodyguard, thereby ensuring his visiting partner's personal safety—and the continued supply of his trade goods (Harner 1972, 131; Karsten 1935, 563; Kelekna 1985, 229).

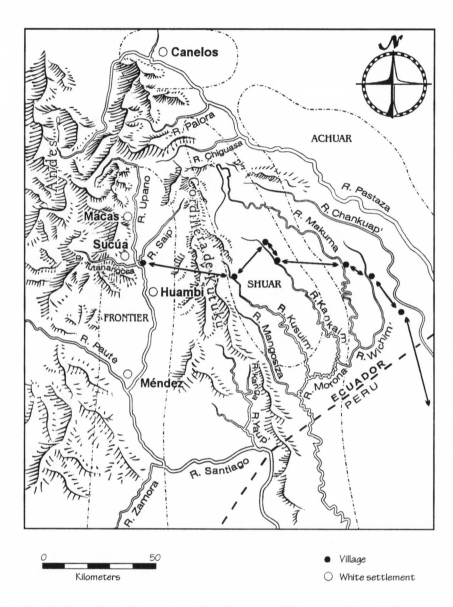

Fig. 3.1. Intertribal exchange networks of native and Western trade goods between trade partners in the Jivaroan area (adapted from Harner 1972, map 2, fig. 5).

The gray-haired Achuar trader Aiju, whom Frank Drown visited on the Huasaga River in 1959, was living testimony of the degree to which traders can benefit from this blanket security offered them in the territories of their trade partners. Aiju, who boasted to Drown that in his prime he had killed his four fists of enemies, now traded peccary hides, which he received from many widely distributed Achuar sources and exchanged for Western goods from traders far downstream in the Peruvian Amazon. Drown wrote of Aiju: "An Indian with a hoary head such as Aiju's is rare among either the Atshuaras or the Jivaros. Most of them die of disease or in war long before their hair turns white. But Aiju, as a valued middle man, had achieved a kind of neutrality" (Drown and Drown 1961, 223–24). Like all traders, Aiju also exchanged nonmaterial goods, in the form of information, ideas, stories, and foreign ways. Through his regional network of trade ties, Aiju was in the position of being able to provide Drown with the names of some 400 people in neighboring communities. Aiju also informed the Achuar party of men led by Tsantiacu, which included Tukup' and Frank Drown, that their enemies (Timas and his brother, Kashíjint) had vowed to kill Tsantiacu. Finally, Aiju and the members of his household were familiar with foreigners from distant places and with their goods and ways (Drown and Drown 1961, 221, 223–24; Kelekna 1985, 238–39). We will see how men who wish to become shamans obtain their shamanic power through such trade partnerships as well.

This amikri relationship is highly valued, for not only do the trade partners acquire goods that are not usually available in their regions, but they assume a redistributive role in the movement of these trade goods, which they dispense to their fellow villagers and neighbors. Harner (1972, 126) points out that the relationship between a trader and his neighbors is of key significance, for the people to whom the trader distributes the goods he receives through his amikri relationships become obligated to him. The trader's fellow villagers and neighbors grow dependent on his supply of trade goods, and their obligation and dependence enhance his standing in the community and in the wider region into which he funnels trade goods. Moreover, his neutral ties with many other villages enable him to act as a peaceful emissary to settle disputes and hostilities between groups (Harner 1972, 126; Kelekna 1985, 239–41, 244–46). Indeed, Kelekna concludes that through his wide-ranging amikri relationships, the Achuar trader gains material goods, wives, information, and contacts beyond his region. The trader becomes a supralocal authority figure, whose multiple roles have important social and political implications for the development of centralized leadership. Although his decision-making authority is not that of an official chief, the trader's wide-ranging ties and multiple roles in the wider region "are a minimal manifestation of authority and direction and as such represent a radical departure from kin-based social organization and the embryonic development of supra-local political integration" (Kelekna 1985, 249).

Blowing Natém

With the decline of intertribal warfare, a growing number of Yanomamö and Jivaroan men are becoming shamans or, to use the Shuar expression, "blowing natém" (Hendricks 1993, 163–64). By the time of Harner's field-work (1956 to 1969) among the Shuar and Achuar, approximately one out of every four adult men was a shaman (uwíshin) (Harner 1972, 122, 202). It is worth noting that three of the five Jivaroan war leaders whose careers I have examined here became shamans as they got older. Anguasha, who was a fierce war leader in the 1920s, was referred to as being a shaman in 1945 (Cotlow 1953, 130). Similarly, the great curaca Tuki of the Upano and Paute rivers in the 1920s and 1930s was sought out for his shamanic powers in 1945 (Cotlow 1953, 149, 151). Then there is the case of Tukup' on the Makuma River, who as a young adult had been tempted to participate in an ill-fated visit to an enemy community by the prospect of acquiring shamanic knowledge from a shaman there. But it was only when his war-ring days were finally over that Tukup' began acquiring shamanic power, and he was still in the process of becoming a shaman in 1971. By the time Hendricks met him in 1982, Tukup' had become a curing shaman whose renown extended throughout Shuar and Achuar territory. He was a re-spected elder (uunt) with five wives and many children. He was also the community's headman (Hendricks 1993, 4, 15, 20, 164–66). Yet Tukup' maintained that it was only by "blowing natém" that one could be certain of "seeing" who one's enemy was, making it clear that he still considered himself a warrior—who would resume killing if the need arose (Hendricks 1993, 165, 290).

These men who seek shamanic knowledge must acquire it through an exchange relationship with an established shaman who lives at some dis-tance. The man wishing to become a shaman journeys to the master sha-man and presents him with valuable trade goods, such as a blowgun and curare, a hunting dog, loincloth, or feather crown; and increasingly with firearms, ammunition, and steel tools. In return the practitioner instructs the novice and eventually bestows him with shamanic power. Under the master shaman's instruction, the novice takes tobacco water and natém repeatedly over several days at the same time that he fasts and is taught the incantations and other shamanic knowledge necessary for acquiring the magical darts (*tsentsak*) of shamanic power. The novice then cuts his hair; bathes at a waterfall; and for several months must drink only specified liquids, must eat only certain foods using stick utensils, and must abstain from sexual intercourse (Harner 1972, 118–19, 121, 155–56; Karsten 1935, 400–403).

It is common for Shuar and Achuar men to seek their shamanic power to the north in eastern Ecuador, from Canelos Quichua shamans, whose tsentsak are considered to be the most powerful and most highly valued due to their possession of foreign tsentsak from the "white world" (Taylor 1981, 666). Moreover, even after becoming a practicing shaman, a shaman must periodically renew his supply of magical darts from other, more powerful shamans, preferably from Canelos shamans. The consequent demand for tsentsak has resulted in a chainlike exchange of shamanic power from north to south, wherein the more powerful donor shaman in the north grants the lesser shaman from the south some tsentsak in return for substantial gifts of valuables at regular intervals. Unlike the equal footing that exists between trade partners in other exchange relationships, however, the relationship between the powerful master shaman and the lesser shaman is a hierarchical one (Harner 1972, 119–22, 165).

Upon his return home, the practicing shaman begins to dispense his services as a curing shaman, or as a diviner, or as a bewitching shaman. For their various services, shamans take much tobacco water and natém to mediate with the supernatural world. Curing shamans can then discover the source of an illness or the identity of the killer or the bewitching shaman responsible, and can proceed to cure by removing the magical darts from the bodies of their patients. By taking natém and tobacco water, bewitching shamans can shoot their tsentsak, which have the power to kill, into the bodies of intended victims. A bewitching shaman strikes his victim like an armed warrior on a hit-and-run raid, by stealthily approaching the enemy's household, shooting his magical dart at the intended target, and retreating quickly. This shamanistic practice that has the power to kill is another way of "doing battle" (Godelier 1986), only with magical darts. Shamans also drink tobacco water almost continuously as a preventive shield against enemy tsentsak. It seems that shamans who are under the influence of natém appear to be sporting a rainbow-hued halo over their heads (Harner 1972, 157–64, plate 24; Kelekna 1981, 92–93). Although only shamans can see the natém-induced halos of other shamans, in their outward appearance and manner shamans "form an easily recognizable class of people" (Karsten 1935, 404).

In spite of the dangers of traveling over great distances to acquire shamanic power and of being on the alert for any enemy tsentsak thrown at them, Jivaroan shamans wield considerable power and influence in their neighborhoods and amass unprecedented wealth. They are paid handsomely in valuable trade goods for their services, and are exempt from having to participate in the usual reciprocal exchange of material goods. They are likewise exempt from the customary bride-service and bride-price demanded of other men. Kelekna (1981, 150–51) cites the case of an elderly Achuar shaman who demanded a fourteen-year-old girl as his wife in payment for curing, and then when she escaped, he prevailed upon all the men in his settlement to pursue and capture her. Shamans can count on the services of their fellow villagers, as in the manual labor to help clear their land, without having to reciprocate in turn. They are treated deferentially by others and are offered gifts of goods and food. Consequently, shamans accumulate significant wealth in valuable material goods, which they use to renew their supply of exotic tsentsak from powerful Canelos Quichua shamans (Harner 1972, 117–18, 165; Kelekna 1981, 212).

In response to the increase in the number of shamans and the development of individual differences of wealth in trade goods and exotic shamanic power, hierarchies of shamans have emerged within neighborhoods, across regions, and even across intertribal boundaries. We have seen how the hierarchical partnerships between master shamans and their novices involve the flow of material goods northward to Canelos Quichua shamans and the flow of powerful shamanic power southward in a chainlike exchange from shaman to shaman. As Harner (1972, 120, fig. 3) specifies, if the seeker of tsentsak is relatively fortunate, he may be able to get his power from a shaman who has obtained his darts directly from a Canelos shaman. But if he lives farther south, he may find he can only obtain the darts from a shaman who got them from another shaman who got them from a third shaman who got them from a Canelos shaman. On the neighborhood or regional level, where many shamans now coexist and compete for valuables and tsentsak, they establish secret shaman partnerships that are similarly hierarchical in nature (Harner 1972, 123–24, 202). Four to five shamans may be linked together, under the leadership of a formally recognized leader, or "higher" shaman, who bestows tsentsak to his lower shamans in return for valuable material goods (fig. 3.2).

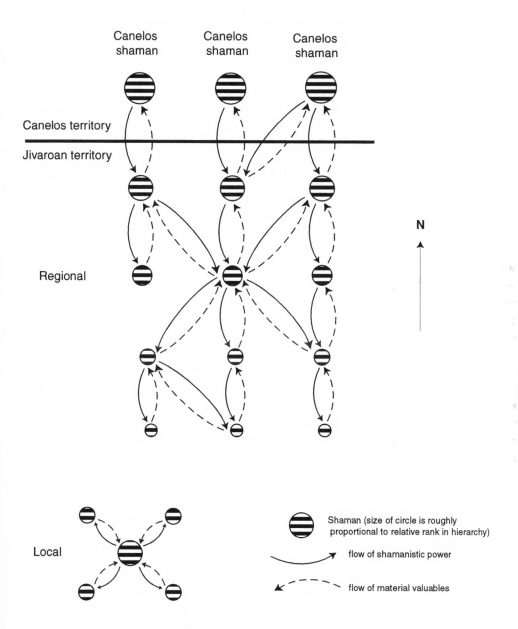

Fig. 3.2. Hierarchies of Jivaroan shamans within neighborhoods, across regions, and beyond tribal boundaries (following Harner 1972, figs. 3, 4).

Shamans and would-be shamans readily admit that they blow natém in order to benefit from the esoteric and material advantages that accrue to them through their participation in these shaman partnerships and inter-tribal shaman hierarchies. Shamanic power assumes the form of a "Chinese-box" series of enclosed domains, their symbolic and territorial space widening with positions further up the hierarchy of shamans. As purvey-ors of superior tsentsak and other Western valuables, the Canelos Quichua shamans are the mediators of shamanic power, which is derived ultimately today from the "white world." That shamanic power, which is valued the most highly and considered the strongest because of its source outside the Jivaroan world, is further sanctioned because of its capacity to produce unprecedented wealth in foreign goods (Taylor 1981, 666, 672–73, 675).

Through their travels to distant regions and their accumulation of for-eign sources of shamanic power and wealth, shamans gain renown in their communities and beyond. They are revered for their curing and divinatory powers and for the supernatural protection they can offer their fellow vil-lagers. They are likewise feared for their bewitching powers (see Kelekna, chap. 7 this volume). Consequently, they are exempt from many social ob-ligations. As their renown increases—in part through their increasing wealth, with which they acquire more powerful, exotic tsentsak—patients come from far away to be treated, and others come to acquire shamanic power from them. They become wealthy men who wield considerable power in their regions. They are sought after for their supernatural powers, whereby they can play decision-making roles in the processes of peace-making, warmongering, or choosing a curaca's successor (Cotlow 1953, 47; Stirling 1938, 121). In most matters, shamans get their way. Accordingly, shamans are poised to cast aside the tribal ethic of being simply greaters among equals, to begin acting in more self-serving ways and to become more than just men of renown.[3]

Conclusion

Through their pursuit of intervillage and intertribal warfare, tribesmen have traditionally sought power and gained renown as warriors, eventu-ally as distinguished warriors, and ultimately as war leaders. For their as-tuteness and their allied victories, war leaders achieve prominence among the many villages in their region. Sometimes their renown reaches far be-yond their regions. At the same time that they are reaping the material and social rewards of their successes in warfare and in deterring counterraids by their enemies, war leaders are building networks of obligations and allegiances among the member villages of their war and marriage alliances. In times of war, they can actually exert centralized authority over the many subordinate villages of the war alliances they head. We have seen how the regional authority and renown of some war leaders persist for many years.

Tribesmen also attain regional prominence through their participation in intervillage trade partnerships and shaman partnerships. These non-warring intervillage relations provide tribesmen with a relatively peaceful arena in which to compete for the accumulation of prestige and power. They travel over great distances—frequently across tribal boundaries—and withstand certain risks in their pursuit of partners with whom to conduct reciprocal, delayed exchanges of material goods and esoteric shamanic power. Yet through the intervillage and intertribal partnerships that traders and shamans establish and nurture, they build contacts well beyond their villages and begin to participate in a larger network of regional and interregional relationships. Through the pursuit of warfare, but also of exchange and shamanic power, tribesmen can achieve renown over the widest fields (Godelier 1986, 167, 170). They reap the social, material, and esoteric bounty of these far-flung alliances and begin to wield an unprecedented amount of influence verging on outright authority over their fellow villagers as well as over other villages in their regions.

An example can be drawn from the Yanomamö village of Hasupuweteri, in which component sublineages were headed by shamans in 1975. Fifty-year-old or so Orawe headed the lesser sublineage. Orawe was a great shaman acclaimed for his curing, his ability to protect the village from any evil forces sent by enemy shamans, and for his easygoing manner. The forceful Yarimowe or "Longbeard" headed the larger sublineage. Yarimowe was reputedly an even more powerful shaman than Orawe and was the village's most influential leader and headman. His authority was almost palpable in the rousing, night-long speeches he delivered to the village and in his bullying of foreigners for trade goods, some of which he would use to build alliances with visiting headmen (Good 1991, 66, 79). The supervillage renown and authority of this powerful shaman and great headman was such that his death ten years later was a "thunderous event that had shaken not only the Hasupuweteri, but the Patahamateri and all the other communities in the region. . . . There had been a massive funeral ceremony and far-flung mourning" (Good 1991, 291).

With their many external contacts and their experience and knowledge of foreign ways, these men of renown—war leaders, traders, shamans, and headmen alike—are destined to serve as the "culture brokers" for their villages in dealings with visitors, who come increasingly from outside the tribesmen's world. The headman of Puunapiwei-teri in the 1950s, Porawë, who was considered the most powerful shaman in the region, became such a culture broker. His superior shamanic power was evident when Porawë was summoned to Witokaya to cure a sick child; he began by taking the hallucinogenic *ebene* and curing the other shamans gathered of wounds induced by evil spirits (*hekura*) (Valero 1984, 446–90; Cocco 1972, 222). As a headman Porawë led by example, and he could literally snuff out any disputes among villagers simply by appearing on the scene (Valero 1984, 513, 515). This great shaman and headman came to be sought out repeatedly by Westerners in their dealings with the Puunapiwei-teri and neighboring villages; in return for plantains and sending men to work as laborers, Porawë received machetes, fishhooks, salt, and other Western goods, which he distributed among the villagers (Valero 1984, 499–500, 508, 515). Men of supravillage renown like Porawë succeed in enhancing the external dimension of centralized leadership as Spencer (1994, 35) has defined this key aspect in the development of permanent centralized authority.

However, permanent centralized leadership is not born of supravillage renown alone. The long-term advantages of such centralized authority must outweigh and counter the forces of intravillage factionalism, to the extent that such centralized leadership needs to be institutionalized, perpetuated, and inherited. We have seen how the sons of distinguished war leaders have an advantage in inheriting their fathers' chieftaincies under conditions of heightened warfare, when all the lessons in the art of warfare instilled in them by their great fathers together with their own accomplishments in warfare will be urgently needed and sought by their fellow villagers.

In times of relative peace, and today, sons of traders, shamans, and headmen as well might hold a similar advantage. It so happens that in 1972, the forty-five-year-old headman of the Yanomamö village of Iyëwei-teri, Hioduwä (Justo Núñez), was a powerful shaman like his elderly father, Badaxiwë. Neighboring villages maintained good relations with Iyëwei-teri in order to benefit from their superior curing abilities as well as to avoid any evil hekura being fired their way. Indeed, Badaxiwë's renown extended from the Padamo and Ocamo rivers up the Orinoco to the Mavaca River, a territory wherein villages solicited his services. So powerful a shaman was Badaxiwë that his son predicted that his death would bring torrential thunderstorms produced by the grieving, departing hekura. Like the shaman and headman Porawë discussed earlier, Badaxiwë had the authority to intervene and single-handedly resolve disputes that erupted and that threatened intervillage relationships (Cocco 1972, 111, 424, 426, 430).

Hioduwä was poised to inherit his father's superior shamanic powers, for through his own 25-year-long pursuit of shamanic power he had acquired knowledge, experience, and supernatural powers second only to his father's and considered critical for curing the gravest of illnesses. Hioduwä had even traveled as a native emissary to visit Pope Paul VI at the Vatican in 1972 and upon his return had visited villages along the Padamo and Orinoco rivers to deliver the greetings from the pope ("great shaman of the white men"). Moreover, in 1970 Hioduwä's twenty-year-old son, Renato, had begun training to become a shaman, under the instruction of his father and grandfather. Renato's initiation as a shaman was considered a most welcome development by the inhabitants of Iyëwei-teri, one that would bring good hunting to their village and that would assure their continued well-being (Cocco 1972, 427, 437–38, 473; Chagnon 1983, 196; Ritchie 1996, 65, 80, 96). The supernatural protection that this young shaman-in-training offered his people by his being the son and grandson of powerful shamans was a clear sign of his future chieftaincy.

The protective hegemony of centralized leadership will be sought, selected for, and eventually made permanent through the institutionalization of hereditary leadership among the autonomous villages of tribal societies. A lineage of hereditary leaders who by their genealogy and training are disposed to do what is in the best interests of their people will emerge to head the member villages of that region in perpetuity.

A final point concerns the regional administrative hierarchy that will administer and rule the subordinate villages within an emergent chief's region. Generally, paramount chiefs exert centralized authority over a regional administrative hierarchy composed minimally of local village chiefs; sometimes paramount chiefs are assisted in their decision-making activities by deputy chiefs, including war chiefs, and by ritual specialists. The autonomous village societies examined here lack such regional administrative hierarchies, of course. However, an incipient administrative hierarchy does exist episodically among certain South American tribal societies. It is most apparent in the conduct of intervillage affairs, which occurs in a ritual context. As described by Niels Fock, when the headman of a Waiwai village in Guyana wishes to invite a neighboring village to a dance festival, that invitation makes its way through a clear, village-level administrative hierarchy (fig. 3.3). The headman (*yayalitomo*) gives the message in the form of an official *oho* chant to his deputy (e.g., son, brother-in-law), who in turn passes it on to another man, whom Fock refers to as an employee (e.g., younger man, second son-in-law). The employee travels to the neighboring village in ceremonial dress and delivers the invitation to the yayalitomo of

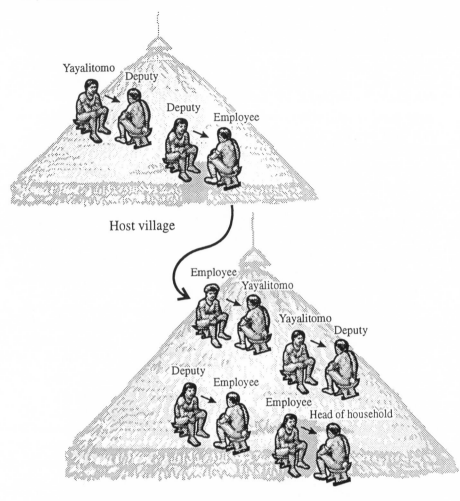

Fig. 3.3. Village-level administrative hierarchy for intervillage affairs among Wai-wai villages in Guyana (adapted from Fock 1963, 208, 231).

that village, sitting on a stool opposite him, by means of the following ceremonial oho dialogue, wherein the recipient answers "oho" (yes) at the end of each sentence: "My leader sends me (oho) to invite you to come and drink (oho), let everyone who wants to, come, (oho), and everybody who does not want to come, stay home" (Fock 1963, 172, 218). The oho chant requires quickness in speech, peculiar diction, and the use of archaic language, which means that only men with certain experience can deliver it.

The invited headman, by means of an oho chant, informs his deputy about the invitation to the dance festival. The deputy passes the information on to the employee, who then goes to inform the head of each family in the village, always in the form of an oho chant.

There seem to be no native designations for these oho functionaries, whose specialized roles drop out in ordinary domestic village affairs. Aside from the shaman, the headman and these two oho functionaries who deliver invitations to intervillage dance festivals are the only cases of individual specialization in Waiwai villages; they represent a graduated organization of village administration through persons who are practically considered to be substitutes and official employees of the leader (Fock 1963, 208, 218).

Like the the incipient hierarchy manifested by an intervillage raiding party led by a war leader, and for that matter like the asymmetrical shaman partnerships and intertribal hierarchies of Jivaroan shamans, the kind of village administrative hierarchy that operates only on the occasion of intervillage dance festivals among the Waiwai will emerge as a full-time institution to administer a greater variety of activities within the emergent regional chief's domain. Under conditions that favor the readiness or efficiency of centralized leadership (see also Redmond 1994, 128–30), the administrative demands of the emergent paramount chief will be easily met by this incipient administrative hierarchy in existence among autonomous village societies. In peace just as much as in war, then, such centralized leadership can emerge and be made permanent.

Notes

1. In a departure from his etic behavioral approach to the study of Yanomamö warfare, Brian Ferguson addresses the leading role that such ambitious war leaders play in inciting warfare. Ferguson considers the Namowei-teri (Wãnitima-teri) headman and war leader Husiwë "a study in agency" (Ferguson 1995, 210, 366–67). In assessing the objectives underlying the escalating hostilities between the Namowei-teri and the Pishaasi-teri, Ferguson (1995, 238) cites a comment made by Husiwë's wife, Helena Valero, in an early, translated version of her narrative (Biocca 1970, 232–33), in which the possibility is raised that Husiwë was seeking to defeat the Pishaasi-teri in warfare in order become a regional chieftain.

2. I am indebted to Matt Gerhart of Yale University, Class of '95, for bringing Lemonnier's study to my attention.

3. This increase in the number of men becoming shamans, with all the benefits and power that accrue to them, is exactly the route to cultural success that Chagnon predicts tribesmen would pursue under peaceful conditions, "when one's neighbors are nice guys" (Chagnon 1992b, 240). Such an increase in the number of Yanomamö shamans was reported by the Salesian missionary José Berno at Mavaca, where of the 30 adult men residing there in 1972, 25 were shamans (Cocco 1972, 424).

References

Biocca, Ettore, ed.
1970 *Yanoáma: The Narrative of a White Girl Kidnapped by Amazonian Indians.* New York: E. P. Dutton.
Carneiro, Robert L.
1981 The chiefdom: Precursor of the state. In *The Transition to Statehood in the New World,* edited by G. D. Jones and R. R. Kautz, 37–79. Cambridge: Cambridge University Press.
Chagnon, Napoleon A.
1968 Yanomamö social organization and warfare. In *War: The Anthropology of Armed Conflict and Aggression,* edited by M. Fried, M. Harris, and R. Murphy, 109–59. Garden City, N.Y.: The Natural History Press.
1983 *Yanomamö: The Fierce People.* 3rd ed. New York: Holt, Rinehart and Winston.
1988 Life histories, blood revenge, and warfare in a tribal population. *Science* 239:985–92.
1990 Reproductive and somatic conflicts of interest in the genesis of violence and warfare among tribesmen. In *The Anthropology of War,* edited by J. Haas, 77–104. School of American Research. Cambridge: Cambridge University Press.
1992a *Yanomamö.* 4th ed. Fort Worth: Harcourt Brace College Publishers.
1992b *Yanomamö: The Last Days of Eden.* San Diego: Harcourt Brace Jovanovich.
Cocco, P. Luis
1972 *Iyëwei-teri: Quince Años entre los Yanomamos.* Caracas: Escuela Técnica Popular Don Bosco.
Cotlow, Lewis
1953 *Amazon Head-Hunters.* New York: Henry Holt.
Descola, Philippe
1981 From scattered to nucleated settlement: A process of socioeconomic change among the Achuar. In *Cultural Transformations and Ethnicity in Modern Ecuador,* edited by N. E. Whitten Jr., 614–46. Urbana: University of Illinois Press.
Drown, Frank, and Marie Drown
1961 *Mission to the Head-Hunters.* New York: Harper and Row.
Feil, D. K.
1987 *The Evolution of Highland Papua New Guinea Societies.* Cambridge: Cambridge University Press.

Ferguson, R. Brian
1995   *Yanomami Warfare: A Political History.* Santa Fe: School of American Research Press.

Fock, Niels
1963   *Waiwai: Religion and Society of an Amazonian Tribe.* Ethnographic Series of the National Museum, no. 8. Copenhagen: National Museum.

Godelier, Maurice
1986   *The Making of Great Men: Male Domination and Power among the New Guinea Baruya.* Cambridge: Cambridge University Press.

González Holguín, Diego
1989   *Vocabulario de la Lengua General de todo el Peru llamada Qquichua o del Inca* (1608). Edited by R. Matos Mendieta. Lima: Editorial de la Universidad Nacional Mayor de San Marcos.

Good, Kenneth
1991   *Into the Heart: One Man's Pursuit of Love and Knowledge among the Yanoama.* London: Hamish Hamilton.

Gregor, Thomas
1990   Uneasy peace: Intertribal relations in Brazil's Upper Xingu. In *The Anthropology of War,* edited by J. Haas, 105–24. School of American Research. Cambridge: Cambridge University Press.

Harner, Michael J.
1972   *The Jívaro: People of the Sacred Waterfalls.* Garden City, N.Y.: Doubleday–Natural History Press.

Hendricks, Janet W.
1988   Power and knowledge: Discourse and ideological transformation among the Shuar. *American Ethnologist* 15: 216–38.
1993   *To Drink of Death: The Narrative of a Shuar Warrior.* Tucson: University of Arizona Press.

Karsten, Rafael
1935   *The Head-Hunters of Western Amazonas.* Societas Scientiarum Fennica. Commentationes Humanarum Litteratum VII (1). Helsingfors: Centraltryckeriet.

Kelekna, Pita
1981   Sex Asymmetry in Jivaroan Achuara Society: A Cultural Mechanism Promoting Belligerence. Ph.D. dissertation, University of New Mexico. Ann Arbor: University Microfilms.
1985   Achuara trade: Counterpoise and complement to war. In *Political Anthropology in Ecuador: Perspectives from Indigenous Cultures,* edited by J. Ehrenreich, 217–56. Society for Latin American Anthropology and Center for the Caribbean and Latin America. Albany: State University of New York.

Lemonnier, Pierre
1990   *Guerres et Festins: Paix, Echanges et Compétition dans les Highlands de Nouvelle-Guinée.* Paris: Editions de la Maison des Sciences de l'Homme.
1991   From great men to big men: Peace, substitution and competition in the High-

lands of New Guinea. In *Big Men and Great Men: Personifications of Power in Melanesia,* edited by M. Godelier and M. Strathern, 7–27. Cambridge: Cambridge University Press.

Lévi-Strauss, Claude

1943   Guerre et commerce chez les indiens de l'Amérique du Sud. *Renaissance* 1:122–39.

Lizot, Jacques

1984   *Les Yanomami Centraux.* Paris: Editions de l'Ecole des Hautes Etudes en Sciences Sociales.

1985   *Tales of the Yanomami: Daily Life in the Venezuelan Forest.* Cambridge: Cambridge University Press.

1989   Sobre la guerra. *La Iglesia en Amazonas* 44:23–34.

1991   Palabras en la noche. *La Iglesia en Amazonas* 53:54–82.

Lowie, Robert H.

1949   Social and political organization of the tropical forest and marginal tribes. In *Handbook of South American Indians,* vol. 5, *The Comparative Ethnology of South American Indians,* edited by J. H. Steward, 313–50. Bureau of American Ethnology Bulletin 143. Washington, D.C.: Smithsonian Institution.

Mauss, Marcel

1954   *The Gift: Forms and Functions of Exchange in Archaic Societies.* Glencoe, Ill.: Free Press.

Redmond, Elsa M.

1994   *Tribal and Chiefly Warfare in South America.* University of Michigan Museum of Anthropology, Memoirs, no. 28. Ann Arbor.

Ritchie, Mark A.

1996   *Spirit of the Rainforest: A Yanomamö Shaman's Story.* Chicago: Island Lake Press.

Rivière, Peter

1971   The political structure of the Trio Indians as manifested in a system of ceremonial dialogue. In *The Translation of Culture: Essays to E. E. Evans-Pritchard,* edited by T. O. Beidelman, 293–311. London: Tavistock Publications.

Ross, Jane B.

1984   Effects of contact on revenge hostilities among the Achuara Jívaro. In *Warfare, Culture, and Environment,* edited by R. B. Ferguson, 83–109. New York: Academic Press.

Sahlins, Marshall D.

1972   *Stone Age Economics.* Chicago: Aldine-Atherton.

Salomon, Frank

1986   *Native Lords of Quito in the Age of the Incas.* Cambridge: Cambridge University Press.

Siverts, Henning

1972   *Tribal Survival in the Alto Marañon: The Aguaruna Case.* IWGIA Document 10. Copenhagen: International Work Group for Indigenous Affairs.

1975   Jívaro head hunters in a headless time. In *War, Its Causes and Correlates*, edited by M. A. Nettleship, R. D. Givens, and A. Nettleship, 663–74. The Hague: Mouton Publishers.

Smole, William J.

1976   *The Yanoama Indians: A Cultural Geography.* Austin: University of Texas Press.

Spencer, Charles S.

1994   Factional ascendance, dimensions of leadership, and the development of centralized authority. In *Factional Competition and Political Development in the New World*, edited by E. M. Brumfiel and J. W. Fox, 31–43. Cambridge: Cambridge University Press.

Stirling, Matthew W.

1938   *Historical and Ethnographical Material on the Jívaro Indians.* Bureau of American Ethnology Bulletin 17. Washington, D.C.: Smithsonian Institution.

Strathern, Andrew J.

1971   *The Rope of Moka: Big-men and Ceremonial Exchange in Mount Hagen, New Guinea.* Cambridge: Cambridge University Press.

Taylor, Anne-Christine

1981   God-wealth: The Achuar and the missions. In *Cultural Transformations and Ethnicity in Modern Ecuador*, edited by N. E. Whitten Jr., 647–76. Urbana: University of Illinois Press.

1985   L'art de la réduction: La guerre et les mécanismes de la différenciation tribale dans la culture Jivaro. *Journal de la Société des Américanistes* 71:159–73.

Urban, Greg

1986   Ceremonial dialogues in South America. *American Anthropologist* 88(2):371–86.

Valero, Helena

1984   *Yo Soy Napëyoma.* Fundación La Salle de Ciencias Naturales Monografía no. 35. Caracas: Editorial Texto.

Velasco, Juan de

1842   *Historia del Reino de Quito en la America Meridional* (1789). Vol. 3. Quito: Imprenta de Gobierno.

Zikmund, Miroslav, and Jiří Hanzelka

1963   *Amazon Headhunters.* Prague: Artia.

CHAPTER 4

Investigating the Development
of Venezuelan Chiefdoms

CHARLES S. SPENCER

Recent years have seen an increase in archaeological research aimed at the Intermediate Area, lying south of Mesoamerica and north of Peru, where aboriginal societies of considerable complexity, though not true states or urban civilizations, developed in pre-Hispanic times (Bray 1980–88; Cooke and Ranere 1984; Drennan 1985; Lange 1984, 1992; Lange and Stone 1984; Lathrap et al. 1977; Linares and Ranere 1980; Linares 1979). Accompanying this growing interest has been a new orientation, away from the concerns with diffusion and migration that characterized the work of earlier Intermediate Area researchers, toward a focus on indigenous processes of long-term cultural evolution, which in some regions led to the development of complex societies (Cooke and Ranere 1992; Creamer and Haas 1985; Drennan and Uribe 1987a; Linares 1977). In an effort to understand the nature of this complexity, some investigators have found the chiefdom concept to be a useful analytical tool.

The Chiefdom Concept in Anthropology

There is no lack of controversy surrounding the chiefdom. On the one hand, there are evolutionary scholars who recognize the considerable empirical variability that exists in human sociopolitical organization but feel that a relatively small number of basic designs underlie the evident diversity. One of these designs can be recognized as the chiefdom and defined as follows: a human society that has centralized political authority and institutionalized social status differentiation but lacks an internally specialized central government (Spencer 1987; Wright 1977). The chiefdom is thus interposed between uncentralized "egalitarian" societies and bureaucratic states, in terms of sociopolitical complexity as well as general evolutionary sequencing (Earle 1987a, 1989; Spencer 1990). Evolutionary anthropologists recognize that some developmental sequences have proceeded to state formation while others have not, and they see in this a fertile field for comparative analysis and, ultimately, theory construction and assessment.

By contrast, other scholars question the utility of the chiefdom concept and, indeed, the evolutionary approach in general. Taking a more particularistic view, they argue that the wide variability observed among the societies that some would classify as chiefdoms renders such a cross-cultural classification moot (Feinman and Neitzel 1984; Upham 1987). Greater weight is given to the differences between developmental sequences rather than to similarities, and comparative analyses are viewed with suspicion (Hodder 1982; Yoffee 1979, 1988). From this perspective, cultural change is a continuous, historical phenomenon that must be studied relativistically; attempts to impose general evolutionary schemes upon it are seen as misguided and ultimately sterile (Hodder 1986; Kottak 1977; Lewis 1968; Zeidler 1987).

It is unlikely that a reconciliation will soon occur between these discordant outlooks. At the same time, it seems unwarranted to conclude that the chiefdom has been so tainted by controversy that it has become diminished as a topic for sober investigation. To the contrary, I would argue that the skirmishing actually reflects the enduring importance and vitality of the chiefdom as both a theoretical concept and a subject for empirical research (see Earle 1991). I also think there is more than a little common ground underlying the apparently dissonant positions. In the first place, there seems to exist a shared understanding of the basic cultural features of the phenomenon under study. One need only say that one's research deals with prehistoric chiefdoms in a certain area, and most contemporary anthropologists will know what is meant, though some might prefer a different label, such as ranked society or middle-range society. In addition, most will recognize that such a study is a worthwhile endeavor, being both a contribution to culture history and an enhancement of the empirical data base against which competing theories (of whatever ilk) can be evaluated. There is also relatively widespread agreement that addressing these concerns will require the careful linking of ethnohistoric and ethnographic data concerning chiefdoms with archaeological information on sequences of long-term development in as many regions as possible (Carneiro 1981; Drennan and Uribe 1987b; Earle 1987a; Wright 1986).

It is particularly incumbent on evolutionary anthropologists to seek a better understanding of why chiefdoms developed in some places and not in others, and why in a few cases the trajectory of cultural evolution led on to something rather more complex: true state societies. Yet, to make headway toward such a goal, it is important to do more than just demonstrate the existence of chiefdoms at particular times and places. These systems and their evolutionary trajectories must be described in some detail, including the environmental and historical contexts of their development. This requires the application of multilevel research designs that emphasize the collection of long-term diachronic data on various levels of cultural organization—such as the household, community, regional, and interregional levels (Flannery 1976a; Lathrap et al. 1977; Roosevelt 1987; Struever 1971). Key variables of the cultural systems under study must be monitored, including population size and distribution, the relationships between human settlement and critical environmental variables, the organization of primary production and craft activities, the nature of social differentiation, political centralization, religious behavior, exchange relationships, and warfare (Cooke and Ranere 1984; Drennan 1985; Spencer and Redmond 1984). Because collecting such information is neither quick nor easy, archaeologists will have to commit themselves to lengthy research projects in a variety of suitable regions. Fortunately, such research has begun, in some cases building upon the work of previous scholars whose interests did not focus on chiefdoms per se.

Recognizing Chiefdoms in the Archaeological Record

An essential step in any analysis of prehistoric chiefdom development is the identification of chiefdoms in the archaeological record. Many conceptions of chiefly organization stress political centralization and socioeconomic differentiation as central features (Carneiro 1981; Earle 1987a, 1989; Flannery 1972; Peebles and Kus 1977; Spencer 1987). In multilevel research designs, these features should manifest themselves in the structure of variability on the various organizational levels of the cultural system in question.

On the regional level of a chiefdom, for example, one would expect to find evidence of centralized political control exerted by a regional leadership over a number of communities (Carneiro 1981; Earle 1987a; Roosevelt 1987). Archaeologically, this should be seen in a regional settlement hierarchy of two or three levels based on settlement size; if a histogram or bar graph of settlement size is constructed, such a hierarchy will be manifested by a frequency distribution with two or three modes. The higher levels should exhibit their greater political importance by having relatively more public architecture than lower levels (Creamer and Haas 1985; Peebles and Kus 1977; Spencer 1982, 58; Steponaitis 1981). At the very top of this hierarchy should be an identifiable regional capital or first-order center, largest in size and with the grandest public architecture in the region (Flannery 1976b; Hansell 1987; Lathrap et al. 1977). At the same time, one does not ordinarily expect to find a great deal of morphological or functional diversity among public buildings on any level, in keeping with the generalized internal structure of chiefly administration (Flannery and Marcus 1976; Spencer 1987, 1990).

To assess the community and household levels of chiefdom organization, one's perspective shifts to individual sites, where there should be evidence for centralized leadership as well as social differentiation. Of course, we must bear in mind that the nature of this evidence will surely vary according to the site's position in the regional settlement hierarchy. For example, the community plan of a first-order center can be expected to have a relatively formalized layout focused on a central zone of public architecture (such as a plaza), befitting its role as the seat of centralized regional administration, while smaller sites will likely have a less formal and less imposing arrangement (Hasemann 1987; Lathrap et al. 1977; Oyuela 1987).

Social differentiation may be expressed through variability among household units in terms of size and elaborateness of construction and associated artifacts (Castaño 1987; Creamer and Haas 1985; Spencer 1982, 79–149; Whalen 1983). The social ranking of individuals is another key feature of chiefly society; social differences can be manifested archaeologically through patterns of differential burial treatment and variable health or nutritional status (Castaño 1987; Creamer and Haas 1985; Hatch 1987; Peebles 1987; Peebles and Kus 1977; Powell 1988).

The inevitable energy costs incurred by a chiefly administration usually must be met though the development of an effective political economy, which stimulates and mobilizes the production of surplus (Earle 1978, 1987b; Lightfoot 1987; Sahlins 1972; Steponaitis 1981). Archaeologically, one might find evidence for intensified agricultural or craft production beyond what is required for local subsistence needs, coupled with infrastructural improvements in transportation, communication, or storage facilities that enhance the leadership's control over such surplus (Brumfiel and Earle 1987; Creamer and Haas 1985; Earle 1987b; Spencer 1979, 1982, 151–97).

On the interregional level, separate chiefdoms often interact with one another through exchange and warfare. The long-distance exchange of prestige or luxury goods is especially characteristic (Helms 1979, 1987) and can be archaeologically manifested by the presence of exotic goods, often in high-status contexts (Peebles 1987; Sanoja and Vargas 1987; Snarskis 1987; Spencer 1982, 152–97). Warfare, usually in the form of sporadic raids directed by the leadership against another chiefly polity, can be archaeologically expressed in the form of artifacts, features, and facilities that reflect offensive and defensive warfare activities, including weapons, fortifications, and sacrificed captives (Carneiro 1981; Redmond 1990, 1994; Snarskis 1987; Wilson 1987).

Venezuela as a Setting for Chiefdom Research

Although few archaeological projects in Venezuela have focused explicitly on pre-Hispanic chiefdoms, the nation holds great potential for such research. Ethnohistoric sources reveal that chiefly societies existed in various parts of the country during the sixteenth century. *Caquetío* is a term that was apparently used to refer to a number of independent but ethnically related chiefly polities in several river drainages over a large area extending from the sub-Andean valley of Barquisimeto well into the *llanos* (humid savanna grasslands) of the Orinoco Basin (Morey 1975; Oliver 1988). They were encountered by Nicolás Federmann on his first expedition to the llanos in 1530 (Federmann 1962), and also by Georg Hohermuth von Speyer in 1535 (Jahn 1927, 207). In 1538 Caquetío were reported along the Río Casanare, south of the Apure River (Castellanos 1962, 98–99), but Morey (1975, 33) has argued that this was a postcontact phenomenon and that their aboriginal distribution was limited to the llanos north of the Apure. *Achagua* and *Otomaco* are ethnic designations for other somewhat less well known chiefdoms that occupied areas along the Apure River, although the Achagua may have extended into southern parts of Barinas state (Morey 1975, 37–38).

Federmann reported that the Caquetío occupied large, well-fortified villages on the savanna, usually near a major tributary stream of a large river (Morey 1975, 96). Along one river valley were 23 villages politically united under the direction of a paramount chief; one of the member villages contained some 4,000 inhabitants. Federmann (1962, 191–92) estimated that this paramount chief could raise a fighting force of 30,000 men. Two other such chiefdoms on the llanos, he claimed, could muster 16,000 and 8,500 fighting men, respectively (Morey 1975, 96, 108, 309).

There are no detailed descriptions of Caquetío communities, but it appears that two or three related families would often build their houses adjacent to one another in the form of a compound (Morey 1975, 92). Federmann (1962, 212) described one Caquetío chief sitting in a spacious structure, which might have been his residence or perhaps a public or ceremonial building where he carried out his chiefly duties. Social differentiation in Caquetío society was manifested not only by house size but also by shell-bead necklaces and the number of wives a man had (Morey 1975, 100–1, 109, 259).

Agriculture provided the Caquetío with the bulk of their subsistence, though contributions also came from hunting, fishing, and gathering. Among the crops grown by the Caquetío were two varieties of maize, squash, manioc, sweet potatoes, cotton, and tobacco (Morey 1975, 51, 85). The Caquetío appear to have engaged in intensive agriculture. One river valley was said to have had some 12 miles of irrigated fields on both banks (Morey 1975, 51). In addition, Gumilla described the use of artificially drained or raised fields by llanos groups generally, which presumably would also apply to the Caquetío (Gumilla 1963, 429–33; Morey 1975, 147).

Caquetío chiefdoms interacted with other groups through both trading and raiding. Among the items known to have been produced and exchanged by llanos groups were strings of fresh-water shell disks, turtle eggs and oil, slaves, pottery, foodstuffs, the hallucinogen *yopo*, cotton, palm products, tree resins, and animal skins (Morey 1975, 257–69). Coming into the llanos proper from areas to the east and southeast were the poison *curare*, various vegetable dyes, and manioc graters. From the Andes came salt and gold, woven cotton fabric, and probably workable stone (Morey 1975, 252–55). Warfare occurred frequently between the Caquetío and neighboring groups (Federmann 1962, 189–92, 215–19). The Caquetío fortified their villages and were able to muster a fighting force on short notice; aside from defensive actions, most warfare took the form of surprise raids on villages for the purpose of looting and taking captives (Morey 1975, 282–83).

Chiefdoms also existed during the sixteenth century along the middle and lower reaches of the Orinoco River, as Whitehead (1988) has documented. Antonio de Sedeño led an expedition into the lower Orinoco in 1531. He came upon a village called Aruacay, which had 200 houses and was led by a "chief-priest" (Oviedo y Valdés 1959, 391, in Whitehead 1988, 12). During a 1583 journey to the mouth of the Orinoco River, Jorge Griego encountered a chief named Carapana, who lived in village of 2,000 people and was said to have ruled over "many more" villages (Whitehead 1988, 13). Another chief, Morequito, ruled a village of 4,000 people (Whitehead 1988, 13). These chiefdoms were raided frequently by other groups living farther upstream; attacking forces of 40 dugout canoes are reported (Whitehead 1988, 13).

During a trip along the middle Orinoco in the seventeenth century, Jacinto de Carvajal encountered a chief named Tavacare, who was accompanied by a war party of 3,000 men (Carvajal 1956, 166, in Roosevelt 1980, 255, 257). Tavacare was said to rule over a large domain composed of several districts (each with its own district chief) and a large number of villages, each of which had a community chief or *capitán* (Carvajal 1956, 164–65, in Roosevelt 1980, 256). This political unification appears to have occurred in a context of offensive warfare directed by Tavacare against other groups along the Orinoco River (Roosevelt 1980, 257–58).

Previous Archaeological Research on Venezuelan Chiefdoms

Archaeologists have recently begun to recover data bearing on the development and organization of pre-Hispanic chiefdoms in Venezuela. In the Parmana region along the middle Orinoco River (fig. 4.1), Anna Roosevelt carried out a regional-scale project during the mid-1970s (Roosevelt 1980). She documented a long sequence of pre-Hispanic occupation here, beginning around 2100 B.C. and lasting until the contact period (Roosevelt 1980, table 15). Her settlement pattern survey and excavations yielded diachronic data on human demography and subsistence practices. An important conclusion of her research was that maize agriculture makes its appearance during Corozal II times (400 B.C.–A.D. 100) and is associated with a growing human population in the Parmana region (Roosevelt 1980, 243).

When did a chiefdom form of organization emerge at Parmana? Although information on variability among households and burials is not yet available, we can address this question by analyzing the published settlement pattern data for the nine periods of pre-Hispanic occupation (Roosevelt 1980, tables 16–18). As noted earlier, one manifestation of chiefdom organization is a regional settlement hierarchy of at least two levels. Sufficient evidence of this would be at least a bimodal frequency distribution in a bar graph of settlement sizes.

The first three phases of the Parmana chronological sequence (La Gruta, Ronquín, and Ronquín Sombra) comprise the La Gruta tradition (2100–800 B.C.). This period is one of sedentary villages, the earliest known in Venezu-

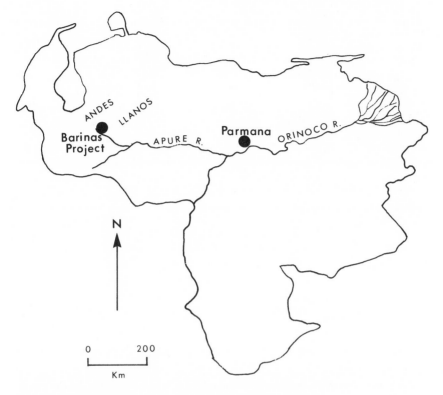

Fig. 4.1. Venezuela, showing locations mentioned in the text.

ela, in which people pursued a subsistence procurement strategy that combined hunting and collecting with manioc agriculture; maize had not yet
appeared (Roosevelt 1980, table 20). Human population was low and there
is no evidence of a regional settlement hierarchy. The La Gruta phase (2100–
1600 B.C.) has a single site with 1.6 hectares of occupation (Roosevelt 1980,
table 16). Ronquín phase (1600–1100 B.C.) also has but one habitation site,
covering 1.7 hectares (Roosevelt 1980, table 16). Ronquín Sombra phase
(1100–800 B.C.) likewise occurs at one site; the occupation covers 1.5 hectares (Roosevelt 1980, table 16).

The three Corozal phases (800 B.C.–A.D.400) see the appearance of maize,
sporadically in the proveniences of the first two Corozal phases but quite
uniformly in the proveniences of the last Corozal phase (Roosevelt 1980,
table 20). Regional population undergoes considerable growth, although a
clear regional settlement hierarchy is not in evidence; the frequency distributions of site sizes are unimodal for all three Corozal phases. Corozal I
phase (800–400 B.C.) is reported at four sites with a total of 7.55 hectares of

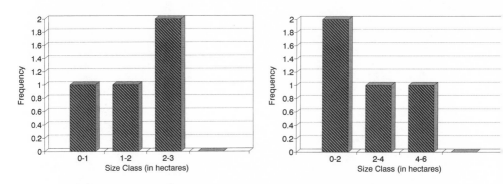

Left: Fig. 4.2. Settlement sizes, Corozal I phase, Parmana region. *Right:* Fig. 4.3. Settlement sizes, Corozal II phase, Parmana region.

occupation; the data yield a unimodal frequency distribution, skewed to the left (fig. 4.2). Corozal II phase (400 B.C.–A.D. 100) also appears at four sites, but occupation area increases to 10.05 hectares (Roosevelt 1980, table 17). The frequency distribution continues to be unimodal, in this case skewed to the right (fig. 4.3). In Corozal III phase (A.D. 100–700), regional occupation area more than doubles, to 23.25 hectares on four sites (Roosevelt 1980, table 17). The frequency distribution, however, is unimodal and symmetrical (fig. 4.4).

Regional population grows only a little in the Camoruco I phase (A.D. 400–700), reaching a total of 24.1 hectares on five sites (Roosevelt 1980, table 18). The frequency distribution is unimodal and skewed slightly to the right (fig. 4.5). In Camoruco II times (A.D. 700–1100), regional population is relatively stable, edging up slightly to 24.8 hectares on six sites (Roosevelt 1980, table 18). The frequency distribution is unimodal and skewed to the right (fig. 4.6). In the last phase of the prehistoric sequence, Camoruco III (A.D. 1100–1500), regional population grows dramatically, with the total occupied area reaching 34.05 hectares on eight sites (Roosevelt 1980, table 18). It is in the Camoruco III phase that we get the first solid evidence of a regional settlement hierarchy in the Parmana region: the frequency distribution of site sizes is clearly bimodal (fig. 4.7). Thus, the regional settlement pattern data lead us to conclude that chiefdom organization first appeared along the middle Orinoco River during the last four centuries prior to European contact. This is an admittedly provisional interpretation that ought to be evaluated through future research in the middle Orinoco; what is especially needed is more information on variability in community layouts, household size, and burial patterns.

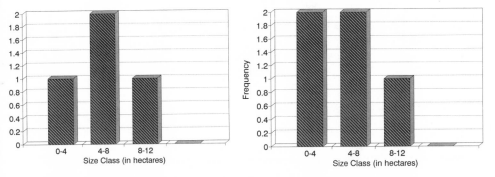

Left: Fig. 4.4. Settlement sizes, Corozal III phase, Parmana region. *Right:* Fig. 4.5. Settlement sizes, Camoruco I phase, Parmana region.

In the western llanos area of Barinas state (fig. 4.1), recent research has also produced information concerning chiefdom development. Based on her fieldwork at La Betania and La Calzada in the middle llanos (fig. 4.8), Alberta Zucchi defined the Osoid Series composed of two phases: the La Betania phase (A.D. 650–1200) and the Caño del Oso phase (230 B.C.–A.D. 650). She concluded that mounded earthworks were associated with the later La Betania phase, though the very first such structures may have been erected as early as the middle of the sixth century A.D. (Zucchi 1967, 1972a, 1972b, 1973).

The map of the La Betania site reveals that the site covers 15–20 hectares. There are five earthen mounds, the tallest of which is 3.6 meters high (Zucchi 1967, fig. 4). Although it is quite probable that the site is the largest in its vicinity, this cannot be stated with certainty until a systematic re-

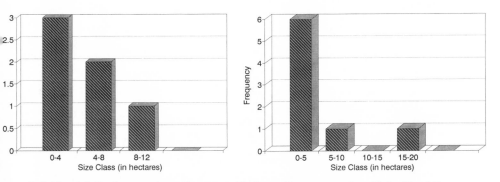

Left: Fig. 4.6. Settlement sizes, Camoruco II phase, Parmana region. *Right:* Fig. 4.7. Settlement sizes, Camoruco III phase, Parmana region.

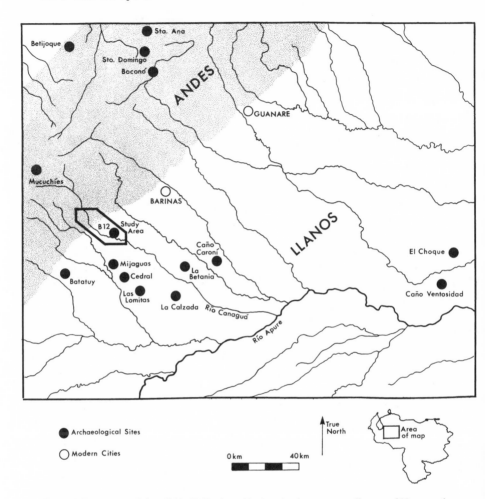

Fig. 4.8. Location of the 1983–88 Barinas Project in the western llanos of Venezuela.

gional settlement pattern survey is carried out. Zucchi excavated seven burials, which produced some evidence of social differentiation at the site. Four of the burials lacked burial accompaniments, but the other three had two items apiece: in two cases a pair of ceramic vessels, and in one case a ceramic vessel and a stone ax (Zucchi 1967, 117–20).

A drained-field system was the focus of research in 1972 by Zucchi and William Denevan along the Caño Ventosidad in southeastern Barinas (fig. 4.8). Mapping and excavations were conducted at this field system, which the investigators argued was a man-made extension of the natural riverine levees and would have permitted the harvesting of more than one crop per year (Denevan and Zucchi 1978; Zucchi and Denevan 1979).

In the Hato La Calzada de Páez area, Adam Garson conducted a settlement pattern survey followed by the excavation of 19 test pits at five sites in 1976 (Garson 1980). Garson found a total of 22 Osoid Series habitation sites, dating to either the Caño del Oso or La Betania phases, in a study region of 120 square kilometers (Garson 1980, 89, 98). In addition, he located nine *calzadas* (earthen causeways) that he assigned to the Osoid Series (Garson 1980, 98). He also discovered a drained-field system just 1.3 kilometers from an Osoid settlement, though he was reluctant to associate the two sites because he found the field system by examining aerial photographs after the fieldwork period (Garson 1980, 129–30).

Earthen mounds occurred at 13 of Garson's 22 Osoid sites. There was also considerable variation in site area, which led him to conclude that the Osoid occupation exhibited a regional settlement hierarchy (1980, 99–121, 291–302, 305–7). The largest site in the study region is the La Calzada site itself (fig. 4.8). Garson classified the site as "larger than 15 hectares" and reported ceramics eroding for "several hundred meters" along the banks of the adjacent Caño del Oso (Garson 1980, 105, 294). As of this writing, only a small part of the La Calzada site has been mapped: a four-hectare portion that contains the three principal mounds (Zucchi 1972a, fig. 3; also reproduced as Garson 1980, map 11). The only excavation thus far at this site is a trench that Zucchi placed in the tallest mound, which reaches 12.9 meters in elevation and is the highest mound in the Hato La Calzada study region (Garson 1980, 105; Zucchi 1972a, 1972b, 1973). Charcoal samples from hearths located at its base and top were radiocarbon dated to A.D. 550 and 540, respectively, indicating a mid–sixth century A.D. construction date (Zucchi 1973, 187).

The settlement pattern, architectural, and burial data resulting from Zucchi's and Garson's work can be drawn together to suggest that at least two chiefdoms had emerged in the lower llanos of Barinas by about A.D. 500–600. The La Calzada chiefdom has a regional settlement hierarchy probably centered on the La Calzada site, though additional mapping and excavation should be carried out here to substantiate this conclusion. The other chiefdom is most likely centered on the La Betania site, though a good regional survey and more mapping and excavation of individual sites of varying sizes should be conducted to improve our understanding of this system's regional organization.

The 1983–88 Barinas Project

In 1983 the author and Elsa M. Redmond began a project on the prehistory of the Andean piedmont and high llanos in Barinas (Redmond and Spencer 1989, 1994; Spencer and Redmond 1992).[1] Five seasons of survey and excavation were carried out in a portion of the Río Canaguá drainage, about 50 kilometers to the northwest of La Calzada (fig. 4.8). The study region of 450 square kilometers overlaps portions of the high llanos and the adjacent Andean piedmont, each of which has a lengthy occupation history. Three seasons of intensive regional survey (1983–85) yielded 103 archaeological sites. During the fourth and fifth seasons (1986–88), we excavated a total of 201 test pits at 10 sites (three in the piedmont and seven in the llanos). Also in the fifth season we completed three areas of horizontal excavation at the site of Gaván (B12), which was the largest prehistoric settlement in the study region. I here discuss the Early Gaván and Late Gaván phases (A.D. 300–1000) in the high llanos.

Early Gaván phase (A.D. 300–550) is the earliest period of occupation that we detected in the high llanos. Early Gaván pottery (which is similar to Zucchi's Caño del Oso material) was found at sites B12, B97, and B21, making a total of 11 hectares of human occupation at this time. B97 and B21 are each three hectares in size, while B12 covers five hectares (fig. 4.9) I have previously suggested (Spencer 1993, 60) that the slightly larger size of B12 during the Early Gaván phase may reflect the faction-building activities of an aspiring elite there, perhaps a manifestation of the short-term "chieftaincy" phenomenon defined by Redmond in the introduction of the present volume. However, there is no evidence of chiefdom organization at this time. The survey data do not show a regional settlement hierarchy of two or more levels, the pattern generally associated with chiefdoms. A bar graph of Early Gaván site sizes exhibits a unimodal distribution (fig. 4.10).

By Late Gaván phase (A.D. 550–1000), human habitation in the study region had greatly increased, to 32 sites covering a total of 124 hectares (table 4.1). Moreover, the Late Gaván settlement pattern (fig. 4.11) also reflects the appearance of a regional settlement hierarchy. A bar graph of Late Gaván site sizes shows a clearly bimodal distribution (fig. 4.12). If mounded architecture is considered along with site size, a maximum of three hierarchical levels can be discerned (fig. 4.11). From this viewpoint, the bottommost level contains 26 habitation sites that range from 1 to 4 ha and lack mounded architecture; the intermediate level comprises five sites (B97, B21, B17, B25, and B30) that cover 6–10 ha and have 2–4 mounds reaching 2–6 m in height.

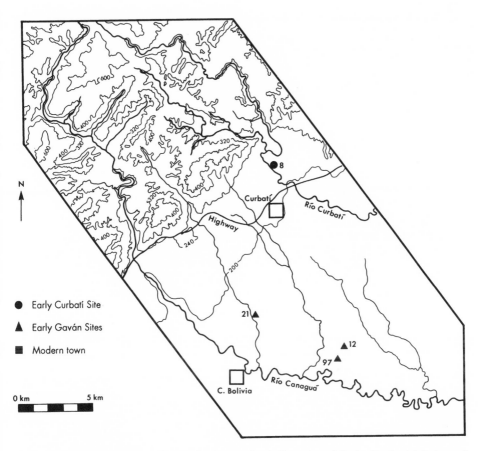

Fig. 4.9. Settlement patterns for Early Gaván (high llanos) and Early Curbatí (piedmont) phases (A.D. 300–550).

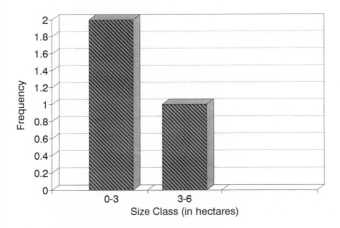

Fig. 4.10. Site sizes, Early Gaván phase.

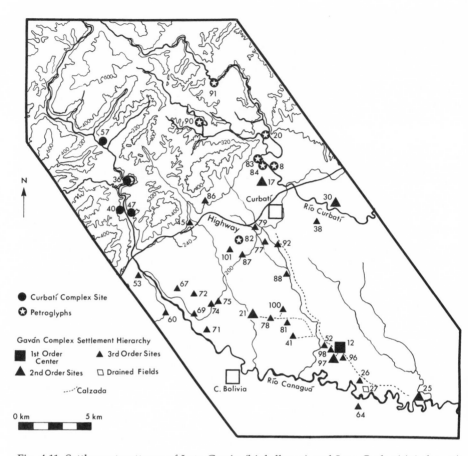

Fig. 4.11. Settlement patterns of Late Gaván (high llanos) and Late Curbatí (piedmont) phases (A.D. 550–1000).

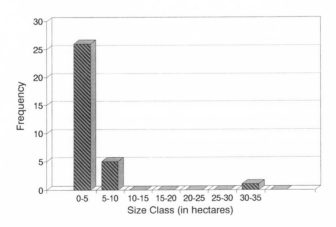

Fig. 4.12. Site sizes, Late Gaván phase.

Table 4.1. Late Gaván site sizes

Site	Site size (ha)	Site	Site Size (ha)
B12	33.0	B75	1.25
B97	6.0	B69	4.4
B21	8.8	B72	3.0
B30	9.4	B67	1.0
B17	7.5	B60	3.0
B25	10.0	B53	1.0
B98	1.0	B88	2.5
B52	1.25	B87	0.5
B96	1.25	B101	1.0
B26	3.0	B77	1.0
B64	3.0	B92	3.0
B41	4.4	B79	1.25
B81	2.5	B38	3.75
B78	0.5	B45	2.5
B100	1.25	B86	0.5
B71	0.5	B74	1.0

Occupying the top level of the Late Gaván regional hierarchy is the Gaván site (B12), where we excavated 55 test pits and three areas of horizontal excavation (fig. 4.13). The Gaván site covers some 33 hectares and has a number of earthworks, including two large mounds (12 meters and 10 meters tall) at either end of a plaza 500 meters long. The taller of these mounds, on the southeast side of the site, has a maximum basal diameter of 90 meters and was apparently ascended by a ramp that extends 80 meters into the plaza. Our Test 183 recovered, in the very first or lowest construction level of the mound, radiocarbon (charcoal) and thermoluminescence (pottery) dates with midpoints of A.D. 650 and 410, respectively (Spencer and Redmond 1992, tables 2, 3). A reasonable date for the initial construction of this mound would be about A.D. 500–600.

We feel that a nondomestic or public use can reasonably be attributed to the two largest mounds at the B12 site (fig. 4.13). Both mounds have a roughly conical form with top areas that seem too small to support a residence, unlike the other 134 mounds at the site that could have served this purpose. Indeed, on two of these smaller mounds we carried out horizontal excavations (Area A and Area D), which uncovered the remains of residences (fig. 4.13). We also placed six test excavations in and around the largest mound (T.8, T.9, T.33, T.174, T.183, and T.184) and 49 other tests throughout the rest of the site, many of them associated with housemounds

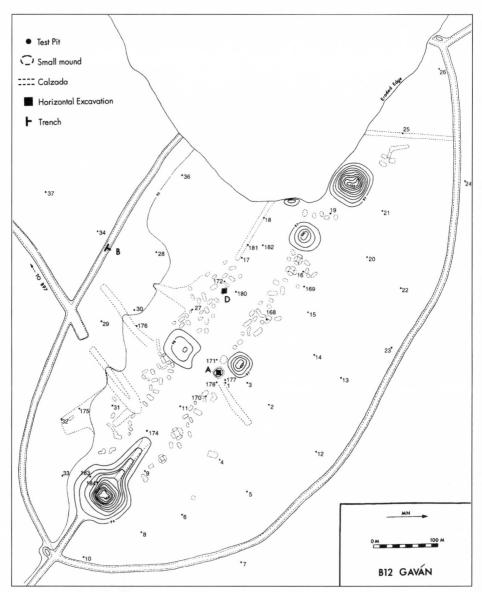

Fig. 4.13. Gaván site (B12), showing the major mounds, *calzadas*, the encircling earthwork, smaller housemounds, the areas of block excavation, and the numbered test pits.

Table 4.2. Distribution of *manos* and *metates* in excavation operations at the Gaván site (B12)

Excavation operation	Manos	Metates
T.4	1	0
T.16	1	0
T.18	1	0
T.19	1	0
T.20	1	1
T.171	0	1
T.175	0	1
T.177	1	0
T.182	1	0
Area A	3	0
Area D	1	1

(fig. 4.13). Time limitations unfortunately prevented us from excavating at the second-largest mound.

If our interpretation of the main mound as nondomestic is correct, then there should be far fewer domestic artifacts in the half-dozen tests there than in the other excavations at the site. Because Milagro Rinaldi's pollen analysis (1990) showed that maize was the staple of the Late Gaván phase diet (Spencer et al. 1994), *manos* and *metates* should be among the artifacts that were most clearly domestic in nature. The sample is not large, but it can be seen that manos and metates were excavated at the Area A and Area D housemounds and elsewhere at the site but were not recovered in the excavations in and around the largest mound (table 4.2; fig. 4.13). Thus, we have at least one, and at most two, nondomestic or public mounds at B12. Societies with bureaucratic governments usually have many more public buildings than this at their first-order centers (Flannery and Marcus 1976; Spencer 1990). In sum, the settlement pattern and public architecture data for Late Gaván phase point to a chiefly regional political organization, one that was centralized but nonbureaucratic.

It is likely that public ceremonies were more frequent and conducted on a larger scale at the B12 site than at other Late Gaván phase settlements. Not only does this site have the region's largest plaza area and the grandest earthen mounds, but also ritual artifacts such as figurines were much more frequent than at the other excavated Late Gaván phase sites (table 4.3). The regional prominence of B12 is further underscored by the network of calzadas or earthen causeways that radiate out from the large center, connecting it to a number of smaller sites (fig. 4.11).

Table 4.3. Distribution of figurine heads and burned daub at five excavated Late Gaván sites

Site	Number of excavations	Figurine heads	Burned daub
B12	55 tests, 3 areas	12	25.44 kg
B97	28 tests	2	3.36 kg
B21	33 tests	1	0.07 kg
B17	6 tests	0	0.02 kg
B26	16 tests	0	0.00 kg

The Gaván site is also circumscribed by a calzada-like earthwork that still stands one meter or more high in many places and is usually about six to eight meters wide at the top and some 20–25 meters wide at the base. Although a portion of the construction has been destroyed by stream erosion on the site's northwest side, it is clear that this earthwork originally had the shape of a large oval measuring about 950 meters by 470 meters. Since no potsherds were found in the fill of this earthwork, it is reasonable to assume that it was built at the beginning of the Late Gaván phase, before the site's population had begun to fill up the circumscribed area. Our Area B excavation did locate an alignment of postmolds down the centerline of the earthwork, probably indicating that a palisade had originally stood upon it (fig. 4.14). The carbonization of the postmolds and the presence of ash and burned earth are evidence that the palisade was burned, probably

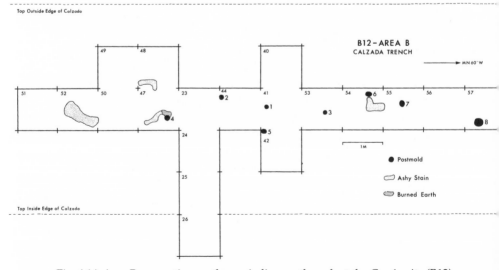

Fig. 4.14. Area B excavation on the encircling earthwork at the Gaván site (B12).

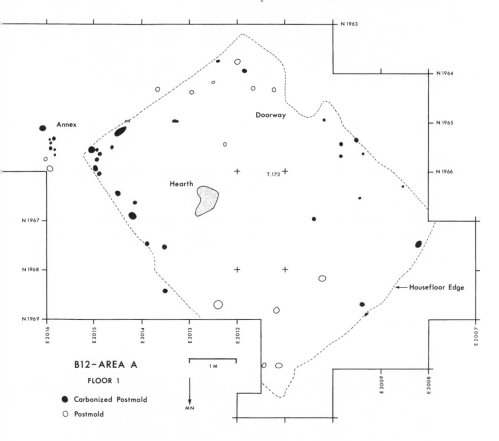

Fig. 4.15. Area A housefloor at the Gaván site (B12).

when the site was abandoned around A.D. 1000. Large quantities of burned daub were found throughout our excavations at B12, especially in the uppermost (or latest) levels.

Patterns of social differentiation in Late Gaván phase society have also been documented at the Gaván site. We observed that the 134 visible housemounds at B12 (fig. 4.13) were variable in terms of mound height, moundtop area (presumably reflecting house size), and associated artifacts. A more detailed comparison view was gained through horizontal excavations at Area A and Area D (fig. 4.13). In Area A we exposed a housefloor in good condition, atop a housemound one meter high (fig. 4.15). The principal structure is rectangular in shape and is defined by 41 postmolds and a hard-packed earthen surface, called Floor 1. The house has a roofed-over area (defined by the postmolds) of 27.9 square meters. Thermoluminescence dates (on pottery) with midpoints of A.D. 760 and 900 are associated

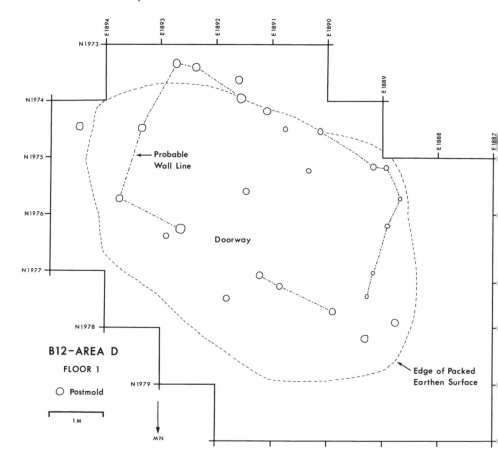

Fig. 4.16. Area D housefloor at the Gaván site (B12).

with this Late Gaván house (Spencer and Redmond 1992, table 3). Like the Area B palisade, this house was evidently burned when the Gaván site was abandoned.

In Area D, we exposed another house characterized by a hard-packed earthen surface (called Floor 1) and 26 postmolds (fig. 4.16). The postmolds of this house define a rectangular roofed-over area of just 16.6 square meters (59 percent of the size of the Area A house). Further, the Area D house sits on a housemound only 55 centimeters high (a bit over half the height of the Area A housemound). These differences in house size and housemound height suggest that the members of the Area A household enjoyed a somewhat higher social standing than those of Area D.

The social differentiation suggested by interhousehold variability is consistent with a pattern of differential treatment of individuals at death. We excavated a total of eight human burials, seven at B12 and one at B97, an adjacent second-order site. Four of these (Burials 1, 2, 3, and 8) were actually not "burials" in the ordinary sense of the term but rather pieces of disarticulated human skeletons. Burials 4, 5, 6, and 7, on the other hand, were normal interments: articulated skeletons, carefully laid to rest in extended position. Moreover, they were all associated with residential features: Burial 4 was found in Test 27, adjacent to a housemound; Burial 5 was beneath a housefloor at the B97 site; Burials 6 and 7 were underneath the Area A housefloor. These adult individuals did not all receive the same burial treatment. Burial 6 had three ceramic vessels in accompaniment, while Burial 5 and Burial 4 had none (Spencer and Redmond 1992, figs. 10, 11). It is not possible to state whether Burial 7 had any accompaniments, because there was not enough time to excavate the lower half of the body that protruded into the excavation wall.

In contrast to the domestic contexts of the complete burials, the deposits containing disarticulated partial skeletons were found in test pits placed in what were probably nondomestic, public, or ceremonial contexts. Burial 1 was found in Test 17, while Burials 2 and 3 were in Test 18; both test pits were excavated in the elongated earthen structure on the northwest side of the plaza area at B12 (fig. 4.13). Burial 8 was found in Test 183, in the lowest construction level of the main mound of the site; given the radiocarbon and thermoluminescence dates already mentioned, Burial 8 probably dates to the initial years of the Late Gaván phase. In none of these cases were enough bones found to account for a complete individual, and some of the individual bones were themselves incomplete. We think that the deposits may represent captives or sacrificial victims whose bodies were dismembered and interred in the mound fill of public constructions.

The Late Gaván phase has also produced some data on agricultural intensification and the operation of a chiefly political economy in Late Gaván phase times. There are several calzadas that emanate from B12; one of them leads to the southeast, passing alongside B26. Just one kilometer southeast of B26, and also connected by calzada to the B12 site, is a 35-hectare area of drained fields that we have labeled B27 (fig. 4.17). A soil sample that we excavated at B27 was shown to have a predominance of maize pollen (Rinaldi 1990), suggesting that the drained-field system was largely planted in maize. Recently, Milagro Rinaldi, Redmond, and I have concluded that this drained-field system was capable of generating a con-

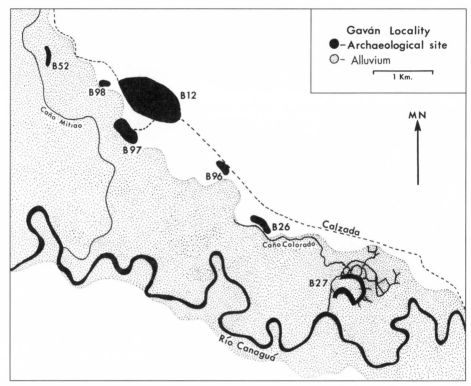

Fig. 4.17. The Gaván locality, showing the first-order center (B12), an adjacent sec-ond-order site (B97), four nearby third-order sites (B52, B98, B96, B26), the drained fields (B27), and the calzada system.

siderable surplus beyond the subsistence needs of the people at the nearby village (B26) who probably farmed it; this surplus was probably sent along the calzada to the Gaván site, for use by the chiefly elite (Spencer et al. 1994).

Long-distance exchange in the Late Gaván phase is evidenced by arti-facts made of materials not native to the llanos but rather to the Venezuelan Andes, Maracaibo Basin, and even farther afield. Several excavated high-status contexts contain polished stone ornaments made of serpentinite, "greenstone," malachite, slate, amphibolyte, and phyllite (Carlos Schubert and Ramón Sifontes, personal communication, 1986–88). The high Venezu-elan Andes contain source areas for slate, amphibolyte, and phyllite, while the Andes of southern Colombia or Ecuador have malachite sources (Ra-món Sifontes, personal communication, 1988). The nearest natural sources of serpentinite or greenstone are the Caribbean mountains in the Caracas area, or the Paraguaná and Guajira peninsulas, on either side of the Gulf of Venezuela and Maracaibo Basin (Wagner and Schubert 1972). Near Mucuchíes, at 3,000 meters of elevation in the high Andes above our study region (fig. 4.8), Wagner excavated a prehistoric serpentinite workshop (Wagner 1973a; Wagner and Schubert 1972). Her radiocarbon dates have midpoints ranging from A.D. 830 to 1500, which overlaps the latter part of the Late Gaván phase.

Warfare was also prevalent in the Late Gaván phase. The B12 site in particular has yielded signs of hostilities. These include the encircling earthwork with its palisade, the partial skeletons buried in nonresidential mound fill, and the widespread conflagration at the site when it was abandoned. These features have not been found in Early Gaván phase deposits or at any other Late Gaván phase sites. As table 4.3 shows, burned daub was vastly more prevalent at B12 than at the other four Late Gaván phase sites where we conducted excavations. We would suggest, first, that such violence appeared or became much more common in Late Gaván times; and second, that the first-order center was more involved in both offensive and defensive activities than were the smaller villages of the region. If the mobilization of warriors from the region's villages was part of the warfare strategy of the regional elite, this could have been accomplished with the help of the calzada network, which would have expedited the rapid movement of warriors into the regional center. Although most evidence of hostilities was found at the Gaván site, it seems clear that warfare had profound consequences for all the villages of the region, as shown by the general depopulation of the region that accompanied the burning and abandonment of B12 at the end of the Late Gaván phase.

Conclusion

In the western llanos of Barinas, the first sedentary villages had appeared by 200 B.C., while the first chiefdoms emerged around A.D. 550. The latter are manifested by (1) the appearance of a clear settlement hierarchy focused on a large regional center; (2) population growth, evidenced by a substantial increase in occupied area; (3) the construction of pyramid mounds and other earthworks; (4) social status differentiation seen in residences and burial treatment; (5) the implementation of complex agricultural and transportation technologies (the drained fields and calzadas); and (6) expanded relationships of exchange and warfare.

In the middle Orinoco River region, sedentary villages were in existence by 2100 B.C.; these are currently the earliest known occupations by sedentary agriculturalists in Venezuela. Chiefdom organization makes its appearance much later in the middle Orinoco, around A.D. 1100; this interpretation, I should reiterate, is based on published settlement pattern data and could change if new data are collected on site structure, household variability, and burial patterns. For the present, however, we are left with an interesting contrast: the first sedentary villages in Venezuela appeared in the middle Orinoco River area, but the earliest chiefdoms emerged in the western llanos.

To account for this developmental contrast, allow me to propose a trial model of chiefdom development in Venezuela. Let us assume that the earliest sedentary agricultural villages were along rich alluvial levees of the middle Orinoco River, as Roosevelt (1980, 195, 221) and Rouse (1978) have proposed. Let us further assume that human population began to grow around 800–400 B.C., associated with a shift from manioc to maize as the staple crop, as documented by Roosevelt (1980, 225–28, 235–38). I suggest that this growing population of maize agriculturalists expanded up the Orinoco River to the mouth of the Apure River and then up the Apure into the western llanos. The expansion probably occurred through a budding-off process whereby daughter villages were established farther and farther upstream along the alluvial zone.

This expanding agricultural population reached the southeastern Barinas area by about 200 B.C. (Zucchi 1967, 1972b, 1973) and the study area of the 1983–88 Barinas Project by A.D. 300 (Spencer and Redmond 1992). It is in this part of northern Barinas, where the high llanos give way to the Andean piedmont, that the expanding agriculturalists would have found themselves in an area that was more environmentally circumscribed than any they had previously encountered. The best land for cultivation, the alluvial zone, becomes narrower and narrower as one approaches the piedmont, where cultivable land is indeed scarce, and ultimately there are the high Andes themselves, reaching heights of 5,000 meters above sea level. Moreover, there is evidence that the Andean zone was already inhabited when the expanding llanos agriculturalists reached northern Barinas. Erika Wagner has documented pre-Hispanic occupations beginning around A.D. 300 in several Andean valleys, including the Boconó and Mucuchíes regions (Wagner 1967, 1972, 1973a, 1973b, 1979). The Santa Ana area also has evidence of occupation at this time (Tarble 1977). In the upper reaches of our own study region, there is an Early Curbatí (A.D. 300–550) occupation at site B8, a village that overlooked a stretch of alluvium in the Andean piedmont (Spencer 1991; Spencer and Redmond 1992). Thus, along with the greater *environmental circumscription* of the zone where the llanos meet the

Andes, there was probably also a degree of *social circumscription* operating by A.D. 300, when the first agriculturalists expanded into northern Barinas from the south.

Robert Carneiro has long maintained that these conditions—a growing agricultural population in an area with pronounced environmental and/or social circumscription—are likely to lead to extensive warfare and ultimately to the appearance of chiefdom organization, as war leaders institutionalize themselves and their descendants into a permanent regional chiefly elite (Carneiro 1970, 1981). This line of argument, I think, is applicable to the Barinas case. The Barinas data show considerable population growth between Early Gaván and Late Gaván phases (from 11 hectares to 124 hectares of occupation area), probably the result of continued immigration as well as internal processes of demographic increase. Even though Late Gaván population levels appear never to have risen to the point where they severely pressed upon the overall carrying capacity of the region (Spencer et al. 1994), I nonetheless suspect that the combination of demographic growth plus social and environmental circumscription fostered an increasingly competitive climate in the higher llanos by the middle of the first millenium. The appearance of chiefdom organization around A.D. 550 is clearly associated with evidence of warfare. The onset of the Late Gaván phase sees both the defensive earthwork and the disarticulated human skeletons at the base of the largest mound at B12. I suggest that an aspiring elite at B12 directed the construction of this defensive feature, and also the sacrificing of captives, in order to present themselves as effective military leaders against enemies who may have included some of the piedmont inhabitants as well as other groups of immigrating agriculturalists from elsewhere in the llanos. That the region's villagers chose to follow this aspiring elite is shown by the emergence of chiefdom organization here and its persistence throughout the Late Gaván phase, a span of 450 years.

Notes

1. Our work in Barinas was funded by grants to Spencer and Redmond from the National Science Foundation (BNS-85-06192), the Wenner-Gren Foundation (No. 4798), the Connecticut Research Foundation, and a University of Connecticut Faculty Summer Fellowship. In Venezuela, we have worked closely with the Departamento de Antropología of the Instituto Venezolano de Investigaciones Científicas (IVIC), where we have been *colaboradores visitantes* since 1983. For their professional support and friendship, we thank Dra. Erika Wagner, Dra. Alberta Zucchi, the late Dr. Carlos Schubert, Dr. Jesús Eduardo Vaz, Dr. Rafael Gassón, Inés Frías, Dr. Lilliam Arvelo, Milagro Rinaldi, Luís Molina, and Prof. Ramón Sifontes. During the Barinas

fieldwork, we were helped in the field by many good friends, including María An-
dueza, Rafael Gassón, Inés Frías, Javier Fernández, Theodora Meijers, Pablo Novoa,
Alejo Novoa, Lucio Laviano, and Raiza Ron.

References

Bray, Warwick
1980–88 *Pro Calima: Archäologisches Projekt im Westlichen Kolumbien/Südamerika.* 5
     vols. Basel: Vereinigung Pro Calima.
Brumfiel, Elizabeth M., and Timothy K. Earle
1987   Specialization, exchange, and complex societies: An introduction. In *Special-
     ization, Exchange, and Complex Societies,* edited by E. M. Brumfiel and T. K.
     Earle, 1–9. Cambridge: Cambridge University Press.
Carneiro, Robert L.
1970   A theory of the origin of the state. *Science* 169:733–38.
1981   The chiefdom: Precursor of the state. In *The Transition to Statehood in the New
     World,* edited by G. D. Jones and R. R. Kautz, 37–79. Cambridge: Cambridge
     University Press.
Carvajal, Jacinto de
1956   *Relación del Descubrimiento del Río Apure Hasta Su Ingreso en el Orinoco* (1648).
     Prólogo y notas por M. Acosta Saignes. Caracas: Ediciones Edime.
Castaño Uribe, Carlos
1987   La vivienda y el enterramiento como unidades de interpretación: Anatomía
     de dos casos de transición del modelo de cacicazgo. In *Chiefdoms in the Ameri-
     cas,* edited by R. D. Drennan and C. A. Uribe, 231–49. Lanham, Md.: Univer-
     sity Press of America.
Castellanos, Juan de
1962   *Elegías de Varones Ilustres de Indias* (1569–1589). Introducción y notas de Isaac
     J. Pardo. Biblioteca de la Academia Nacional de la Historia, no. 57. Fuentes
     para la Historia Colonial de Venezuela. Caracas: Italgráfica, C.A.
Cooke, Richard G., and Anthony J. Ranere
1984   The Proyecto Santa María: A multi-disciplinary analysis of prehistoric adap-
     tations to a tropical watershed in Panama. In *Recent Developments in Isthmian
     Archaeology,* edited by F. W. Lange, 3–30. British Archaeological Reports In-
     ternational Series, no. 212. Oxford: Oxford University Press.
1992   The origin of wealth and hierarchy in the central region of Panama (12,000–
     2,000 BP), with observations on its relevance to the history and phylogeny of
     Chibchan-speaking polities in Panama and elsewhere. In *Wealth and Hierar-
     chy in the Intermediate Area,* edited by F. W. Lange, 243–316. Washington, D.C.:
     Dumbarton Oaks, Trustees for Harvard University.
Creamer, Winifred, and Jonathan Haas
1985   Tribe versus chiefdom in lower Central America. *American Antiquity* 50(4):
     738–54.

Denevan, William, and Alberta Zucchi
1978   Ridged-field excavations in the central Orinoco llanos, Venezuela. In *Advances in Andean Archaeology,* edited by D. Browman, 235–45. The Hague: Mouton Publishers.

Drennan, Robert D.
1985   Introduction. In *Regional Archaeology in the Valle de La Plata, Colombia: A Preliminary Report on the 1984 Season of the Proyecto Arqueológico Valle de la Plata,* edited by R. D. Drennan, 1–13. University of Michigan Museum of Anthropology, Technical Reports, no. 16. Ann Arbor.

Drennan, Robert D., and Carlos A. Uribe, eds.
1987a   *Chiefdoms in the Americas.* Lanham, Md.: University Press of America.

Drennan, Robert D., and Carlos A. Uribe
1987b   Introduction. In *Chiefdoms in the Americas,* edited by R. D. Drennan and C. A. Uribe, vii–xii. Lanham, Md.: University Press of America.

Earle, Timothy
1978   *Economic and Social Organization of a Complex Chiefdom: The Halelea District, Kaua'i, Hawaii.* University of Michigan Museum of Anthropology, Anthropological Papers, no. 63. Ann Arbor.
1987a   Chiefdoms in archaeological and ethnohistorical perspective. *Annual Review of Anthropology* 16:279–308.
1987b   Specialization and the production of wealth: Hawaiian chiefdoms and the Inka empire. In *Specialization, Exchange, and Complex Societies,* edited by E. M. Brumfiel and T. K. Earle, 64–75. Cambridge: Cambridge University Press.
1989   The evolution of chiefdoms. *Current Anthropology* 30(1):84–8.

Earle, Timothy, ed.
1991   *Chiefdoms: Power, Economy, and Ideology.* School of American Research. Cambridge: Cambridge University Press.

Federmann, Nicolás
1962   *Historia Indiana o Primer Viaje de Nicolás Federmann.* In *Descubrimiento y Conquista de Venezuela: Textos Históricos Contemporáneos y Documentos Fundamentales.* Tomo II. *Cubagua y la Empresa de los Belzares* (1557). Biblioteca de la Academia Nacional de la Historia, no. 55. Fuentes para la Historia Colonial de Venezuela. Caracas: Italgráfica C.A.

Feinman, Gary, and Jill Neitzel
1984   Too many types: An overview of sedentary prestate societies in the Americas. In *Advances in Archaeological Method and Theory,* vol. 7, edited by M. B. Schiffer, 39–102. New York: Academic Press.

Flannery, Kent V.
1972   The cultural evolution of civilizations. *Annual Review of Ecology and Systematics* 3:399–426.
1976a   (ed.) *The Early Mesoamerican Village.* New York: Academic Press.
1976b   Evolution of complex settlement systems. In *The Early Mesoamerican Village,* edited by K. V. Flannery, 162–73. New York: Academic Press.

1976c   Empirical determination of site catchments in Oaxaca and Tehuacán. In *The Early Mesoamerican Village*, edited by K. V. Flannery, 103–17. New York: Academic Press.

Flannery, Kent V., and Joyce Marcus

1976   Evolution of the public building in Formative Oaxaca. In *Cultural Change and Continuity*, edited by C. Cleland, 205–22. New York: Academic Press.

Garson, Adam G.

1980   Prehistory, Settlement and Food Production in the Savanna Region of La Calzada de Paez, Venezuela. Ph.D. dissertation, Yale University. Ann Arbor: University Microfilms.

Gumilla, P. José.

1963   *El Orinoco Ilustrado y Defendido* (1745).Biblioteca de la Academia Nacional de la Historia, no. 68. Fuentes para la Historia Colonial de Venezuela. Caracas: Italgráfica, C.A.

Hansell, Patricia

1987   The Formative in central Pacific Panama: La Mula-Sarigua. In *Chiefdoms in the Americas*, edited by R. D. Drennan and C. A. Uribe, 119–39. Lanham, Md.: University Press of America.

Hasemann, George

1987   Late Classic settlement on the Sulaco River, central Honduras. In *Chiefdoms in the Americas*, edited by R. D. Drennan and C. A. Uribe, 85–103. Lanham, Md.: University Press of America.

Hatch, James W.

1987   Mortuary indicators of organizational variability among late prehistoric chiefdoms in the southeastern U.S. interior. In *Chiefdoms in the Americas*, edited by R. D. Drennan and C. A. Uribe, 9–19. Lanham, Md.: University Press of America.

Helms, Mary W.

1979   *Ancient Panama: Chiefs in Search of Power.* Austin: University of Texas Press.

1987   Art styles and interaction spheres in Central America and the Caribbean: Polished black wood in the Greater Antilles. In *Chiefdoms in the Americas*, edited by R. D. Drennan and C. A. Uribe, 67–84. Lanham, Md.: University Press of America.

Hodder, Ian

1982   Theoretical archaeology: A reactionary view. In *Symbolic and Structural Archaeology*, edited by I. Hodder, 1–16. Cambridge: Cambridge University Press.

1986   *Reading the Past.* Cambridge: Cambridge University Press.

Jahn, Alfredo

1927   *Los Aborígenes del Occidente de Venezuela.* Caracas: Litografía y Tipografía del Comercio.

Kottak, Conrad

1977   The process of state formation in Madagascar. *American Ethnologist* 4:136–55.

Lange, Frederick W., ed.

1984   *Recent Developments in Isthmian Archaeology*. British Archaeological Reports International Series, no. 212. Oxford: Oxford University Press.

1992   *Wealth and Hierarchy in the Intermediate Area*. Washington, D.C.: Dumbarton Oaks, Trustees for Harvard University.

Lange, Frederick W., and Doris Z. Stone, eds.

1984   *The Archaeology of Lower Central America*. Albuquerque: University of New Mexico Press.

Lathrap, Donald A., Jorge G. Marcos, and James A. Zeidler

1977   Real Alto: An ancient ceremonial center. *Archaeology* 30(1):2–13.

Lewis, Herbert S.

1968   Typology and process in political evolution. In *Essays on the Problem of Tribe*, edited by J. Helm, 101–10. Proceedings of the 1967 Annual Spring Meeting of the American Ethnological Society. Seattle: University of Washington Press.

Lightfoot, Kent G.

1987   A consideration of complex prehistoric societies in the U.S. Southwest. In *Chiefdoms in the Americas*, edited by R. D. Drennan and C. A. Uribe, 43–57. Lanham, Md.: University Press of America.

Linares, Olga F.

1977   *Ecology and the Arts in Ancient Panama: On the Development of Rank and Symbolism in the Central Provinces*. Studies in Pre-Columbian Art and Archaeology, no. 17. Washington, D.C.: Dumbarton Oaks, Trustees for Harvard University.

1979   What is lower Central American archaeology? *Annual Review of Anthropology* 8:21–43.

Linares, Olga F., and Anthony J. Ranere, eds.

1980   *Adaptive Radiations in Prehistoric Panama*. Peabody Museum Monographs, no. 5. Cambridge: Harvard University Press.

Morey, Nancy K.

1975   Ethnohistory of the Colombian and Venezuelan Llanos. Ph.D. dissertation, University of Utah, Provo. Ann Arbor: University Microfilms.

Oliver, José R.

1988   The Archaeological, Linguistic, and Ethnohistorical Evidence for the Expansion of Arawakan into Northwestern Venezuela and Northeastern Colombia. Ph.D. dissertation, University of Illinois, Urbana-Champaign.

Oviedo y Valdés, Gonzalo Fernández de

1959   *Historia General y Natural de las Indias* (1535). Madrid: Biblioteca de Autores Españoles.

Oyuela C., Augusto

1987   Implicaciones de las secuencias locales y regionales en los aspectos culturales de los Tairona. In *Chiefdoms in the Americas*, edited by R. D. Drennan and C. A. Uribe, 213–29. Lanham, Md.: University Press of America.

Peebles, Christopher S.

1987   Moundville from 1000 to 1500 AD as seen from 1840 to 1985 A.D. In *Chiefdoms in the Americas,* edited by R. D. Drennan and C. A. Uribe, 21–42. Lanham, Md.: University Press of America.

Peebles, Christopher, and Susan M. Kus

1977   Some archaeological correlates of ranked societies. *American Antiquity* 42(3): 421–48.

Powell, Mary L.

1988   *Status and Health in Prehistory: A Case Study of the Moundville Chiefdom.* Washington, D.C.: Smithsonian Institution Press.

Redmond, Elsa. M.

1990   Tribal and chiefly warfare in northern South America. Paper presented at Non-Imperial Polities in the Lands Visited by Christopher Columbus during his Four Voyages to the New World. Congress sponsored by the Smithsonian Tropical Research Institute, Panama.

1994   *Tribal and Chiefly Warfare in South America.* University of Michigan Museum of Anthropology, Memoirs, no. 28. Ann Arbor.

Redmond, Elsa M., and Charles S. Spencer

1989   Investigaciones en el Piedemonte Andino y los Llanos Altos de Barinas. *Boletín de la Asociación Venezolana de Arqueología* 5:4–24.

1994   Savanna chiefdoms of Venezuela. *National Geographic Research and Exploration* 10(4):422–39.

Rinaldi, Milagro

1990   Informe de las Muestras 54, 114, 442. Laboratorio de Paleoecología, Centro de Ecología y Ciencias Ambientales. Instituto Venezolano de Investigaciones Científicas. Unpublished manuscript on file, Department of Anthropology, American Museum of Natural History.

Roosevelt, Anna C.

1980   *Parmana: Prehistoric Maize and Manioc Subsistence along the Amazon and Orinoco.* New York: Academic Press.

1987   Chiefdoms in the Amazon and Orinoco. In *Chiefdoms in the Americas,* edited by R. D. Drennan and C. A. Uribe, 153–85. Lanham, Md.: University Press of America.

Rouse, Irving B.

1978   The La Gruta sequence and its implications. In *Unidad y Variedad: Ensayos Antropológicos en Homenaje a José M. Cruxent,* edited by E. Wagner and A. Zucchi, 203–29. Caracas: Ediciones del Centro de Estudios Avanzados.

Sahlins, Marshall

1972   *Stone Age Economics.* Chicago: Aldine-Atherton.

Sanoja O., Mario, and Iraida Vargas A.

1987   La sociedad cacical del Valle de Quíbor (Estado Lara, Venezuela). In *Chiefdoms in the Americas,* edited by R. D. Drennan and C. A. Uribe, 201–12. Lanham, Md.: University Press of America.

Snarskis, Michael J.
1987   The archaeological evidence for chiefdoms in eastern and central Costa Rica. In *Chiefdoms in the Americas*, edited by R. D. Drennan and C. A. Uribe, 105–17. Lanham, Md.: University Press of America.

Spencer, Charles S.
1979   Irrigation, administration, and society in Formative Tehuacán. In *Prehistoric Social, Political, and Economic Development in the Area of the Tehuacán Valley*, edited by R. D. Drennan, 13–109. University of Michigan Museum of Anthropology, Technical Reports, no. 11. Ann Arbor.
1982   *The Cuicatlán Cañada and Monte Albán: A Study of Primary State Formation.* New York: Academic Press.
1987   Rethinking the Chiefdom. In *Chiefdoms in the Americas*, edited by R. D. Drennan and C. A. Uribe, 369–90. Lanham, Md.: University Press of America.
1990   On the tempo and mode of state formation: Neoevolutionism reconsidered. *Journal of Anthropological Archaeology* 9(1):1–30.
1991   Coevolution and the development of Venezuelan chiefdoms. In *Profiles in Cultural Evolution: Papers from a Conference in Honor of Elman R. Service*, edited by A. T. Rambo and K. Gillogly, 137–65. University of Michigan Museum of Anthropology, Anthropological Papers, no. 85. Ann Arbor.
1993   Human agency, biased transmission, and the cultural evolution of chiefly authority. *Journal of Anthropological Archaeology* 12(1):41–74.

Spencer, Charles S., and Elsa M. Redmond
1984   Prehistory of the Andean piedmont and high llanos in Barinas, Venezuela. Proposal BNS-85-06192 submitted to the Anthropology Program, National Science Foundation.
1992   Prehispanic chiefdoms of the western Venezuelan llanos. *World Archaeology* 24(1):134–57.

Spencer, Charles S., Elsa M. Redmond, and Milagro Rinaldi
1994   Drained fields at La Tigra, Venezuelan llanos: A regional perspective. *Latin American Antiquity* 5(2):119–43.

Steponaitis, Vincas P.
1981   Settlement hierarchies and political complexity in nonmarket societies: The Formative period in the Valley of Mexico. *American Anthropologist* 83(2):320–63.

Struever, Stuart
1971   Comments on archaeological data requirements and research strategy. *American Antiquity* 36(1):9–19.

Tarble, Kay
1977   *Comparación Estilística de Dos Colecciones del Noroeste de Venezuela: Una Nueva Metodología.* Caracas: Instituto Venezolano de Investigaciones Científicas, Centro de Estudios Avanzados.

Upham, Steadman
1987   A theoretical consideration of middle range societies. In *Chiefdoms in the*

Americas, edited by R. D. Drennan and C. A. Uribe, 345–68. Lanham, Md.: University Press of America.

Wagner, Erika

1967 *The Prehistory and Ethnohistory of the Carache Area in Western Venezuela*. Yale University Publications in Anthropology, no. 71. New Haven.

1972 La protohistoria e historia inicial de Boconó, Estado Trujillo. *Antropológica* 33:39–60.

1973a The Mucuchíes phase: An extension of the Andean cultural pattern into western Venezuela. *American Anthropologist* 75(1):195–213.

1973b Chronology and cultural relationships of the Betijoque phase in western Venezuela. *Relaciones Antropológicas: A Newsletter Bulletin on South American Anthropology* 1(1):13–17.

1979 Arqueología de los Andes Venezolanos: Los páramos y la tierra fría. In *El Medio Ambiente Páramo*, edited by M. L. Salgado-Labouriau. Caracas: Ediciones del Centro de Estudios Avanzados.

Wagner, Erika, and Carlos Schubert

1972 Pre-Hispanic workshop of serpentinite artifacts, Venezuelan Andes, and possible raw material source. *Science* 175:888–90.

Wagner, Erika, and Kay Tarble de Ruíz

1975 Lagunillas: A new archaeological phase for the Lake Maracaibo Basin, Venezuela. *Journal of Field Archaeology* 2:105–18.

Whalen, Michael E.

1983 Reconstructing Early Formative village organization in Oaxaca, Mexico. *American Antiquity* 48(1):17–43.

Whitehead, Neil L.

1988 *Lords of the Tiger Spirit: A History of the Caribs in Colonial Venezuela and Guyana, 1498–1820*. Dordrecht: Foris Publications.

Wilson, David J.

1987 Reconstructing patterns of early warfare in the lower Santa Valley: New data on the role of conflict in the origins of complex north coast society. In *The Origins and Development of the Andean State*, edited by J. Haas, S. Pozorski, and T. Pozorski, 56–69. Cambridge: Cambridge University Press.

Wright, Henry T.

1977 Recent research on the origin of the state. *Annual Review of Anthropology* 6:379–97.

1986 The evolution of civilizations. In *American Archaeology Past and Future*, edited by D. J. Meltzer, D. D. Fowler, and J. A. Sabloff, 323–65. Washington, D.C.: Smithsonian Institution Press.

Yoffee, Norman

1979 The decline and rise of Mesopotamian civilization: An ethnoarchaeological perspective on the evolution of social complexity. *American Antiquity* 44(1):5–35.

1988   Orienting collapse. In *The Collapse of Ancient States and Civilizations*, edited by N. Yoffee and G. L. Cowgill, 1–19. Tucson: University of Arizona Press.

Zeidler, James A.

1987   The evolution of prehistoric "tribal" systems as historical process: Archaeological indicators of social reproduction. In *Chiefdoms in the Americas*, edited by R. D. Drennan and C. A. Uribe, 325–44. Lanham, Md.: University Press of America.

Zucchi, Alberta

1967   La Betania: Un Yacimiento Arqueológico del Occidente de Venezuela. 2 vols. Ph.D. dissertation, Universidad Central de Venezuela, Caracas.

1972a Aboriginal earth structures of the western Venezuelan llanos. *Caribbean Journal of Science* 12(1–2):95–106.

1972b New data on the antiquity of polychrome painting from Venezuela. *American Antiquity* 37(3):439–46.

1973   Prehistoric human occupations of the western Venezuelan llanos. *American Antiquity* 38(2):182–90.

Zucchi, Alberta, and William M. Denevan

1979   *Campos Elevados e Historia Cultural Prehispánica en los Llanos Occidentales de Venezuela*. Caracas: Universidad Católica Andres Bello.

CHAPTER 5

Tupinambá Chiefdoms?

WILLIAM C. STURTEVANT

The literature on chiefdoms in the Americas emphasizes building models of societies of this sort, by elaborating appropriate social, economic, and political characteristics and the functional interrelations between them and by contrasting these, explicitly or implicitly, with characteristics appropriate for tribal organizations on the one hand and for state systems on the other. These models are then compared, usually, with archaeological evidence. In most cases little of the archaeological evidence is directly indicative of the characteristics of the models, so there remains ample room for further theoretical and methodological discussion. It would seem useful, however, to test the models not only against archaeological evidence but also against ethnographic and historical evidence, as I attempted some years ago for some models of the nature of tribes (Sturtevant 1983).

There is evidently no case of a chiefdom directly observed by a modern ethnographer. Furthermore, the American chiefdoms for which there is ethnohistorical evidence have a rather strange distribution, for they are concentrated in (if not quite limited to) the regions first explored by Europeans: the Antilles, northeastern South America, Panama, and the Gulf and south Atlantic coasts and interior of North America (Carneiro 1981, 48; Feinman and Neitzel 1984; Creamer and Haas 1985; Drennan and Uribe 1987; Knight 1990). Most of the Indian societies in these regions were extinct, or drastically changed, by the eighteenth century, so that our understanding of them is based on the surviving documents written by Europeans in the sixteenth and seventeenth centuries (supplemented by archaeological evidence in some places).

It seems possible that this rather striking distribution of historical chiefdoms in America is not a phenomenon of the real world but rather is the result of the nature of our sources of evidence. Europeans of the early colonial period originated in hierarchical societies and tended to describe and interpret the American Indian societies and behavior they observed on the basis of contemporary European ideas about the normal structure and workings of society. To them, individual differences in demeanor and in dress and ornament indicated differences in social rank, and they were predisposed to look for kings and nobles. Warfare was understood to be motivated by hegemonic ambitions, territorial expansion, and the collection of tribute.

If there were no chiefdoms on the Northwest Coast of North America—if the distribution map by Sanders and Price (1968, 50) is wrong—it may be because European exploration and colonial dominance in this region came quite late. "Pristine" societies here were first seen by Europeans in the late eighteenth century and described by observers who were influenced by the European enlightenment (and by stereotypes of the Noble Savage). Furthermore, the best evidence on Northwest Coast societies comes from memory ethnography recorded only a century or so later by good anthropologists at the beginning of the period of Boasian fieldwork. Earlier, in the "tribal zones" (compare Ferguson and Whitehead 1992) bordering Mesoamerica and the Andes, chiefdoms may have been missed because the major, dominant societies of Nuclear America obviously met sixteenth-century European standards for states and even empires.

Of course one should not expect to find the label *chiefdom,* or its equivalent in any language, before the mid–twentieth century. However, not only had the concept not yet been invented, but also it may be that the characteristics now held to typify chiefdoms were overlooked by Europeans of earlier periods.

Yet Patrick Menget (1985, 190–91) has pointed out that as early as 1590, the Jesuit José de Acosta characterized three types of political organization in the New World, even suggesting that they represented historical stages. According to Acosta, there were many "totally barbarous" Indians, without laws or leaders, living as mobs like savages and wild animals. "As far as I can understand, the first inhabitants of these Indies were of this kind," as were, in his day, most Brazilians, the Chiriguanos, Chanchos, Yscaycingas, Pilcozones, most of the Floridas, and all the Chichimecos of New Spain. However, most of the "nations and peoples of Indians" had somewhat more order and agreement although they lacked kings and absolute rulers and lived as independent groups (*behetrías*), governing themselves by consent. Among them some principal men were recognized as superior to the common people, and joined together in councils for important affairs, but leaders were chosen and obeyed only for certain purposes, especially during war. Such societies included the Araucanians, Muisca, and Otomí. Acosta's third type exhibited well-established kingdoms or empires, of which "only two have been discovered" in America, those of the Mexicans and the Incas. These two societies he compared with respect to the buildings and grandeur of their courts, the richness of their treasures, the size of provinces, their antiquity, conquests, and manner of succession (by election in Mexico, "like the Roman Empire"; by inheritance in Peru, "as the kings of France and Spain"). At least in Mexico, the kingdom began with rule by a consul or *dux*, without absolute authority, but as the king gained power his rule became absolute and tyrannical. Acosta summarized this strikingly modern typology in three separate chapters (see bk. 6, chaps. 11, 19, and bk. 7, chap. 11 in Acosta 1940, 471–72, 489–90, 537–38).

The Tupinambá of coastal Brazil may be examined as a test of the hypothesis that American chiefdoms are an artifact of postmedieval European preconceptions. The documentation for them is probably better than that for any other American society of the sixteenth and seventeenth centuries, except for some of the native states of Mesoamerica and the Andes. The available ethnohistorical data on Tupinambá culture of the sixteenth and seventeenth centuries is much better than what we have for the Natchez of the sixteenth and eighteenth centuries or the Timucua of the seventeenth century, and is comparable to what is available on Hawaii at the end of the eighteenth century. Like the Natchez (Knight 1990) and the Hawaiians (Earle 1977), the Tupinambá merit close examination by typologists and theorists of sociopolitical evolution.

The name Tupinambá here refers to the groups speaking mutually intelligible dialects of a single Tupian language (see Rodrigues 1958, 1986) and sharing essentially the same culture. The Tupinambá occupied the coast from the region of São Paulo to the mouth of the Amazon River. European descriptions of the Tupinambá begin with Cabral's discovery of Brazil in 1500. Over the next two centuries there are excellent materials written in Portuguese and French and important primary sources also in German, Spanish, Italian, Dutch, Latin, and English. The sources are usefully diverse in other ways: they derive from Protestants as well as Catholics, from missionaries, soldiers, administrators, traders, slavers, and even the philosopher Michel de Montaigne, who interviewed Tupinambá and Indianized Frenchmen in Normandy (Métraux 1963). There are no modern ethnographies or recent historical documents, because the Tupinambá have been extinct since about 1700 and since almost a century earlier in the southern part of their range. However, there are excellent modern synthetic historical ethnographies: two monographs by Alfred Métraux published in 1928, on Tupinambá material culture and religion, and his sketch in the *Handbook of South American Indians* (Métraux 1948), and especially two monographs by Florestan Fernandes first published in 1948 and 1952, on the social function of warfare among the Tupinambá and in particular on Tupinambá social organization. These are classic historical ethnographies, recasting into ethnographic formats the information from the historical sources, very thoroughly and critically searched out and cited (see the analyses by Viveiros de Castro 1985, 1986, 81–117). Useful supplements are more recent ethnographic works on related Tupi-Guarani societies, especially an important monograph by Viveiros de Castro (1986, 1992).

In a sense this is an independent test, for Fernandes and Métraux wrote before the modern anthropological interest in evolutionary typology; their descriptions of Tupinambá society were not influenced by Oberg, Service, Fried, and Carneiro (although Fernandes [1963, 23] does thank Kalervo Oberg among his teachers at the University of São Paulo).

To determine whether available information indicates that the Tupinambá were organized into chiefdoms it is not necessary to apply a narrow or precise definition of chiefdom. It is sufficient to use a polythetic definition and examine the Tupinambá evidence for the presence of various attributes that have been proposed to characterize or typify chiefdoms. In the following, the attributes of chiefdoms are those described by Service (1962), Fried (1967), Peebles and Kus (1977), Carneiro (1981), Sanders (1984), Feinman and Neitzel (1984), Wright (1984), Upham (1987), Spencer (1987), and Drennan (1987).

Chiefdoms are multicommunity political units, with fairly dense populations that may total some 10,000, living in several (perhaps at least 10) different villages or districts united under a single leadership. The maximum and the average community size are significant, and there should be a bimodal distribution, for example with several smaller communities dependent on a larger ceremonial center. Usually there is a geographical patterning of settlements by size, with an architecturally distinctive central or capital settlement surrounded by smaller villages, and this distribution will probably reflect the economic potentials of the natural environment.

The minimal sociopolitical unit of the Tupinambá was the *maloca* or longhouse, some 5 to 10 meters wide and perhaps 100 meters long (some accounts say twice that long). Each maloca was occupied by an extended family of at least 40 people, more usually 50 to 200 people, and according to some sources as many as 600 to 850 people. Each local group or *aldeia*—called a *taba* in Tupinambá—had a distinctive name and was composed of one to seven or eight malocas, arranged around a central plaza which was the locus of important activities such as ritual sacrifices, feasts, dances, and chiefly council meetings. On the frontiers between traditional enemies the aldeias were fortified with stockades.

There were hundreds of aldeias, many of them named in the early sources that also mention larger territorial groupings (Fernandes 1963, 63). The latter include Tupinambá (in a narrow sense), Tupinikin, Potiguara, Caeté, Piratininga, Tamoyo, Temimino, Tupina, Amoipira, Tobayara, and Tapuitapera. All these are Tupinambá in the larger sense of Métraux (1948), sharing cultural patterns although with local differences. The terminological problem seems comparable to that for the poorly understood "tribal hierarchy" of the Roman sources on North Africa (Mattingly 1992), although for sixteenth-century coastal Brazil there is no evidence for a political hierarchy; the aldeia was the largest political unit. It ranged in size from a minimum population of perhaps 300 to a maximum of perhaps 6,000 to 8,000 (Fernandes 1963, 68–69). The total Tupinambá population in 1500 may have been about 400,000; this is the sum of the figures given by Hemming (1978, 492–501) for the territorial groupings listed as Tupinambá by Métraux (1948). These numbers, like other estimates of sixteenth-century population sizes, should not be taken very seriously, but they probably do indicate the order of magnitude of Tupinambá local groups.

It remains to be explained how a great many independent, mutually antagonistic Tupinambá societies occupied such a long stretch of coast over which only one language was spoken. Either the expansion was very recent, or there were mechanisms for maintaining communication and hence intelligibility. On the other hand, perhaps the many sixteenth-century Tupinambá societies spoke several (related) languages rather than only one.

There seems to be no evidence in the documents for a bimodal distribution of the sizes of local groups. Fernandes estimates, with little confidence, that an average aldeia controlled a territory of some 45 square kilometers but with much variation, depending on such factors as the fertility of the soil, the total population, and the proximity of other groups.

In a chiefdom one expects to find specialized nonresidential structures within the community. The society should be socially stratified, with at least two levels—or, according to some analysts, a maximum of two, the chief and associated nobility versus the rest—or three (village chiefs, district chiefs, paramount chief), states then being characterized by more levels, either three or four. There may well be a class of captives and/or slaves.

Social rank is ascribed rather than achieved, and the inequality of individuals or groups may be based on seniority, military effectiveness, or differential access to goods or political power. A permanent paramount chief is likely, with well-established, usually genealogical, principles for succession and legitimacy. The chief has judicial, economic, and ritual authority. There are other institutionalized leadership positions, with differentiated functions. There is, however, little delegation of authority; bureaucratic organization typifies the level of states, not chiefdoms. In a chiefdom markers of high status are to be expected, such as sumptuary rules, residential segregation, special modes of behavior (including obeisance), multiple wives, specialized servants, and differential mortuary practices. The chief may well control productive activities above the household or local level. There may be craft specialization, but it will be only part-time.

Among the Tupinambá there is no evidence for the existence of ceremonial centers, nor for any differential functions of aldeias, whether political, economic, or ritual. There is also no evidence for specialized structures within the aldeia, until, under Portuguese influence, some aldeias erected special meeting houses.

The occupants of a maloca were consanguineal and affinal relatives—an extended family, dependent on the senior man. The household could be four generations deep, with the senior man at the apex as the chief of the maloca, and his wives (for leading men were polygynous), then his married son who was to be his successor (usually the firstborn son) and therefore resided patrilocally. In addition there were the daughters of the household head and their married-in husbands, and their children and occasionally grandchildren. Each wife had a hearth area that was distinct but not walled off from the rest. Some malocas housed more than one extended family, each with its chief. Each maloca chief controlled agricultural land, which was worked in individual plots by each wife in the maloca. The chief also organized the preparation of *cauim* (manioc beer). Each hearth within the maloca was an independent production and consumption unit, although there was continual sharing throughout the maloca, and indeed throughout the aldeia. The aldeia was the unit within which there was redistribution of goods.

The population of an aldeia was organized in age categories, of which there were six for each sex, the first, newborn infants, being common for both sexes. These categories to a large extent determined activities and privileges, which tended to be reciprocal and egalitarian within the category and asymmetrical across categories, the elders exerting social control.

The aldeia is described as an independent, self-sufficient economic unit. The men of the aldeia cooperated in clearing fields and no doubt in hunting and fishing. The location of the aldeia was selected by the council made up of the elders and chiefs of the constituent malocas and was determined mainly by the availability of resources.

In a chiefdom there are mechanisms for the redistribution of goods, including luxury goods, by means of tribute or taxation. There are likely to be organized productive activities transcending the level of the household. Warfare is conducted for conquest, for defense, and to acquire captives. Warfare may be the source of the social ranking that is a necessary character of the chiefdom (Carneiro 1981), and the paramount chief is especially important in the conduct of war. There are probably mechanisms (in addition to warfare) for dealing with unpredictable environmental conditions, such as specialized means of food storage or strategies for the collection of famine foods.

Among the Tupinambá trade between local groups seems to have involved only luxury goods such as feathers and crystals. There are apparently no references either to means for regulating the distribution of resources or to economic inequalities. There was nothing resembling tribute or special labor for the chiefs.

Indeed, even the form of the political organization of the aldeia seems poorly documented. There was a council of chiefs who dealt with organizing daily activities, the treatment of guests and visitors, and especially planning warfare. For the aldeia was the minimal offensive and defensive social unit, although war expeditions were often undertaken by several local groups together, and when an aldeia suffered an attack, messengers were sent to nearby aldeias requesting help. Warfare was conducted for the purpose of vengeance, to acquire captives for eventual sacrifice and cannibalistic consumption. Ritual feasts associated with these sacrifices did draw on more than one aldeia and presumably food in addition to the cooked sacrificial victims was shared on these occasions. Warfare was not carried on to establish economic or political dominance over another group, nor for territorial gain except to dislocate other groups during an expansive movement or migration.

War captives were in a sense enslaved, and although all were eventually sacrificed, it was often only years after they had been captured. But these captives did not form a low-status class, for they were nearly completely integrated into the society of their captors. They were in effect adopted, and they shared almost equally in the economic and social activities of their captors. Ultimately not only were they sacrificed and eaten, but so were the children they had by the women of the local group—the Tupinambá were strongly patrilineal, although evidently also largely matrilocal (or matri-patrilocal). Women as well as men were captured in warfare and ultimately sacrificed and eaten, but the details of their treatment are less well described in the sources available.

Social stratification did not involve a category of war captives at the bottom, and it is not clear that there was any upper stratum either. Fernandes (1963, 320–23) describes the council of chiefs as essentially a gerontocracy or oligarchy, and in principle an egalitarian body, although each aldeia is said to have had at least one head chief. Often there were two, and sometimes three or four aldeia chiefs. They were not formally elected, and probably had quite limited authority. Obedience of the chief was said to be entirely voluntary. Especially in peacetime the chiefs were listened to, rather than obeyed. They did have special ritual duties and played supervisory roles during the ceremonies and feasts involving the sacrifice of prisoners.

Chiefs were men of higher status, which they had gained especially through prowess in war, through the taking of captives and later sacrificing them and supervising their cooking and eating to avenge dead relatives and friends. Men with outstanding abilities in subsistence pursuits also had higher status. Men of high status had multiple wives, and a man gained status from having many daughters, for their husbands increased the number of warriors he could field, and that increased the number of captives likely to become part of his group. It is clear that the leader of a war party (who was usually the chief of a local group—an aldeia or taba) had considerable power and authority as such, and gained prestige therefrom, but it is not clear that his authority extended beyond the activities of the war party. Tupinambá war leaders were evidently similar to the tribal war leaders of northern South America described in recent ethnographies. Although for the Tupinambá we lack many details that are known for these modern tribal leaders as analyzed by Redmond (1994), there is little or no evidence that Tupinambá chiefs had the power and authority described by Redmond for the paramount chiefs of chiefdoms.

Other than chiefs, the only specialized office mentioned for the Tupinambá is that of *pajé* or shaman. In the process of carrying out his duties, the pajé served neighboring aldeias. Pajés were mobile, visited widely, and enjoyed the benefits of free transit; they could even enter enemy territory relatively safely.

Apparently the chiefs of malocas and aldeias had no judicial authority and no special economic privileges, indeed no power or authority beyond what they had as war leaders. Some chiefs of local groups were more prestigious, more renowned, than others, but there is little evidence for any one of them exercising dominance over aldeias other than his own. In fact, Fernandes cites no evidence for any political organization above the level of the aldeia, although different aldeias sometimes cooperated, especially in warfare and in major rituals such as those involving the sacrifice and eating of long-term war captives.

The Tupinambá exhibit hardly any of the characteristics of chiefdoms and lack those considered crucial by most theorists. That they can be shown not to have been organized in chiefdoms may be the result of the unusually high quality of the surviving documentary evidence. The Tupinambá were perhaps the first American society to be well understood by literate Europeans and therefore to be quite well documented. The contrast is remarkable—and unfortunate—with the fragmentary and biased evidence on the presumed chiefdoms first encountered by Europeans, those of the Taino and others in the West Indies. On the other hand, sixteenth-century evidence on the Calusa of southwest Florida is sufficient to identify them as a chiefdom (Goggin and Sturtevant 1964; Widmer 1988) with considerably more certainty than is permitted by the evidence on the Taino (and many others).

Sixteenth-century European preconceptions about hierarchy and status differentiation were not so strong as to obscure the fundamental nature of Tupinambá societies before they were destroyed. Perhaps it is reasonable to agree with the early commentators who said that the Tupinambá had no faith, law, or king—in French *foi, loi, roi;* in Portuguese *fé, lei, rei*—at least in the strict contemporary European senses of those words (although not for the reason suggested by Magalhães in 1576 [1922, 33^r], namely that their language lacked the letters *f, l,* and *r*). Yet the European understanding of Tupinambá society was soon simplified and overgeneralized, providing the foundation for the influential Noble Savage stereotype.

References

Acosta, José de
1940 *Historia Natural y Moral de las Indias en que se tratan las Cosas Notables del Cielo, y Elementos, Metales, Plantas y Animales dellas: y los Ritos, y Ceremonias, Leyes y Gobierno, y Guerras de los Indios* (1590). México: Fondo de Cultura Económica.
Brumfiel, Elizabeth M., and John W. Fox, eds.
1994 *Factional Competition and Political Development in the New World.* Cambridge: Cambridge University Press.

Carneiro, Robert L.
1981   The chiefdom: Precursor of the state. In *The Transition to Statehood in the New World*, edited by G. D. Jones and R. R. Kautz, 37–79. Cambridge: Cambridge University Press.

Creamer, Winifred, and Jonathan Haas
1985   Tribe versus chiefdom in lower Central America. *American Antiquity* 50(4): 738–54.

Drennan, Robert D.
1987   Regional demography in chiefdoms. In *Chiefdoms in the Americas*, edited by R. D. Drennan and C. A. Uribe, 307–23. Lanham, Md.: University Press of America.

Drennan, Robert D., and Carlos A. Uribe, eds.
1987   *Chiefdoms in the Americas*. Lanham, Md.: University Press of America.

Earle, Timothy K.
1977   A reappraisal of redistribution: Complex Hawaiian chiefdoms. In *Exchange Systems in Prehistory*, edited by T. K. Earle and J. E. Ericson, 213–29. New York: Academic Press.

Earle, Timothy K., ed.
1984   *On the Evolution of Complex Societies: Essays in Honor of Harry Hoijer 1982*. Malibu: Undena Publications.
1991   *Chiefdoms: Power, Economy, and Ideology*. School of American Research. Cambridge: Cambridge University Press.

Feinman, Gary, and Jill Neitzel
1984   Too many types: An overview of prestate societies in the Americas. In *Advances in Archaeological Method and Theory*, edited by M. B. Schiffer, 7:39–102. New York: Academic Press.

Ferguson, R. Brian, and Neil L. Whitehead, eds.
1992   *War in the Tribal Zone: Expanding States and Indigenous Warfare*. Santa Fe: School of American Research Press.

Fernandes, Florestan
1963   *A Organização Social dos Tupinambá* (1948). São Paulo: Difusão Européia do Livro.
1970   *A Função Social da Guerra na Sociedade Tupinambá* (1952). São Paulo: Livraria Pioneira Editôra.
1975   Um balanço crítico da contribuição etnográfico dos cronistas. In *Investigação Etnológica no Brasil e Outros Ensaios*, by F. Fernandes, 191–289. Sociologia Brasileira 2. Petrópolis: Vozes.

Fried, Morton H.
1967   *The Evolution of Political Society: An Essay in Political Anthropology*. New York: Random House.

Goggin, John M., and William C. Sturtevant
1964   The Calusa: A stratified nonagricultural society (with notes on sibling marriage). In *Explorations in Cultural Anthropology: Essays in Honor of George Peter Murdock*, edited by W. H. Goodenough, 179–219. New York: McGraw-Hill.

Hemming, John
1978   *Red Gold: The Conquest of the Brazilian Indians*. Cambridge: Harvard University Press.

Knight, Vernon James Jr.
1990   Social organization and the evolution of hierarchy in southeastern chiefdoms. *Journal of Anthropological Research* 46(1):1–23.

Magalhães de Gandavo, Pero de
1922   *Historia da prouincia sãcta Cruz a que vulgarmẽte chamamos Brasil* (1576). Facsimile and English translation by J. B. Stetson Jr., 2 vols. New York: Cortes Society.

Mattingly, D. J.
1992   War and peace in Roman North Africa: Observations and models of state-tribe interaction. In *War in the Tribal Zone: Expanding States and Indigenous Warfare*, edited by R. B. Ferguson and N. L. Whitehead, 31–60. Santa Fe: School of American Research Press.

Menget, Patrick
1985   Notes sur l'ethnographie jésuite de l'Amazonie portugaise (1653–1759). In *Naissance de l'Ethnologie?: Anthropologie et missions en Amérique, XVIe–XVIIIe siècle*, edited by C. Blanckaert, 175–92. Paris: Éditions du Cerf.

Métraux, Alfred
1928a *La Civilisation Matérielle des Tribus Tupi-Guarani*. Paris: Librairie Orientaliste Paul Geuthner.
1928b La religion des Tupinamba et ses rapports avec celle des autres tribus Tupi-Guarani. *Bibliothèque de l'école des hautes études, sciences réligieuses*, vol. 45. Paris.
1948   The Tupinamba. In *Handbook of South American Indians*, vol. 3, *The Tropical Forest Tribes*, edited by J. H. Steward, 95–133. Bureau of American Ethnology Bulletin 143. Washington, D.C.: Smithsonian Institution.
1963   Les précurseurs de l'ethnologie en France du XVIe au XVIIIe siècle. *Cahiers d'Histoire Mondiale* 7(3):721–38. Neuchâtel.

Peebles, Christopher S., and Susan M. Kus
1977   Some archaeological correlates of ranked societies. *American Antiquity* 42(3): 421–48.

Redmond, Elsa M.
1994   External warfare and the internal politics of northern South American tribes and chiefdoms. In *Factional Competition and Political Development in the New World*, edited by E. M. Brumfiel and J. W. Fox, 44–54. Cambridge: Cambridge University Press.

Rodrigues, Arion D.
1958   Classification of Tupi-Guarani. *International Journal of American Linguistics* 24(3):231–34.
1986   *Línguas Brasileiras: Para o Conhecimento das Línguas Indígenas*. São Paulo: Loyola.

Sanders, William T.
1984   Pre-industrial demography and social evolution. In *On the Evolution of Complex Societies: Essays in Honor of Harry Hoijer 1982*, edited by T. Earle, 7–39. Malibu: Undena Publications.

Sanders, William T., and Barbara J. Price
1968   *Mesoamerica: The Evolution of a Civilization.* New York: Random House.

Service, Elman R.
1962   *Primitive Social Organization.* New York: Random House.

Spencer, Charles S.
1987   Rethinking the chiefdom. In *Chiefdoms in the Americas*, edited by R. D. Drennan and C. A. Uribe, 369–89. Lanham, Md.: University Press of America.

Sturtevant, William C.
1983   Tribe and state in the sixteenth and twentieth centuries. In *The Development of Political Organization in Native North America*, edited by E. Tooker, 3–16. 1979 Proceedings of the American Ethnological Society. Washington, D.C.: American Ethnological Society.

Upham, Steadman
1987   A theoretical consideration of middle range societies. In *Chiefdoms in the Americas*, edited by R.D. Drennan and C. A. Uribe, 345–67. Lanham, Md.: University Press of America.

Viveiros de Castro, Eduardo [=Castro, Eduardo Batalha Viveiros de]
1985   Bibliografia etnológica básica Tupi-Guarani. *Revista de Antropologia* 27–28:7–24.
1986   *Araweté: Os Deuses Canibais.* Rio de Janeiro: Jorge Zahar Editor Ltda.
1992   *From the Enemy's Point of View: Humanity and Divinity in an Amazonian Society.* Translated by C. V. Howard. Chicago: University of Chicago Press. [Translation of Viveiros de Castro 1986, somewhat revised and omitting a chapter and many notes on the Tupi-Guarani literature.]

Widmer, Randolph J.
1988   *The Evolution of the Calusa: A Nonagricultural Chiefdom on the Southwest Florida Coast.* Tuscaloosa: University of Alabama Press.

Wright, Henry T.
1984   Prestate political formations. In *On the Evolution of Complex Societies: Essays in Honor of Harry Hoijer 1982*, edited by T. K. Earle, 41–77. Malibu: Undena Publications.

CHAPTER 6

Colonial Chieftains of the Lower Orinoco and Guayana Coast

Neil L. Whitehead

My fundamental premise here is that anthropology should go further than the archaeological record in seeking to understand the chiefdom. Undoubtedly the importance of an extended time scale to analysis of the evolution of such political forms is a compelling reason for the dominance of the archaeological paradigm in current debates, but by the same token this reflects an overemphasis on questions as to the origins with a corresponding lack of attention to the dynamics of chieftaincy itself. Chiefdoms, as they are conceived in the archaeological literature, are only one aspect of this broader phenomenon, and it seems unlikely that the theoretical problems of typology that have become apparent in the definition of chiefdom (Upham 1990; Earle 1991) can be resolved without recasting the debate in its wider anthropological context, as has been the case for tribes (Haas 1990; Ferguson and Whitehead 1992).

I therefore begin by considering the relevance of ethnohistoric evidence and ethnographic testimony with a view to suggesting that it has generally been treated as "second-class," thereby theoretically blinding us to certain critical features of chiefdoms, which, once recognized, may permit a more adequate modeling of their development and decay. Examples of both precolonial and colonial period chieftaincies are then discussed in order to elucidate these features as they existed in Orinoquia and Guayana.[1] I conclude with some further remarks on the concepts of chiefdom and chieftaincy. Since issues of definition have been to the fore in this debate, I first clarify the usage of those terms here.

Chieftaincy is understood as being present in any supradomestic political unit that defers to individual leadership; as such the range of this political phenomenon is wide indeed, including a small raiding-party at one extreme, right through to political complexes such as divine kingship at the other. *Chiefdom* is then understood to be a special case of chieftaincy, one that is coincident with other forms of leadership and control in the spheres of economy and ideology, such as the management of irrigation works or the social relationships with the divine. In theoretical terms the intractability of providing a definition of the category *chiefdom* stems from a conflation of these differing aspects of political power.

Use of Historical and Contemporary Testimony

Although archaeology frequently makes use of ethnohistorical and ethnographic information, it is often argued, as in the case of Drennan and Uribe (1987, viii), that the cultural biases and truncated nature of this information, supposedly due to the rapidity and facility of European conquest, means that such sources can only be relevant to relatively short time spans and to a limited range of such societies.

While this may indeed be the case for some of those chieftaincies for which considerable archaeological presence can already be shown, it begs the question of whether we are interested in particular historical incidences of chiefdoms or the general phenomenon of chieftaincy. I suspect it ought to be the latter but that we are theoretically inhibited by a necessity, derived from studying the evolution of political forms, to respond to the evidence from particular archaeological contexts. For example, there is no a priori reason why archaeological chiefdoms, such as those evinced by the remains at Moundville or Marajoara, should be taken as critical to the understanding of the general phenomenon, other than the fact that we have archaeological information on these situations and not others; that is, they represent a probabilistic sample rather than the full distributional picture. To make these chiefdoms the sole exemplars of the social context for chieftaincy would unnecessarily exclude many other legitimate examples of the phenomenon. This is the case in the lower Orinoco River, where the historical evidence is strong but physical remains have yet to be recovered; and there are cases where, in the absence of clear ethnographic or historical evidence, the physical remains are not of themselves seen as sufficiently convincing, as in the Southwest of the United States.

The theoretical priority of the archaeological evidence thus derives only from its possible role in the search for pristine situations of development and, given the problems with the notion of pristine social development, there is no necessary reason to import this assumption into the discussion of chiefdoms, as has been done in the case of tribes (Haas and Creamer 1993). However, the functional priority of the archaeological record in the Americas certainly means that it will constrain any argument on native political evolution before 1492. Indeed, in the case of Moundville, the archaeological sequence is so detailed that it is equivalent to a single phase for most other archaeological cultures (Peebles 1987) and could certainly act as an effective parameter for the interpretation of historical sources, were they to exist. However, this archaeological example only emphasizes the point that we are dealing with different types of information, not different realities revealed by that information.

This consideration is particularly important when issues of the credibility of European records are raised since it is a common misapprehension that these pose unique problems of interpretation in the Americas, being the product of an invasive culture. However, since almost all written records are the product of the cultural activity of states, this would seem to be more a methodological problem in the study of nonstate societies, rather than an absolute limit on the value of ethnohistorical data.

Complementing this misapprehension is the notion that in the Americas most chiefdoms promptly collapsed in the face of European onslaught. Undoubtedly this did occur, but not uniformly—some chiefdoms, such as those of the Orinoco and Amazon rivers, survived well into the sixteenth century, while others had their origins in this very same period, reaching a zenith of development only in the seventeenth and eighteenth centuries. Such considerations are also the source of a theoretical concern to distinguish the contingent histories of particular chiefdoms from the study of the general conditions and dynamics of chieftaincy, the latter concept being readily generalizable through time and across culture.

This then brings us to a third, related issue, that of the supposed brevity of time span to which historical sources refer. Again the Americas pose special problems but not unique ones. Certainly the historical record is deafeningly silent about events prior to 1492 beyond the realms of the Andean and Mesoamerican states. This might be said of many other regions of the world in virtue of the close relationship between literacy and state organization already suggested. However, even in the Americas, there is still half a millennium of political evolution to be studied, which, though it may not comprise a single uninterrupted evolutionary sequence from band to state, may nevertheless illustrate well the processes of change—both between and within these typological classes of political formation.

In this context we need not specially privilege ethnographic information either and, as Drennan and Uribe (1987, ix) point out, in the context of Amazonia it has been used to produce a false notion of past society and polity, undermining in turn the authority of ethnographic analysis of contemporary society. But since ethnographic activity is the only opportunity that exists for the integrated observation, rather than mere retrospective analysis, of social phenomena, its importance is absolutely irreducible. Nonetheless, the written results of such endeavors are themselves ethnohistorical sources, albeit still lingering on the edge of memory: but it is with a consideration of times "immemorial" that this paper is primarily concerned.

Chieftaincy in Orinoquia
and Guayana before Spanish Settlement

Roosevelt (1980, 1987) has outlined the main features of the evidence concerning chiefdoms along the Amazon and Orinoco floodplains. Suffice it to say here that those organizational features most often considered archaeologically diagnostic of chiefdoms—such as centralized rule over extensive domains incorporating large populations, intensive production of seed crops, differential social practices or statuses, and the practice of external warfare—are all identified from the area under discussion.

Historical and ethnographic research since that date has served to confirm Roosevelt's summary analysis (see Langebaek 1987, Porro 1994, Whitehead 1996, 1994, 1995) as well to suggest ways in which it may be elaborated to take account of more complex phenomena associated with these societies that are not immediately evident in physical remains (see Kelekna, chap. 7 this volume; Rappaport 1987).

For example, evidence reviewed in Whitehead (1996, 1997) suggests that *guanin* (golden metals) had a critical role to play in the validation of political and social authority, particularly where this involved an exchange of persons, whether through warfare, marriage, or some other form of contractual relationship. This does not imply that gold items were exchanged directly for persons, in the manner of later European slave trading, but the belief systems that supported the valorization of golden objects also signaled the appropriateness of persons as items in a wider cycle of exchange. This is evident from the fact that exchanges were both commercial and military in form, the distinction between trading and raiding being, as ever, a fine one.

While there is no evidence to suggest that the wearing of golden objects was explicitly reserved for the elite only, ornamentation with golden objects was nonetheless a symbol of an exalted status, and the accumulation of such objects was unlikely to have been achieved by those who were not to the fore in either the external relations of trade and war or the internal relations of leadership. The various native beliefs that have been conflated into the European myth of El Dorado clearly testify to this and also serve to alert us to the connections between the chieftains of the lower Orinoco River and those of the Colombian sierras. Although the ritual parameters that expressed such beliefs were not identical in the Colombian and Guayanan contexts, as the Europeans assumed, the existence of sustained, if indirect, interaction between the elites of these regions is also amply demonstrated by the longevity and wide dispersion of the mid-Orinocan Barrancoid and western Venezuelan Dabajuroid ceramic series. This contradicts earlier assumptions as to the isolated and parochial aboriginal society in the lower Orinoco, assumptions largely derived from an ethnographic record that was itself the product of observation of the consequences of the colonial era for native society and culture. So great was the devastation of native society in the first phases of contact with Europeans that, even as early as the seventeenth century (Whitehead 1994, 1995), little, if anything, remained of the continental systems of political and economic interaction that are evinced in the native use of golden metals.

However, the presence of diagnostic or suggestive features such as those outlined by Roosevelt (1987)—to include agricultural/habitation mounds, extensive cemeteries, earthworks, complex ceramic repertoire, seed-crop usage, and a prevalence of human iconography—do not in themselves mark out any chiefdom in particular. Obviously such suggestive features may combine with varying emphasis on different elements in different regions (Drennan and Uribe 1987, xi). This has rightly led some to doubt the utility of the chiefdom concept at all. Equally, while accepting a polythetic system of classification, others have sought to isolate one or more of these elements as causal in the origin of historic chiefdoms. Thus, Carneiro (1981), for example, draws attention to the role of warfare consequent on a physical and social circumscription in causing a wide variety of societies to organize as chiefdoms. Similarly, Upham (1987), although ultimately renaming chiefdoms as "middle-range societies," identifies the management of environmental risk as the key factor to which chiefdom organization and alliance formation can be considered the response. Thus baldly stated, there actually need be little disagreement between these positions, since the processes of incorporation, be they warfare or alliance formation, are not the critical element—rather, "environmental risk" is precisely "circumscription" viewed from another analytical perspective.

However, the attempt by Upham (1990) to integrate the discussion of chiefdoms with that of tribes is useful since it draws our attention to the question of the origins of chiefdoms and brings us up sharply, once again, to the question of the importance of historical data. Certainly the origin of the chiefdoms first encountered in Orinoquia and Guayana is not accessible to historical study, but the manner of their eventual collapse may yet tell us much about their actual functioning, in particular the uses of ethnicity (intergroup definition) and of kinship and descent (intragroup definition)—social processes that are notoriously difficult to inspect archaeologically.

At the mouth of the Orinoco River from about 1520 onward, three chiefdoms may be identified that persisted for another hundred years; they may be politically identified as Yao, Orinoqueponi, and Tivetive (Whitehead 1997). According to the criteria offered by Carneiro (1981, 47) these would qualify as "typical," perhaps even "maximal" chiefdoms. They would comfortably exceed the demographic threshold suggested by Upham (1987, 355) of incorporating a population of over 10,000 persons. Indeed the population of one town alone was estimated at over 4,000. The authority of local chieftains, or *casiqui,* and by extension that of paramount chiefs, or *aquerewana,* seems to have been the product of their control over long-distance trade in specialist manufactures, such as goldwork and cotton goods, as well as their control within this region of the exploitation of variable resources, such as metals and sources of pottery clays. A tradition of warfare is implied by the presence of military capabilities and the effectiveness of resistance to the Spaniards as well as by native accounts of "civil war" at the beginning of the sixteenth century. Although lying outside the circum-Caribbean area, these chiefdoms certainly interacted with those of the Venezuelan littoral and were not considered at all distinctive, at least as regards political organization, by contemporary witnesses. Notably other groups were so distinguished according to their political features, particularly the "Caribes" of the northern llanos of the Orinoco River and the "Aruacas" to the south of the Essequibo River, with whom these chiefdoms were increasingly at war by the end of the sixteenth century.

The regional links of these chiefdoms spread north into the Caribbean via satellite communities on Trinidad and Grenada, and south along the Guayana coast as far as the Essequibo River, until the late sixteenth century when the Yao paramount chief, Anacajoury, invaded the region between the Oyapock and Amazon rivers, carving out new "chiefdoms" for his casiquis. To the west the Orinoco chieftains sent traders into the llanos of the Apure and Meta rivers, probably to sustain a system of elite exchanges with the Muisca (Chibcha) as well as with chiefly societies of the Venezuelan spur of the Andes, either directly or through the mediation of the Achagua. Indeed, following the description by Langebaek (1987; see also Lleras Pérez and Langebaek Rueda 1987), there appear to have been many analogous features between the Chibcha and the lower Orinoco chiefdoms, not just in the presence of various diagnostic traits but also in the ethnic and linguistic pattern of organization that was reported in the sixteenth century; that is, a common linguistic base alongside a multiplicity of ethnic units—eight in the Chibcha case, and, for example, three in the case of the Orinoqueponi (Nepoyo, Shebayo, Guayano). Notably, in view of my earlier comments, without the historical accounts, the archaeological remains would actually have belied the importance of the Chibchan chiefdoms (Feidel 1984, 313).

With intensification of European penetration into this area during the sixteenth century there was no sudden extinction of the Orinoco chiefdoms, but the conditions for the exercise of chieftaincy certainly changed— and in highly unpredictable ways. Thus, elite control of external exchange was directly undermined by Spanish trading activities, as lesser chiefs jockeyed for lead position in exchanges with the Spaniards, especially for metal tools and European guanin (i.e., brass, copper) in the form of bells and mouth harps. By the mid–sixteenth century we may infer a chronic instability in chiefly authority from the evidence of attempts to prohibit altogether such exchanges with the Spaniards, especially of native guanin (goldwork). Alongside these developments there were also, of course, direct campaigns of military conquest by various conquistadors, most notably the *entradas a fuego y sangre*, "invasions by fire and blood," by Sedeño and Ordaz in the 1530s (Ramos 1955, 2–3). There was as well a steady demand for slaves for use in the Cubaguan pearl fisheries, which effectively neutralized the chiefdoms of Hororotomaka and Pallamos—ancestral to the modern Warao—by the end of the century. Similarly, the paramount chief (aquerewana) of the Orinoqueponi, Morequito, eventually failing to exploit the conflicts on the Spanish side, was executed during a visit to Margarita. His nephew was promoted as the Spanish pretender in his place, following the rules of avunculate succession. In fact Topiawari, Morequito's aged uncle, succeeded briefly instead, suggesting some resilience in the traditional organization of this chiefdom; but this could not prevent the ultimate military occupation of his province of Arromaia with the aid of one of Morequito's former casiqui, Carapana ("the mosquito").

The Spanish foundation of Santo Tomé on the lower Orinoco in 1596 effectively signaled the collapse of the then extant chiefdoms of this region. The system of ethnic identity that underlay them also broke up, but the exercise of chieftaincy was still possible and it is from the subsequent process of ethnic redefinition, founded on the economics of European trading, that the new colonial chieftains of the seventeenth century emerge. It is thus important to note—contrary to Service's conjecture that "no one has observed the actual origin of a chiefdom" (quoted in Carneiro 1981, 56)— that with the use of the ethnohistorical data, we are actually in a good position to do just this. Accordingly, the genesis of colonial chieftains will now be briefly examined.

Colonial Chieftaincy along the Orinoco and Guayana Coast

From around 1540 onward, and clearly related to the events described above, there began to emerge significant new groupings among the native population in this region (Whitehead 1992). Initially they were given the notoriously fluid designations of Aruaca and Caribe on the basis of their attitude to the Spaniards. This instability of reference transpires to have been far less than earlier commentators have allowed, and it is entirely appropriate that such realignments in the native polity should have appeared confusing and inconsistent, for this was the actual nature of social change for contemporary observers.

Of course these new groupings within the native polity did not arise from thin air, and obviously the emergence of the Caribes as a social movement in the Orinoco Basin must be tied into the events on the Caribbean Islands; but that story, because of its ideological overlay, is too complex to have the time to unravel here (see Whitehead 1995). Suffice it to say then that the so-called "Island Caribs" were neither islanders nor indeed were they Caribs, in the ethnological sense of that term; nonetheless their position at the forefront of contact with the Europeans, from which they derived considerable trading opportunities without ever quite succumbing to the ensuing effects of disease and enslavement, gave them a great source of prestige and power among the continental native groups. This political and economic eminence was deployed by the Dominican Caribe chieftain known as Le Baron to create a powerful island polity at the beginning of the seventeenth century (Whitehead 1995:91–111).

With the advent of Dutch, English, and French settlement on the mainland as well as the islands, in the early seventeenth century the locus of opportunity moved to the Orinoco and Essequibo rivers, and accordingly, the emergence of powerful Caribe chieftains, such as Taricura along the Barima River (Whitehead 1988, 61), may be observed right across this area, though with a different ethnic base to those of the islands.

It is in these contexts that the purpose of making a theoretical distinction between chiefdoms and chieftaincy can begin to be understood, for these chieftains controlled no defined territory, took no preeminent role in food production, claimed no divinity for their lineage—as the Dominican kings had done—and did not indulge in monumental architecture. Yet the reality of their chiefly power can be seen clearly enough in their extremes of polygamy, their military effectiveness against the Europeans, and their extraction of tribute from other groups, in which features they are reminiscent of the Páez colonial chieftaincies described by Rappaport (Rappaport 1987, 272). Moreover, in the Caribe case the origins of chiefly power are equally clearly identifiable, as well as quantifiable, through the study of their control over the distribution of European goods from the coast into the interior (see Whitehead 1988, 82–85). This kind of emergent chiefly power connected to the redistribution of European manufactures is often seen in the history of other post-1500 chieftaincies.

Similar considerations apply to the rise of the Aruaca chieftains, or *adumasis*, along the Guayana coast and at the mouth of the Orinoco River. Essentially where the Caribes had benefited from the trade in European manufactures with Spain's colonial rivals, the Aruacas derived their dominance primarily from their trade in *aru* or manioc flour to the Spanish enclaves and from a close political identification and economic cooperation with the European colonial elites throughout the region. The Spanish alliance also led to joint military incursions against the remnants of the precolonial chiefdoms of Orinoco as well as against the emergent Caribe chieftains in Essequibo and Surinam—necessitated by decisive military defeats for the Aruacas in 1587 and again in about 1596; indeed, it seems likely that the Caribe kings of Dominica also have their origins in these events of the late sixteenth century.

However, unlike their Caribe competitors, the Aruaca adumasis of the Guayana coast emerged from the collapse of a preexisting highland chiefdom that was socially based on the ethnolinguistic group the Lokono. Accordingly, much of the clan structure that had underlain the earlier highland chiefdom was carried over into the colonial era and non-Lokono groups were incorporated wholesale as new "clans," some still extant today. The collapse of this highland polity may be related to the economic draw of coastal trading with the Europeans and especially the trade in aru north to Spanish ports at Margarita. This was directly initiated, in 1539, by a Morisco (Spanish North African) who had been shipwrecked on the Guayana coast and adopted by the Aruaca some 12 years previously.

It is known that not all sections of the Lokono went along with these developments, and one might therefore infer, following Renfrew's (1974, 74–82) suggestion, a change from "group oriented" to "individualizing" chieftaincy—the more so since it was as leaders of particular clans or extended families, rather than as paramount or pan-ethnic chieftains, that individuals rose to prominence in the colonial period. Such an inference is further reinforced by evidence that some clans of the Aruacas incorporated the children of marriages with non-Amerindians, as well as non-Lokono.

Conclusion

The problem for the ethnohistorian and ethnographer, thus faced with what are evidently clear examples of exercise of chieftaincy, is that it seems possible that such polities would fail to register firmly as archaeological chiefdoms. Some striking examples of this paradox outside the region under discussion would be the case of the Calusa of southern Florida (Goggin and Sturtevant 1964) or the chieftaincies of California (Bean and King 1974), which, like the Cuiva and Guayqueri of the Orinoco Basin (Federmann 1962), all seem to have been essentially hunter-gatherer chiefdoms, not practicing formal horticulture or agriculture. Although there is a methodological necessity for archaeologists to define chiefdoms in such a manner that they can be identified from material remains (after Milisauskas in Carneiro 1981, 52), an *anthropological* understanding of the phenomenon must go further than this and must integrate the data from direct observation. In this case it may be more appropriate to model the process theoretically as pertaining to the archaeology of power, rather than to the archaeology of any particular expression of that power, such as of a particular historical chiefdom. This much has already been recognized by Renfrew (1984), Trigger (1974), and Steponaitis (1978).

Thus, any given archaeological field study is concerned with a specific and limited situation only. However, although archaeology has evolved sophisticated archaeological criteria for the study of social relations, since some social relations may leave no material trace there can be no complete understanding of the anthropological phenomenon of chieftaincy from archaeological data alone—no matter how thoroughly particular archaeological chiefdoms come to be understood.

One response to this, following Renfrew (1984), is to find an operational definition of power, such as through central place theory; and this approach works well in many archaeological contexts. However, as was suggested in the case of the Páez and the Caribes, whose dispersed mode of settlement was actually a critical factor in the development of chieftaincy in the face of European colonial activity, such spatial criteria do not capture all instances of the phenomenon. As Shennan (1989) has indicated, much the same sort of problem applies to the question of cultural or ethnic identity. Thus, just as the dynamics of group power over that of the domestic unit underlay the processes of group identity and coordination that historically produce tribes (i.e., ethnic formations), so too the dynamics of individual power over that of the group (i.e., chieftaincy) underlay the historical inception of particular chiefdoms—in which case, as suggested earlier, it is the parameters of these dynamic systems, not the various clusters of diagnostic traits that they create, that should be the locus of our attention.

In this context, and in view of the evidence for colonial chiefdoms, it would then appear that long time spans are not sufficient of themselves for the understanding of chieftaincy. But extended time spans are critical for the practice of archaeological theory, since the significance of positional relations between inert objects takes a far greater sample to establish than does the significance of relations between active persons whose behavior is precisely the source of significance for the positional relations between those objects. Such considerations, incidentally, are thus the basis of a rationale for ethnoarchaeology. Given these considerations, the "problem" of the chiefdom, and its place in political evolution, will be not be resolvable in its own terms because the taxonomic categories derived from the archaeological evidence are only heuristic devices.

Rather, by situating "chiefdoms" within the general field of the study of the organization and expression of power—that is, "chieftaincy"—we are then able to use a unitary framework for the discussion of the evidence as to the forms of political power in the past and present; be that evidence archaeological, historical or ethnographic, and whatever the demographic or technological origins of the chiefdom configuration. It is the inequality of individual access to the sources of social power that creates each new opportunity for dominance over others to be exercised. Extant environmental and cultural features, such as the nature of circumscription or military and religious traditions, then operate to create a specific historical trajectory in which the inequality of individual access over that of the group will repeatedly recreate the material conditions for the exercise of chieftaincy and sometimes produce that which we already recognize as the chiefdom.

Note

1. The term *Guayana* delineates the geographical area encircled by the Amazon and Orinoco rivers and the Atlantic Ocean. *Guianas* refers to the colonial political units of the eastern coast of this vast region and *Guyana* to the postcolonial state that supplanted the British administration, just as *Surinam* supplanted Dutch Guiana.

References

Bean, Lowell J., and Thomas F. King
1974   *Antap: California Indian Political and Economic Organization.* Ballena Press Anthropological Papers no. 2. Ramona, Calif.: Ballena Press.
Carneiro, Robert L.
1981   The chiefdom: Precursor of the state. In *Transition to Statehood in the New World,* edited by G. D. Jones and R. R. Kautz, 37–79. Cambridge: Cambridge University Press.
Drennan, Robert D., and Carlos A. Uribe, eds.
1987   *Chiefdoms in the Americas.* Lanham, Md.: University Press of America.
Earle, Timothy, ed.
1991   *Chiefdoms: Power, Economy, and Ideology.* School of American Research. Cambridge: Cambridge University Press.
Federmann, Nicolás
1962   *Historia Indiana o Primer Viaje de Nicolás Federmann.* In *Descubrimiento y Conquista de Venezuela: Textos Históricos Contemporáneos y Documentos Fundamentales.* Tomo II. *Cubagua y la Empresa de los Belzares* (1557). Biblioteca de la Academia Nacional de la Historia, no. 55. Fuentes para la Historia Colonial de Venezuela. Caracas: Italgráfica C.A.
Feidel, S. J.
1984   *Prehistory of the Americas.* Cambridge: Cambridge University Press.
Ferguson, R. Brian, and Neil L. Whitehead, eds.
1992   *War in the Tribal Zone: Expanding States and Indigenous Warfare.* Santa Fe: School of American Research Press.
Goggin, John M., and William C. Sturtevant
1964   The Calusa: A stratified, nonagricultural society. In *Explorations in Cultural Anthropology: Essays in Honor of George Peter Murdock,* edited by W. H. Goodenough, 179–219. New York: McGraw-Hill.
Haas, Jonathan
1990   Warfare and the evolution of tribal politics in the prehistoric Southwest. In *The Anthropology of War,* edited by J. Haas, 171–89. School of American Research. Cambridge: Cambridge University Press.
Haas, Jonathan, and Winifred Creamer
1993   *Stress and Warfare among the Kayenta Anasazi of the Thirteenth Century A.D.* Fieldiana: Anthropology n.s., no. 21. Chicago: Field Museum of Natural History.

Langebaek R., Carl H.
1987   *Los Muiscas.* Bogotá: Banco de la República.

Lleras Pérez, Roberto, and Carl H. Langebaek Rueda
1987   Producción agrícola y desarollo sociopolítico entre los Chibchas de la Cordillera Oriental y Serranía de Mérida. In *Chiefdoms in the Americas,* edited by R. D. Drennan and C. A. Uribe, 251–70. Lanham, Md.: University Press of America.

Peebles, Christopher S.
1987   Moundville from 1000 to 1500 AD as seen from 1840 to 1985 AD. In *Chiefdoms in the Americas,* edited by R. D. Drennan and C. A. Uribe, 21–42. Lanham, Md.: University Press of America.

Porro, Antonio
1994   Social organization and political power in the Amazon floodplain: The ethnohistorical sources. In *Amazonian Indians from Prehistory to the Present: Anthropological Perspectives,* edited by A. Roosevelt, 79–94. Tucson: University of Arizona Press.

Ramos, D.
1955   Las misiones del Orinoco a la luz de pugnas territoriales. *Anuario de Estudios Americanos* 12:1–37.

Rappaport, Joanne
1987   Los cacicazgos de la sierra Colombiana: El caso Páez. In *Chiefdoms in the Americas,* edited by R. D. Drennan and C. A. Uribe, 271–88. Lanham, Md.: University Press of America.

Renfrew, Colin
1974   Beyond a subsistence economy: The evolution of social organisation in prehistoric Europe. In *Reconstructing Complex Societies,* edited by C. B. Moore, 69–96. Supplement to the Bulletin of the American Schools of Oriental Research no. 20.
1984   *Approaches to Social Archaeology.* Cambridge: Harvard University Press.

Roosevelt, Anna C.
1980   *Parmana: Prehistoric Maize and Manioc Subsistence along the Amazon and Orinoco.* New York: Academic Press.
1987   Chiefdoms in the Amazon and Orinoco. In *Chiefdoms in the Americas,* edited by R. D. Drennan and C. A. Uribe, 147–52. Lanham, Md.: University Press of America.

Shennan, Stephen
1989   Introduction: Archaeological approaches to cultural identity. In *Archaeological Approaches to Cultural Identity,* edited by S. Shennan, 1–32. London: Unwin Hyman.

Steponaitis, Vincas P.
1978   Location theory and complex chiefdoms: A Mississippian example. In *Mississippian Settlement Patterns,* edited by B. D. Smith, 417–53. New York: Academic Press.

Trigger, Bruce

1974 The archaeology of government. *World Archaeology* 6:95–106.

Upham, Steadman

1987 A theoretical consideration of middle range societies. In *Chiefdoms in the Americas,* edited by R. D. Drennan and C. A. Uribe, 345–68. Lanham, Md.: University Press of America.

Upham, Steadman, ed.

1990 *The Evolution of Political Systems: Sociopolitics in Small-Scale Sedentary Societies.* School of American Research. Cambridge: Cambridge University Press.

Whitehead, Neil L.

1988 *Lords of the Tiger Spirit: A History of the Caribs in Colonial Venezuela and Guyana, 1498–1820.* Dordrecht: Foris Publications.

1992 Tribes make states and states make tribes: Warfare and the creation of colonial tribes and states in northeastern South America. In *War in the Tribal Zone: Expanding States and Indigenous Warfare,* edited by R. B. Ferguson and N. L. Whitehead, 127–50. Santa Fe: School of American Research Press.

1994 The ancient Amerindian polities of the Amazon, the Orinoco, and the Atlantic coast: A preliminary analysis of their passage from antiquity to extinction. In *Amazonian Indians from Prehistory to the Present: Anthropological Perspectives,* edited by A. Roosevelt, 33–53. Tucson: University of Arizona Press.

1996 The Mazaruni dragon: Golden metals and elite exchanges in the Caribbean, Orinoco and Amazon. In *Chieftains, Power and Trade: Regional Interaction in the Intermediate Area of the Americas,* edited by C. H. Langebaek and F. Cardenas-Arroyo, 107–32. Bogota: Universidad de los Andes.

Whitehead, Neil L., ed.

1995 *Wolves from the Sea: Readings in the Anthropology of the Native Caribbean.* Leiden: KITLV Press.

1997 *The Discoverie of the Large, Rich and Beautiful Empyre of Guiana. By Sir Walter Ralegh.* Manchester/Norman: Manchester University Press/Oklahoma University Press.

CHAPTER 7

War and Theocracy

PITA KELEKNA

In the study of New World ranked societies, distinction was early drawn between theocratic and militaristic chiefdoms (Steward and Faron 1959, 177). Following this analysis, it has traditionally been assumed that theocratic chiefdoms are small, peaceful, homogeneous populations, in which settlements are consolidated through religion, a temple-idol complex serving as ancestral burial site, pilgrimage center, and place of community activity. Managerial control of labor is generally inferred from the extent of irrigation works, causeway construction, or megalithic tombs. In the social interaction of theocracies, group contacts are peaceful with elite primary concern focused on religion, the hereditary priesthood serving an oracular function (Steward and Faron 1959, 240–41). By contrast, militaristic chiefdoms are considered to be more heterogeneous in composition, expansionistic in terms of territorial conquest, fortifications, and exaction of tribute, their elites pragmatically oriented toward economic activity and sociopolitical domination (Steward and Faron 1959, 209). From this evolutionary perspective then, theocracies appear to be stable, militaristic chiefdoms dynamic; as Webster (1976, 814) reservedly notes, religion has come to be viewed as a stabilizing rather than a dynamic force.

In this chapter I diverge markedly from this position. Rather than viewing theocracy as a cultural dead end, I contend that religion plays a vital role in the evolution of political systems. Furthermore, my claim is that, far from being antithetical to war, religion frequently is instrumental in promoting militarism and legitimizing political inequality in society.

To trace and characterize the role of religion in the promotion of societal belligerence, chieftaincy, and the emergence of centralized authority, several New World societies are considered: the tribal Jivaroan of the Ecuador-Peruvian Amazon, the chiefdoms of the Cauca Valley of Colombia, the Maya polities and upstart Aztec state of Mesoamerica.

Along this gradient of sociopolitical complexity, religion is examined according to the manner in which myth and ritual project images of cosmic order onto the plane of human experience. The dual-faceted character of religious symbols (Geertz 1972, 169) is examined in the sense of *model of*, as an expression of structure in synoptic form, and *model for*, as the shaping and manipulation of human action in terms of the symbols of the envisaged order. Attention is given the interplay of solar, avian, feline, and serpentine symbols in Amerindian mythico-religious systems and how these relate to war and hierarchy. Contrary to the notion that innovation and militarism break with theology, interaction between material factors of existence and human symbology is posited. In the evolutionary process, it is shown that sacred and secular are intertwined as new symbols emerge from old.

Jivaroan Warrior-Shaman Complex

In terms of circumscription theory (Carneiro 1970)—which predicts that in warfare, subjugation of defeated populations, socioeconomic hierarchization, and concentration of power develop more readily in agricultural regions environmentally delimited by geographic features such as deserts, mountains, and oceans—the first people to be considered here are the least circumscribed and the least centralized politically. Subsequent sections, however, address religion in situations of increasing population pressure and greater environmental circumscription. The Jivaroans, inhabitants of the Amazon rain forest of Ecuador and Peru, traditionally practice extensive slash-and-burn horticulture, hunting, and fishing.[1] Settlements, comprising a single extended family household or a small cluster of family dwellings, are dispersed throughout the tropical forest. In this atomistic society, each settlement enjoys a fair degree of political autonomy, with internal disputes resolved through simple fission. Due to unrelenting pressure of demographic expansion eastward from the Andes, frequent inter-settlement feuding (Hendricks 1993, 19; Redmond, chap. 3, this volume) compels communities to enter into military alliances for purposes of assault and defense. Upon completion of a raid a war party commonly disperses. With strong affinal alliance, however, political alignment may persist for a significant period.

In this acephalous situation, religion is an accessory to aggression in several different ways. In myth the sun god Etsa epitomizes the warrior role. In deeds of daring and tenacity, the deity combats and vanquishes *iwia*, anthropophagous demons of the forest that prey on men and threaten social existence. Forest animal personifications of the solar deity—the capuchin monkey, squirrel, golden fox, and promethean hummingbird—defeat the enemy in trickster ordeals of cunning and violence. These detailed accounts of Etsa's exploits convey a morality of revenge killing, an ethic that impels men to undertake assassination and to participate in retaliatory raiding (Kelekna 1981, 101–4).

Training for the role of warrior begins early. At a young age, the boy gains familiarity with weaponry and acquires basic skills in tracking, stalking, and hunting that equip him well to accompany war expeditions by the age of seven. Politically, ceremonial narratives of past warring exploits and recent raids orient the boy as to his family's allies and enemies. Spiritually, in preparation for his martial role, the young boy is inducted into the *arutam* cult. Arutam represents the warring aspect of the sun god and refers to ancestor or forefather. Ancestor worship not only emphasizes transgenerational continuity and peer solidarity; it also serves as a mechanism of territorial definition (Flannery 1972). Under the direction of an eminent warrior, initiands trek far into the forest to a distant waterfall, where sky, earth, and water meet, there to undergo rigorous ordeals. They consume the hallucinogen *maikiua* (*Datura arborea*) to experience sacred visions of terrifying spirits in the form of jaguar, eagle, a disembodied head, a spinning sun, a shooting star. The initiand is required to strike the apparition with his staff, thereby gaining the male energy that ensures his success in the adult world (Harner 1972, 136–38; Kelekna 1994, 240–41). Initiation is thus an exercise in daring, assault, and dominance. To gain greater spiritual strength, a youth is also encouraged to make a shrunken head from a sloth (Harner 1972, 149). After his first killing, the young warrior ritually consumes the heart of a jaguar in order to acquire the strength and ferocity of the beast. And as a mature adult he greets each dawn with jaguar roars to deter raiders who might be gathering for attack.

Arutam is also sought during the world-renewal festival that occurs at approximately 10-year intervals. In the early predawn hours, the rhythmic playing of the *tuntui* log-signal drum summons all to attend from miles around. As the drumming is continued by adult males throughout the day, young girls, to ensure fertility, ritually perform horticultural tasks in the gardens while boys search the forest for the sacred *natém* (*Banisteriopsis caapi*) vine. Just before dusk, a line of freshly painted pottery drinking vessels, product of each married woman's hearth, is extended from west to east across the plaza to form the *axis mundi* of the ceremony. When the sun dips to the horizon, grandmothers ladle from huge bowls the sacramental hallucinogen. As they imbibe, youths are subject to ritual hazing by the seasoned warriors present, then hasten to shelters along the forest trails to experience supernatural visions. The following day, they consume maikiua in order to commune with the ancestors.

As the warrior relates to the solar male aerial sphere of the forests and skies, so the religious figure of the Jivaroan shaman is linked to the aquatic realm of the rains and rivers. In the depth of the river lies a house of writhing snakes, the abode of the shamanic deity Tsunki, whose tutelary spirits are the anaconda and caiman. As Tsunki exists betwixt earth and sky, so the shaman mediates between natural and supernatural, life and death, health and sickness, fertility and birth (Kelekna 1981, 118). In a culture in which all illness, misfortune, and death are attributed to malign witchcraft, the shaman is greatly valued for shielding the community against alien sorcery and for healing the sick. But he is also feared for the spiritual power he commands of killing at a distance. For this reason a strong shaman wields extraordinary influence in society. Out of dread of supernatural retribution, others show him extreme deference and routinely fulfill his directives (Harner 1972, 117).

Whether curing or killing, the shaman is assisted by spirit helpers, which on the one hand combat the malignant darts of disease lodged in a victim's body or conversely project bewitching darts against the enemy (Redmond, chap. 3, this volume). Curing takes place at night after the shaman has consumed natém. Kneeling by the patient, he perceives the malevolent sorcerer's darts, which he sucks out to relieve the torment. During the ceremony, the assembled family members and the shaman, summoning all his powers to rid the patient of disease, form an emotionally supportive group around the individual. Just as the warrior provides military defense against enemy attack, so the shaman is the spiritual protector against life's uncertainties and calamities.

In face of uncertainty, the shaman also acts as diviner. In a hallucinogenic trance, the divining shaman is able to identify the alien sorceror who inflicted disease. When this identity is established, the victim's kin leave on a raid. Assassination of the bewitching shaman restores the invalid to health or, in the event of fatality, appeases the *emesak* soul of the deceased, which might harm surviving family members if death is left unavenged (Kelekna 1981, 118–23).

In Jivaroan hostilities, close political alignment of warrior-shaman pairs is not infrequent and confers mutual advantage. The warrior protects the shaman from assassination raids, while the shaman's spiritual powers complement the warrior's tactical strength. In supernatural divination, the ritual attribution of disease and death to malign sorcery has crucial strategic significance for the success of the raiding party. It taps the emotions of a threatened community and establishes the critical we/they distinction, the in- versus out-group identification, so fundamentally important to organized intergroup conflict.

Religious observances prevail throughout the raid. Warriors assemble ritually painted and resplendent with feather crowns and ornamentation, emblematic of their fine marksmanship and affinity with Etsa, god of the hunt and war. During the trek, the war leader at intervals intones sacred hymns. On the eve of the attack, all warriors come together to describe the sacred visions experienced, from which they derive supernatural strength. From this point on, it becomes imperative that the raiders kill. Once the visions are described, arutam power dissipates during the attack. Unless the raiders take a life, they will be unable to regain spiritual vigor (Harner 1972, 140). Following assassination, head trophies are taken if the enemy is of another tribe. If the slain warrior of another tribe is greatly feared, he may also be dismembered (Hendricks 1993, 137–38).

Raiders flee through the forest until all pursuit is eluded. The war expedition then stops by the side of a stream to detach the skins from the skulls, which are cast into the river as an offering to the anaconda. The purpose of shrinking a head (*tsantsa*) is to capture the emesak, avenging soul of the deceased, as it hovers alongside the retreating war expedition. Rubbing the headskin with hot pebbles and sand reduces it to the size of a man's fist. *Chonta* palm pins fasten the lips together to prevent the emesak from escaping. Charcoal is rubbed over the skin to neutralize the spirit and prevent it from inflicting harm. Perforation is made in the top to allow suspension of the tsantsa from the warrior's neck (Harner 1972, 187–89), there simulating fertilizing testis. In the ensuing ritual of male gestation, identity is stripped from the victim and transferred to the group of the victor. On return to the settlement, the victor paints his legs with hen's blood, symbolizing perhaps the fertility of menses. Women greet the tsantsa seductively to allay its vengeful powers (Taylor 1985, 161). Rites are enacted to mortify and subdue the spirit of the slain, to promote the material wealth of the slayer, and to ensure in the community female fecundity, horticultural fertility, and male prowess in hunt and war. A feast is held to symbolize ritual consumption of the enemy. During the feast the fertilizing power of the slain foe is passed to the killer and his family, where it becomes the principle of production of a child, a new member for the group (Descola 1992, 118; Harner 1972, 146–47; Pellizzaro 1980).

Through multiple killings, a great warrior increases his spiritual vigor to the point that he is known as *kakáram* (powerful one; for fuller discussion, see Redmond, chap. 3, this volume); he is regarded as invincible (Harner 1972, 113), even a demigod, precursor perhaps of the messianic leader or divine king of more complex social structures. In these first steps toward chieftaincy, the supernatural strength the great war leader possesses is believed to be manifested in the forcefulness of his ceremonial oratory and address. Thus intertwined in Jivaroan life, cosmology, theory of disease, sorcery accusation, fear of supernatural retribution, and quest for power compel the individual to embrace the ethos of revenge killing and to participate fully in internecine warfare.

Chiefdoms in the Cauca Valley

Northwest of the Amazon in Colombia, in the circumscribed valley of the Cauca River, concentrations of population and corresponding intensification of warfare are documented ethnohistorically for pre- and early contact times (Trimborn 1949, 277, 284). As discussed by Carneiro (1990), in this region sociopolitical integration was at the chiefdom level, although at varying levels of complexity. There existed numerous allied multivillage aggregations of political consequence as well as polities that were exceptionally large and powerful, such as Guaca and Popayán, each with several previously independent chiefdoms under its suzerainty (Trimborn 1949, 289, 330, 334–35).

In Cauca Valley warfare, economic considerations featured more prominently than in Amazon rain forest feuding. Outbreaks of armed conflict stemmed from disputes over territorial expansion, control of trade routes, exaction of tribute, or access to mineral resources such as salt deposits or gold mines (Trimborn 1949, 283). Revenge for past killings and retaliation for offenses against persons of rank were also contributing factors. Additionally—unlike in Jivaroan raiding, in which solely women were abducted for purposes of polygyny—in Cauca Valley warfare the capture of prisoners of either sex was a primary motive (Trimborn 1949, 284). Captives were held in servitude, as domestic retainers or agricultural slaves. Slaves could additionally be bestowed as gifts or exchanged across transregional networks for commodities such as food, gold, or cotton cloth (Hernández de Alba 1948, 317–18). Human fat was also extracted for use as illumination in mines (Hernández de Alba 1948, 319; Trimborn 1949, 393).

In this Colombian region, warfare was markedly escalated in terms of extent and intensity of hostilities. Military alliances were forged among polities (Trimborn 1949, 277, 331–34), with hundreds of warriors and sometimes several thousand participating in a campaign (Trimborn 1949, 335–37). The battlefield was an arena in which men could achieve distinction and gain status as warriors. Weaponry was varied and of fair sophistication: slings, bows, poisoned arrows and darts, and lances for fighting at a distance; for hand-to-hand fighting, clubs, spears of fire-hardened palmwood, and shields for defense (Hernández de Alba 1948, 312). In wars of annihilation, settlements were commonly besieged, inhabitants slaughtered, homes and fields devastated. As a consequence, fortifications were highly developed (Trimborn 1949, 294). Tall palisades reinforced by deep pitfalls filled with sharp spikes surrounded the settlements (Trimborn 1949, 351). Trails were also snared with heavy log traps. In ultimate emergency hilltop redoubts provided refuge (Hernández de Alba 1948, 318; Trimborn 1949, 340).

Significant ritual surrounded warfare. Combat discipline was impressive; warriors fought heroically in close formation (Trimborn 1949, 339). Like the Jivaroans, Cauca Valley combatants painted their bodies with magical representations and were decorated with a variety of ornaments (Trimborn 1949, 317, 323). Plumed headdresses and sometimes helmets and light armor were worn. Great effort was made to intimidate the adversary with taunts, threats, and challenges. Musical instruments, conch shells, whistles, drums of flayed human skin, and trumpets fashioned from human limb bones were played to perpetuate the torment of the victim and to instill terror in the enemy (Trimborn 1949, 359–62). War trophies were also displayed (Hernández de Alba 1948, 319).

Dramatic sacrifice accompanied war. Men went to battle equipped with special ropes in order to secure captives for sacrifice (Trimborn 1949, 389). It was believed that the spirit and valor of the slain warrior could be appropriated through cannibalism. As part of the victory celebrations, because the heart and blood were considered seats of supernatural energy, first the victim's blood was drunk then the heart and viscera were ingested crude to incorporate this vital substance (Trimborn 1949, 394–97, 415). The remainder of the body was cooked and eaten on the battlefield. At times, the skin of the victim was flayed and stuffed with ashes to serve as a trophy displayed along with skulls and other skeletal remains outside a chief's residence (Hernández de Alba 1948, 319; Trimborn 1949, 347). Oriented toward the rising sun in the east, these trophies of the vanquished foe validated chiefly status and authority and inspired fear and respect in the onlooker (Hernández de Alba 1948, 312; Trimborn 1949, 372, 400).

Other captives were not immediately killed but reserved for sacrifice at a later feastday (Trimborn 1949, 369). Often fort and temple were the same edifice. Oriented eastward, the deity was represented by a wooden sculpture, a head disk symbolizing the rising sun (Trimborn 1949, 418). In the Muisca region north of the Cauca Valley, an origin myth recounts how at the first dawn the god illumined all that had been chaos and sterile, dispatching ravens to the end of the earth. As the birds flew, light emanated from their beaks, revealing all the creations of the omnipotent god (Pérez de Barradas 1951, 372). Cauca temples had zoomorphic jaguar or serpentine motifs (Hernández de Alba 1948, 320). Like the Jivaroan shamans, the priests of these temples in trance communicated with the supernatural and interpreted the will of the deities with regard to war and agriculture (Trimborn 1949, 283). They also performed the central role of sacrificers (Trimborn 1949, 193).

Birds were sacrificed in great numbers. Especially valued were parrots that had first been taught to speak; then after sacrifice their heads were preserved. Among the Muisca (see Kurella's discussion, chap. 8, this volume), young boys acquired in trade from adjoining tropical forest tribes were reared in temples to converse in song with the sun god. To placate the sun in times of drought, a child would be sacrificed before sunrise on a mountain peak. As the first rays touched the crest, the east-facing rocks were anointed with the blood and the body was exposed to be devoured by the sun (Kroeber 1946, 907; Trimborn 1949, 411). In the foundation of a house, posts were driven into the ground through the bodies of young girls to give greater strength to the construction and to ensure the well-being of the residents (Trimborn 1949, 416). In the funerary rites of Cauca Valley dignitaries, numerous sacrificial victims were interred with the deceased (Trimborn 1949, 417). Just prior to battle, human sacrifice was the final preparatory ritual for war. In religious ceremony the victim was suspended, his heart excised and offered to the sun, his body devoured (Trimborn 1949, 424). Such rites engendered an ever-increasing tide of merciless hatred and vengeance.

Maya Ballgame and Political Alliance

In Mesoamerica, early reconstruction of Maya culture as pacific and stable (Thompson 1954) has been contradicted by more recent archaeological findings (Coe 1966, 147; Schele and Miller 1986; Webster 1977). During the first millenium B.C., mounting evidence shows an upward demographic trend with concomitant stress, leading to aggressive population movement in the lowlands. During the Formative era, this militant expansion with resultant feedback in sociopolitical organization contributed to precocious development in the Maya area: emergence of social hierarchies, increase in political centralization, and the establishment of civic-religious centers (Webster 1977, 343–49).

Among Maya polities, there existed a high degree of local and regional competition. As in the Cauca Valley region, conflict stemmed from disputes over material resources and access to distribution networks. Epigraphic and iconographic evidence attest that the Maya were continually involved in alliance formation and warfare. One notable feature of the Maya ceremonial centers is the near-ubiquitous occurrence of the ballcourt. This section addresses this important aspect of Maya religion, the cosmic drama of this ritual contest and the political ends in relation to warfare.

The ballgame, a deeply religious rite, appears to have originated circa 1200 B.C. in the Gulf Coast lowlands, whence it diffused widely over the Mesoamerican region (Brundage 1979, 9). Despite local variation in certain procedures of the ballgame, an underlying unity in the ritual symbolism of the game and the principles for which it was played prevailed over a wide area. The ballcourt and the ballgame constituted one motif within a broad ritual sphere related to sacrifice and the descent of the sun (Gillespie 1991, 317).

In common with Jivaroan and Cauca societies, the Maya placed special emphasis on the sun as the focal element in religion. Cyclic solar descent and reappearance furnished a paradigm of transformation. The green Feathered Serpent was said to carry the sun between its jaws across the sky (Fox 1991, 235). At dusk, in nocturnal passage, the sun plunged to the nadir, there to struggle with the forces of the underworld. At dawn it again emerged heroically to ascend the heavens (Cohodas 1991, 255).

Linked to the solar cycle, the ballcourt represented the surface of the earth with its four cardinal directions (Cohodas 1991, 270). Often the court was partially sunken into ground, its center the axis mundi. At midcourt, a perforated stone ring was positioned on each sidewall to mark the solar dusk and dawn passage, into and out of the underworld. Orientation of the ballcourt was commonly aligned with astronomical movements. As a rite, the ballgame, the symbolic reenactment of the struggle between celestial and infernal forces, functioned to assure the continuation of the sun, moon, and planets and, with their diurnal and annual cycles, the alternating dualities of sky and underworld, solstice and equinox, dry and rainy seasons, night and day, dusk and dawn, death and rebirth. Celestial periodicity was inextricably linked to agricultural fertility (Gillespie 1991, 319). During the summer solstice it was believed the sun mated with the moon to conceive the maize deity, who was the sun reborn (Gillespie 1991, 321). Solar movement was thus a metaphor for the alternation of the seasons, the regeneration of maize and vegetation, and the renewal of life.

The ballgame contest between opposing teams was the crucial equivalent of the sun's descent in the west, its underworld passage, and its ultimate transformation and rebirth in the east. Ritual life-death symbolism of the ballgame was reflected in the art engraved on stelae and reliefs associated with the ballcourt. Death and descent of the sun were depicted in the form of sun vultures, skeletal deities, sacrificial death by decapitation or dismemberment, and *hacha* trophy-head surrogates (Gillespie 1991, 318). In some scenes, the victim was trussed up as a ball and thrown down the staircase before decapitation (Miller and Houston 1987, 53–54). The obverse, rebirth, was portrayed in the *palma* fertility symbols featuring watery scrolls, spurting blood, and decapitated players with vegetation or snakes emerging from their necks. The culminating sacrifice of the loser or enemy captive provided the blood to propel the sun and moon across the heavens (Gillespie 1991, 320).

Symbolically, participation in the ballgame located the player within a sacred, mythical context. It was the enactment of a cosmogonic rite, a mode of communication with the supernatural, a game of divine chance. Although the game was played by mortals, its outcome was controlled by the gods alone. The ballgame marked both disjunction and transition, separating opposing categories yet at the same time maintaining a balanced relationship between categories. But the dynamic cyclicity of celestial bodies, so essential to seasonal fertility, was also directly connected to Maya political structure and to the rhythms of war. For war too furnished resolution of conflict, and the ballgame symbolized segmentation and alliance between sociopolitical units (Gillespie 1991, 343). As "root paradigm," the ballgame referenced not merely existing social structures but also "cultural goals, means, ideas, outlook, currents of thought, and patterns of belief," which varyingly inclined toward alliance or divisiveness (Turner 1974, 64).

Strong parallels existed between warfare and the ballgame. At the risk of injury or death, teams representing two separate communities competed for high stakes. On occasions the ballgame secured ends ordinarily achieved by fighting. It also relieved intercommunity conflict (Stern 1949, 96–97). In a society of limited political hegemony, the ballgame served as an arena in which through complementary opposition, inherently fractious lineage communities could be bound into regional alliance. In segmentary sociopolitical organization, particular lineage groups were ascribed to specific directions (Fox 1991, 233), distinctive headdresses denoting their differential allegiance (Eckholm 1991, 247). The ballcourt provided the political centrality to cement linkage between autonomous land-holding groups, "coalesced into uneasy alliances of varying sizes and levels, generally in response to pressures of conquest or rebellion" (Fox 1991, 217). For opposing groups sharing a common belief system, the ballcourt was the forum in which to vie for social and political status.

Relations between sociopolitical units varied from rivalry at one time to mutual assistance at another. These shifting alliances paralleled the fundamental ballgame myth of cosmic forces at war and the victory of vital forces over those of death. Given the oracular quality of the game, myth eased the inherent tension among divisive lineages. Substitute and symbol for war, the ballgame acted to resolve conflicts. Its ritual setting legitimized decisions and mediated communication across segmental and regional boundaries.

The central precinct of the ballcourt had both sacred and profane components, which accommodated all segments of society. Not solely for the expression of religious doctrine, "in addition the game was a public spectacle drawing the diversity of society under one ideological standard" (Scarborough 1991, 130). The hereditary priesthood's mathematical command of calendrics determined the precise date of the ceremonial gathering. Much excitement surrounded the game as it coincided with many feasts and pilgrimages. As a sport, it was accompanied by spirited wagering by most in attendance, the stakes varying according to the status of the gamblers. Yet ballplaying was integrally related to soldiery and the growth of military institutions; it helped maintain martial readiness, trained individuals to take punishment, and inculcated elite ideology among key cadres. For the elite, it served as a vehicle through which to acquire wealth and territory, to reaffirm power, and to demonstrate publicly the prerogatives of status. In processual terms, the ballgame instilled awareness of solidarity while affirming the authority of the elite (Scarborough 1991, 142). In the accelerating competition and hierarchy among Maya polities, the ritual ballgame provided supernatural legitimation of dominance.

Mexica Religion and Militarism

In this fourth section, consideration is given to the rise of Mexica military might. In viewing briefly the history of early Aztec steppe migrations, it is possible to identify primitive shamanic elements similar to traits discussed earlier with reference to Jivaroan and Cauca Valley societies, and then to trace, in the space of a few centuries, their transformation into mechanisms legitimizing exalted political position—their evolution into the oppressive Mexica state religion.

As Chichimeca, Aztec origins lay in the northern deserts. Their early gods were *mimixcoa*, cloud serpents of the thorny wilderness. Born of the earth mother, these first ancestors were believed to have emerged from the serpentine tunnel of the Sevenfold Cave of Aztlán (Luckert 1976, 111), an island shrine in the middle of a lake. Initially the Aztec were not warlike. But, driven by increasing desiccation of the steppe, they itinerantly encroached and raided southward, forming a loose alliance with the Toltec polity. The origin myth recounts how in the course of these legendary wanderings, as a tree split, their oracle ordained that the Mexica divide from the rest of the tribe. In obeisance, the Mexica broke away from other Aztecs and resumed their peregrination to Coatepec, the Snake Mountain (Brundage 1972, 24–25), where according to legend, the earth mother Coatlicue became impregnated by floating feathers, the soul of a slain hero warrior. On learning of her pregnancy, Coatlicue's children decided to kill her. But the Mexica god Huitzilopochtli emerged from her womb fully grown, armed with a fire serpent with which he slaughtered many of his Centzonhuitznahua Star siblings and dismembered his elder sister Coyolxauhqui Moon, scattering her body parts (Gillespie 1991, 63).

As in Jivaroan, Cauca Valley, and Maya religions, the sun played an important central role. Equated with the spring and summer sun during the ascending period of the ecliptic, Huitzilopochtli, "hummingbird on the left/south," was the Mexica god of war, par excellence. The spectacular iridescent plumage of the male hummingbird shines like the sun, its blue-green hues signifying the renewal of vegetation. The bird also flies in a distinctive manner: up, down, forward, and back. It both reverses its flight and hovers in the sky, as the sun does at each solstice. Territorial, the hummingbird is a fearless fighter, known to engage a hawk with well-aimed thrusts of its sharp beak. A man preparing to fight consumed the heart of the hummingbird to gain agility and quicksightedness (Hunt 1977, 67–68). As the hummingbird-sun soared high in the sky it became the white solar eagle, which led the Mexica southward to their sacred destination (Hunt 1977, 60). The sacred fetish bundle of Huitzilopochtli was carried on the back of the *teomama*, the oracle-shaman who during crises heard the instructions of the sun god in twittering voices (Clendinnen 1991, 22). This shaman represented the most primitive of priesthoods. As the simulacrum of the deity, the teomama was responsible for interpreting divine will, upholding tribal morale, and guiding the path of the wandering group (Brundage 1972, 23–24).

In the wake of Toltec decline, the Mexica pillaged with impunity through the interstices of the crumbling society to enter the Valley of Mexico. Latecomers to the valley, the Mexica secured and fortified the rock of Chapultepec on Lake Texcoco. But in 1349, other lake communities took concerted action to destroy the Mexica (Conrad and Demarest 1984, 22). In the rout, the Mexica god Huitzilopochtli was captured, their leader was executed, and the people were massacred, enslaved, or put to flight. Later as mercenary warriors to Culhuacan, the Mexicas' ferocity in battle soon won them the right to reclaim their god. Civil war in Culhuacan, however, forced the Mexica to flee with the sacred appurtenances of their deity. Huitzilopochtli guided them along the western lakeshore; on shoaling grounds not far from the island of Tlatilulco, they came upon a sacred scene that had been prophesied from the earliest years of their wanderings. Perched upon a cactus that bore the red-fleshed nopal fruit representing the stylized human heart was a great eagle with a serpent in its mouth. Here the awed Mexica built a sod altar to Huitzilopochtli and founded their city of Tenochtitlán (Brundage 1972, 25–34).

In this manner the twin founding of Mexico was accomplished. From these miserable beginnings, the Mexica of Tenochtitlán and Tlatilulco were able to expand their island bases and to forge a military theocracy of un-precedented scope and intensity. During the Tepanec war, with the defeat of Azcapotzalco in 1428, broad mainland territories came under Mexican control. The Triple Alliance of Tenochtitlán, Texcoco, Tlacopan imposed harsh tributary labor on the vanquished in the form of porter service for the armies, heavy construction work in building causeways and water chan-nels to Tenochtitlán, and the erection of engineering works (Conrad and Demarest 1984, 49). Agricultural foodstuffs, cotton, animal hides, feathers, and precious stones were also exacted as tribute. Coercive markets were organized with resultant population influx (Hassig 1985, 85–126).

To administer these diverse elements, Tenochtitlán was divided militar-ily into the sacred number of four, corresponding to the cardinal directions (Brundage 1972, 50). An oligarchic council, again of four, was instituted to serve as the principal advisors to the distinguished warrior elected leader—*tlatoani* (Conrad and Demarest 1984, 36). Each quarter of the city was composed of several parishes or *calpulli*. The symbol bestowing legiti-macy on the calpulli was the *calpulco* temple where the talismanic deity was held, weapons of war were stored, and the *telpochcalli* warrior school was organized. As a correlate of their politico-military dominance, the Mexica grafted their tribal gods onto the ancient religion of Mesoamerica. Their patron Huitzilopochtli was identified with the warrior sun, Tonatiuh, who daily battled his way across the sky, and Tezcatlipoca of the south, the young growing sun of the spring and summer (Conrad and Demarest 1984, 36–38). And Mexica rituals came to embrace the age-old rites of Mesoamerica, the ballgame, sacrifice, death, and regeneration of life.

At the juncture of the four quarters of Tenochtitlán stood the focal pyramid of Mexico (Brundage 1972, 50–51). To commemorate Mexica historical association with Tollan, the pyramid surrounded by a serpent wall represented Coatepec, sacred Snake Mountain, site of Huitzilopochtli's rebirth (Coe 1962, 161). At the summit the dual shrines of Tlaloc, god of the waters, and Huitzilopochtli, god of the sun—oldest and youngest deities of Mesoamerica—divided the annual calendar into the semester of agriculture and the semester of war. The columns of the Huitzilopochtli shrine symbolized the sacred pillars supporting the sky. Congelation of military ambition and might, the temple stood architecturally to elevate Tenochtitlán into the empyrean (Brundage 1979, 146).

This syncretization of the Huitzilopochtli cult with more ancient beliefs had important ramifications for the long-established cults of warfare and human sacrifice in Mesoamerica. In the mid–fifteenth century, an unprecedented freeze and drought had caused desperate famine and widespread emigration throughout the entire valley. These events were attributed to the wrath of the gods. To avert such disasters, Mexica cosmology held that captives must be taken relentlessly in warfare for sacrifice. *Xochiyaoyotl* flower wars were organized in which warriors seeking military glory voluntarily engaged in chivalric contests expressly to provide sacrifical victims for the gods (Brundage 1979, 205–6). The spiritual strength of the sacrificed enemy warriors strengthened the sun and staved off its inevitable destruction by the forces of darkness. To preserve the universe from the daily threat of annihilation, religion thus prescribed it as Mexica duty to pursue a course of endless warfare, human sacrifice, conquest, and exploitation of the Mesoamerican provinces (Brundage 1972, 130–33).

Sacrificial victims were procured from enemy warriors captured in battle, tributary or purchased slaves of subjugated cities, Mexica's own criminals and destitutes, and even infants at the breast. In this latter case, Mexica children born with a double cowlick under a particular day sign were purchased by priests. Over the first few months of the calendar year, they were sacrificed to the rain god Tlaloc, either by drowning in the whirlpools of Lake Texcoco or by burial in mountain caves. Their tears augured rain for the crops (Brundage 1979, 213; Clendinnen 1991, 98–100).

In the mass sacrifices that attended the celebration of victory or the dedication of a monument, the victim, having ascended the pyramid of

Huitzilopochtli, was pinned down on the killing stone. The pulsing heart was excised and offered to the sun, the blood daubed on the mouths of the stone idols, and the pillaged body released to roll down to the base of the pyramid for dismemberment and distribution. This tragic ascent and descent paralleled the diurnal passage of the sun, the victim becoming at the point of sacrifice *cuauhtecatl,* the solar eagle, the sun poised at its zenith (Brundage 1979, 217).

Form of sacrifice varied according to calendar event. In the festival of Tlacaxipehualiztli, gladiatorial combat was organized in which a captive of distinction was tethered by the waist to an elevated stone. Equipped with a feathered club, the captive fought a series of four Mexica champions, in full battle gear. The objective was a prolonged display in the art of weapon handling, during which the victim was slowly cut to shreds (Clendinnen 1991, 94–95). At the feast of Xipe Totec, the ancient Mesoamerica god of fertility, springtime sun, flowers, and young corn, a man hung on a frame of poles was shot to death with arrows. In sexual insinuation, the fructifying blood was allowed to drip down upon a round stone representing the earth (Brundage 1979, 74). The flayed skin of the victim, symbol of the regrowth of vegetation, was then worn by the priest in a sacred dance. Inside out, the skin signified rejuvenation and resembled the serpent shedding, husking of the maize ear, even the foreskin and human penis (Luckert 1976, 57, 133).

In the spring ceremony of Toxcatl, which celebrated the appearance of the first shoots of maize, a young male captive was selected for his beauty and bearing to impersonate Tezcatlipoca, fickle god of destiny. For a year the impersonator was adorned and feted as he roamed the streets of the town playing flutes. Shortly before his death, Tezcatlipoca, dressed as the seasoned warrior, danced with his four wives, impersonators of the spring goddesses. Finally, breaking his flutes on the steps of the temple, he ascended to his ceremonial death. Following the sacrifice, in ritual rebirth, the flutes of the newly chosen Tezcatlipoca sounded through the streets (Clendinnen 1991, 105).

Each year, in sacred religious context, some 15,000 to 20,000 persons were sacrificed in the central and neighborhood temples of Tenochtitlán (Brundage 1979, 215; Conrad and Demarest 1984, 47). The primary executioners, the priests received long preparation for their duties. Sacerdotal training emphasized toughness and composure. Extensive discipline in self-mortification entailed fasting; purificatory ordeals of endurance to solicit rain for agriculture; fertility rites involving laceration of the tongue and penis with maguey spines; and, in the ancient shamanic tradition as protector of the community, solitary vigils of nocturnal patrol around the perimeter of the city. In major campaigns, the warrior squads of each city, grouped according to calpulli, were led to battle by priests, each carrying the image of his god on his back. In confronting the enemy, it was priests who sounded the attack with a conch trumpet and who on the battlefield sacrificed the first captives. And it was they who, in the spectacle of public ceremonial, with magisterial composure ascended pyramids, subdued victims, and enacted mass sacrifice (Clendinnen 1991, 128–31).

But the populace too participated in this drama of death. As part of the religious observances, the swathed thighbones of "god captives" were enshrined in household compounds. Individuals were routinely recruited to obligatory service in the central and local temple precincts. If duties were onerous they were also celebratory. When a warrior of the calpulli offered his captive in triumphant festival, the neighborhood people were implicated in the care and preparation of the victim; the rounds of feasting, dancing, and flower offerings; the delivery to the place of death; and finally in the ritual consumption of the corpse (Clendinnen 1991, 2, 43).

The central character in the religious theater of Huitzilopochtli, however, was the warrior. The birth of the Mexica boy was welcomed by war cries. Hailed as eagle, ocelot, troupial, the child was held aloft in dedication to the sun, his umbilical cord entrusted to a seasoned warrior to be buried on the battlefield. At the naming ceremony, the infant's hand was closed around a tiny bow, arrow, and shield, signaling his warrior destiny. Periodically during childhood, his arms, chest, and stomach were incised to symbolize the boy's future fortitude in combat (Clendinnen 1991, 112, 153). At the age of ten a boy began his warrior training in the telpochcalli. First in training then in combat, physical toughness was developed and tested. Under strict discipline, with severe hazings the inevitable penalty for transgression, skills of combat and weapon handling were taught. Initiation in battle followed. The objective was to fell the opponent with a crippling sword-strike to the lower leg, so that he could be wrestled to the ground and subdued. Assistants were on hand to bind the captive. As the tally of captives taken in battle grew, honors, elaboration in dress, privileges, select ranking, and insignia of valor accrued to the successful warrior. The most accomplished warriors were eligible to join the distinguished orders of the eagle and jaguar knights. And the most exalted warrior, the commander in chief, assumed the title *tlaccatecatl,* defender of the Temple of Huitzilopochtli (Brundage 1972, 115).

Discussion

By tracing the relationship of religion to war from tribal to state levels, it is possible to discern certain themes, polysemous yet persistent across time and space, in the growing complexity of sociopolitical organization. The most salient theme is that of the sun, energizing principle linked to war and the hunt, symbol of virility, power, and domination. Associated with the sun are celestial and aerial entities: planets and stars, the majestic jaguar, the bird emissaries—eagle, quetzal, condor, raven, troupial, parrot, hummingbird of the south—the rubber ball, the skull. For the Amerindian, identity and spiritual force are concentrated in the head, hence the vivid plumed crown of the warrior, the fantastic Mexica helmets emulating the valiant animal avatars of the sun god. Conversely, for the vanquished, there exist the Jivaroan tsantsa, the decapitated enemy heads adorning the Cauca Valley temple, and in Mesoamerica the Maya shrunken-head ornaments emblematic of chiefly status (Tompkins 1990, 46) and the sinister Mexica *tzompantli* rack of skulls (Conrad and Demarest 1984, 38). Solar themes are also evident in the jaguar predawn roar of the Jivaroan warrior, daring the enemy lurking in the forest to attack; in the Maya jaguar-claw obsidian knife used to mangle the corpse of the sacrificial victim (Robicsek and Hales 1990, 73); and in the Mexica elite knights of Tlacaxipehualiztli gladiatorial combat, two eagles and two jaguars, who spar with the prestigious captive. In the creation myth, eagle and jaguar hurled themselves into the sacrificial flames to emerge from the immolation as celestial bodies. Day raptor, the eagle was totally consumed by the fire and became the sun. Night predator, the jaguar was singed only in spots and became the moon (Brundage 1972, 110).

Counterposed to the solar sphere lie the serpentine waters and underworld, linked with fertility, birth, and resurgence of life. The snake is represented in multivariant forms: the anaconda tutelary spirit of the Amazon shaman; the snakes surging from the neck of the decapitated Maya ballplayer; the sevenfold snake cave of Aztec emergence; the lakes and caves of Mexica infant sacrifice to Tlaloc, god of fertilizing rain; and Coatepec, serpent mountain, sacred locality of the birth of Huitzilopochtli, point of emergence of the day sun, "threshold between natural and supernatural domains" (Gillespie 1989, 86–87). At the meeting place of upper and lower worlds where all elements converge, sacred ritual is enacted: at the waterfall in the arutam quest, on the eastward-facing rocks of the Colombian mountain peak, on the Maya ballcourt, and on the central pyramid of Tenochtitlán, dual shrine of solar deity Huitzilopochtli and Tlaloc, god of the waters.

But whereas in battle the protagonist is the eagle or jaguar warrior, in ritual the shaman-priest is officiant. Among the Jivaroans, when sickness or fatality strikes, the shaman through divinatory ritual identifies the bewitching sorcerer. By assigning culpability for death and disease to the alien sorcerer, the shaman draws de jure distinction between in-group and out-group. Most important, the war party he emboldens represents a sodality that extends beyond immediate kinship and the local community. In accordance with the shamanic denunciation, this broader sodality becomes morally obligated to undertake revenge killing. Similarly, prior to battle, Cauca Valley priestly oracle and human sacrifice are the preparatory rites that commit the assembly of warriors to heroic action and that launch concerted attack against the enemy. In the case of the Maya, astronomical knowledge empowers the hereditary priesthood to set the calendric rhythms of war and agriculture throughout the year. Within the cosmic context of diurnal victory of vital forces over death, the ceremonial ball-game maintains men in military readiness, legitimizes decisions among fractious lineages, and mediates communication and alliance across segmental and regional boundaries.

Clearly religion plays a critical role, by providing the pan-group identity, the operational framework, and moral justification for the acts of war. Rather than declining with material advance, religious faith intensifies, sanctifying new concepts of sociopolitical order. In the particular case of the Mexica rise to power in Mesoamerica, the series of changes by which shamanic practice became transformed into state religion occurred within the time frame of a scant 200 years. Originally in the northern wilderness the Aztec were not warlike. At the split tree of legend, the Mexica diverged from this existence. In the epoch of Toltec dissolution, Huitzilopochtli was reborn sun god at Coatepec amid sibling hostility and bloody slaughter. The mythical break with other Aztecs and the violent contest between cosmic siblings, as *model of* (Geertz 1972, 169), reflect the mounting hostility in society and are omens of the impending political struggle in the Valley of Mexico, "crowded with related but consciously separate and highly competitive peoples" (Clendinnen 1991, 197). The metaphor of conflict is again apparent in the Mexica eagle perched upon the cactus, surrounded by fallen adversaries—the scattered bones and feathers of many birds, in its beak the serpent alternatively interpreted as hieroglyph for war (Clendinnen 1991, 23), and, in the sky above, shield and arrows, symbols of conquest (Durán 1971).

Historically, the tale of Huitzilopochtli's rebirth likely also masks the transfiguration of a human chieftain into a deity (Clendinnen 1991, 22; Conrad and Demarest 1984, 27). After the fall of Tollan, the most powerful Chichimec leader was named Xolotl, Evening Star (Gillespie 1989, 155). In tribal society it was previously seen that the outstanding kakáram war leader could assume the trappings of divinity. The religious shift from mimixcoa (cloud serpents) to Huitzilopochtli therefore possibly reflects a messianic revitalization (Wallace 1972) that propelled the barbarian Mexica into central Mexico during a period of cultural disintegration. At all events, with rising Mexica dominance in the area, their patron Huitzilopochtli came to usurp divine images of older solar deities belonging to other ethnic groups.

The Jivaroan shaman's accusation of malign sorcery, delivered in sacred trance, unites contentious tribesmen and bestows identity upon the raiding party, strengthening warrior resolve to win health and security for their families. In the case of chiefdoms, divinity similarly embodies the identity of the entire polity. With the increasing societal complexity and diverse ethnicity of Tenochtitlán, this cohesion is necessarily accomplished by ritual at multiple levels. At the highest level, members of the Triple Alliance were bound in amphictyony through the exchange of gods and cult practices (Brundage 1972, 120). In Tenochtitlán the central pyramid united the four quadrants with their calpulli, each organized around its parish temple, mascot deity, and warrior school. Just as during the northern exodus, the shaman-teomama guided the Mexica in times of adversity, so from each calpulli, troops were led into battle by the parish priest-teomama. At inauguration the Mexica monarch was proclaimed *tlatoani*—great speaker, he who gives orders—a parallel perhaps to the oratorical prowess and military-political leadership of the Jivaroan kakáram. In ceremony he also assumed the sacred duties of the ancestral teomama, carrier of Huitzilopochtli, thus combining both military and religious functions.

For identity to exist, boundaries must be declared. At the tribal boundary anthropophagous monsters prey on people; tribesmen take head trophies and dismember victims of other tribes. Chiefdoms torture and cannibalize the enemy. Mexica boundaries were defined by its sacrificial victims, captives from subjugated cities or Mexica's own criminals and deviants. For the tributary chief, whose attendance is compulsory, the spectacle of mass sacrifice served as deterrent to rebellion (Conrad and Demarest 1984, 59). The central performances that awed the nobles and commoners alike were orchestrated by priests intent upon displaying their dread supernatural powers (Clendinnen 1991, 44). The sacrificial drama inspired adherence to established norms. The endless public bloodshed, while providing momentary exhilaration, reconciled—perhaps even inured—the populace to the inevitability of their own suffering, either in the form of personal demise or through loss of beloved family members. Doubtless the frequent bloody spectacle steeled men for the gore of battle. No doubt too, the obligatory was converted into the desirable (Turner 1969, 30) as the prospect, after heroic death, of an honored place in the glorious retinue of the sun god (Brundage 1979, 48) lured warriors to their fate on the battlefield or the sacrificial altar. Women's fertility, the constant production of fresh warriors, was venerated in the *mociuaquetzque* funerary rites for mothers martyred in childbirth; as goddesses they too were believed to ascend the heavens as companions to the warrior sun in its daily march across the sky (Conrad and Demarest 1984, 171–72). In this pageant of war, ritual and the practicality of military strategy were linked. The political contribution of the *pochteca,* hereditary traders and shrewd spies of distant territories, was also honored by the sumptuary extravagance of the Panquetzaliztli merchants' feast (Clendinnen 1991, 101, 138).

In all the cultures considered here, as *model of,* the drama of cyclic solar transformation reflects the alternations, oppositions, and conflicts of the natural and social worlds, ecological and demographic pressures. Also, embedded in the collective history of a culture is the parallel multivocality of myth and ritual which, as *model for,* projects societal values and prescribes participatory roles appropriate to those exigencies. In the Jivaroan world-renewal festival, girls' fertility horticultural rites are the accompaniment of the youths' ritual hazing. In myth, by vanquishing the forces of the underworld, the sun returns each spring to regenerate life and vegetation. So on the human plane in the triumph of military victory, the defeat, degradation, and death of the alien foe feed the vitality, prosperity, and efflorescence of warrior society.

Part of a broad population movement from the less favored northern lands, the Mexica, as nomadic hunters entering the Valley of Mexico, encountered a circumscribed region of diverse habitats with concentrated resources in the rich lacustrine bottomlands (Carneiro 1992, 187; Conrad and Demarest 1984, 13). In the fierce competition among polities of the valley, they were forced to fight for their very existence. As mercenaries they learned from their masters the techniques of conquest (Conrad and Demarest 1984, 23). For the fledgling island polity of Tenochtitlán, the motives for military ascendancy were prestige, the acquisition of agricultural land, and the economic advantage of tribute (Hassig 1985, 103). The sacred campaigns of Huitzilopochtli were synchronized with these economic and political needs (Conrad and Demarest 1984, 49). With battle success the Mexica exacted cruel tribute from subjugated peoples and, in alliance with Texcoco and Tlacopan, dominated a hegemony of 38 tributary provinces, stretching from one ocean to the other.

Contrary to the view that militarism is secular in character, it is clear that religion played a prominent and indispensable role in Mexica expansion. In the language of myth and ritual, authority of the ruler was validated with sacred pomp, alliances were forged with puissant neighbors, internal rivalries among knightly orders were articulated, priestly control permeated daily activities, and members of each calpulli around the neighborhood deity and under one god, Huitzilopochtli, fought for military glory. In its sanguinary view of the universe, Mexica religion—northern messianism interwoven with the rich cosmogony of ancient Mesoamerica—escalated to an unprecedented level the pace and scale of human killing.

Yet the richly elaborated symbols of Mexica religion were in large part the same symbols accreted over the millennia in the cultural experience of earlier, simpler societies. The sun, eagle, jaguar, and snake were part of the primitive repertory of tribes and chiefdoms, where shaman and warrior, ritual and war went hand in hand. As we have seen, in the tsantsa ritual the Jivaroan warrior returning from an assassination raid pauses to feed the skull of his slain victim to the anaconda, patron of shamans. Similar juxtaposition of solar and serpentine symbols was evidenced in Maya myth, in which daily the sun is carried across the sky by the snake monster, alternatively represented as a human head emerging from the jaws of the feathered serpent (Smith 1982, 239–40). The same motifs were also apparent in the central pyramid of Tenochtitlán, itself the juncture of snake mountain and sky, dual shrine of Tlaloc, ancient god of the underworld and fertilizing waters, and Huitzilopochtli, solar god of war. High priests of this shrine embodied the duality of serpentine shaman and solar warrior, thereby representing the close alignment of religion and military might. Articulated in ancient myth and rite, across cultures at varying levels of sociopolitical complexity, religion played a vital and integral role in the promotion of militarism and increasing hierarchization in society.

Notes

1. I am indebted to the Comisión Fulbright del Ecuador, the Organization of American States, Sigma Xi Research Society of North America, and the Frieda Butler Foundation of the University of New Mexico, whose financial support made possible research in the Jivaroan area. In Ecuador my research was sponsored by the Instituto Nacional de Antropología e Historia and the Instituto Nacional de Patrimonio Cultural del Ecuador. Earlier drafts of this chapter were presented at the South American Indian Caucus at Bennington College, Vermont, and at the seminar of Ecological Systems and Cultural Evolution at Columbia University, New York.

References

Brundage, B. Cartwright
1972   *A Rain of Darts: The Mexica Aztecs.* Austin: University of Texas Press.
1979   *The Fifth Sun: Aztec Gods, Aztec World.* Austin: University of Texas Press.
Carneiro, Robert L.
1970   A theory of the origin of the state. *Science* 169:733–38.
1990   Chiefdom-level warfare as exemplified in Fiji and the Cauca Valley. In *The Anthropology of War,* edited by J. Haas, 190–211. School of American Research. Cambridge: Cambridge University Press.
1992   Point counterpoint: Ecology and ideology in the development of New World civilizations. In *Ideology and Pre-Columbian Civilizations,* edited by A. A. Demarest and G. W. Conrad, 175–203. Santa Fe: School of American Research Press.
Clendinnen, Inga
1991   *Aztecs: An Interpretation.* Cambridge: Cambridge University Press.
Coe, Michael D.
1962   *Mexico.* New York: Praeger.
1966   *The Maya.* New York: Praeger.
Cohodas, Marvin
1991   Ballgame imagery of the Maya lowlands: History and iconography. In *The Mesoamerican Ballgame,* edited by V. L. Scarborough and D. R. Wilcox, 251–88. Tucson: University of Arizona Press.
Conrad, Geoffrey W., and Arthur A. Demarest
1984   *Religion and Empire: The Dynamics of Aztec and Expansionism.* Cambridge: Cambridge University Press.
Descola, Philippe
1992   Societies of nature and the nature of society. In *Conceptualizing Society,* edited by A. Kuper, 107–26. London: Routledge.
Durán, Diego
1971   *Book of the Gods and Rites and the Ancient Calendar.* Translated and edited by Fernando Horcasitas and Doris Heyden. Norman: University of Oklahoma Press.

Eckholm, Susanna M.

1991   Ceramic figurines and the Mesoamerican ballgame. In *The Mesoamerican Ballgame*, edited by V. L. Scarborough and D. R. Wilcox, 241–49. Tucson: University of Arizona Press.

Flannery, Kent V.

1972   The origins of the village as settlement type in Mesoamerica and the Near East: A comparative study. In *Man, Settlement, and Urbanism*, edited by P. J. Ucko, R. Tringham, and G. W. Dimbleby, 23–53. London: Gerald Duckworth.

Fox, John W.

1991   The lords of light versus the lords of dark: The Postclassic highland Maya ballgame. In *The Mesoamerican Ballgame*, edited by V. L. Scarborough and D. R. Wilcox, 213–38. Tucson: University of Arizona Press.

Geertz, Clifford

1972   Religion as a cultural system. In *Reader in Comparative Religion: An Anthropological Approach*, edited by W. A. Lessa and E. Z. Vogt, 167–78. New York: Harper & Row.

Gillespie, Susan D.

1989   *The Aztec Kings: The Construction of Rulership in Mexican History.* Tucson: University of Arizona Press.

1991   Ballgames and boundaries. In *The Mesoamerican Ballgame*, edited by V. L. Scarborough and D. R. Wilcox, 317–45. Tucson: University of Arizona Press.

Harner, Michael J.

1972   *The Jívaro: People of the Sacred Waterfalls.* Garden City, N.Y.: Anchor Press–Doubleday.

Hassig, Ross

1985   *Trade, Tribute, and Transportation.* Norman: University of Oklahoma Press.

Hendricks, Janet W.

1993   *To Drink of Death.* Tucson: University of Arizona Press.

Hernández de Alba, Gregorio

1948   Sub-Andean tribes of the Cauca Valley. In *Handbook of South American Indians*, vol. 4, edited by J. H. Steward, 297–327. Bureau of American Ethnology Bulletin 143. Washington, D.C.: Smithsonian Institution.

Hunt, Eva

1977   *The Transformation of the Hummingbird: Cultural Roots of a Zinacantecan Mythical Poem.* Ithaca: Cornell University Press.

Kelekna, Pita

1981   Sex Asymmetry in Jivaroan Achuara Society: A Cultural Mechanism Promoting Belligerence. Ph.D. dissertation, University of New Mexico. Ann Arbor: University Microfilms.

1994   Farming, feuding, and female status: The Achuar case. In *Amazonian Indians from Prehistory to the Present*, edited by A. Roosevelt, 225–48. Tucson: University of Arizona Press.

Kroeber, Alfred L.

1946 The Chibcha. In *Handbook of South American Indians,* vol. 2, edited by J. H. Steward, 887–909. Bureau of American Ethnology Bulletin 143. Washington, D.C.: Smithsonian Institution.

Luckert, Karl V.

1976 *Olmec Religion: A Key to Middle America and Beyond.* Norman: University of Oklahoma Press.

Miller, Mary E., and Stephen D. Houston

1987 The Classic Maya ballgame and its architectural setting: A study in the relations between text and image. *Res* 14 (Autumn):47–66.

Pellizzaro, Siro

1980 *Tsantsa: Celebración de la Cabeza Cortada.* Sucúa: Mundo Shuar.

Pérez de Barradas, José

1951 *Pueblos Indígenas de la Gran Colombia 2: Los Muiscas Antes de la Conquista.* Madrid: Consejo Superior de Investigaciones Científicas.

Peterson, Frederick A.

1962 *Ancient Mexico: An Introduction to Pre-Hispanic Cultures.* New York: Capricorn Books.

Robiscek, Francis, and Donald M. Hales

1984 Maya heart sacrifice. In *Ritual Human Sacrifice in Mesoamerica,* edited by E. H. Boone, 49–90. Washington, D.C.: Dumbarton Oaks Research Library and Collection.

Scarborough, Vernon L.

1991 Courting in the southern Maya lowlands: A study in pre-Hispanic ballgame architecture. In *The Mesoamerican Ballgame,* edited by V. L. Scarborough and D. R. Wilcox, 129–144. Tucson: University of Arizona Press.

Schele, Linda

1984 Human sacrifice among the Classic Maya. In *Ritual Human Sacrifice in Mesoamerica,* edited by E. H. Boone, 7–48. Washington, D.C.: Dumbarton Oaks Research Library and Collection.

Schele, Linda, and Mary E. Miller

1986 *The Blood of Kings: Dynasty and Ritual in Maya Art.* New York: Fort Worth and Braziller.

Smith, A. Ledyard

1982 *Excavations at Seibal, Department of Petén, Guatemala: Major Architecture and Caches.* Memoirs of the Peabody Museum of American Archaeology and Ethnology 15, no. 1. Cambridge, Mass.: Harvard University.

Stern, Theodore

1949 *The Rubber Ballgame of the Americas.* Monographs of the American Ethnological Society, no. 17. New York: J. J. Augustin.

Steward, Julian H., and Louis C. Faron

1959 *Native Peoples of South America.* New York: McGraw-Hill.

Taylor, Anne-Christine

1985   L'art de la réduction: La guerre et les mécanismes de la différenciation tribale dans la culture Jivaro. *Journal de la Société des Américanistes* 71:159–73.

Thompson, J. Eric S.

1954   *The Rise and Fall of Maya Civilization.* Norman: University of Oklahoma Press.

Tompkins, Ptolemy

1990   *This Tree Grows Out of Hell: Mesoamerica and the Search for the Magical Body.* San Francisco: Harper.

Trimborn, Hermann

1949   *Señorío y Barbarie en el Valle del Cauca.* Translated from the German by José María Gimeno Capella. Madrid: Consejo Superior de Investigaciones Científicas, Instituto Gonzalo Fernández de Oviedo.

Turner, Victor W.

1967   Symbols in Ndembu ritual. In *The Forest of Symbols: Aspects of Ndembu Ritual,* 19–47. Ithaca: Cornell University Press.

1969   *The Ritual Process: Structure and Anti-Structure.* Chicago: Aldine.

1974   *Dramas, Fields and Metaphors: Symbolic Action in Human Society.* Ithaca: Cornell University Press.

Wallace, Anthony F. C.

1972   Revitalization movements. In *Reader in Comparative Religion: An Anthropological Approach,* edited by W. A. Lessa and E. Z. Vogt, 503–15. New York: Harper & Row.

Webster, David L.

1976   On theocracies. *American Anthropologist* 78:812–28.

1977   Warfare and the evolution of Maya civilization. In *The Origins of Maya Civilization,* edited by R. E. W. Adams, 335–71. School of American Research Book. Albuquerque: University of New Mexico Press.

CHAPTER 8

The Muisca

Chiefdoms in Transition

Doris Kurella

The Colombian part of the north Andean region, seen as part of a culture area designated the Intermediate Area, has received little attention over the last few decades compared to the central Andes or Mesoamerica.[1] At the beginning of the 1980s, a new and strong interest in the Andean part of Colombia evolved and many important archaeological projects as well as ethnohistorical studies led to new results, permitting a far better understanding of this region than existed ten years ago.[2]

At the time of the Spanish Conquest, many sociopolitical groups with different ethnic origins lived within this territory (fig. 8.1). Most of these may be characterized as chiefdoms (Carneiro 1990, 1991a, 1991b; Drennan 1991).[3] Occupying different ecological zones, these chiefdoms differed in size and complexity, and formed a "network of interacting societies" (Spencer 1991, 141) in which groups of various sizes were connected to each other through trade (fig. 8.2), conflict, political alliances, and kinship (Bischof 1971; Carneiro 1990; Kurella 1993; Langebaek Rueda 1991; Trimborn 1948, 1949).

The aim in this chapter is to provide a detailed picture of one of the most important groups that lived within this region: the Muisca chiefdoms as they existed at the time of the Spanish Conquest.[4] The outlines of the political and economic organization of the Muisca, their interaction with surrounding groups, and the consequences of war for the structure of their society are discussed.

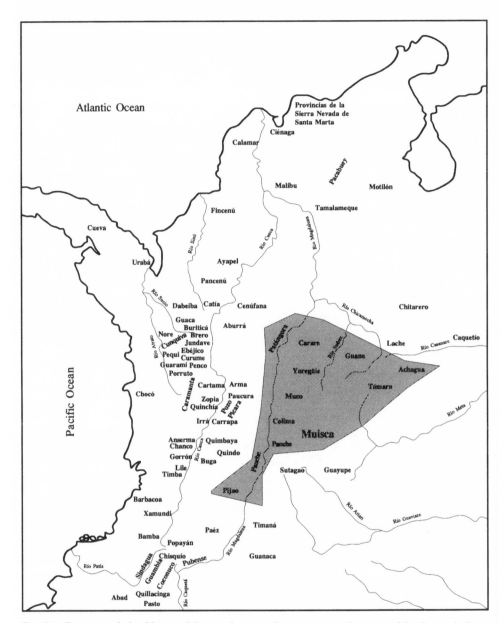

Fig. 8.1. Groups and chiefdoms of the northern Andean region at the time of the Spanish Conquest.

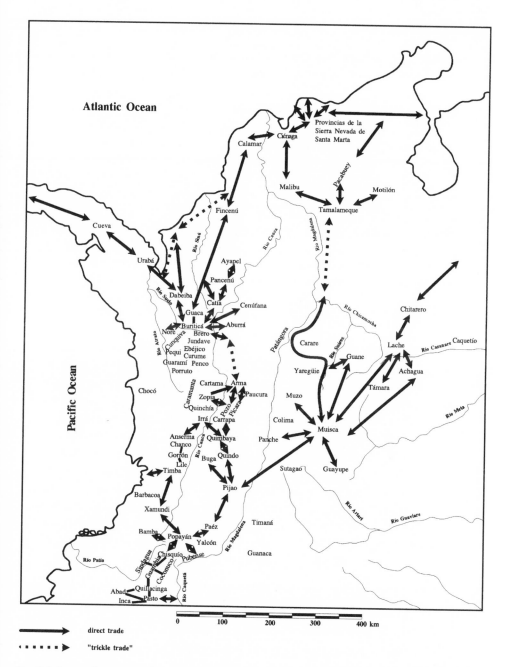

Atlantic Ocean

Pacific Ocean

Cueva

Urabá

Río Sinú

Río Cauca

Río Atrato

Río Sucio

Calamar

Ciénaga

Provincias de la
Sierra Nevada de
Santa Marta

Malibu

Fincenú

Ayapel

Pancenú

Dabeiba

Guaca

Catía

Buriticá

Nore

Cenúfana

Aburrá

Brero

Cunquiva

Jundave

Pequi

Ebéjico

Curume

Guaramí

Penco

Porruto

Chocó

Cartama

Arma

Zopia

Paucura

Quinchía

Carrapa

Irrá

Anserma

Chanco

Quimbaya

Gorrón

Buga

Lile

Quindío

Timba

Barbacoa

Xamundi

Bamba

Popayán

Paéz

Yalcón

Sindagua

Chisquío

Guachicono

Colomuco

Pubense

Abad

Quillacinga

Inca

Pasto

Río Patía

Río Caquetá

Guanaca

Timaná

Río Magdalena

Río Cauca

Caramanta

Pozo

Picara

Muzo

Colima

Panche

Sutagao

Pijao

Muisca

Guayupe

Río Ariari

Río Guaviare

Río Meta

Patángora

Río Magdalena

Carare

Río Suárez

Yaregüie

Guane

Río Chicamocha

Lache

Río Casanare

Caquetío

Achagua

Támara

Chitarero

Tamalameque

Pacabuey

Motilón

0   100   200   300   400 km

→ direct trade

⋯▸ "trickle trade"

Fig. 8.2. Long-distance trade relations of the groups and chiefdoms at the time of the Spanish Conquest.

The Environment

Jiménez de Quesada was the first European to encounter the Muisca, in 1536.[5] They formed a part of the Chibchan language group and, at that time, inhabited the Altiplano Cundiboyacense, a high plateau in the Eastern Cordillera with altitudes ranging between 1,800 and 2,800 meters above sea level.[6] The size of the population can only be estimated. One million people, Kroeber's estimate (1946, 892), now seems too high. Results from some recent ethnohistorical projects, however, suggest numbers around 500,000 (Reichel-Dolmatoff 1982, 97). Their settlement area, which can be relatively well reconstructed on the basis of the chroniclers' reports, spread out over about 22,000 square kilometers. It centered on the Sabana de Bogotá, the largest plateau in the Altiplano, and lay mainly at altitudes ranging from 2,400 to 2,800 meters above sea level. Favorable conditions included a moderate climate and yearly average temperatures of around 14°C in this part of the *tierra fría* inhabited by the Muisca (Guhl 1968, 196).[7] There are no extreme temperature changes on the Altiplano Cundiboya-cense as, for example, in the central Andes.

Only some groups living in the north, northwest—that is, in Vélez (fig. 8.3)—and in certain marginal zones of Muisca territory had access to warmer stretches of *tierra templada* or *tierra caliente* within their territories. These lands provided additional possibilities for agricultural production (Aguado 1956, 2:238). The natural resources of the former Muisca territory, such as the emerald mines of Somondoco and the salt wells of Tausa, Zipaquirá, and Nemocón, constituted inexhaustible resources for the production of goods that played an important role in trade within the Muisca territory as well as in trade relations with other groups outside this area.

The Muisca lived on the Altiplano in a situation that was socially circumscribed (Carneiro 1970, 737; 1991b, 22). They were surrounded on all sides by other groups of different ethnic origins. The Muisca were also circumscribed in an environmental sense (Carneiro 1970, 734; 1991b, 22); their settlement areas were limited to regions within the tierra fría.

Political Structure and Social Organization

Supralocal Organization

The ethnically and economically integrated network of politically independent Muisca units has been wrongly described as a "confederation of chiefdoms" by Reichel-Dolmatoff (1982, 90). It consisted mainly of many independent chiefdoms, which were mostly separated from one another by

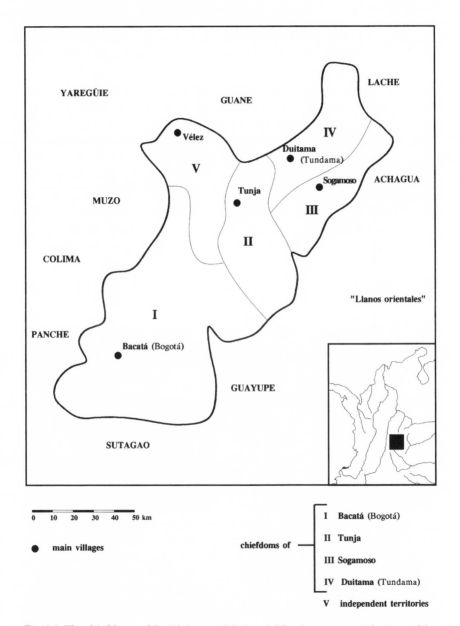

Fig. 8.3. The chiefdoms of the Muisca and their neighboring groups at the time of the Spanish Conquest.

geographic barriers. Small mountain ranges, which subdivide the high altitude plateau into many wide and easily accessible valleys, were the most typical of such natural frontiers between groups. The inhabitants of one valley, living in scattered farmsteads near their fields (Broadbent 1964a, 21; 1968, 141), have been perceived as one social unit: "cada valle es su poblazón por si" (Jiménez de Quesada 1972, 287). They shared the same tribal name based on the name of the most powerful local chief (Aguado 1956, 1:263; Fernández de Oviedo 1959, 3:125; Guillén Chaparro [1583] 1975, 8:162). Larger villages outside of these valleys were separate units with their own local chiefs (Aguado 1956, 1:259). The people in such a chiefdom would have spoken the same dialect and practiced a similar religion (Aguado 1956, 1:163, 264). Large communities are known to have existed in the south and north. These were the centers of the chiefdoms of Tunja and Bogotá (or Bacatá) and contained the palaces of the chiefs holding the titles *zipa* and *zaque* respectively. All Muisca buildings were wooden constructions. The houses of the chiefs were often enclosed by palisades and thus were clearly separated from the houses of the rest of the population (Jiménez de Quesada 1972, 295).

By the time of the Spanish Conquest, large parts of the Muisca lands had been split between two centers of power held by the aforementioned zipa of Bogotá and the zaque of Tunja. This special status of Tunja and Bogotá, which was achieved only a few generations before the Spanish Conquest (Broadbent 1981, 261), was due to the submission of other chiefdoms through warfare (Aguado 1956, 1:259). The chiefs of the vanquished groups were permitted to stay in power but had to pay tribute to the conqueror (AGI Patr.R.27, R.14/f.3r.). Not all the other chiefdoms, however, capitulated. Some chiefs in marginal Muisca areas remained politically autonomous to a large extent until the Spanish Conquest. Their territories included the region of Vélez (Fernández de Piedrahita 1973, 1:223) in the northwest and lands of the chiefs of Duitama (or Tundama) and Sogamoso (fig. 8.3). They were in no sense part of the spheres of influence of the zipa or the zaque. None of the four principal *caciques* paid tribute to any of the others, nor were they in any way subservient (Kurella 1993, 109; Langebaek Rueda 1987, 35; Tovar Pinzón 1980). The process of the conquest of smaller chiefdoms by stronger ones, combined with the intention of both zipa and zaque to consolidate their spheres of influence, not only resulted in continuous warfare between zipa and zaque but also in attempts by conquered chiefs to regain their autonomy (Aguado 1956, 1:259; Simón 1981, 3:425, 4:195).

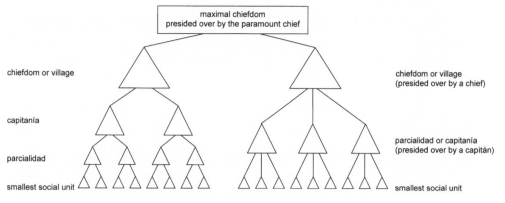

Fig. 8.4. Levels of social organization in Muisca society.

Local-Level Organization

The smallest territorial and social unit was probably a group related by kinship ties, people who lived in a single dwelling and labored together in the same fields (Visita [1560], 75). Whether these represented nuclear families, extended families, lineages, or larger groups is unclear (Broadbent 1964a; Villamarín and Villamarín 1975). Several of these small groups formed *partes* or *parcialidades*.[8] A number of small parcialidades could constitute a *capitanía*, headed by a *capitán*. However, if a parcialidad was of sufficient size it could be considered by the Spaniards to have the status of a capitanía (Kurella 1993, 96; Langebaek Rueda 1987, 27). This has created some confusion in the literature. A few large parcialidades or capitanías together constituted a *cacicazgo* or chiefdom (ANC Vis.Boy.17/f.262v.), presided over by a local chief. Several villages were organized together with the chiefdoms in the valleys into a "maximal chiefdom"[9] (Carneiro 1981, 47) headed by the paramount chief (figure 8.4). All these positions were inherited by the leader's oldest sister's son (ANC Vis.Boy.3/f.479v; Castellanos 1955, 4:143; Tovar Pinzón 1980, 71). Thus, the Muisca practiced a sort of matrilineal inheritance, which is characteristic of tribes belonging to the Chibchan language family.

The Hierarchy among the Chiefly Class

One of the functions of the capitanes was to represent their parcialidad or capitanía before the cacique. In addition, they oversaw the paying of tribute to the chief (ANC Vis.Boy.17/f.546r.). As payment for their work they would receive a painted cotton blanket. The capitanes themselves were also required to pay tribute and they played a role as leaders in military matters as well, but their status was below that of a chief (ANC Vis.Boy.17/ f.446v.). Among the Muisca, the chiefs were the most powerful and privileged persons even if there was a strict hierarchical ranking among them. They held a superior position vis-à-vis the rest of the population (Anónimo 1943, 475; Peebles and Kus 1977, 422) and the right to practice polygamy (Guillén Chaparro [1583] 1975, 8:162). Chiefs were entitled to receive tribute from their subjects in the form of labor—for working the fields of the chiefs and constructing their houses (ANC Vis.Sant.6/f.714r.)—and military conscription as well as gold, emeralds, and foodstuffs (ANC Vis.Boy.17/f.545r.; Tovar Pinzón 1980, 15, 64). The wearing of gold ornaments and painted cotton blankets (AGI Patr.R.27, R.34/f.1r.) and the consumption of deer meat were restricted to the chiefly class (fig. 8.5). Other members of society had to ask permission to bypass any of these rules (Guillén Chaparro [1583] 1975, 8:162; Visita [1560], 75).

According to Castellanos (1955, 4:150–51), jurisprudence was the privilege of this upper class; every criminal transgression had a specific punishment (Jiménez de Quesada 1972, 296; Tovar Pinzón 1980, 178). Where there was no legitimate successor to the village cacique, the paramount chief had the right to take over his lands and give them away as a reward to warriors or other persons (Simón 1981, 3:391).

There was also a religious aspect to the role of the chief, which further enhanced his status. The cacique and the village priest were often, as in Sogamoso and Duitama, one and the same. The Muisca also had other kinds of priests, the *xeques* (Castellanos 1955, 4:158) or *chuques* (Langebaek Rueda 1990, 88). They cared for the temples, made offerings to the gods, buried the dead (Castellanos 1955, 4:155, 167), and gave advice in political and everyday matters (Rojas 1965, 221). These priests were healers as well (Castellanos 1955, 4:155, 167). The xeques held a status that was clearly below that of the chief. Offerings presented by the inhabitants of the chiefdom first went through the hands of the chief, who then passed them on to the temple priest (Castellanos 1955, 4:158). In spite of the fact that every chiefdom had its own priests, all inhabitants of the Muisca territory respected the same gods and attended the same ceremonies. The Sun Temple of Sogamoso, for example, was considered a common sanctuary, and all inhabitants had unrestricted access to it.

Uzaques are mentioned for the chiefdom of Bogotá. These were caciques who lived in the palace of the zipa and were responsible for his security. Their rank fell between that of the zipa, who also held the title of uzaque, and those of the other caciques of the chiefdom of Bogotá (Castellanos 1955, 4:151, 155; Juicio de res., 1979, 2:86; Langebaek Rueda 1987, 27).

Fig. 8.5. Muisca ceramic figurine of a cacique, 24.5 cm tall, of unknown provenience; in the collection of Dr. L. Petersen, Linden-Museum Stuttgart, Germany (Inventory number 120868; Negative number P1855/18; courtesy of the Linden-Museum Stuttgart).

Professional warriors or *guechas* were considered members of the privileged classes as well. Guechas were only to be found in the chiefdom of Bogotá, which was directly adjacent to the territories of the Panche (fig. 8.3), with whom they were constantly at war (AGI Patr.R.27/R.14,f.6r.; Aguado 1956, 1:275; Castellanos 1955, 4:201, 259). They came from different districts of the Bogotá chiefdom and were selected personally by the paramount chief. They had access to certain privileges, which they gained by meritorious service in the wars against the Panche. Thus, they were allowed to wear gold ornaments and, when a cacique died leaving no legitimate successor, the zipa himself could install one of them in the place of the deceased chief (Castellanos 1955, 4:201; Simón 1981, 3:214). By order of the paramount chief they occupied border villages to protect the population from attacks by the Panche (Simón 1981, 3:213). The Muisca would kill captured Panche warriors, taking trophy heads. Others were captured and brought into Muisca territory. Some of these men were also used in sacrifices or were forced to work as slaves in the palace of the zipa (AGI Patr.R.27/R.14,f.6r.).

The Economic Basis of the Muisca Chiefdoms

Food Production

The Muisca agricultural economy was based on corn and beans. In order to achieve maximum productivity, these crops were cultivated on raised fields, called *camellones* by the Spanish chroniclers (Aguado 1956, 1:439; Castellanos 1955, 4:182; Fernández de Oviedo 1959, 3:110; Langebaek Rueda 1984, 13; 1987, 62–63). These were laid out in the *pantanos* (swamps) in such a way as to assure optimal drainage and probably also to protect the crops from frosts (Broadbent 1964b, 1968; 1987, 425). This method of cultivation resulted, most probably, in two corn harvests per year (Salomon 1986, 59), enabling the inhabitants of the Muisca territory to produce a significant surplus in basic foodstuffs.

Other methods of food production were less important; the cultivation at higher altitudes of certain plants, such as squashes and potatoes, as well as the production of cotton, coca, tobacco, and tropical fruit in the tierra caliente were rendered possible by obtaining fields that were situated in other ecological zones. The Muisca grew coca and cotton in drier and warmer valleys within Muisca territory as well as in regions close to the territories of the Muzo and Panche. These regions were located within one day's travel, making it possible to return to the village for the night (cited in

Langebaek Rueda 1984, 22; Visita [1560], 85), a strategy that has been called "microverticality" by Oberem (1978, 54).[10] In some regions they also stayed away from their homes for several weeks to work their fields but then returned to their villages (Guillén Chaparro [1583] 1975, 8:165), a method that had been applied in pre-Hispanic times in a very similar way by the inhabitants of the Sierra Nevada de Santa Marta (Herrera de Turbay 1985, 26), a mountain range in the north of Colombia (fig. 8.1). In any case, the applicability of both methods was limited to small areas because of the well-defined borders with other ethnic groups and should be seen only as a supplement to the basic food production within Muisca territory.

Abundant fish in the rivers of the Altiplano Cundiboyacense (Jiménez de Quesada 1972, 295) and probably pisciculture in the ditches between the raised fields (Broadbent 1987, 435) as well as in the lagoons (Anónimo 1943, 455) also provided an important contribution to the protein supply of the Muisca. Although hunting is mentioned in many sources (e.g., Simón 1981, 3:164, 174), consumption of meat was often restricted to the ruling chiefs and their families (Visita [1560], 1988, 75).

Manufacturing Production

The most important goods produced by the Muisca economy were salt, cotton blankets, pottery, ornaments and sacrificial objects made from gold, and emeralds mined in Muisca territory. Within these production spheres, a remarkable degree of interregional specialization developed.[11] The villages situated near the most important salt springs at Zipaquirá, Nemocón, and Tausa were mainly occupied in the production of salt (Aguado 1956, 1:256; Castellanos 1955, 4:187; Cardale de Schrimpff 1981, 30; AGI Santa Fé 188/f.77v.).[12] Through the evaporation of brine in huge ceramic vessels, called *gachas*, the Muisca produced salt in the form of bricks. These were traded not only within their territory but also as far away as the territories of the Panche, Muzo, Colima, and the Pijao at the southern end of the Magdalena Valley (AGI Patr.R. 27/R.14,f.3v.; ANC Tributos 16/f.902r.; Fernández de Oviedo 1959, 3:86; Simón 1981, 3:123, 232). To the north of Muisca territory, the salt bricks reached the regions of the Carare and Patángora (Simón 1981, 3:123, 232) (fig. 8.2).

Ceramics were mainly produced in villages situated in hot and dry, and therefore less fertile, regions of Muisca territory. A few of the most important centers were at Sutamarchán, Tinjacá, Raquirá, and Cucaita.[13] In these villages, the ceramic output clearly exceeded domestic requirements. The inhabitants of these communities produced pottery primarily for trading (AHT 18/f.108r.; Falchetti de Sáenz 1975, 195–96). Agricultural production was neglected for other activities, although not abandoned altogether. There were still fields to be worked in the vicinity of the villages, but the majority of the population was involved in other production activities. All other necessary goods such as clothing, food, cotton, and salt were bartered in Muisca markets for locally made products (Kurella 1993, 159).

In spite of producing little cotton of their own, and thus being forced to import raw cotton through trade from the tierra caliente regions, the Muisca of the Altiplano Cundiboyacense developed one of the most important centers for finely woven cotton textiles in the entire northern Andean region. The Muisca were certainly not the only producers of cotton blankets, but given the quantity and the quality of their blankets, they nearly approached industrial standards. The simple white blankets, called *mantas chingamanales* by the Spaniards (Aguado 1956, 1:406), were woven in almost every household. These blankets served as clothing for the population, or as trade items in the local markets. In addition to the weaving of simple blankets, the Muisca also fabricated *mantas finas,* or finely woven and richly painted cotton blankets.[14] Unfortunately, it is not possible to reconstruct who was in charge of the production of the respective kinds of blankets or where they were manufactured. Few local centers of cotton weaving are mentioned in the available sources (AGI Patr.R.27, R.14/f.2v.; ANC Vis.Sant.6/718r.). Mantas finas served as clothing exclusively for the chiefly classes, but could, on the other hand, be used as trade goods by everyone (Kurella 1993, 158). These textiles also served as offerings during religious ceremonies (Langebaek Rueda 1990, 93). The number of mantas finas in circulation at a given time in the Muisca territory must have been so considerable that it is reasonable to assume that a substantial part of the population was occupied in their production. It is not known if this kind of work was carried out by specialists. Langebaek Rueda (1990, 94) mentions the possibility that some of the priests made those blankets to be used in religious ceremonies.

Gold had an outstanding importance in Muisca society. It is remarkable that most of the manufactured gold was imported from the territories of enemy groups in the tierra caliente because the Muisca did not have any important gold sources within their territory. There were only minor sources of gold in their lands (Langebaek Rueda 1987, 88). It is not known whether they were exploited to any extent in pre-Columbian times. On the other hand, copper mines were abundant in Muisca territory. The ore was extracted and used together with gold to produce the alloy *tumbaga* (Visita [1560] 1988, 76). At least some of the Muisca goldsmiths were full-time specialists. Castellanos (1955, 4:142–43) refers to them as subjects of the chief of Guatavita. These people moved from place to place offering their services. Their tools have been found in many places in Muisca territory (Bright 1972; Langebaek Rueda 1990, 94; Plazas de Nieto 1975, 66; Schuler-Schömig 1974, 1). Most Muisca ornaments were made of the gold-copper alloy tumbaga (Plazas de Nieto and Falchetti de Sáenz 1986, 239).

Gold ornaments could be worn only by the chiefs, capitanes, and other privileged persons. It emphasized their special status (Visita [1560] 1988, 75). The huge central temples of the Muisca, such as the Sun Temple of Sogamoso, were partially covered with gold and contained numerous golden objects as offerings to the gods (Castellanos 1955, 4:240; Rojas 1965, 359). *Tunjos,* small anthropomorphic figurines made of tumbaga, were put into ceramic vessels and served as funerary goods (Aguado 1956, 1:289; Langebaek Rueda 1987, 49; Mayer 1983, 366).[15]

At least some of the Muisca goldsmiths were full-time specialists. Castellanos (1955, 4:142–43) refers to them as subjects of the chief of Guatavita. These people moved from place to place offering their services. Their tools have been found in many places in Muisca territory (Bright 1972; Langebaek Rueda 1990, 94; Plazas de Nieto 1975, 66; Schuler-Schömig 1974, 1). Emeralds first and foremost had religious functions. They were offered on household altars and in temples (Jiménez de Quesada 1972, 298, 301). Emeralds have been found in some Muisca graves (Silva Celis 1945, 295), and some of the mummy burials of the chiefs had emeralds attached to their clothing (Simón 1981, 3:406; Langebaek Rueda 1987, 108). As trade goods, they were mainly important inside Muisca territory. The emerald mines were situated at Somondoco.[16] These mines were only in use during certain seasons when the rivers had enough water. Topsoil was washed away with water from canals while the emeralds themselves were extracted using digging sticks. This labor was carried out exclusively by the population from the chiefdoms of Somondoco (AGI Patr.R.27/R.14,f.2v.). With accompanying ceremonies, laborers left for the mines situated at some distance from their villages. The mined emeralds then were traded in markets throughout the Muisca lands for goods such as gold, necklaces, and cotton blankets (AGI Patr.R.27/R.14,f.2v.). People from other villages could also come directly to Somondoco in order to trade for emeralds. There was probably an interregional market for emeralds at Tinjacá, held at regular intervals (Langebaek Rueda 1987, 109).

The Network of Muisca Chiefdoms

In spite of differences in dialect, subjection to different paramount chiefs, and the individual names given to the chiefdoms, the Spaniards seem to have perceived the existence of an entity that they later called "los Muisca." By contrast, the Guane, another Chibchan-speaking group, who settled far-ther north (fig. 8.1), have always been considered as clearly separate from the Muisca and called the "Provincia de los Guane" (Castellanos 1955, 4:314; Aguado 1956, 3:69; ANC Vis.Sant.2/f.467r.). It is the network of trade relations, religion, and common cultural norms that appears to have linked the politically autonomous polities of the Muisca.

The Economic System of the Chiefdoms

The economic system of the chiefdoms on the Altiplano Cundiboyacense may be divided into four different spheres, each one embedded in a social institution of the Muisca society: barter in local markets, long-distance trade, tribute, and elite exchange (or gift giving among the elite) were char-acteristics of the Muisca economic system (Kurella 1993, 157).[17] Each of these spheres was embedded in the social structure in the form of an insti-tution or a group of people (corporate groups, chiefs). Through the interac-tion among these spheres and their respective institutions, the needs of all social classes were satisfied. The "analytical separation of these spheres as well as the identification of their points of interaction" (Berdan 1975, 1) permits a clearer insight into the linking elements of the Muisca dominions and, at the same time, the social positions of the chiefs within the caci-cazgos (Kurella 1993, 37).

All the goods produced by the Muisca, as well as the necessary raw materials, circulated in the first sphere, the local market trade (fig. 8.6). Foodstuffs, luxury goods, and items used in everyday life, such as pottery and clothing, could be found in these markets. Every individual in the lands of the Muisca had the right to buy and sell these goods, although not always the right to use them. Examples of limited use would be the mantas finas worn only by people of privileged classes, the gold, and the emeralds (Kurella 1993, 158). Trading prices were fixed in the local markets, often held in many places at regular intervals (ANC Tributos 14/672v.; Aguado 1956, 1:341). At the same time, the markets were considered to be big feasts held in honor of the chief (Langebaek Rueda 1987, 120). There were also occasions when the inhabitants of different villages visited one another to exchange goods (Kurella 1993, 159). Goods were bartered at set values (Aguado 1956, 1:406–7; Simón 1981, 3:403).[18]

The second economic sphere was that of long-distance trade, which op-erated under different rules. Only a limited variety of goods were traded. These included cotton, cotton blankets, salt, coca, gold and gold objects, tropical fruit, feathers from tropical birds, marine molluscs (*Oliva* sp.), as

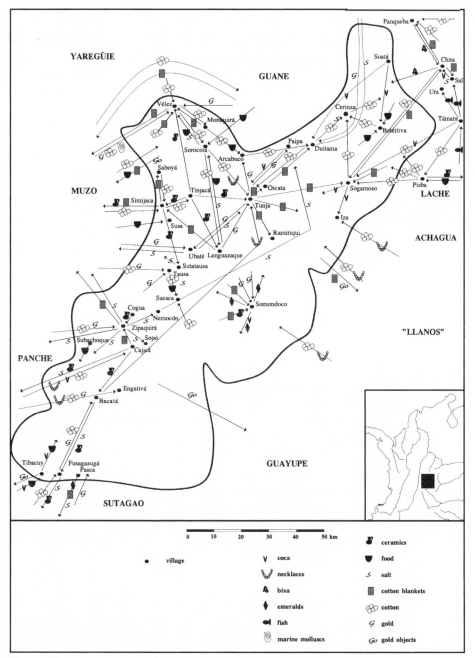

Fig. 8.6. The trade relations of the Muisca. Raw material such as cotton and gold comes in at Pasca and manufactured goods like cotton blankets as well as salt are taken out to the Panche region. From Pasca, for example, the raw material is traded to the main markets at Tunja, Sorocotá, or Vélez in the north where people could exchange it for blankets, ceramics, or other manufactured goods.

well as necklaces made of small disc-shaped beads cut from marine molluscs (fig. 8.6) (Kurella 1993, 166).[19] In order to obtain products like cotton and gold, the inhabitants of border villages such as Pasca, Vélez, and Simijaca or people living in communities with big markets, such as Tinjacá and Duitama, had to go to the tierra caliente, offering salt bricks and manufactured goods like cotton blankets and gold objects. Markets were held there, for example in the territory of the Pijao (AGI Patr.R.27/R.14,f.3v.). In the lands of the Panche (ANC Tributos 16/f.902r.) or the Muzo (ANC Vis.Boy.17/f.303r.), the Muisca would go directly to individual farmsteads, where they would barter for the desired goods. At the border of the Carare River, Muisca traders met with people from other groups in small huts, where the exchange took place. The most important products the Muisca had to offer were salt bricks and cotton blankets, which they exchanged for gold and other goods (Fernández de Oviedo 1959, 3:86). The organization of this long-distance trade lay directly in the hands of the inhabitants of Muisca villages situated close to the borders, like Pasca in the south or Duitama in the north, and not in the hands of an elite (Visita [1560] 1988, 75). Nor were there any professional traders such as the *pochteca* of the Aztecs (Berdan 1975, 144) or the *mindalaes* of the Pasto (Salomon 1978). In the Muisca form of "administered trade," the tradesperson was part of the village social organization and the kinship group.

Differentiation must be made between direct and indirect tribute in the third economic sphere; the Muisca populations paid direct yearly tribute into the hands of their chiefs or capitanes. Indirect tribute was paid when brine or salt bricks were acquired. For the right to extract salt from the wells on the chief's territory he received a portion of the trade goods (AGI Santa Fé 188/f.77v.). The greater part of these trade goods remained in the hands of the chief and only a small portion was used in rewarding people who worked for the chief—for example, in the construction of the chiefly houses (ANC Vis.Boy.17/f.546r.,v.).

Elite exchange or gift giving among the elite, seen as the fourth economic sphere (Kurella 1993, 172), only took place between the privileged classes. This exchange, in general, consisted of rewards bestowed upon capitanes or lower-ranking chiefs for services rendered (ANC Vis.Boy.17/f.546r.,v.). These rewards consisted of jewelry and cotton blankets and took as well the form of privileges such as the right to wear gold ornaments or the fine, painted cotton blankets. This exchange served to enhance the prestige and the power of the chief. At the same time, it motivated the lower-ranking chiefs to fulfill obligations to their paramount chief while improving their own social position and maintaining their status.

The Interaction of the Economic Spheres

Not only did local markets provide all necessary goods for the Muisca; they served as distribution centers for long-distance trade goods. The dominating principle operating within as well as between these two economic spheres was that of reciprocity. The third sphere was dominated by the principle of redistribution, in which the chiefs played an economically decisive role; through tribute all the necessities of life also came into the hands of the chiefly classes. In this manner, the upper classes were fed as well as supplied with prestige items. Some of these extracted goods were redistributed.[20] The elite exchange, in which reciprocity again predominated, can be seen as a mechanism for maintaining power (Kurella 1993, 174). The first two spheres extended over the whole Muisca area, which means that together they formed a unified economic entity. Within the last two spheres the chiefdoms were independent of one another. Gifts were only handed out within a given chiefdom.

The Muisca: Chiefdoms in Transition

The sociopolitical units on the Altiplano Cundiboyacense never formed a homogeneous state or even an empire.[21] On the one hand, in the "independent territory," we are dealing with autonomous villages; and in the case of the cacicazgos, on the other hand, we can identify chiefdoms of differing social complexity. Compared to the other polities on the Altiplano Cundiboyacense, the chiefdom of Bogotá would have to be seen as being at the upper end of the scale of social complexity, as a chiefdom developing into a state. But, before we can start to discuss the points that show this development, a few critical remarks should be made about the ethnohistorical sources. To decide whether a society is still a chiefdom or has already developed into a state, the information considered must be very precise. The Muisca case indeed shows some difficulties in this respect. The written sources on the Muisca were documents by Europeans for Europeans and therefore provide a restricted point of view of Muisca society. In addition, the amount of ethnohistoric information available about different regions or polities is in direct proportion to the presence of a Spanish administrative center therein. In this way, it is hardly astonishing that the quality of the sources concerning the chiefdom of Bogotá is so much more thorough than are those concerning Duitama, Tunja, and Sogamoso, since Bogotá later became the Spanish center of the Audiencia de Santa Fé.[22] So, keeping these problems in mind, we should discuss Bogotá as the entity that is best documented, compared to the others.

There is no evidence for centralized control of the production or procurement of basic resources in Muisca society, as for example in the Inca state. One of the most critical questions is who controlled the use of the land, that most important of resources. Did the chief have "possession" of land in the first place, or did it only come to him in cases where the line of inheritance was broken? Or was it "owned" by the gods and the chief decided who was allowed to work it? This is one of the questions that cannot be clearly answered with reference to the known sources.

As to the internal organization of Muisca society, chiefdoms tend to have their administrative functions still embedded in social institutions, whereas a state does have a professional bureaucracy. The beginnings of such a bureaucracy can be perceived in the groups of uzaques and capitanes. First and foremost chosen to be responsible for the security of the paramount chief, the uzaques, little by little, could have achieved more power and become another decision-making level of society. Capitanes could also have moved from simple tribute-collecting activities to coordinating functions.

Pressure from the outside also led to internal changes within Muisca society. The intermittent warfare between the Muisca and the Panche at the southern border of the chiefdom of Bogotá had a singular character; it could be neither won nor lost by either side. The Muisca were too strong an adversary to be overcome by the Panche, while access to Panche lands was too difficult for the Muisca warriors to achieve victory. This irreconcilable situation led to the creation by the Muisca of a class of warriors, the guechas, who had a social rank just under that of the paramount chief and equal to the uzaques. Once having come into existence, this group of specialized warriors may have exerted an influence on the frequency of the conflicts in order to solidify or even enhance their status within the society (McCauley 1990, 9). The Muisca-Panche war could also have led to a confederacy between Bogotá and one of the other chiefdoms, or one or all of the others might have been conquered by Bogotá, creating a new level of organization by the former ruling classes and thus forming a new centralized regional state.

In spite of huge gaps in the information on Muisca society, the Chibchan-speaking groups of the Colombian highlands provide excellent examples for studying processes of social development as well as economic systems and offer a clearer view of how pre-state societies were organized.

Notes

I am indebted to Robert L. Carneiro for inviting me to contribute to this volume, to Martin Kurella and Alice Choyke for their help in translating the manuscript, and to Christian Guksch and Monica Barnes for their never-ending patience and valuable criticisms of various drafts of the manuscript.

1. Until the beginning of the 1980s, the most important publications on the north Andean region were Broadbent (1964a, 1964b, 1966, 1968); Friede (1974) and Villamarín (1972), Villamarín and Villamarín (1975) on the Muisca; Trimborn (1942, 1948, 1949) and Friede (1963) on the Cauca Valley; Romoli de Avery (1962, 1977–78) on southern Colombia; Bischof (1971) on the Sierra Nevada de Santa Marta; and Reichel-Dolmatoff (1951, 1961, 1982) and Bray (1978) concerning the region as a whole.

According to Lange (1992, 3), the prehistoric Intermediate Area includes eastern Honduras, Nicaragua, Costa Rica, Panama, northern Ecuador, Colombia, and western Venezuela.

2. Some of the archaeological projects that have been carried out are in the Valle de Calima (Cardale de Schrimpff et al. 1991), along the Río del Oro in the Sierra Nevada de Santa Marta (Soto Holguín 1988; Serje 1987; Plazas de Nieto 1987; Falchetti de Sáenz 1987), and in the Fúquene and Susa valleys (Langebaek Rueda 1995). The most important ethnohistorical studies are by Langebaek Rueda (1987) on the Muisca and by Rappaport (1987) on the Páez of southern Colombia.

3. The term *chiefdom* is defined as "a regionally organized society with a centralized decision-making hierarchy coordinating activities among several village communities" (Earle 1987, 288), or, in other words, "an autonomous political unit comprising a number of villages or communities under the permanent control of a paramount chief" (Carneiro 1981, 45). Moreover, "chiefdoms possess institutionalized offices of leadership: the chief and his associates. Such offices can exert control and exercise some power over persons, products, and situations" (Peebles and Kus 1977, 422).

4. This article is based on the results of an ethnohistorical study of sixteenth-century documents mostly in the Archivo de Indias (Seville), the Archivo Nacional de Colombia (Santa Fé de Bogotá), and several smaller archives in Colombia as well as printed sources from the sixteenth and early seventeenth centuries (Kurella 1993).

5. The name Muisca was given to the inhabitants of the Altiplano by the Spaniards. It derives from the indigenous term *muexca*, meaning "person" (Aguado 1956, 1:263).

6. Results of recent archaeological research suggest an occupation of the Altiplano Cundiboyacense by the Muisca of about 700 years, from the ninth to the sixteenth century A.D. (Boada Rivas 1987, 11–12; Lleras Pérez 1989, 12; Peña León 1991, 14). Some of the Muisca origin myths report that they also inhabited a part of the Magdalena Valley but had been forced back by the Muzo and other Carib-speaking

groups (AGI Santa Fé 188/f.499r.; Guillén Chaparro [1584] 1985, 15; Friede 1968, 37). Those Carib groups, however, started to settle in the Magdalena Valley about 1000 A.D.

7. In some regions (Mexico, Central America, northern Andes) the mountains are divided into four climatic zones: the *tierra caliente* (hot lands), including the lowlands up to about 700 meters above sea level; the *tierra templada* (temperate lands), including temperate zones between 700 and 1,700 meters above sea level; the *tierra fría* (cold lands), covering the areas between 1,700 meters and the upper limit of vegetation; and finally the *tierra helada* (frozen lands), the region of the snow-covered mountain peaks (Neef 1975, 417–18).

8. Both terms, *partes* and *parcialidades*, can be translated as "parts." "They are synonymous and often used interchangeably in the same document to refer to the same unit" (Broadbent 1981, 261).

9. A "maximal chiefdom" is "one that has become large and complex enough to approach the threshold of a state" (Carneiro 1981, 47).

10. "Microverticalidad quiere decir que los habitantes de un pueblo tenían campos situados en diferentes pisos ecológicos alcanzables en un mismo día con la posibilidad de regresar al lugar de residencia por la noche" [Microverticality means that the inhabitants of a village had fields in different ecological zones, accessible within one day, with the possibility of returning to their homes for the night; Oberem 1978, 54, translation by Doris Kurella].

11. The increased production of certain goods in individual villages does not mean that these goods were not made elsewhere. In the aforementioned places, production far exceeded the needs of individual households. This surplus was mainly used for trade. Pottery was produced in most of the Muisca villages while salt was also extracted from many little saltwells for local use.

12. For all production centers and trade routes see fig. 8.6.

13. In the chronicles and documents these places are called *pueblos de los olleros* (villages of the pottery makers) or *ollerías* (AHT 18/f.90v.; Castellanos 1955, 4:298).

14. Due to the acidity of the soil, few blankets and no backstrap looms have survived (Cortés Moreno 1990, 62). All known Muisca blankets come from caves at higher altitudes and regions where the dead were buried as mummy bundles, as for example the Páramo de Pisba (Cortés Moreno 1990). Similar blankets have been found at the Mesa de Geridas within the Guane territory (Schottelius 1946).

15. The Muisca most commonly used the lost-wax casting technique when making gold or tumbaga objects (Mayer 1981, 474; Schuler-Schömig 1974, 2).

16. At the time of the Spanish Conquest the emerald mines of Muzo no longer lay in Muisca territory (AGI Santa Fé 188/f.499r.).

17. The economic system of the Muisca has been analyzed applying the definitions and concepts of Karl Polanyi (Polanyi et al. 1957). Polanyi (1957, 70) postulates that every economy consists of "institutionally separate and motivationally distinct economic spheres of exchange." Each of these spheres is connected to a certain social institution of the society; it is "embedded in noneconomic institutions, the economic

process itself being instituted through kinship, marriage, age-groups, secret societies, totemic associations, and public solemnities" (Polanyi 1957, 70–71). The whole "primitive economy for Polanyi was conceived of as submerged in social relations" (Stanish 1992, 12).

18. The description of Aguado clearly mentions fixed prices as being a pre-Hispanic mechanism of exchange.

19. The Muisca also obtained necklaces from the eastern lowlands of Colombia and Venezuela (*llanos orientales*), traded directly from the Achagua or indirectly through the Lache, who were in permanent contact with groups on the llanos orientales (figs. 8.2, 8.6) (Kurella 1993, 58; Morey 1975, 251–53).

20. This kind of exchange is seen as redistribution even if it is not used in the sense of "pooling" all produced items and redistributing all of them among the whole population. Redistribution is here seen as "simply an elementary form of taxation whereby goods mobilized from subsistence producers are used to compensate governmental and warrior personnel, religious functionaries, craft specialists, and other 'nonproducers'" (Johnson and Earle 1987, 235). This definition still goes along with Polanyi's: "When the status of the dominant individual is constituted along political lines, we may properly speak of redistribution in the sense originally defined by Polanyi" (Stanish 1992, 25).

21. Chiefdoms "vest leadership in generalized regional institutions" (Johnson and Earle 1987, 246), whereas "a state is defined as a society with specialized administrative activities" (Johnson and Wright 1975, 267).

22. An *audiencia* was a Spanish supreme court and administrative council in the colonies.

References

Primary Sources

AGI   Archivo General de Indias, Seville, Spain
AHT   Archivo Historico de Tunja, Tunja, Colombia
ANC   Archivo Nacional de Colombia, Bogotá, Colombia

Unpublished Documents

AGI Audiencia de Santa Fé 188
1555   Carta del licenciado Briçeño a S.M. (16.3.1555). F.77r.–78r.
AGI Audiencia de Santa Fé 188
1564   Carta a S. M. de Juan de Senagos (12.12.1564). F.497r.–503r.
AGI Patronato Real 27, Ramo 14
1537–39 Relación maravillosa del descubrimiento de la Provincia de Santa Marta
        firmada por Juan de Martín y Antonio de Lebrija, oficiales reales de Santa

Marta, 1536. Salió para este descubrimiento el adelantado Don Hernández de Lugo, quien nombró por su teniente al licenciado Don Gonzalo Jiménez y con este fueron el capitán Juan de Céspedes que en muchas hambres, trabajos y muchas muertes en el Julio de 1539. Descubrió esta provincia Antonio de Ojeda en 1509, y la conquistó Rodriguo de Bastidas. F.1r.–8r.

AGI Patronato Real 27, Ramo 34

1583 Carta del Oidor Don Francisco Guillén Chaparro en que refiere los usos y costumbres de los indios de la tierra fría en el Nuevo Reino de Granada. Marzo 1583. F.1r.–2r.

AHT Legajo 18

1586 Juicio criminal de María Herrezuelo, contra Diego, Cacique de Indios de Tinjacá, por abusos en sus tierras. F.81r.–133v.

ANC Tributos 14

1578–95 Vélez: pleito de su cabildo y encomenderos con el fiscal real, por los quintos de oro del rey, que el dicho funcionario les demandara. F.597r.–713v.

ANC Tributos 16

1559 Hernández, Francisco, escribano real, verifica el censo de población indígena de la provincia de Mariquita, haciendo el computo de los tributos pagados por ella. F.237r.–428v., 878r.–986v.

ANC Visitas de Boyacá 17

1594a Investigaciones que hiciera en los repartimientos indígenas de Sutatausa y Tausa, el Oidor Miguel de Ibarra, sobre la administración de Gonzalo de León Venero, encomendero de ellos. F.262r.–460v.

ANC Visitas de Boyacá 17

1594b Información judicial que levantara el Oidor Miguel de Ibarra, sobre la administración de los indígenas de Simijaca y cargos que se le formularan a Gonzalo de León Venero, encomendero de ellos. F.487r.–650v.

ANC Visitas de Boyacá 3

1601 Documentos referentes a la visita del Oidor Luis Henríquez, a los resguardos indígenas de Sichacá y Cormechoque, de la jurisdicción de Tunja, encomienda del capitán Martín de Rojas. F.401r.–552v.

ANC Visitas de Santander 2

1560 Documentos referentes a la visita del Oidor Tomás López, a las parcialidades indígenas de Macaregua, Guayaca, y otras de la jurisdicción de Vélez. F.466r.–519r.

ANC Visitas de Santander 6

1602 Información judicial, tomada por el Oidor Luis Enríquez, en las poblaciones indígenas de Onzaga, Chicamocha y Suacón, sobre la administración de Hernándo Mateus, encomendero de ellas. F.669–778.

Secondary Sources

Aguado, Pedro de
1956 *Recopilación historial de Santa Marta y Nuevo Reino de Granada* (1581). 4 vols.

Bogotá: Biblioteca de la Presidencia de Colombia.

Anónimo

1943 Descripción de la ciudad de Tunja, sacada de las informaciones hechas por la justicia de aquella ciudad en 30 de mayo de 1610 años. *Boletín de historia y antigüedades* 30(342–43):451–88.

Berdan, Frances F.

1975 Trade, Tribute, and Market in the Aztec Empire. Ph.D. dissertation, University of Texas, Austin.

Bischof, Henning

1971 *Die Spanisch-Indianische Auseinandersetzung in der Nördlichen Sierra Nevada de Santa Marta (1501–1600).* Bonner Amerikanistische Studien, Nr. 1. Bonn: Rheinische Friedrich-Wilhelms-Universität.

Boada Rivas, Ana María

1987 Asentamientos indígenas en el Valle de la Laguna (Samacá-Boyacá). Bogotá: Fundación de Investigaciones Arqueológicas Nacionales, Banco de la República.

Bray, Warwick

1978 *The Gold of El Dorado.* London: Times Books.

Bright, Alec

1972 A goldsmith's blowpipe from Colombia. *Man,* n.s. 7(2):311–13.

Broadbent, Sylvia

1964a *Los Chibchas: Organización Sociopolítica.* Serie Latinoamericana No.5. Bogotá: Facultad de Sociología, Universidad Nacional de Colombia.

1964b Agricultural terraces in Chibcha territory, Colombia. *American Antiquity* 29(4):501–4.

1966 The site of Chibcha Bogotá. *Ñawpa Pacha* 4:1–14.

1968 A prehistoric field system in Chibcha territory, Colombia. *Ñawpa Pacha* 6:135–48.

1981 The formation of peasant society in central Colombia. *Ethnohistory* 28(3):268–77.

1987 The Chibcha raised-fields system in the Sabana de Bogotá, Colombia: Further investigations. In *Prehispanic Agricultural Fields in the Andean Region,* part 2, edited by W. M. Denevan, K. Mathewsen, and G. Knapp, 425–42. BAR International Series 359 (ii). Oxford: BAR.

Cardale de Schrimpff, Marianne

1981 *Las Salinas de Zipaquirá: Su Explotación Indígena.* Bogotá: Fundación de Investigaciones Arqueológicas Nacionales, Banco de la República.

Cardale de Schrimpff, Marianne, et al.

1991 *Calima: Trois Cultures Précolombiennes dans le Sud-ouest de la Colombie.* Lausanne: Editions Payot.

Carneiro, Robert L.

1970 A theory of the origin of the state. *Science* 169:733–38.

1981 The chiefdom: Precursor of the state. In *The Transition to Statehood in the New*

World, edited by G. D. Jones and R. R. Kautz, 37–79. Cambridge: Cambridge University Press.

1990　Chiefdom-level warfare as exemplified in Fiji and the Cauca Valley. In *The Anthropology of War*, edited by J. Haas, 190–211. School of American Research. Cambridge: Cambridge University Press.

1991a　The nature of the chiefdom as revealed by evidence from the Cauca Valley of Colombia. In *Profiles in Cultural Evolution: Papers from a Conference in Honor of Elman R. Service*, edited by A. T. Rambo and K. Gillogly, 167–90. University of Michigan Museum of Anthropology, Anthropological Papers, no. 85. Ann Arbor.

1991b　The ecological basis of Amazonian chiefdoms. Unpublished MS on file, Department of Anthropology, American Museum of Natural History.

Castellanos, Juan de
1955　*Elegías de Varones Ilustres de Indias* (1601). 4 vols. Bogotá: Edición de la Presidencia de Colombia.

Cortés Moreno, Emilia
1990　Mantas Muiscas. *Boletín Museo del Oro* 27:61–75.

Drennan, Robert D.
1991　Cultural evolution, human ecology, and empirical research. In *Profiles in Cultural Evolution: Papers from a Conference in Honor of Elman R. Service*, edited by A. T. Rambo and K. Gillogly, 113–35. University of Michigan Museum of Anthropology, Anthropological Papers, no. 85. Ann Arbor.

Earle, Timothy
1987　Chiefdoms in archaeological and ethnohistorical perspective. *Annual Review of Anthropology* 16:279–308.

Falchetti de Sáenz, Ana María
1975　*Arqueología de Sutamarchán, Boyacá*. Bogotá: Fundación de Investigaciones Arqueológicas Nacionales, Banco de la República.

1987　Desarollo de la orfebrería tairona en la provincia metalúrgica del norte colombiano. *Boletín Museo del Oro* 19:3–24.

Fernández de Oviedo y Valdés, Gonzalo
1959　*Historia General y Natural de las Indias, Islas y Tierra-Firme del Mar Océano* (1548). 5 vols. Biblioteca de Autores Españoles. Madrid: Ediciones Atlas.

Fernández de Piedrahita, Lucas
1973　*Noticia historial de las conquistas del Nuevo Reino de Granada* (1666). 2 vols. Bogotá: Ministerio de Educación Nacional, Instituto Colombiano de Cultura Hispánica.

Friede, Juan
1963　*Los Quimbayas Bajo la Dominación Española*. Bogotá: Talleres Gráficos del Banco de la República.

1968　Informe colonial sobre los indios de Muzo. *Boletín Cultural y Bibliográfico* 11(4):36–46.

1974　*Los Chibchas Bajo la Dominación Española*. Medellín: Ediciones La Carreta.

Guhl, Ernesto
1968   Los páramos circundantes de la Sabana de Bogotá, su ecología y su impor-
       tancia para el régimen hidrológico de la misma. In *Geo-ecology of the Moun-
       tainous Regions of the Tropical Americas*, edited by C. Troll, 195–212. Proceed-
       ings of the UNESCO Mexico Symposium, August 1–3, 1966. Bonn: Dümmler
       in Kommission.
Guillén Chaparro, Francisco
1975   Relación de tierra fría (1583). In *Fuentes Documentales para la Historia del Nuevo
       Reino de Granada (1550–1590)*, edited by J. Friede, 8:161–66. Bogotá: Biblioteca
       Banco Popular.
1985   Visita vom 6.5.1584, durchgeführt in "Trinidad de los Indios Muzos y Coli-
       mas" (1584). In *Zur Situation der Muzos und Colimas im Jahre 1584 nach dem
       Bericht von Francisco Guillén Chaparro*, edited by J. Steininger. *Wiener Ethno-
       historische Blätter* 28:3–19.
Herrera de Turbay, Luisa F.
1985   *Agricultura Aborigen y Cambios de Vegetación en la Sierra Nevada de Santa Marta.*
       Bogotá: Fundación de Investigaciones Arqueológicas Nacionales, Banco de
       la República.
Jiménez de Quesada, Gonzalo
1972   Epítome de la conquista del Nuevo Reino de Granada. In *Jiménez de Quesada
       en su Relación con los Cronistas y el Epítome de la Conquista del Nuevo Reino de
       Granada*, edited by D. Ramos Pérez, 277–307. Sevilla: Escuela de Estudios
       Hispanoamericanos.
Johnson, Allen W., and Timothy Earle
1987   *The Evolution of Human Societies: From Foraging Group to Agrarian State.* Stan-
       ford: Stanford University Press.
Johnson, Gregory A., and Henry T. Wright
1975   Population, exchange, and early state formation in southwestern Iran.
       American Anthropologist 77:267–89.
Juicio de residencia contra Gonzalo Jiménez de Quesada (n.d.)
1979   In *El Adelantado Don Gonzalo Jiménez de Quesada. Tomo 1: Estudio Biográfico,
       Tomo 2: Documentos*, edited by J. Friede, 81–89. Bogotá: Carlos Valencia
       Editores.
Kroeber, Alfred L.
1946   The Chibcha. In *Handbook of South American Indians*, vol. 2, *The Andean Civili-
       zations*, edited by J. H. Steward, 887–909. Bureau of American Ethnology
       Bulletin 143. Washington, D.C.: Smithsonian Institution.
Kurella, Doris
1993   Handel und Soziale Organisation im Vorspanischen Nördlichen Anden-
       raum. Ph.D. dissertation, Freie Universität Berlin. Bonn: Holos.
Lange, Frederick W.
1992   The Intermediate Area: An introductory overview of wealth and hierarchy
       issues. In *Wealth and Hierarchy in the Intermediate Area*, edited by F. W. Lange,

1–14. Washington, D.C.: Dumbarton Oaks Research Library and Collection.

Langebaek Rueda, Carl Henrik

1984 Comentarios sobre teorías acerca de las limitaciones de la agricultura Muisca. *Memorias III Congreso de Antropología*:11–27. Bogotá: ICFES.

1987 *Mercados, Poblamiento e Integración Etnica entre los Muiscas, Siglo XVI*. Bogotá: Colección Bibliográfica, Banco de la República.

1990 Buscando sacerdotes y encontrando chuques: De la organización religiosa Muisca. *Revista Antropológica y Arqueológica* 7:81–103.

1991 Highland center and foothill periphery in 16th century Eastern Colombia. *Research in Economic Anthropology* 13:323–37.

1995 *Regional Archaeology in the Muisca Territory: A Study of the Fúquene and Susa Valleys*. University of Pittsburgh Memoirs in Latin American Archaeology, no. 9. Pittsburgh.

Lleras Pérez, Roberto

1989 Arqueología del alto Valle de Tenza. Bogotá: Fundación de Investigaciones Arqueológicas Nacionales, Banco de la República.

Mayer, Eŭgen F.

1981 Zur funktion der sogenannten formsteine der Muisca-kultur Kolumbiens. *Beiträge zur Allgemeinen und Vergleichenden Archäologie* 3:472–75.

1983 Vergleichende untersuchung von entwicklungsabläufen in der metalltechnik des vorspanischen Amerika. *Beiträge zur Allgemeinen und Vergleichenden Archäologie* 5:361–77.

McCauley, Clark R.

1990 Conference overview. In *The Anthropology of War*, edited by J. Haas, 1–25. School of American Research. Cambridge: Cambridge University Press.

Morey, Nancy K.

1975 Ethnohistory of the Colombian and Venezuelan Llanos. Ph.D. dissertation, University of Utah, Salt Lake City.

Neef, Vera

1975 Die subtropischen und tropischen Gebiete. In *Das Gesicht der Erde: Physische Geographie*, edited by E. Neef, 416–18. Leipzig: Brockhaus.

Oberem, Udo

1978 El acceso a recursos naturales de diferentes ecologías en la Sierra Ecuatoriana (siglo XVI). *Actes du XLII Congrès des Américanistes* 4:51–64. Paris, 1976.

Parsons, James, and William Bowen

1966 Ancient ridged fields of the San Jorge River floodplain, Colombia. *Geographical Review* 56:317–43.

Peebles, Christopher S., and Susan M. Kus

1977 Some archaeological correlates of ranked societies. *American Antiquity* 42(3): 421–48.

Peña León, Germán A.

1991 *Exploraciones Arqueológicas en la Cuenca Media del Río Bogotá*. Bogotá: Fundación de Investigaciones Arqueológicas Nacionales, Banco de la República.

Plazas de Nieto, Clemencia
1975   *Nueva Metodología para la Clasificación de la Orfebrería Prehispánica.* Bogotá: Ediciones Jorge Plazas.
1987   Forma y función en el oro Tairona. *Boletín Museo del Oro* 19:25–33.
Plazas de Nieto, Clemencia, and Ana María Falchetti de Sáenz
1986   Cultural patterns in prehispanic metalwork of Colombia. 45th International Congress of Americanists, 239–41. Bogotá: Colección Bibliográfica, Banco de la República.
Polanyi, Karl
1957   Aristotle discovers the economy. In *Trade and Market in the Early Empires,* edited by K. Polanyi, C. M. Arensberg, and H. W. Pearson, 64–94. Glencoe: Free Press.
Polanyi, Karl, Conrad Arensberg, and Harry W. Pearson, eds.
1957   *Trade and Market in the Early Empires.* Glencoe: Free Press.
Rappaport, Joanne
1987   Los cacicazgos de la sierra colombiana: El caso Páez. In *Chiefdoms in the Americas,* edited by R. D. Drennan and C. A. Uribe, 271–87. Lanham, Md.: University Press of America.
Reichel-Dolmatoff, Gerardo
1951   *Datos Histórico-Culturales sobre las Tribus de la Antigua Gobernación de Santa Marta.* Bogotá: Banco de la República.
1961   The agricultural basis of the sub-Andean chiefdoms of Colombia. In *The Evolution of Horticultural Systems in Native South America: Causes and Consequences,* edited by J. Wilbert, 83–100. Antropológica Suplemento no. 2. Caracas: Sociedad de Ciencias Naturales La Salle.
1982   Colombia indígena-período prehispánico. In *Manual de la historia de Colombia* edited by J. J. Uribe, 1:33–115. Bogotá: Ediciones Printer Colombiana.
Rojas, Ulises
1965   *El Cacique de Turmequé y su Epoca.* Tunja: Imprenta Departamental.
Romoli de Avery, Kathleen
1962   El suroeste del Cauca y sus indios al tiempo de la conquista española según documentos contemporáneos del distrito de Almaguer. *Revista Colombiana de Antropología* 11:240–99.
1977–78 Las tribus de la antigua jurisdicción de Pasto en el siglo XVI. *Revista Colombiana de Antropología* 21:11–55.
Salomon, Frank
1978   Pochteca and mindalá: A comparison of long-distance traders in Ecuador and Mesoamerica. *Journal of the Steward Anthropological Society* 9(1–2):231–46.
1986   *Native Lords of Quito in the Age of the Incas.* Cambridge: Cambridge University Press.
Schottelius, Jŭstŭs W.
1946   Arqueología de la Mesa de Los Santos. *Boletín de Arqueología* 2(3):213–25.

Schuler-Schömig, Immina von
1974   Patrizen im goldschmiedehandwerk der Muisca Kolumbiens. *Baessler Archiv, Neue Folge* 22:1–22.
Serje, Margarita
1987   Arquitectura y urbanismo en la cultura Tairona. *Boletín Museo del Oro* 19:87–96.
Silva Celis, Eliécer
1945   Investigaciones arqueológicas en Sogamoso. *Boletín de Arqueología* 1(4):283–97; 1(6):467–89.
Simón, Pedro
1981   *Noticias Historiales de las Conquistas de Tierra Firme en las Indias Occidentales* (1625). 6 vols. Bogotá: Biblioteca Banco Popular.
Soto Holguín, Alvaro
1988   *La Ciudad Perdida de los Tayrona: Historia de su Hallazgo y Descubrimiento.* Bogotá: Centro de Estudios del Neotrópico.
Spencer, Charles S.
1991   Coevolution and the development of Venezuelan chiefdoms. In *Profiles in Cultural Evolution: Papers from a Conference in Honor of Elman R. Service,* edited by A. T. Rambo and K. Gillogly, 137–65. University of Michigan Museum of Anthropology, Anthropological Papers, no. 85. Ann Arbor.
Stanish, Charles
1992   *Ancient Andean Political Economy.* Austin: University of Texas Press.
Tovar Pinzón, Hermes
1980   *La Formación Social Chibcha.* Bogotá: Centro de Investigación y Educación Cooperativa.
Trimborn, Hermann
1942   Der handel im Caucatal. *Zeitschrift für Ethnologie* 74:112–26.
1948   *Vergessene Königreiche.* Braunschweig: Limbach.
1949   *Señorío y Barbarie en el Valle del Cauca.* Madrid: Instituto Gonzalo Fernández de Oviedo, Consejo Superior de Investigaciones Científicas.
Villamarín, Juan A.
1972   Encomenderos and Indians in the Formation of Colonial Society in the Sabana de Bogotá, Colombia, 1537–1740. Ph.D. dissertation, Brandeis University.
Villamarín, Juan, and Judith Villamarín
1975   Kinship and inheritance among the Sabana de Bogotá Chibcha at the time of the Spanish Conquest. *Ethnology* 14(2):173–79.
Visita de 1560
1988   In *No hay Caciques ni Señores: Relaciones y Visitas a los Naturales de América, Siglo XVI,* edited by H. Tovar Pinzón, 21–120. Barcelona: L'Hospitalet de Llobregat, Sendai Ediciones.

CHAPTER 9

Social Foundations of Taino *Caciques*

WILLIAM KEEGAN, MORGAN MACLACHLAN, AND BRYAN BYRNE

The Spaniards who conquered the West Indies at the turn of the fifteenth century were fascinated by the ways in which native West Indian societies were organized. Cristóbal Colón (Dunn and Kelley 1989; Henige 1991), Ramón Pané (Bourne 1906), Andrés Morales (Mártir de Anglería 1989), Hernando Colón (Keen 1959), Bartolomé de Las Casas (1967, 1985), Gonzalo Fernández de Oviedo y Valdés (1959), and Pedro Mártir de Anglería (1989) each produced detailed accounts of Taino lifeways and Spanish-Taino interactions. Although the Spaniards detected many differences, the chroniclers also reported that the Tainos had a hierarchical social organization that mirrored Spanish society. Such descriptions certainly overhispanicized Taino social organization, and the chroniclers were inaccurate in some of their interpretations of the Taino social formation (Moscoso 1986; Wilson 1990a, 1990b); nevertheless, their accounts are of sufficient detail to provide the historical continuity needed to create a model of Taino society at contact and to use this model to evaluate ethnological models for the evolution of matrilocal and avunculocal societies (Keegan and Maclachlan 1989; Maclachlan and Keegan 1990).

In our initial study we concluded that the Tainos traced descent through the female line and lived in extended matrilocal or avunculocal residence units (Keegan and Maclachlan 1989), and that Melvin Ember was essentially correct in his model for the evolution of avunculocal residence (Ember 1974; Ember and Ember 1971). However, our initial study emphasized only two aspects of social organization, residence and descent; other aspects of the political economy were left open. We have followed up that work by continuing our examination of archaeological remains in the West Indies for evidence of the mechanisms by which avunculocal chiefdoms emerged (Keegan 1992, 1994). Our investigation of the ethnohistoric and cross-cultural literature also continues (Byrne 1991; Keegan 1996; Keegan et al. 1992).

In the present chapter we examine the political ramifications of the social formation we call the avunculocal chiefdom. Here we are concerned with the social context from which chiefs emerged and the structural relationships that produce social hierarchies. Our discussion is presented in three parts. First, we briefly discuss the term *chiefdom* as we have used it in our study of the Tainos. Second, we examine in some detail the special characteristics of avunculocal chiefdoms. Finally, we examine the social nexus from which avunculocal chiefs, and their aristocracy, emerged among the Tainos.

Chiefdoms

Our definition of chiefdoms has tended to follow Timothy Earle (1978, 1987) and Allen Johnson (Johnson and Earle 1987), who define chiefdoms as regionally integrated polities in which the interests of a dependent population are balanced against those of an emerging aristocracy (Carneiro 1981, 45; Earle 1987, 297). Spanish descriptions of Taino society leave little doubt that the Tainos in Puerto Rico, Hispaniola, and eastern Cuba were complex chiefdoms by the date of European contact (Wilson 1990b; Keegan 1991a). In addition, the archaeology of the Bahamas, Jamaica, central Cuba, and possibly the Leeward islands (see fig. 9.1) indicates that populations on these islands were within the Taino political sphere and were characterized by simple chiefdoms (Keegan and Maclachlan 1989; Allaire 1987; Rouse 1992).

The distinction between simple and complex chiefdoms is one of scale versus size. Chiefdoms, in contrast to chieftaincies (e.g., "Big Man" or "local group" polities), are regional in the sense that they extend beyond the village or local group (Johnson and Earle 1987). To a large degree the main difference between simple and complex chiefdoms is that simple chiefdoms have fewer members. Because they both use similar mechanisms to integrate regional populations, they share more with each other than they do with local group polities of similar size. In other words, a simple chiefdom with 1,000 members is more similar to a complex chiefdom with 10,000 members than it is to a chieftaincy with 1,000 members.

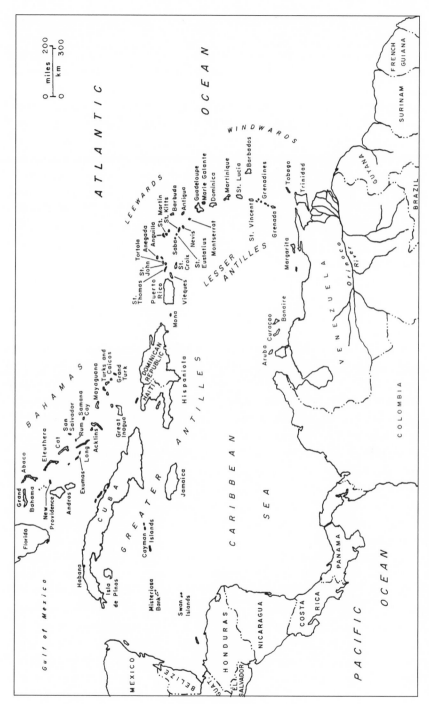

Fig. 9.1. Map of native West Indian peoples in 1492.

Earle (1987, 291) reports that almost all efforts to explain the rise of chiefdoms have stressed the importance of economic relations. These relations are characterized as either managerial, in which the chief organizes and manages aspects of the economy, or controlling, in which there is differential access to productive resources and/or exchanged wealth. Johnson and Earle (1987) have shown that such hierarchical relations of production should be viewed as complementary behaviors comprising the economic role of chiefs.

We view Earle's dichotomy of "management" and "control" as representing mechanisms for achieving the more basic objective of chiefdom-level economies. We define this objective as economic growth under conditions of locally diminishing marginal returns to production. Chiefdoms emerge from subsistence economies. The economic goal of subsistence production is usually given as the satisfaction of needs or wants using a cost-minimization strategy (Johnson and Earle 1987). Yet, for a cost-minimization strategy to be effective, some other aspect of the economy must be satisfied, optimized, or maximized. Taken to an extreme, cost minimization ends with the death of its practitioners. We believe that the major goal of subsistence economies is population growth either through the production of offspring or the recruitment of new members. This goal is not surprising given that labor is typically the major limiting factor in subsistence economies.

In sum, we view chiefdoms as hierarchically organized, kinship-based polities that are organized to promote economic growth. Economic growth occurs through the recruitment of new members, by either immigration or procreation. In a sense chiefdoms can be compared to a pyramid scheme. The cost of membership is not severe, and everyone benefits as long as growth continues. However, when population size exceeds the organization capabilities of the kinship system or when growth stops, the pyramid collapses under its own weight (often with a shove from a neighboring competitor).

The preceding is a slightly modified description of a system of staple finance, a type of finance that is sometimes referred to as "redistribution" (Earle 1987). The use of staples to create a financial institution begins in economies in which the subsistence output of every household is autonomous. In order to make certain that needs are met, every household must produce somewhat more than it actually uses. When a leader or chieftain emerges who is able to mobilize the surplus production of the individual households, the opportunity for political action also emerges. In other words, the initial step involves appropriating the surplus production of individual households.

In return for their otherwise unused produce the chieftain must provide at least the same level of subsistence security as was represented by the appropriated surplus. By accepting responsibility for their security and managing subsistence risk, the chieftain obtains the means to finance other activities and there is no additional cost to the individual household. For such a system to work there must be trust among the participants. The producers must trust their leader to bail them out in times of subsistence stress, and the chieftain must trust the producers to maintain the same level of subsistence overproduction. Such trust, what behavioral ecologists would call reciprocal altruism (Trivers 1971; Maynard Smith 1981), is achieved through the manipulation of kinship relations.

To this point leadership can be strictly situational. In other words, an individual who is able to garner the support of relatives helps the group respond to an acute problem. Once the problem has passed, the leadership role may vanish or remain as an honorific. There is no mechanism for transferring the leadership role either laterally or generationally. It is only after a situation becomes chronic that leadership becomes formalized. Such formalization occurs through the manipulation of traditional kinship-defined roles, which leads to the creation of rules of succession. The variability observed in rules of succession is largely the result of underlying differences in the kinship system from which leadership roles emerged.

From this initial economy of scale, the jump to a regionally integrated economy is easily achieved. First, because kinship relations typically extend over a wide area, the basis for collaborative effort is already in place. Through marriage alliances, and the more formal expression of rules of residence and descent, the social fabric is ever more tightly knit. Second, subsistence security is more easily maintained over a larger area and with a more diversified economy. Shortfalls in one area can be offset by the allocation of surplus products from other areas. Thus, so long as crop failures and other disasters are localized and not severe, the economy can grow at a rapid rate for no additional investment in subsistence production. Lastly, as the economy grows households are ever more distant from the leaders who appropriate their surplus production. In the process, the surplus is converted from a household need to a political necessity.

Competition between households and larger aggregations (clans, lineages, etc.), the intensification of wealth finance as a means to integrate the ever-growing regional polity (D'Altroy and Earle 1985), and increasing

demands on the organization and output of household production all contribute to the emergence of chiefdoms as a recognizable social formation.
At their inception, simple chiefdoms provide benefits to most, if not all, of
their members. By the time hierarchical inequalities have developed, the
household may have no other option than to accept the dictates of the
emerging elites.

Avunculocal Chiefdoms

In defining chiefdoms as regional-scale growth economies, which are organized by principles of kinship, we have identified kinship, and more generally social organization, as the key element in the emergence of chiefs. It is
our contention that one cannot understand the political formation called
chiefdoms without first understanding the social foundations in which
their political economies are embedded.

We find avunculocal chiefdoms interesting for three reasons. First, they
are comparatively rare, yet they evolved in a series of widely separated
areas of restricted size, with a remarkable degree of similarity. Avunculocal
chiefdoms evolved independently in Africa, Oceania, and the Americas, in
tropical forests and Arctic tundra, and in economies practicing foraging,
horticulture, and agriculture (Ember 1971; Rosman and Rubel 1986; Weiner
1976). Thus it is a matter of theoretical interest to understand why this unusual and complex pattern of kinship organization should be arrived at by
disparate, unrelated peoples. Second, we believe that the Taino represent
one of the clusters of societies in which conditions favoring the avunculocal
chiefdom occurred, although scholars long failed to recognize that this was
so. Third, avunculocal chiefdoms serve as an excellent vehicle for illustrating the ways in which economic relations and social organization evolve in
concert.

The notion of infrastructural primacy that underlies the cultural materialist perspective is often misunderstood to mean a mechanical materialism
in which a given set of material conditions is viewed as leading inevitably
to similar social organization and ideology. In fact, the primacy attributed
to infrastructural determination suggests instead that infrastructural stability promotes social stability whereas infrastructural change regulates
social change, with the character of the change reflecting prevailing cultural patterns. In other words, entirely new organizational structures are
not created out of thin air. For example, a society does not suddenly change
its descent reckoning from matrilineal to patrilineal. Instead, change is op-
portunistic. Existing organizational structures are modified or rearranged

to meet new conditions. Thus, it is hardly surprising that chiefdoms are found with cognatic, matrilineal, and patrilineal descent and several patterns of marital residence. The question is why do societies take one turn rather than another in their development in response to comparable infrastructural change? Part of the answer lies in the antecedent social organization on which infrastructural change goes to work.

The idea that infrastructurally driven social change is mediated by a society's antecedent structure is illustrated by Ember's arguments cited in Keegan and Maclachlan (1989, 619–20). Matrilocal residence and the subsequent development of matrilineality, he suggests, emerges from external warfare. With men absent much of the time, women are obliged to rely heavily on one another, and extended households centered on groups of related women are the result. Internal warfare and heavy reliance on male labor, by contrast, favor patrilocal residence. Avunculocal residence is seen as a response to internal warfare emerging in a previously matrilineal and matrilocal society, as powerful men rally their clansmen around them to form extended households of matrilineally related men.

This argument would seem to imply an incompatibility between matrilocal residence and the competition of men for control of local resources. It is not difficult to see how this might be so. Divale (1984) has viewed matrilocality and external war as elements in an expansionist migratory strategy, such as that of the Bantu-speaking peoples in Africa or the settlement of island chains such as the West Indies. The matrilocal family is also congenial with a pattern of low intensity horticulture reliant on female labor coupled with hunting or fishing by men over large areas. It may be too that absent men and the relatively high divorce rates typical of matrilocal societies inhibit population growth. In any case, the matrilocal pattern seems suitable to a society that can deal with the crowding of local subsistence resources by migration or by expansion of catchment areas. This pattern of residence is not, however, suited for the intensification of labor in farming or growth in population density. This is so, first, because the intensification of effort requires the labor of previously absent men, and second, because population pressure on local resources suitable for intensified production engenders internal conflict.

Here we observe the structural mediation of infrastructurally driven processes quite clearly. When infrastructural conditions conducive to the emergence of chieftains and then chiefs occur in a previously patrilocal society, no change in marital residence occurs because the existing pattern is compatible with new political and economic realities. In the matrilocal case, the existing pattern deprives the male would-be entrepreneur of both

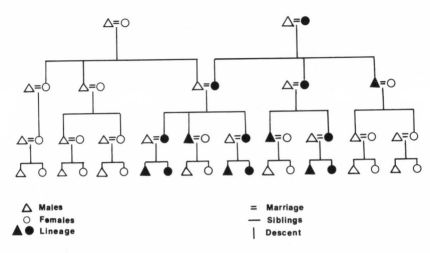

Fig. 9.2. Matrilineal kinship.

a domestic group of related males and the resource base he needs to advance his interests. Something has to change.

Much of what we have said thus far echoes our earlier work. What remains to be added are observations concerning what chiefs do to transform slow-growth matrilineal societies into societies with denser populations and higher productivity. Our thoughts on these matters have been strongly influenced by Abraham Rosman and Paula Rubel (1989) who employed a controlled comparison of the Southwest Pacific and the Northwest Coast of North America, somewhat similar to that employed for the Taino by Keegan and Maclachlan (1989).

Rosman and Rubel (1989) point to the marked similarities between the Trobriand on the one hand and the Haida and Tlingit on the other. In both areas there is an aristocracy of chiefs with avunculocality, and matrilineal descent, as well as Crow-type kinship terminology and patrilateral cross-cousin marriage (fig. 9.2). They then address the question of how these societies reached this state from an antecedent state by comparing them to their culturally related neighbors, on the assumption that these may reflect both an antecedent baseline state and transitional states on the path to an avunculocal chiefdom. In one case these are neighboring Melanesian horticulturalists; in the other, Athapaskan foragers. In both instances the baseline state involves a matrilocal society that practices direct marital exchange, usually bilateral cross-cousin marriage, and the transitional stages involve growth in matrilineal kinship, in political integration, and in the frequency of avunculocal residence.

Rosman and Rubel describe their comparisons as the investigation of developmental potential in two contrasting environments. They demonstrate that the sociopolitical organizations of the Trobriand and the Haida and Tlingit are virtually identical, despite dramatic differences in their ecology and economy. The results appear to undercut traditional materialist theories, which view ecology and/or economy as the major determining factors. It thus appears that structural principles have priority in the evolution of social complexity. How else can one explain identical sociopolitical organizations in such radically different environments (arctic versus tropical island) and among people with radically different economies (e.g., foragers versus horticulturalists)? This is similar to the question raised by Marquardt (1992, 2), who asks how the Calusa were able to achieve complexity and power without controlling agricultural surpluses.

The solution is found in looking at variables at the appropriate scale. Our position is that such macrocomparisons of ecology and economy overlook more basic similarities. We prefer to reconstrue Rosman and Rubel's analysis in terms of differing potentials for economic and demographic growth in relation to their neighbors. What matters to us is not the difference between Melanesian horticulture and Northwest Coast foraging but the fact that the avunculocal chiefdoms in both areas enjoyed distinct advantages over their neighbors due to superior subsistence resources and strategic locations for trade. Thus, the features of infrastructure that may be most important in the transformation of relatively egalitarian matrilineal societies into aristocratic avunculocal chiefdoms have less to do with the character of subsistence technologies or environments than they do with locational concentration of resources within regions and factors circumscribing the opportunities of individuals and groups.

Occupation of a regionally advantageous position lays the way open for the development of social organization capable of controlling resources and of arranging them in a way leading to the economic and population growth that consolidates the advantaged group's regional position. It should be remembered that throughout this process, these societies are not simply responding to the independent growth of their population but are actively promoting the production of offspring. At the same time the process is attended by growing differences of rank and privilege within the advantaged society. The fact that the less advantaged are members of an advantaged society may be what holds them in place (if indeed they have somewhere else to go, migration may entail unacceptable opportunity costs). Better to be a low-ranking Haida or Trobriander than a nomadic hunter or the tiller of an impoverished atoll.

The Tainos and Their Islands

The West Indies extend over 4,000 kilometers like stepping stones between the South, Central, and North American mainlands (fig. 9.1). The islands exhibit a bewildering level of diversity in landform, geology, and history. For example, all but the northernmost Bahamas fall within the tropics, all but the southernmost Antilles fall within the North Atlantic hurricane track, and all of the islands are influenced by persistent trade winds, while variations in topography and rainfall create landscapes which range from steep mountain peaks to depressions below sea level and from rain forest to desert.

At the time of Spanish contact all of the Greater Antilles, except extreme western Cuba, and the Windward islands of the Lesser Antilles were occupied by peoples we today call Tainos (Rouse 1992).[1]

The Greater Antilles comprise 88 percent of the land area in the West Indies (207,968 square kilometers). The main islands—Cuba (110,922 sq. km.), Jamaica (11,424 sq. km.), Hispaniola (76,484 sq. km.; shared by Haiti and the Dominican Republic), and Puerto Rico (8,897 sq. km.)—are formed around two sections of mountain ranges that originate in northern Central America and a southern range, which forms the Blue Mountains of Jamaica and the Sierra de Baharuco on Hispaniola (Watts 1987, 9; West and Augelli 1976, 31–32). One of the northern ranges rises in southernmost Cuba as the Sierra Maestra, forms the Cordillera Central of Hispaniola and central range of Puerto Rico, and ends in the Virgin Islands. The second, lower range, the Cordillera Septentrional, runs along the northern coast of the Dominican Republic. The highest mountain in the Antilles, Pico Duarte (3,175 meters), is a huge gold-bearing batholith, which intrudes into the Cordillera Central in the Dominican Republic (Watts 1987; West and Augelli 1976, 31). The surfaces of these islands are mostly weathered limestone, sedimentary, and metamorphic rocks.

The Bahama archipelago is a chain of 29 calcareous islands, 661 cays, and 2,387 rocks stretching over 1,000 kilometers, from 100 kilometers east of West Palm Beach, Florida, to within 100 kilometers of Haiti and Cuba (Sealey 1985). Today composed of the Commonwealth of the Bahamas and the Turks and Caicos Islands, they occupy about 5 percent of the land area in the West Indies (11,826 sq. km.).

The Lesser Antilles, which account for 3 percent of the land area (7,164 sq. km.), form a double arc of islands "along an arcuate zone of instability which roughly coincides with the Atlantic edge of the Caribbean tectonic plate" (Watts 1987, 11). The inner arc is built around high volcanic cones, while the discontinuous outer arc is limestone islands built on older volcanic or crystalline bases (Watts 1987, 11–12; Watters et al. 1992). Antigua, eastern Guadeloupe (Grandterre), Anguilla, Barbuda, and Marie Galante are the main outer-arc islands. Water passages in the Lesser Antilles are short, with every island visible from its neighbors. Traditionally the Lesser Antilles have been divided into Windward and Leeward groups, designations that originated as British colonial administrative units (West and Augelli 1976, 194–95). This division remains useful for two reasons. The Leewards (3,207 sq. km.) are almost all much smaller than the Windwards (3,957 sq. km.). In fact, the island of Guadeloupe (1,702 sq. km.) is larger than all of the other Leewards combined. The Windward-Leeward division also coincides with protohistoric cultural distributions, with Island Carib societies occupying the Windward islands and eastern Tainos on the Leewards (Rouse 1992; Allaire 1987, 1996).

Colonization of the West Indies

Groups of pottery-using horticulturalists, called Saladoids after the type site in Venezuela, entered the Antilles from coastal Guiana and the Orinoco River Valley in Venezuela sometime prior to 400 b.c. (Haviser 1997; Rouse 1992; Siegel 1992). Their migration is easily traced by the distinctive ways they decorated their pottery vessels. Recent evidence suggests that the earliest Saladoid sites in the West Indies are in Puerto Rico and the Leeward islands. This distribution indicates that most of the Lesser Antilles were by-passed during the initial migration(s) such that their arrival in the Greater Antilles was almost simultaneous with their departure from South America (Keegan 1995).

The Saladoid peoples were extensive horticulturalists who lived in villages along the coast or adjacent to rivers. In addition to exploiting the numerous plants indigenous to the Antilles, they also brought with them familiar cultigens, the most important of which was manioc. Manioc was supplemented by other root crops and fruits, land animals, marine mollusks, and fishes. Siegel (1992) has argued that the Saladoids practiced ancestor worship, as is reflected in the spatial arrangement of their settlements with structures surrounding a central plaza/cemetery.

During the initial phase of island colonization, the population grew at a rapid rate as groups moved quickly through the islands. Opportunities for individuals to assume positions of leadership would have been fairly common but short-lived. We believe these initial colonists practiced matrilineal descent and matrilocal residence because these patterns of residence and descent characterize the mainland Arawakan peoples who today live closest to the river mouths from which the ancestors of the Tainos departed (Steward and Faron 1959, 300–1). Furthermore, matrilineal descent is usually accompanied by a preference for matrilocal residence (Aberle 1961, 666), which is necessary for avunculocal residence to emerge (Fox 1967; Murdock 1949). Finally, ethnohistoric reports identify matrilineal descent and avunculocal residence as the predominant patterns among the Classic Taino at contact (Alcina Franch and Galán Mayo 1990; Keegan and Maclachlan 1989, 623).

Within these social arrangements males fill the major political roles as leaders of the matrilineage (Schneider 1961, 5). Such male leaders—headmen or chieftains—would have come forward in a number of instances, for example, (1) in the formation of marriage alliances with other matri-sibs, which were needed to ensure reproductive continuity; (2) during the fissioning of local settlement units and the movement of people between islands; (3) in the management of economic and demographic risk inherent in island colonization though the continuation of inter-island trading and visiting; and (4) in hostile relations with Archaic groups, called Casimiroids, already in residence on at least some of the islands. These, and other, opportunities for leadership were short-lived and could be abrogated through the fissioning and moving away of dissatisfied individuals.

After colonists reached Puerto Rico there was a pause of almost 1,000 years before population expansion continued to the west and north (Keegan 1995). By the time a second wave of expansion began around A.D. 600, the pottery styles had changed to the point at which the peoples were distinguished as Ostionoid, named for the type site in western Puerto Rico. The second wave moved rapidly westward along northern and southern routes to colonize Hispaniola, Jamaica, the eastern end of Cuba, and the Bahamas (Rouse 1992; Keegan 1992). It is hypothesized that the Casimiroid foragers, who occupied most of Cuba at this time, halted the movement of the Ostionoids into western Cuba. However, too little research has been conducted to explain the fate of the Casimiroid groups living in Hispaniola and possibly Jamaica. The Casimiroids may have perished in the islands either due to poor manipulation of their environment; they may have been exterminated by the Ostionoid immigrants; or they may have become acculturated into Saladoid groups, thus giving rise to the Ostionoid culture (Chanlatte Baik and Narganes Storde 1990; Rouse 1986; Siegel 1989).

Eventually, all of the islands came to be occupied at relatively low densities. Where previously all of the archaeological sites contained common material remains (for example, white-on-red painted pottery, exotic stone pendants and amulets, and a common religious paraphernalia), a period of semi-autonomous development on a subregional scale now took place. This intermediate phase is reflected in divergent regional pottery styles (Rouse 1986).

Trade networks were extensive during the Ostionoid period, encompassing all of the Greater Antilles, Bahamas, and possibly through the Lesser Antilles to mainland South America (Boomert 1987; Watters 1997). Recent excavations on Grand Turk have revealed a specialized shell-bead production center that was in operation in the twelfth and thirteenth centuries A.D., which reflected the strong ties between the Bahamas and Greater Antilles (Carlson 1993). In addition, some researchers have suggested that there was contact with Mesoamerica, based on similarities in the ballgames played both in Mesoamerica and in the Greater Antilles (Alegría 1983; but cf. Walker 1993). Columbus was impressed with the seaworthiness of Taino canoes, and he described canoes that could hold 50 to 100 men in the Bahamas and Cuba (Dunn and Kelley 1989). Trade goods consisted of subsistence items, pottery, cotton, parrots, salt, raw materials for tool manufacture, and ceremonial items such as *zemis* (representations of spirits), beads, and semiprecious stones (Sauer 1966; Sullivan 1981; Rouse 1986; Keegan 1992).

In the final phase of development, which began about A.D. 600 (Curet 1992; Rouse 1992), powerful regional chiefs emerged. The Tainos are regarded as a series of polities whose political power in the fifteenth century was centered on the island of Hispaniola (Keegan 1992; Rouse 1992; Wilson 1990b). Following Las Casas (1967), there has been a tendency to treat all of the northern West Indies as a single culture area with minor local differences.[2] Similarities in material culture support this conclusion. It should be remembered, however, that there was a range of variability; for example, three mutually unintelligible languages were spoken on Hispaniola alone (Las Casas 1967, 1:634, 2:311; Mártir de Anglería 1989, 356; Bourne 1906, 335).

The Tainos lived in large permanent villages in which houses containing several related families were aligned on streets or were irregularly arranged around a central plaza (Rouse 1992). Some villages had several thousand inhabitants. Surrounding the villages were permanent mounded fields, called *conucos,* where manioc, sweet potato, and, to a lesser extent, maize were planted (Sturtevant 1961, 1969). A wide variety of other cultigens were also grown in house gardens, including chili peppers, beans, squash, gourds, cotton, various fruits, *Bixa* (annatto), and tobacco (Keegan

1987; Newsom 1993). The Tainos made extensive use of terrestrial and marine animals and may have domesticated the Muscovy duck and hutia (*Geocapromys* sp.), a cat-sized rodent (Keegan 1992).

The Individual in Taino Society

Before discussing the avunculocal chiefdom as a social formation, it is useful to examine social relations from the perspective of a single individual. Membership in social groups began at birth. Immediately after birth, every individual was given a name identifying him or her as a Taino—a human being (Fewkes 1907, 47). Already each individual belonged to a nuclear family, an extended family, a matri-clan, a matrilineage, and a *cacicazgo* (chiefdom-level polity). Gender and membership in these groups had consequences for one's entire life.

Although there are no records of lateral kin terms in the available ethnographies or histories, Byrne's (1991) cross-cultural analysis suggested that the Tainos used Crow-type kin terms. In the bifurcate-merging Crow system, female patrilateral and matrilateral cross-cousins are differentiated from each other, siblings, and parallel cousins, while patrilateral daughters are lumped with patrilateral aunts and matrilateral daughters are lumped with their brother's daughter (Murdock 1949, 224).

The world was dominated by one's mother's kin, especially the female kin. The most important male was the mother's brother. Between birth and puberty, individuals were socialized in the rights and obligations that accompanied group memberships. Life passages were marked by participation in various ceremonies, including a hair-cutting ceremony in which the child was the focus (Lovén 1935). At puberty, the passage from child to adult was celebrated. Unless they were married at this time, girls remained in the village of their mothers. Boys, particularly those who were expected to participate in leadership roles in their clan, moved to the village of their designated maternal uncle.

Marriage marked one's passage to full adulthood. Commoner males were expected to compensate the wife-giving lineage by providing bride-service (Fewkes 1907, 48). The husband moved to the village of his wife where he worked for his in-laws for several years. It is not clear how long bride-service lasted, but in some societies the end of bride-service (sometimes called suitor-service) coincides with the birth of a child. In effect, bride-service ends with the production of a new member of the wife's clan. The couple would then set up their own household in the most advantageous location. After marriage and bride-service, most commoners would pass through various roles and positions within their lineage and other less formal groups. In addition, certain individuals would receive training as craft specialists or as healers and shamans.

High-status males compensated the wife-giving lineage with payments rather than service. The husband would accumulate a variety of wealth items with the help of his clan and pay these to the wife-giving clan. The wife would then move immediately to live viri-avunculocally with her husband. High-status males were also polygynous, and were able to take as many wives as they could support. Such multiple marriages had an important integrative effect for the society; high-status women from one clan or lineage were given in marriage to a high-status male from another clan or lineage, thus creating a bond between these groups. The bond was strengthened by the fact that all offspring were members of the wife-giving lineage. Moreover, Harris (1991, 145) notes that "bride-price and suitor-service tend to occur where production is being increased, land is plentiful, and the labor of additional women and children is seen as scarce and as being in the best interests of the corporate group."

The highest position our high-status individual could achieve was that of *cacique.* In preparation, a male joined an assembly of nephews in the village of his uncle the cacique (or clanlord). There he would have been instructed in the duties of the position until the moment of succession. The emergence of caciques is discussed in more detail later.

The final passage was death, which was celebrated by a variety of ceremonies depending upon the rank and gender of the individual. For example, it is reported that when a cacique died, at least some of his wives were buried with him (Fewkes 1907, 70). Some individuals "lived" beyond death, their bones curated in shrines to revered family members.

Taino Political Economy

At contact, the Tainos lived in a ranked society in which the primary division was between the aristocratic *nitainos* and the commoners and *naborías* (see Moscoso 1981; Harris 1994). As with other ranked societies, it is likely that there were numerous divisions within these primary ranks. With the exception of naborías, there is little discussion of the divisions within the commoner class. Naboría was translated as "personal slave"; however, the Taino treatment and meaning of "slave" was very different from its European usage (Harris 1994, 18). To the Tainos naboría meant personal servant, war captive, and person of lower status than commoner, but it did not imply personal ownership (Moscoso 1981, 260–61).

Divisions within the nitainos included, for example, the caciques (chiefs), *behiques* (shamans), and *baharí* (clanlords) (Redmond and Spencer

1994, table 10.1). The highest rank was held by the *matunherí* (paramount cacique), a ruler whose leadership extended over a substantial territory. Among the Tainos, lineages were grouped into cacicazgos. Each cacicazgo was headed by a matunherí who had the support of a large number of district caciques and village clanlords. For example, the 30 wives and multiple names ascribed to Behechio, the matunherí of Xaraguá, represent villages allied under his leadership (Fewkes 1907, 34; Wilson 1990b, 117–18).

Caciques had overall command of the processes of production, including agriculture, fishing, hunting, and handicrafts, with surplus products stored in the caciques' warehouses (Moscoso 1981). Ordinary (commoner) Tainos were reportedly extremely obedient to their caciques. The Spaniards noted that ordinary Tainos would suffer torture or commit suicide if this would best serve their cacique (Las Casas 1967, 2:312; Mártir de Anglería 1989, 592). Peter Harris (1994) has argued that such obedience reflected their belief that caciques were semidivine. Their status was reflected in the use of specially carved wooden stools (*duhos*) to keep them off the ground, and, on occasion, by the transport of caciques on litters.

In his initial dealings with the Tainos, Columbus demanded a set level of tribute from each of the matunherí. The caciques were responsible for collecting the tribute from their followers and delivering it to the Spaniards (Moscoso 1981; Wilson 1990a, 1990b). Later, when the Spaniards began to allocate Taino communities in *encomienda* grants, the caciques were exempt from service and other nitainos served as supervisors and overseers. These roles probably reflect the precontact positions of a certain class of nitainos in the tributary chiefdom (Moscoso 1981, 234).

Although most caciques were males, there are records of females who ascended to this rank (Sued-Badillo 1979, 1985). More important, in avunculocal chiefdoms, women are the power behind the throne. Anacaona, the sister of Behechio, was married to Caonabo, the matunherí of Maguana (Wilson 1990b). This marriage cemented the alliance between the two most powerful Taino cacicazgos in Hispaniola. Moreover, Bartolomé Colón reported that Anacaona controlled both production and distribution of a wide variety of high-status goods.

There are two lists of the Taino provinces on Hispaniola in the sixteenth century. Andrés Morales recorded five province groups, which "since time immemorial were used by the Indians," and listed 53 provinces (Mártir de Anglería 1989, 354). Bartolomé de Las Casas recorded five supreme and two independent caciques and 27 provinces (Las Casas 1967, 1:9–54, 2:308–9). Although there are differences between these accounts, Harris (1994) was able to demonstrate a considerable match between what Morales called province groups and Las Casas called supreme caciques. Harris's reconciliation divides the island into eight pairs, geographical symbols of the two eyes, mouth, forelegs, hindlegs, and vagina of Hispaniola (fig. 9.3), which the Indians viewed as a "monstrous living beast of the female sex" (Mártir de Anglería 1989, 629).

The symbolic beast is also represented in the Taino ceremonial/trading center MC-6 on the island of Middle Caicos, southern Bahama archipelago (Harris 1994; see Sullivan 1981). The pairing of cacicazgos (province groups) appears to be a higher scale reflection of the settlement pairs observed in the Bahamas (Keegan 1992), which formed part of our evidence for the emergence of avunculocal chiefdoms in the region. The main criticism of that formulation is that evidence was lacking for the contemporaneity of settlement pairs. Recent investigations have focused on dating settlement pairs, and the first set of radiocarbon dates from a settlement pair on Middle Caicos are virtually identical (MC-12 and MC-32: cal A.D. 1282 and 1290, respectively).[3]

The Emergence of Caciques

Hereditary ruling classes, headed by a cacique or chief, emerge in stratified societies based on unequal access to the means of production. Johnson and Earle (1987) have summarized the four main pathways by which social stratification is achieved: (1) surplus production for the management of risk; (2) facilitation of large-scale infrastructure, such as irrigation projects; (3) warfare; and (4) long-distance trade. These pathways receive differential emphasis in different societies, as is clear from competing theories regarding the origins of the state (e.g., Wittfogel 1957; Carneiro 1970; Rathje 1971), and it is not necessary for a society to pursue all four. In addition, the use of religious ideology to reinforce the power and authority acquired by chiefs has also been emphasized (Curet 1992). Moreover, the context in which these pathways are pursued is as important as the pathway itself. We contend that in chiefdom-level societies the ultimate objective is population growth, that this objective is pursued in competition with like groups, and that production and reproduction are organized by kinship relations.

The Tainos exhibit all of these characteristics. There is evidence that the population was growing rapidly until at least A.D. 1400 (Curet 1992; Keegan 1992). There is clear evidence of the intensification of food production through mounding, terracing, and irrigation (Moscoso 1981, 1986; Ortíz Aguilú et al. 1991; Sauer 1966), along with the domestication of animals and the elaboration of fishing technologies (Keegan and DeNiro 1988; Wing 1987) and the production of surplus handicrafts (Wilson 1990b). Special-

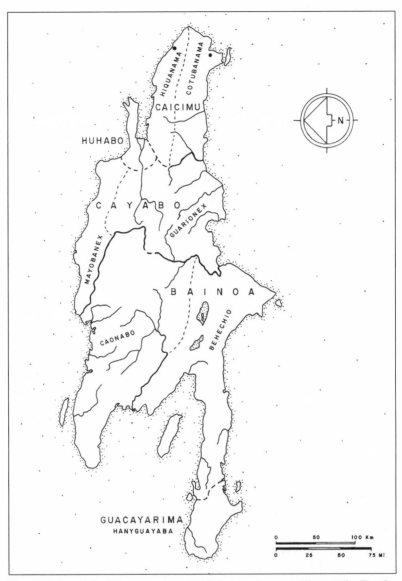

Fig. 9.3. Map of the Taino provinces and their *caciques* on Hispaniola. For the Tainos, the eastern end of the island was the top. Regional boundaries tend to follow major rivers, and they are represented by heavy dashed lines; boundaries between *cacicazgos* tend to follow mountain ranges and are represented by lighter dashed lines. This figure is based on Peter Harris's division of the island into eight pairs of cacicazgos in five major regions; he suggests that these are geographical symbols for the two eyes, mouth, forelegs, hindlegs, and vagina of Hispaniola, which the Indians viewed as a "monstrous living beast of the female sex." The two caves that were the beast's eyes, in the Caicimu region, are represented by dots. (*Source:* Peter O'B. Harris, personal communication, 1997; used with permission.)

ized craft production tied to long-distance exchange is now dated to A.D. 1100 between Hispaniola and the southern Bahamas (Carlson 1993). Large ocean-going canoes were observed by Columbus in both Cuba and the Bahamas (Dunn and Kelley 1989), as were daily "commuter ferries" between Puerto Rico and eastern Hispaniola. Warfare is reflected in a variety of references. Weapons, military adornments, and "war dances" (*areítos*) were observed, and the Tainos were able to assemble, in very short order, large armies to fight the Spaniards. In addition, Wilson (1990b, 116) notes that in the summer of 1496, the paramount cacique of Xaraguá, Behechio, had launched an expedition to conquer the people along the Neiba River as well as some other caciques of the island. In sum, all of the evidence supports the conclusion that the northern West Indies functioned as a system of competing, regionally integrated cacicazgos, between which there were interactions over substantial distances.

Ideology was also important in distinguishing levels of ranking. The use of ritual artifacts to legitimize the power and authority of Taino caciques is well documented (e.g., Curet 1992; Rouse 1992). Furthermore, José Oliver (1997, 145–46) has recently shown how the story of Yayael's banishment, at the beginning of the Taino origin myth recorded by Ramón Pané, supports the social norm of moving to the village of one's maternal uncle at adolescence (avunculocal residence).

In kinship terms, the Taino political machine is best described as an avunculocal chiefdom. We use the term *avunculocal chiefdom* rather than calling it an avunculocal society because the fact that a chiefdom is organized through avunculocal residence does not require the entire society to be so. Avunculocal residence seems to emerge in previously matrilocal, matrilineal societies that have experienced a recurrence of internal warfare (Ember 1974). Because marriage distances are usually short in matrilocal societies, the men of the matrilineage can routinely assemble for political and ritual activities. As internal conflict commences, outbreaks of warfare with nearby neighbors are often intermittent with periods of alliance and trade, which makes them difficult to anticipate. Constant readiness is required because political leaders must always be mindful of potential threats at the same time that they pursue military alliances and actual military campaigns. Under these conditions, the incentive to assemble the men of a matrilineal group more often and for longer periods increases. However, it is not possible to localize all of the men all of the time, so clanlords should attempt to assemble a retinue of capable and loyal followers from among their matri-kin.

Spanish accounts make no mention of intercacicazgo warfare. The reason may be that at the time of European contact the nitainos (elites) were forming marriage alliances between themselves while at the same time increasing the social distance between themselves and the commoners. There is tantalizing evidence that the Taino elite practiced patrilateral cross-cousin marriage in which spouses were exchanged between the five paramount cacicazgos. Our reasoning is as follows. First, avunculocal chiefdoms develop in an environment of within-group hostility. In other words, it is likely that the Taino chiefdoms were sociopolitical groups that at one time waged war on each other. Second, there is compelling evidence that the Tainos used the Crow-type kinship terms expected for patrilateral cross-cousin marriage alliances (Byrne 1991). Third, we have argued that military and political entrepreneurship was the key element in the emergence of the avunculocal chiefdom (Keegan and Maclachlan 1989; see also Wilson 1990a). Faced with a military standoff, in which each chiefdom marshalled roughly equal military forces, an alliance among the nitainos would foster peaceful relations that would increase the productive capacity within each cacicazgo. This standoff may be reflected in the spatial distributions of the 21 known ballcourts on Hispaniola and the 65 ballcourts on Puerto Rico (Wilson 1990b, 22–27). Vescelius noted that in Puerto Rico the most elaborate ballcourts seemed to be located along the boundaries between the cacicazgos, where they served as an outlet for competition between the polities (Rouse 1992, 15).

Peaceful relations would also facilitate the expansion of Taino influences into Cuba, the Bahamas, and the Lesser Antilles. Recent investigations in the southern Bahamas indicate an Antillean Taino presence beginning as early as A.D. 900 and continuing up to contact. This Taino presence has a colonial character, in which a dominant polity is extracting resources from the surrounding periphery. In sum, the notion of "peaceful Arawaks" may in fact be the legacy of competing paramount caciques who manipulated the social and political systems to achieve personal advantage (see Hulme 1986).

It is our contention that the underlying factor in the emergence of chiefs was the creation of a power base through the localization of males who were previously dispersed at marriage. The localization of males provided an underutilized labor force for the intensification of subsistence production, a military force for defense and expansion of territory, and organized long-distance trading expeditions for the purposes of creating and maintaining alliances that were cemented through the exchange of women in marriage. Under these conditions, succession was of supreme importance.

Succession thus became institutionalized in the social formation we call the avunculocal chiefdom.

Conclusions

Our investigations of avunculocal chiefdoms are continuing in both the ethnographic and archaeological arenas. For the present we offer four conclusions.

First, chiefdoms emerge in societies that are experiencing economic and demographic growth under conditions of locally diminishing marginal returns to production. The specific ways in which these societies develop depend on the ways in which production and reproduction unfold within the society's social matrix. In turn, this social matrix is itself subject to change in concert with the evolving infrastructure. Whereas studies of chiefdoms tend to emphasize the relative importance of "control" or "management" by chiefs, we believe that a greater emphasis should be placed on identifying the social relations of production and reproduction that provide structure to the political economy. In sum, explaining the emergence of a chiefdom requires knowledge of the antecedent social organization. It is not sufficient simply to name pathways (e.g., risk management, technology, warfare, and trade) because these have variable effects depending upon the social arrangements through which they are expressed.

Second, as Rosman and Rubel (1989) have shown, the environment and macroeconomy are not determining variables in the emergence of chiefdoms. To these authors, social organization is the crucial factor. While recognizing the significance of their work, we consider relations (e.g., competition) with neighboring groups as the key factor. Thus, the organization of neighboring groups and intergroup relations must also be defined.

Third, the basis for cross-cultural comparisons must be carefully considered, especially by archaeologists. Efforts to understand West Indian prehistory have repeatedly searched the richer ethnographic literature of the Pacific Islands for inspiration concerning the rise of the Tainos (e.g., Moscoso 1981; Watters 1982; Rouse 1986). Yet our investigations, as well as those by Rosman and Rubel (1989), indicate that comparisons may be more appropriately made with Northwest Coast foragers, Central African horticulturalists, and even the Gê societies of the interior Brazilian cerrado (Maybury-Lewis 1989).

Finally, the evolution of social and political systems requires the collaboration of archaeological, ethnohistoric, and cross-cultural ethnographic data evaluated in a well-structured theoretical framework. Having identified the Tainos as an avunculocal chiefdom has enabled us to ask specific questions of the different data sets and to refine our understanding of Taino society. For example, the excavation and dating of settlement pairs on Middle Caicos and the excavation of the shell-bead manufacturing center on Grand Turk were both undertaken with their larger significance in mind. In addition, we have returned to the original chronicles with a clearer notion of the kinds of data that would support or refute our model of Taino social organization.

Notes

1. Debate continues regarding who occupied western Cuba at contact. Those who believe that western Cuba was occupied by nonhorticultural, aceramic Guanahatabeys point to the absence of Taino artifacts from the Pinar del Río province and to the failure of Columbus's native Bahamian interpreter, Diego Colón, to understand the language of an old man picked up on the south coast of Cuba near Bahía Cortés in early June 1494 (Rouse 1992, 20). Those who believe that there is insufficient evidence to support that belief point to the absence of radiocarbon-dated deposits, to the mythical character of the chronicles (e.g., "men with tails" also inhabited western Cuba; Dunn and Kelley 1989, 177), and to encounters with Tainos in Guanahatabey territory (see Rouse 1992, fig. 3) by Columbus at his anchorage near Botabanó (the last anchorage before he encountered the incomprehensible old man) and by Velázquez de Cuéllar near Havana during the entrada of 1511 (Lovén 1935, 5; Keegan 1989, 1994).

2. Las Casas usually refers to "these islands," but the full description is "this island of Hispaniola, and that of Cuba, and that of Sant Juan and Jamaica, and those of the Lucayos" (1967, 1:243).

3. Radiocarbon dates from MC-12 were run by the Illinois State Geological Survey (ISGS) and were provided courtesy of Glen Freimuth and the Caribbean Research Foundation (personal communication, 29 April 1994). The sample was calibrated using the Calib and Display program, version 2.0 (Stuiver and Reimer 1986): ISGS 1098 680 ± 70 bp cal A.D. 1282 2σ cal A.D. 1200 to 1410.

The radiocarbon date from MC-32 was run by Beta Analytic, Inc. on a charcoal sample obtained during excavations on a project sponsored by the National Geographic Society's Committee for Research and Exploration. The sample was calibrated by Beta Analytic, Inc.: Beta-70799 690 ± 50 bp cal A.D. 1290 2σ cal A.D. 1260 to 1400.

References

Aberle, David F.

1961 Matrilineal descent in cross-cultural perspective. In *Matrilineal Kinship*, edited by D. M. Schneider and K. Gough, 655–727. Berkeley: University of California Press.

Alcina Franch, José, and P. L. Galán Mayo

1990 La sociedad Taína como una jefatura. In *Proceedings of the Eleventh International Congress for Caribbean Archaeology*, edited by A. G. Pantel Tekakis, I. Vargas Arenas, and M. Sanoja Obediente, 501–16. San Juan: La Fundación Arqueológica, Antropológica e Histórica de Puerto Rico.

Alegría, Ricardo E.

1983 *Ball Courts and Ceremonial Plazas in the West Indies*. Yale University Publications in Anthropology, no. 79. New Haven.

Allaire, Louis

1987 Some comments on the ethnic identity of the Taino-Carib frontier. In *Ethnicity and Culture*, edited by R. Auger, M. F. Glass, S. MacEachern, and P. H. McCartney, 127–33. Calgary: University of Calgary.

1996 Visions of cannibals: Distant islands and distant lands in Taino world image. In *The Lesser Antilles in the Age of European Expansion*, edited by R. Paquette and S. Engerman, 33–49. Gainesville: University Press of Florida.

Boomert, Arie

1987 Gifts of the Amazons: "Green stone" pendants and beads as items of ceremonial exchange in Amazonia and the Caribbean. *Antropológica* 67:33–54.

Bourne, Edward G.

1906 Columbus, Ramón Pané and the beginning of American Anthropology. *Proceedings of the Antiquarian Society* 17: 310–48.

Byrne, Bryan

1991 Toward the Integration of Kinship Terminology Theory into Ethnoarchaeological Middle-Range Research. Unpublished manuscript in possession of the authors.

Carlson, Lisabeth A.

1993 Strings of Command: Manufacture and Utilization of Shell Beads among the Taino Indians of the West Indies. M.A. thesis, Department of Anthropology, University of Florida, Gainesville.

Carneiro, Robert L.

1970 A theory of the origin of the state. *Science* 169:733–38.

1981 The chiefdom: Precursor of the state. In *The Transition to Statehood in the New World*, edited by G. D. Jones and R. R. Kautz, 37–79. Cambridge: Cambridge University Press.

Chanlatte Baik, Luis A., and Yvonne M. Narganes Storde

1990 *La Nueva Arqueología de Puerto Rico (su proyección en Las Antillas)*. Santo Domingo: Taller.

Curet, L. Antonio
1992   The Development of Chiefdoms in the Greater Antilles: A Regional Study of the Valley of Maunabo, Puerto Rico. Ph.D. dissertation, Arizona State University, Tempe. Ann Arbor: University Microfilms.

D'Altroy, Terence N., and Timothy K. Earle
1985   Staple finance, wealth finance, and storage in the Inka political economy. *Current Anthropology* 26(2):187–206.

Divale, William
1984   *Matrilocal Residence in Pre-Literate Society.* Ann Arbor: University of Michigan Research Press.

Dunn, Oliver, and James E. Kelley Jr., eds.
1989   *The Diario of Christopher Columbus's First Voyage to America 1492–1493* (abstracted by Bartolomé de Las Casas). Norman: University of Oklahoma Press.

Earle, Timothy K.
1978   *Economic and Social Organization of a Complex Chiefdom: The Halelea District, Kaua'i, Hawaii.* University of Michigan Museum of Anthropology, Anthropological Papers, no. 63. Ann Arbor.
1987   Chiefdoms in archaeological and ethnohistorical perspective. *Annual Review of Anthropology* 16:279–308.

Ember, Melvin
1974   The conditions that may favor avunculocal residence. *Behavior Science Review* 9:203–9.

Ember, Melvin, and Carol R. Ember
1971   The conditions that favor matrilocal versus patrilocal residence. *American Anthropologist* 73(3):571–94.

Fernández de Oviedo y Valdés, Gonzalo
1959   *Historia General y Natural de las Indias,* 2 vols. Madrid: Ediciones Atlas.

Fewkes, Jesse W.
1907   The aborigines of Porto Rico and neighboring islands. In *Annual Report of the U.S. Bureau of American Ethnology for 1903–4,* vol. 25: 1–220. Washington, D.C.: Smithsonian Institution.

Fox, Robin
1967   *Kinship and Marriage.* New York: Cambridge University Press.

Harris, Marvin
1991   *Cultural Anthropology.* New York: Harper Collins.

Harris, Peter
1994   *Nitaino* and Indians: A Preliminary Ethnographic Outline of Contact Hispaniola. Master's thesis, Department of Anthropology, University of Florida, Gainesville.

Haviser, Jay B. Jr.
1997   Settlement strategies in the early ceramic age. In *The Indigenous People of the Caribbean,* edited by S. M. Wilson, 57–69. Gainesville: University Press of Florida.

Henige, David
1991   *In Search of Columbus: The Sources for the First Voyage.* Tucson: University of Arizona Press.

Hulme, Peter
1986   *Colonial Encounters: Europe and the Native Caribbean, 1492–1797.* London: Methuen.
1988   Chiefdoms of the Caribbean. *Critiques of Anthropology* 8:105–18.

Johnson, Allen, and Timothy Earle
1987   *The Evolution of Human Society: From Forager Group to Agrarian State.* Stanford: Stanford University Press.

Keegan, William F.
1987   Diffusion of maize from South America: The Antillean connection reconstructed. In *Emergent Horticultural Economies of the Eastern Woodlands,* edited by W. F. Keegan, pp. 329–44, Southern Illinois University, Center for Archaeological Investigations, Occasional Paper 7.
1989   Creating the Guanahatabey (Ciboney): The modern genesis of an extinct culture. *Antiquity* 63:373–79.
1992   *The People Who Discovered Columbus: The Prehistory of the Bahamas.* Gainesville: University Press of Florida.
1994   West Indian archaeology: 1. Overview and foragers. *Journal of Archaeological Research* 2:255–94.
1995   Modeling dispersal in the prehistoric West Indies. *World Archaeology* 26:400–20.
1996   Columbus was a cannibal: Myth and the first encounters. In *The Lesser Antilles in the Age of European Expansion,* edited by R. Paquette and S. Engerman, 17–32. Gainesville: University Press of Florida.

Keegan, William F., ed.
1991a *Earliest Hispanic/Native American Interactions in the Caribbean: A Sourcebook.* New York: Garland Press.

Keegan, William F., and Michael J. DeNiro
1988   Stable carbon- and nitrogen-isotope ratios of bone collagen used to study coral-reef and terrestrial components of prehistoric Bahamian diet. *American Antiquity* 53(2):320–36.

Keegan, William F., and Morgan D. Maclachlan
1989   The evolution of avunculocal chiefdoms: A reconstruction of Taino kinship and politics. *American Anthropologist* 91(3):613–30.

Keegan, William F., Morgan D. Maclachlan, and Bryan Byrne
1992   Los cimientos sociales de los caciques Tainos. *ERES* 3:7–16.

Keen, Benjamin, trans.
1959   *The Life of Admiral Christopher Columbus by His Son Ferdinand.* New Brunswick: Rutgers University Press.

Las Casas, Bartolomé de
1967   *Apologética Historia Sumaria,* 2 vols. Santo Domingo: Sociedad Dominicana de Bibliofilos Inc.

Las Casas, Bartolomé de
1985 *Historia de las Indias,* 3 vols. Santo Domingo: Ediciones del Continente.
Lovén, Sven
1935 *Origins of the Tainan Culture, West Indies.* Göteborg: Elanders Bokfryckeri Akfiebolag.
Maclachlan, Morgan D., and William F. Keegan
1990 Archaeology and the ethno-tyrannies. *American Anthropologist* 92(4):1011–13.
Marquardt, William H.
1992 The Calusa domain: An introduction. In *Culture and Environment in the Domain of the Calusa,* edited by W. H. Marquardt, 1–7. Institute of Archaeology and Paleoenvironmental Studies, Monograph 1. Gainesville: Florida Museum of Natural History, Department of Anthropology, University of Florida.
Mártir de Anglería, Pedro
1989 *Décadas del Nuevo Mundo,* 2 vols. Santo Domingo: Sociedad Dominicana de Bibliofilos Inc.
Maybury-Lewis, David
1989 Social theory and social practice: Binary systems in central Brazil. In *The Attraction of Opposites,* edited by D. Maybury-Lewis and U. Almagor, 97–116. Ann Arbor: University of Michigan Press.
Maynard Smith, John
1981 The evolution of social behaviour: A classification of models. In *Current Problems in Sociobiology,* edited by B. C. R. Bertram et al., 29–44. Cambridge: Cambridge University Press.
Moscoso, Francisco
1981 The Development of Tribal Society in the Caribbean. Ph.D. dissertation, State University of New York, Binghamton.
1986 *Tribu y Clase en el Caribe Antiguo.* San Pedro de Macoris: Universidad Central del Este.
Murdock, George P.
1949 *Social Structure.* New York: Macmillan.
Newsom, Lee Ann
1993 Native West Indian Plant Use. Ph.D. dissertation, University of Florida.
Oliver, José R.
1997 The Taíno cosmos. In *The Indigenous People of the Caribbean,* edited by S. M. Wilson, 140–53. Gainesville: University Press of Florida.
Ortíz Aguilú, J. J., J. Rivera Meléndez, A. Príncipe Jácome, M. Mélendez Maiz, and M. Lavergne Colberg
1991 Intensive agriculture in pre-Columbian West Indies: The case for terraces. Paper presented at the 14th International Congress for Caribbean Archaeology, Barbados.
Rathje, William L.
1971 The origin and development of lowland Classic Maya civilization. *American Antiquity* 43(3):203–22.

Redmond, Elsa M., and Charles S. Spencer

1994   The *cacicazgo*: An indigenous design. In *Caciques and Their People: A Volume in Honor of Ronald Spores,* edited by J. Marcus and J. F. Zeitlin, 189–225. University of Michigan Museum of Anthropology, Anthropological Papers, no. 89. Ann Arbor.

Rosman, Abraham, and Paula Rubel

1986   *Feasting with Mine Enemy: Rank and Exchange Among Northwest Coast Societies.* Prospect Heights, Ill.: Waveland Press.

1989   Dual organization and its developmental potential in two contrasting environments. In *The Attraction of Opposites,* edited by D. Maybury-Lewis and U. Almagor, 209–34. Ann Arbor: University of Michigan Press.

Rouse, Irving

1986   *Migrations in Prehistory.* New Haven: Yale University Press.

1992   *The Tainos: The People Who Greeted Columbus.* New Haven: Yale University Press.

Sauer, Carl O.

1966   *The Early Spanish Main.* Berkeley: University of California Press.

Schneider, David M.

1961   Introduction. In *Matrilineal Kinship,* edited by D. M. Schneider and K. Gough, 1–29. Berkeley: University of California Press.

Sealey, Neil E.

1985   *Bahamian Landscapes.* London: Collins Caribbean.

Siegel, Peter E.

1992   Ideology, Power, and Social Complexity in Prehistoric Puerto Rico. Ph.D. dissertation, State University of New York, Binghamton.

Siegel, Peter E., ed.

1989   *Early Ceramic Population Lifeways and Adaptive Strategies in the Caribbean.* BAR International Series 506. Oxford: B.A.R.

Steward, Julian H., and Louis C. Faron

1959   *Native Peoples of South America.* New York: McGraw-Hill.

Stuiver, M., and P. J. Reimer

1986   A computer program for radiocarbon age calibration. *Radiocarbon* 28:1022–30.

Sturtevant, William C.

1961   Taino agriculture. In *The Evolution of Horticultural Systems in Native America: Causes and Consequences. A Symposium,* edited by J. Wilbert, 69–82. Caracas: Sociedad de Ciencias Naturales La Salle.

1969   History and ethnography of some West Indian starches. In *The Domestication and Exploitation of Plants and Animals,* edited by P. J. Ucko and G. W. Dimbleby, 177–99. London: Gerald Duckworth.

Sued-Badillo, Jalil

1979   *La Mujer Indígena y su Sociedad.* 2nd edition. Río Piedras, Puerto Rico: Editorial Antillana.

1985   Las cacicas Indoantillanas. *Revista del Instituto de Cultura* 87:17–26.

Sullivan, Shaun D.
1981 Prehistoric Patterns of Exploitation and Colonization in the Turks and Caicos Islands. Ph.D. dissertation, University of Illinois.

Trivers, R. L.
1971 The evolution of reciprocal altruism. *Quarterly Review of Biology* 46:35–57.

Walker, Jeffrey
1993 Stone Collars, Elbow Stones and Three-pointers, and the Nature of Taino Ritual and Myth. Ph.D. dissertation, Washington State University, Pullman.

Watters, David R.
1982 Relating oceanography to Antillean archaeology: Implications from Oceania. *Journal of New World Archaeology* 5(2):3–12.
1997 Maritime trade in the prehistoric eastern Caribbean. In *The Indigenous People of the Caribbean,* edited by S. M. Wilson, 88–99. Gainesville: University Press of Florida.

Watters, David R., J. Donahue, and R. Stuckenrath
1992 Paleoshorelines and the prehistory of Barbuda, West Indies. In *Paleoshorelines and Prehistoric Settlement,* edited by L. L. Johnson, 15–52. Boca Raton: CRC Press.

Watts, David
1987 *The West Indies: Patterns of Development, Culture and Environmental Change since 1492.* Cambridge: Cambridge University Press.

Weiner, Annette B.
1976 *Women of Value, Men of Renown.* Austin: University of Texas Press.

West, Robert C., and John P. Augelli
1976 *Middle America: Its Land and Peoples.* 2nd edition. Englewood Cliffs, N.J.: Prentice-Hall.

Wilson, Samuel M.
1990a Taino elite integration and societal complexity on Hispaniola. In *Proceedings of the Eleventh International Congress for Caribbean Archaeology,* edited by A. G. Pantel Tekakis, I. Vargas Arenas, and M. Sanoja Obediente, 517–21. San Juan: La Fundación Arqueológica, Antropológica e Histórica de Puerto Rico.
1990b *Hispaniola: Caribbean Chiefdoms in the Age of Columbus.* Tuscaloosa: University of Alabama Press.

Wing, Elizabeth S.
1987 The versatile Lucayans. Paper presented at the symposium Bahamas 1492: Its People and Environment, Freeport, Grand Bahama.

Wittfogel, Karl A.
1957 *Oriental Despotism.* New Haven: Yale University Press.

CHAPTER 10

Native Chiefdoms and the Exercise of Complexity in Sixteenth-Century Florida

JERALD T. MILANICH

The state of Florida, with its northern end in the southeastern United States and its opposite end dipping down into the tropical Caribbean, provides an excellent laboratory for the study of chiefdoms and chieftaincy. Various late pre-Columbian and colonial period native American groups displayed different levels of chiefly political complexity and practiced an array of economic strategies. For instance, the forested region of the northwest panhandle was home to the pre-Columbian Fort Walton culture, a Mississippian chiefdom (or chiefdoms); one of its early colonial period manifestations was the Apalachee Indians (Scarry 1984, 1990a, 1990b). Prior to their being the focus of Spanish Franciscan missions from 1633 into the early eighteenth century, the political organization of the Apalachee Indians was like that of other complex Native American chiefdoms found in the interior of the southeastern United States during the late pre-Columbian period and the early sixteenth century (Hudson et al. 1985; Hudson 1990; Smith 1990; Williams and Shapiro 1990). It is the only truly Mississippian chiefdom in Florida.

At the same time that the Apalachee Indians lived in the eastern panhandle, the northern half of peninsular Florida was occupied by a number of Timucua-speaking native groups who lived within riverine, forest-lake, coastal, and/or freshwater habitats. Some grew maize and gardened, while others were hunter-gatherer-fishers who cultivated garden crops. Documentary evidence indicates the Timucua, initially composed of 25–30 separate groups, were organized as small, simple chiefdoms, some consisting of literally a handful of villages. These simple chiefdoms, with their single level of political administration, stand in contrast to the complex chiefdoms of the Mississippian societies, which had multiple levels of political administration. And whereas Mississippian complex chiefdoms had populations in the thousands or tens of thousands, the evidence on hand suggests that some of the simple chiefdoms in Florida may only have numbered a thousand people.

At times groups of these Timucuan chiefdoms did join in alliances or confederacies, more complex political structures headed by a dominant chief. We will see how European contact in the colonial period impacted the nature of many of the Timucuan political systems (Deagan 1978; Milanich 1972, 1978, 1996; Milanich and Hudson 1993; Worth 1998a, 1998b).

Southwest Florida was the territory of the Calusa Indians, a group contemporary with the Apalachee and Timucua and whose subsistence economy was based on extensive harvesting of wild resources from the shallow near-shore tropical waters of the Gulf of Mexico (Goggin and Sturtevant 1964; Lewis 1978; Marquardt 1987, 1988, 1992; Widmer 1988). Documentary and archaeological evidence confirms that the sixteenth-century Calusa were organized as a complex chiefdom, as was their late pre-Columbian period manifestation, the Caloosahatchee culture. Other south Florida groups, such as the Tequesta Indians, also were hunter-gatherer-fishers, but they were not nearly as structurally complex as the Calusa. Like the Timucua, the Tequesta and other groups appear to have been small, simple chiefdoms.

Many of the native cultures residing within this cross section of environments and political systems are well-documented, both by archaeology for the pre-Columbian period and by archaeology and documentary research for the colonial period. We have informative diachronic accounts beginning with European contact in the early sixteenth century and continuing through the seventeenth and into the eighteenth centuries, from the time of first contact with European soldiers and sailors through the period of early colonization and into the mission period. In some cases the history of specific groups can be traced from the late pre-Columbian period to the time of their demise. None of the indigenous native American Indian groups survived in Florida after the mid-eighteenth century, although a small number of Apalachee are known to have been living in Louisiana in 1834, remnants of a refugee population from northwest Florida (Covington 1964).

The purpose of this chapter is to introduce readers to the range of chiefly societies present in Florida and to their pertinence for studies of chiefdoms.

With the exception of the Apalachee, all of the Florida native groups were geographically and culturally removed from the better known and more intensively studied Mississippian chiefdoms that flourished in the southeastern United States. Perhaps we can learn more about chiefdoms by focusing on the Florida societies, most of which were exceptions to the Mississippian pattern found to the north.

When the entire cross section of Florida native groups is examined, it is obvious that a taxonomic system classifying a society as either a simple or a complex chiefdom is not an accurate reflection of a changing reality. In Florida there was a continuum of chiefly complexity, a continuum which changed over time. And because Timucuan alliances—attempts to exercise greater political complexity—fluctuated over time, a single diachronic view of the past—one derived, perhaps, from a single document or group of documents from a restricted period—can give modern researchers a skewed view of political complexity. For example, what may appear to be complex or paramount Timucuan chiefdoms encompassing large territories with forty or so villages and a hierarchy of chiefs may in reality be short-term alliances of simple chiefdoms. What documentary evidence suggests was a complex political structure rivaling that of the Apalachee Indians may actually have been a group of simple Timucuan chiefdoms *acting like* a complex chiefdom. In essence, the groups within such an alliance were "exercising complexity." Just as tribal societies—autonomous village societies with achieved leadership—at times exercise chieftaincy (see Elsa Redmond's introduction to this volume), so do simple chiefdoms employ greater hierarchical political organization in specific situations.

Examples of the exercise of chiefdom complexity by Florida Timucuan groups would not necessarily be recognizable were it not for two data sources that help to highlight their existence: (1) a documentary record two centuries long that allows us to see the rise, functioning, and fall of such political structures, and (2) an archaeological record, also diachronic, that provides material evidence of complex chiefdoms with their powerful chiefly lineages persisting over time, evidence contrasting with the material cultural remains of simple chiefdoms at times exercising complexity and forming alliances.

When we use these two sources—a diachronic archival record and archaeological evidence—and apply them to both the late pre-Columbian and early colonial periods, only the Fort Walton culture/Apalachee Indians and the Calusa Indians appear to have been organized as complex chiefdoms that persisted over time. The correlates of such complex political structures are clearly present: large populations and numerous settlements, relatively large territories, chiefly lineages, a hierarchy of lesser chiefs, and a social hierarchy. These characteristics are reflected in the Apalachee and Calusa hierarchical settlement systems with their capital towns/multiple mound centers, lesser towns/mound centers, and other towns and settlements. Archaeological evidence for the presence of elite individuals—chiefs and other hereditary leaders with ascribed status—also is present.

In contrast, although the documentary record does indicate that at times Timucuan simple chiefdoms did form more complex political structures, the archaeological evidence that such structures persisted over time and were not simply instances of the exercise of complexity is lacking. The short-term exercise of complexity was not correlated with "permanent" material manifestations. Were it not for the documentary record, we might not even recognize that the Timucua were organized as simple chiefdoms, much less that some groups formed more complex political entities.

Another material difference between complex chiefdoms and chiefly alliances is that the chiefs of the former were paid actual tribute in the form of goods by lesser, vassal chiefs. The Hernando de Soto narratives of the Apalachee and other Mississippian chiefdoms to the north document the payment of such tribute in the form of cloaks, hides, and rabbits. The elites of complex chiefdoms, including the Florida Apalachee and the Calusa, accumulated other valued items as well. Examples include the exotic goods recovered from the Fort Walton culture Lake Jackson site, a pre-Columbian capital town (Jones 1982) and the site of Mound Key, the Calusa capital, where exotic goods salvaged from Spanish ships were brought (Goggin and Sturtevant 1964; Milanich 1995, 44–49). Such material tribute and exotic goods are not documented for the Timucuan chiefs; nor are such exotic items found in pre-Columbian Timucuan sites (with the exception of the Mount Royal site mentioned later).

Material correlates indicative of complex chiefdoms—such as settlement hierarchies and the *accumulation* of wealth and exotic goods by elites—are not present in simple chiefdoms. As we shall see, this is true not only among the Timucua but elsewhere in Florida as well. This phenomenon leads to our first corollary of chiefdoms and complexity: True complex chiefdoms that persist through time leave evidence in the archaeological record. Simple chiefdoms organized in alliances—exercising complexity—do not.

Why did some groups, such as the Timucua, exercise complexity? Under what conditions did such political structure appear? Some—perhaps all—of the Timucuan alliances appear to have been formed in response to a military threat posed by a complex chiefdom (or another alliance) or by a European colonial power. They formed to counter a politically more complex society. The presence of one alliance could well have led to more alliances among neighboring simple chiefdoms. To be able to confront and deal with a chiefly alliance, one had to be a member of a similar alliance. A second corollary modeling the exercise of complexity might be: To adjust to a threat posed by a politically more complex society, act just as complex. In other words: exercise complexity.

The presence of French and Spanish armies and colonists in the sixteenth century constituted new threats. In the early colonial period, the Timucuan chiefdoms had to contend not only with the diplomatic and military prowess of the Apalachee Indians and other Timucuan alliances; they also came up against the well-armed and organized representatives of European state-level societies. The need to act more complex could only have increased.

The people from Europe also presented another new variable: greater access to exotic items. Whereas the chiefs of the Apalachee Indians might have been able to control access to the wealth that flowed southward to Florida from more northerly Mississippian societies, they could not control all the wealth that was deposited on the coasts of Florida, wealth from South and Central America lost by wrecked Spanish ships. Nor could they control access to the exotic goods brought to the Tampa Bay region by the Pánfilo de Nárvaez (1528) and Hernando de Soto (1539) expeditions, or the goods brought to northeast Florida by the French (at Fort Caroline, 1564–65) and the Spaniards (at St. Augustine after 1565). Shipwreck salvage and opportunities for trade led to chiefly alliances, as did military threats. Alliances provided a means to increase access to new sources of wealth. We might alter our second corollary to read: To adjust to a threat or opportunity posed by a politically more complex society, act just as complex.

In summary, in Florida it was the historical realities of political interaction, especially warfare and the threat of warfare, and the opportunities and threats presented by the colonization of the Americas by European powers that caused some native groups to "act complex." Groups acting complex, as opposed to true complex chiefdoms, cannot be seen in the archaeological record; on the other hand, true complex chiefdoms that persisted over time can be distinguished by means of their material remains. Complex political hierarchy is manifest in complex settlement hierarchy.

In the section that follows we will examine some of the Florida chiefdoms in more detail, contrasting the Apalachee and Calusa complex chiefdoms with simple chiefdoms and chiefly alliances.

Chiefdoms and the Exercise of Complexity

Our first example comes from north-central Florida, where simple Timucuan chiefdoms (appearing in the archaeological record as clusters of small
village sites) existed in 1539 when the de Soto expedition marched through
the area. In that year, leaving the main portion of his army in central Florida, de Soto and a contingent of cavalry and infantry moved rapidly
through the Potano Indian region in Marion and Alachua counties, staying
at five different villages on five different nights. Nothing in the accounts
even hints at any political organization above the village level. The five
towns, of which the corresponding archaeological sites of four are thought
to have been located (Milanich and Hudson 1993, 134–48), are relatively
small and the population density, as can be estimated by these archaeological sites, was not great.

Twenty-five years later both French and Spanish accounts indicate that
the villages of the area through which de Soto had marched were allied
under a single chief, Chief Potano. At that time the Potano alliance was
at war with a second Timucuan chiefly alliance, one dominated by Chief
Outina, whose region encompassed a portion of the St. Johns River valley
east of the Potano (fig. 10.1). In 1564 Outina was able to convince French
soldiers from Fort Caroline to aid his warriors in two raids on Potano's
main town. The raids effectively broke the power of Chief Potano and his
alliance.

What happened? Why had what *appears* to have been a complex chiefdom evolved in such a relatively short time? The best explanation is that
this is an example of the exercise of complexity, of societies acting complex
when it was in their best interests to do so. Having taken a beating when de
Soto passed through the region—in 1606 a village leader still remembered
the cruelty shown by the Spanish army (Geiger 1936, 227–28)—and perhaps under increased attack by St. Johns River natives seeking access to
chert deposits they controlled, the native societies of north-central Florida
had to exercise more complex political organization for protection. The result was probably the ascendancy of a single chief and political unification
for military defense.

The Potano alliance did continue to exist after the French-Outina attacks, but it was greatly weakened. By the 1610s it ceased to exist, the
people having fallen victim to epidemics of disease. By the 1630s the region
was under the control of a Timucuan chief whose main village was to the
north, outside the region.

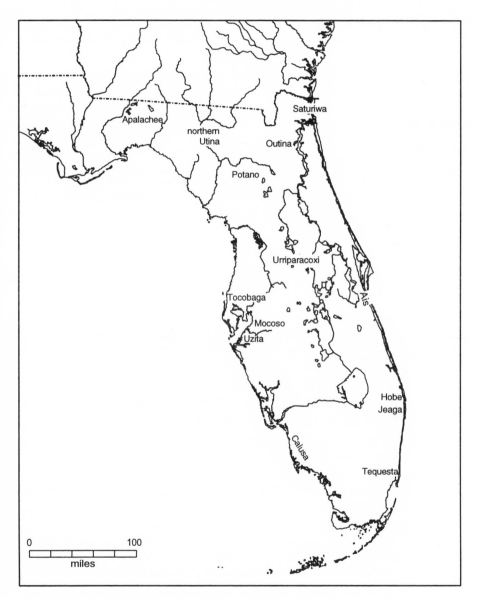

Fig. 10.1. Florida chiefdoms mentioned in text.

If the political complexity of the Potano alliance were reconstructed using only data from the 1539 de Soto *entrada,* a very different conclusion would be reached than if a picture of political organization were reconstructed from documents dating from 1564–1610. The short-lived Potano exercise of complexity, like the other Timucuan chiefly alliances, left not a shred of archaeological evidence of its existence. As noted above, the archaeological signature for simple chiefdoms exercising complexity is quite different from that of groups that incorporated more complex political organization over time.

Another Florida example of the exercise of complexity comes from the central Atlantic coast. By the late seventeenth century an alliance existed among the many small native villages and their chiefs living from the Cape Canaveral locale southward to Fort Pierce. This alliance, headed by the chief of the Ais Indians, probably developed in response to the presence of the Spaniards, French, and later the British and American colonists and the wealth their wrecked ships brought. It may have coalesced as an earlier chiefly alliance, one headed by the paramount chief of the Calusa Indians, was weakening (see later discussion).

The Ais as well as the other Indians along that section of the Atlantic coast were hunter-gatherer-fishers; they did not practice any horticulture. Their economic pursuits were centered on coastal lagoons and other marine habitats and on the extensive freshwater inland marshes and other wetlands found inland for about 15 miles.

Though able to dominate the less numerous Jeaga Indians and other nearby groups, including probably the Hobe Indians, the Ais chief's predecessor had a century earlier been subject to the Calusa chief. The power of the complex Calusa chiefdom in the sixteenth century must have been tremendous, reaching from southwest Florida to the Ais on the east coast. The Ais were not alone in having to pay tribute to the powerful, paramount chief of the Calusa. Other south Florida groups, including the coastal Jeaga, were forced to do likewise.

The salvaging of wrecked ships, the division of spoils among chiefs, and the shifting alliances as Calusa power ebbed are alluded to in both sixteenth- and seventeenth-century documents. One account was written by a shipwrecked Spaniard who witnessed the situation firsthand in about 1545: "I desire to speak of the riches found by the Indians of Ais, which perhaps were as much as a million . . ., or over, in bars of silver, in gold, and in articles of jewelry made by the hands of Mexican Indians, which the [ship's] passengers were bringing with them. These things Carlos divided with the caciques [chiefs] of Ais, Jeaga, Guacata, Mayajuaco, and Mayaca, and he took what pleased him, or the best part" (Fontaneda in True 1945, 34).

Two Spaniards shipwrecked in the Florida Keys and later (1564) ransomed by a French officer gave similar testimony, recorded by the Frenchman: "I questioned them about the places they had been. . . . They answered that fifteen years ago [about 1550] three ships, including one they had been on, were wrecked across from a place named Calos, in the shallows called The Martyrs [the Florida Keys] and the King of Calos had recovered most of the treasure in the ships and saved most of the people, including several women" (Lawson 1992, 88–89).

The apparent demise of the Calusa-dominated alliance is reflected in an extraordinary narrative written by Jonathan Dickinson, a Philadelphian wrecked on the southeast Florida coast in 1695 (Andrews and Andrews 1945). Dickinson and his fellow passengers watched as Hobe Indians began to salvage the wrecked ship and carry off the booty, including chests, trunks, and most of the survivors' clothes as well as corn, rum, sugar, molasses, and Spanish coins.

The survivors of the shipwreck later made their way northward along the coast, eventually reaching the main town of the Ais. When the Ais chief learned of the shipwreck, he immediately went to claim his share of the loot from the Hobe, a subservient group allied with him at the time. Because the Calusa chiefdom no longer dominated southern Florida, the Ais chief no longer had to share his loot in the form of tribute to the Calusa paramount chief. Archaeological evidence from the region of the Ais and their neighbors all indicates simple chiefdoms or even an autonomous village level of political integration. That same evidence has failed to produce data indicating that the chief(s) of the Ais or the chiefs of the other native groups of the region accumulated wealth from their salvage activities.

Like the Apalachee Indians described later, the Calusa are an example of a complex chiefdom, one especially powerful in the early colonial period and able to put its military and political power to use in dominating the native groups of southern Florida. Well documented and described both from archaeological and historical research (Goggin and Sturtevant 1964; Hann 1991; Lewis 1978; Marquardt 1987, 1988; Widmer 1988), the Calusa may originally have sought to maintain hegemony over much of south Florida as a way to obtain foods and other goods from the interior of the region. Later, in the colonial period, those goods came to include the booty salvaged from Spanish and other ships.

The Calusa's alliances with simple chiefdoms were maintained by the threat of force and by arranged marriages. When the Spaniards arrived in the 1560s, the Calusa chief sought to form an alliance with their leader, Pedro Menéndez de Avilés, by arranging for his sister to be given to Menéndez, the governor of Spanish Florida, in marriage. Chief Calos, as he was called by the Spaniards, recognized the military might of the Spaniards and tried to convince Menéndez, his new ally, to join in an attack on the Tocobaga Indians, who lived at the north end of Tampa Bay. Apparently, the chief was seeking to extend his control to a region previously outside his realm.

Archaeological correlates of the Calusa are similar to those of the Apalachee Indians and include a settlement hierarchy and monumental architecture. Mound Key, the site of the Calusa capital in the colonial period, features several large mounds, a plaza, and a canal leading into the site's center. The Calusa typify our first corollary of chiefly complexity: True complex chiefdoms that persisted through time leave evidence in the archaeological record. Groups exercising complexity do not.

In the Florida panhandle well to the northwest of the Timucua-speaking Potano and related groups was the complex chiefdom of the Apalachee Indians. At the time of first contact with Europeans in the early sixteenth century, the Apalachee occupied a region of some 1,375 square miles and had an estimated population of 50,000 people (Hann 1988, 164)—a population density of 36 persons per square mile, in contrast to a density of 10 persons per square mile suggested for the Timucua Indians (Milanich 1996, 60). The Apalachee were the most populous and most densely settled Florida native group and they occupied the largest territory.

Extensive archaeological and documentary studies (Brose 1984; Hann 1988; Jones 1982; Scarry 1981, 1984, 1990b) leave no doubt that the Apalachee and their pre-Columbian ancestors, the people of the Tallahassee Hills variant of the Fort Walton culture, were organized as a complex chiefdom. Characteristics of other Mississippian chiefdoms in the interior of the southeastern United States are present in the Fort Walton culture, including dense populations; site hierarchies; large, patterned villages; monumental architecture; and elite individuals afforded elaborate interment accompanied by special paraphernalia and accumulated wealth. Descriptions by members of the de Soto expedition who wintered among the Apalachee in 1539–40 enhance the archaeological data, providing a picture of a vibrant agricultural society organized as a complex chiefdom.

The development of Apalachee–Fort Walton culture from A.D. 1000 into the period of the Spanish Franciscan missions, A.D. 1633–1702 has been documented (Scarry 1990b). Throughout the period of the missions, the Apalachee themselves still recognized traditional patterns of ascribed social ranking and the hierarchical arrangement of elites, including families, chiefs, and other officials (Hann 1988). Certain villages also were still seen as having greater political importance, reflecting their pre-Columbian status.

The de Soto accounts describe the region's rich agricultural fertility and the ability of the Apalachee to wage effective warfare. Within Florida more maize has been found associated with Fort Walton sites than at all other pre-Columbian sites combined. Other cultigens identified from pre-Columbian Fort Walton sites include beans and sunflowers (Alexander 1984).

What is instructive about the early sixteenth-century Apalachee is not that they were a complex chiefdom but their effect on the native societies living immediately to the east. As with the Calusa of southwest Florida, Apalachee political structure influenced the political structure of nearby groups. One such group was the Uzachile Indians, who spoke Timucua, a language very different from that spoken by the Apalachee, which was a Muskogean language similar to that of many other southeastern native peoples. The Uzachile maintained an uninhabited buffer zone, two days' journey across, between their major town and the river that marked the eastern boundary of Apalachee territory. Apparently this offered some protection against Apalachee raids.

But distance alone was not enough to help them withstand the Apalachee's military prowess. The Uzachile also had to "act complex"—to exercise complexity—to defend themselves against the Apalachee. They formed political alliances with various village leaders of other Timucua-speaking groups, apparently simple chiefdoms, farther east in northern peninsular Florida. Today these groups collectively are known as the northern Utina. Affiliated for defense (and, perhaps, for other reasons), the Uzachile and the towns of Napituca, Aguacaleyquen, and other of the northern Utina chiefdoms, all Timucua speakers, were able to withstand Apalachee military initiatives for at least several centuries by exercising complexity.

When encountered by the de Soto expedition in 1539, each northern Utina simple chiefdom had its own leader, the chief of the main village. The equality of these chiefs was mutually recognized; they referred to one another as "brother," a fictive kin term. These chiefs recognized that the chief of the Uzachile had increased status and deferred to him, at least in military matters. When confronted by de Soto's army, the villages of the northern Utina quickly sought help from the Uzachile leader, who initially sent emissaries in an effort to deal with the situation. Later, an alliance of northern

Utina warriors attacked the army in a desperate attempt to free native hostages the Spaniards had taken. The plan failed and eight captured village chiefs and a number of warriors were slain by the Spaniards (for information on the de Soto expedition among the northern Utina, see Milanich and Hudson 1993).

The geographical buffer zone between the Apalachee and the Uzachile was an archaeological as well as a linguistic boundary. The separate archaeological development of the regions on both sides of the buffer zone can be traced back to about A.D. 900, the time maize agriculture first appears in what would become the Fort Walton/Apalachee region. In that region the Mississippian Fort Walton archaeological culture developed after A.D. 1000 and the language was a Muskogean one. To the east among the Uzachile and the other northern Utina no such Mississippian culture ever was present, and dialects of the Timucuan language were spoken. The Fort Walton people and their Apalachee descendants practiced extensive agriculture; the northern Utina people and their ancestors did not.

When necessary, these northern Utina villages acted complex. They borrowed appropriate chiefly titles and behavioral patterns from the adjacent Apalachee in a successful attempt to maintain their autonomy. Some Muskogean/Apalachee words associated with chiefly titles and some Apalachee signs of chiefly respect (e.g., carrying leaders on litters) were adopted by the Uzachile and other Timucua speakers and are recorded in sixteenth- and early seventeenth-century Spanish documentary sources. The exercise of complexity was a valuable cultural adaptation, one no doubt heavily stimulated (and influenced) by the nearby presence of the Fort Walton/Apalachee chiefdom.

The political structure—simple chiefdoms consisting of a handful or two of small villages—of the northern Florida Timucua Indians was reinforced and supported by the Spaniards in the seventeenth century as part of the mission and hacienda system. On the one hand the Spaniards maintained their own governmental system, part of Spain's New World empire. But they also recognized that it was in their best interests to foster the "Republic of Indians," to support the native leaders who controlled the native population (Bushnell 1989). Working through native chiefs was an effective way to administer the colony of La Florida. Spanish labor drafts of mission Indians, Timucuan as well as Apalachee, were organized through the local chiefs.

During the period of the missions the Timucuan alliances disappeared; they no longer were needed for military protection. It also was in the best interests of the Spaniards not to foster political unification above the level of simple chiefdoms. In essence, the Spaniards placed themselves at the top of the political structure; below them were the Timucuan village chiefs.

Farther east of the northern Utina in the St. Johns River drainage in northeast Florida were two additional Timucuan chiefly alliances. French and Spanish accounts of the 1560s describe two alliances of native villages, one dominated by Chief Outina, mentioned earlier, and the second by Chief Saturiwa. Outina's main village was just west of the St. Johns River, and the villages and chiefs allied with him were found along the river drainage from modern Palatka, Florida, down to Lake George. Chief Saturiwa's village was on the St. Johns River east of modern Jacksonville, and the villages he controlled were on this lower portion of the river and the adjacent coast, well north of the Saturiwa alliance (Milanich 1995, 84–89). Both alliances appear to have been for military purposes, although Saturiwa's may have developed in part in response to the European presence.

The alliances were maintained through the threat of military force, and each chief was eager to use European soldiers and weaponry to punish his enemies and village chiefs who sought to withdraw from the alliance. Documents mention tribute being paid, but it is uncertain if what is meant are actual goods or rather symbols of respect that helped to cement the alliances; the latter seems more likely. The Outina and Saturiwa alliances raided each other, and the Outina alliance also battled the Potano alliance to the west and the Mayaca Indians, a non-Timucua group to the south in the middle reaches of the St. Johns River drainage (Milanich 1995, 70–71, 152–53).

Because the 1564–65 French accounts mention vassal chiefs and tribute, it sounds as though these Timucuan societies were two complex, paramount chiefdoms. But again archaeological data do not suggest that they were organized through time in a complex fashion. Although several large sites with mounds are present in the St. Johns River drainage (Milanich 1994, 267–69), the mounds appear to be monuments associated with lineage interments, rather than the burial mounds of wealthy chiefs. One mound, Mount Royal, does contain copper objects like those worn by the elites of Mississippian societies. The items, thought to date from A.D. 1050, may be evidence that at least for a time, one society did attain some of the trappings of a Mississippian complex chiefdom. But if it did, its level of complexity was not sustained. The importance of individual towns and chiefs must have ebbed and flowed as alliances were formed and broke apart. The colonial period Saturiwa and Outina alliances are examples of the exercise of greater complexity by simple chiefdoms.

Our final examples of Florida chiefdoms and the exercise of complexity come from the Tampa Bay region on the central Gulf coast. In 1539 de Soto and his army landed there and interacted with two small native groups, the Uzita and Mocoso. Each was a political entity consisting of several villages along about 15 miles of the bay coastline. Archaeological sites of these people and their pre-Columbian ancestors, the Safety Harbor culture, are clustered around the bay, most near the shore although a few sites are found on rivers as much as 15 miles inland (Milanich 1994, 394–98). Some villages contain burial mounds and flat-topped pyramidal mounds.

Were these societies organized as complex chiefdoms? The evidence suggests not. The Safety Harbor people and their colonial period descendants were not farmers; populations were small; and nowhere is there archaeological evidence of chiefly interments, settlement hierarchies, or multiple levels of administration. Mound construction, even the presence of mounds on which structures were built, is not necessarily reflective of complex chiefdoms. All of the Safety Harbor mounds studied thus far are either burial mounds or mounds on which charnel houses were erected, or both. The larger mounds all appear to have long histories, with the earlier components dating to pre–Safety Harbor times prior to A.D. 900. One de Soto–era account reports that the chief's house was on a mound, but it is likely that the structure was a charnel temple for the chief's lineage (Milanich 1994, 401–4). Documentary and archaeological evidence is consistent with the Uzita and Mocoso being organized as simple chiefdoms.

The Uzita and the Mocoso told the Spaniards they were allied with and forced to pay tribute (again whether in symbols of respect or in actual goods is not specified) to a powerful chief living in the interior of west-central Florida, a chief named Urriparacoxi, whose main village was some 80 miles away from the coast in a region where agriculture was practiced. The name of this interior chief means "war prince" (*iri-paracoxi*) in the Timucuan language (Granberry 1989, 171, 179), suggesting that the alliance between this Timucuan chief and the coastal Uzita and Mocoso was maintained for military purposes. A variant of the same word, *paracousi*, was given by the French as one of the names for Chief Saturiwa on the St. Johns River (Laudonnière 1975, 61). Like the St. Johns River Utina and Saturiwa alliances, the Mocoso-Uzita-Urriparacoxi alliance was held together by the threat of military force and symbolized in the offering of respect and/or other tribute to the dominant war chief. All three are examples of confederations of simple chiefdoms exercising greater complexity, rather than of the presence of complex chiefdoms with relatively large populations persisting through time.

The Tampa Bay–Urriparacoxi alliance was not to last. Apparently the de Soto expedition's exploits in Tampa Bay caused the demise of the Uzita and Mocoso; after the late fall of 1539 their names disappear from the documentary record. As a result, Urriparacoxi's influence in the Tampa Bay area waned, and by 1567 when an expedition of Calusa and Spaniards entered the area, the most important group was the Tocobaga Indians, who resided in a village at the north end of the bay (Milanich and Hudson 1993, 125–26). No archaeological evidence of settlement hierarchies is present in that region, either.

The chief of the Tocobaga used his influence to assemble 29 village chiefs from the region to meet the Calusa-Spanish entourage, apparently a show of military strength. Pedro Menéndez de Avilés, leader of the Spaniards, left a garrison at the village of Tocobaga but returned the next year to find it destroyed, his soldiers slain, and the village abandoned. The leader of the Tocobaga had exercised complexity when it was in his own best interest and that of other nearby villages.

Further Considerations

From this review of some of the native societies of Florida several points emerge. First, confusion regarding complex chiefdoms versus the short-term exercising of complexity has muddled our understanding of ethnic taxonomies. For instance, some authors (e.g., Milanich 1978, 75–78) have written about the Potano Indians and used that name to refer to all of the native people who lived in a portion of north-central Florida in the early colonial period, a political entity viewed as a single chiefdom. In reality, those people probably never viewed themselves as a single group, nor were they a complex chiefdom. As already noted, it was only after Europeans began to interact with the native people of the region that the societies began to exercise greater complexity, a result of the need for a military confederacy to withstand the threats presented by the French and later the Spaniards. The people we call Potano were originally a number of simple, multivillage chiefdoms, people soon lost under the crush of colonialism.

The second point is that it may not be possible to ascertain whether the exercise of chiefdom complexity was only a post–European contact phenomenon. If the presence of confederacies and the exercise of complexity are not visible in the archaeological record, how can their presence be determined in the absence of documentary evidence? The argument that the exercise of complexity observed by the Hernando de Soto expedition in 1539 in Florida is evidence that alliances of chiefdoms were present in pre-

Columbian times is not supported because that was not the first European encounter with the Florida Indians. Eleven years earlier the expedition of the Spaniard Pánfilo de Nárvaez also marched from Tampa Bay north through peninsular Florida to the territory of the Apalachee Indians in the eastern panhandle. The impact of that expedition on the native peoples could have been tremendous, causing political alliances and realignments, the results of which were witnessed by de Soto's army.

On the other hand, if it is correct that the presence of complex chiefly organization leads to the exercise of more complex political structures in nearby groups, we would expect instances of chiefdom complexity to have been present among Florida groups geographically adjacent to the Apalachee or the Calusa in the pre-Columbian period. This was probably the case, but it cannot be demonstrated as yet.

A third point emerging from an examination of native Florida Indian groups is provided by an attempt to answer the following. Does the exercise of complexity lead to more long-term complex chiefdom formation? If so, why were there not more archaeologically recognizable complex, paramount chiefdoms in pre-Columbian Florida?

As we have seen, in Florida complex chiefdoms only developed and persisted in two regions, each of which is associated with a unique economic system relative to the rest of the state. The Apalachee and their pre-Columbian ancestors associated with the Fort Walton archaeological culture were farmers who practiced extensive, cleared field agriculture, growing maize and other crops (Scarry 1990a). Theirs was the densest population among all the native groups in the state. The Calusa—the densest coastal population—and their pre-Columbian ancestors were economically dependent on the extensive harvesting of wild food sources, especially fish and shellfish, taken from the grass-bottomed, shallow, tropical waters of the Gulf of Mexico and from numerous adjacent estuaries, such as Charlotte Harbor and San Carlos Bay (Marquardt 1992; Widmer 1988).

Elsewhere in the state the economic systems of the native inhabitants did not support complex, paramount chiefdoms and dense populations. Maize agriculture was present in several regions outside of Apalachee territory, including in the lower (northern) St. Johns River drainage and in those parts of northern peninsular Florida where extensive marine or freshwater wetlands were not available. However, in those maize-growing areas farming was not as intensive as it was in Apalachee and populations were not as dense. Where extensive wetlands were present, the majority of the state, the native cultures did not practice maize agriculture; instead, they extensively utilized fish, shellfish, and other wetland-dwelling species for subsistence (Milanich 1994, 325–28). Although most wetlands were economically productive and could support native populations, the level of productivity did not match that found along the southwest Florida coast, a unique ecosystem that was home to the Calusa Indians. Complex chiefdoms did not persist in the absence of extensive, cleared-field maize agriculture or in the absence of the productive waters of the southwest coast.

With the exceptions of the Apalachee and the Calusa, the native peoples of Florida in the sixteenth century were not organized into complex chiefdoms. However, the presence of the Apalachee in the north and the Calusa in the south, endemic warfare, and interaction with European colonial powers all were factors leading to the formation of more complex political structures when needed, especially the exercise of complexity through alliances of simple chiefdoms. These alliances were maintained through the threat of military force and by other means.

The European presence permanently changed the status quo, and in some regions chiefly officials, perhaps war chiefs who headed chiefly confederations, may have become more powerful and more common. Based on the documentary record alone, we might think that complex chiefdoms were everywhere, but when archaeological and diachronic historical data also are examined, it is clear that most of these political structures represented the exercise of complexity.

Had Europeans not invaded Florida in the sixteenth century, would the exercise of complexity in the form of alliances of simple chiefdoms have led eventually to the formation of complex chiefdoms? Does the exercise of greater complexity by simple chiefdoms lead to permanent complex political development? In Florida the answer seems to be no. The pre-Columbian ancestors of the Uzachile, Aguacaleyquen, and other northern Utina peoples lived adjacent to the Fort Walton culture, a Mississippian chiefdom, for a half millennium. Yet the archaeological record of those 500 years contains nothing to suggest pre-Columbian complex chiefdoms among the ancestors of the northern Utina. The exercise of complexity in pre-Columbian Florida was an adaptive tool that was used when needed to create more complex political structures. Those structures apparently did not persist over time, nor did they leave archaeological evidence.

In summary, studies of chiefly political systems should examine specific societies over time. The documentary record needs to be examined to understand the historical events that took place and that may have stimulated simple chiefdoms to act complex. A diachronic approach to understanding the nature of political systems needs also to include archaeological data. True complex chiefdoms persist through time and leave material correlates that can be studied in the archaeological record. Archaeology also enhances a diachronic approach, providing data on pre-Columbian societies as well as providing a check against synchronic documentary sources. When the archaeological record is considered, groups that appear, on the basis of colonial records, to have been organized as complex chiefdoms may be shown instead to have been exercising complexity. It was in their best interest to do so.

References

Alexander, Michelle
1984   Analysis of plant materials from three Fort Walton sites: High Ridge, Velda, and Lake Jackson sites. Paper presented at the 41st Southeastern Archaeological Conference, Pensacola.

Andrews, E., and C. Andrews, eds.
1945   *Jonathan Dickinson's Journal; or God's Protecting Providence.* New Haven: Yale University Press.

Brose, David S.
1984   Mississippian period cultures in northwestern Florida. In *Perspectives on Gulf Coast Prehistory,* edited by D. D. Davis, 165–97. Gainesville: University of Florida Press.

Bushnell, Amy Turner
1989   Ruling the "Republic of Indians" in seventeenth-century Florida. In *Powhatan's Mantle, Indians in the Colonial Southeast,* edited by P. H. Wood, G. A. Waselkov, and M. T. Hatley, 134–50. Lincoln: University of Nebraska Press.

Covington, James W.
1964   The Apalachee Indians move west. *Florida Anthropologist* 17:221–25.

Deagan, Kathleen A.
1978   Cultures in transition: Fusion and assimilation among the eastern Timucua. In *Tacachale: Essays on the Indians of Florida and Southeastern Georgia during the Historic Period,* edited by J. T. Milanich and S. Proctor, 88–119. Gainesville: University Presses of Florida.

Geiger, Maynard
1936   *The Franciscan Conquest of Florida, 1573–1618.* Washington, D.C.: Catholic University of America Press.

Goggin, John M., and William C. Sturtevant
1964   The Calusa: A stratified nonagricultural society (with notes on sibling marriage). In *Explorations in Cultural Anthropology: Essays in Honor of George Peter Murdock,* edited by W. H. Goodenough, 179–219. New York: McGraw-Hill.

Granberry, Julian
1989   *A Grammar and Dictionary of the Timucuan Language.* 2nd edition. Island Archaeological Museum, Anthropological Notes 1. Horseshoe Beach, Fla.

Hann, John H.

1988   *Apalachee: The Land between the Rivers.* Gainesville: University of Florida Press.

1991   *Missions to the Calusa.* Gainesville: University of Florida Press.

Hudson, Charles

1990   *The Juan Pardo Expeditions: Spanish Explorers and the Indians of the Carolinas and Tennessee, 1566–1568.* Washington, D.C.: Smithsonian Institution Press.

Hudson, Charles, Marvin Smith, David Hally, Richard Polhemus, and Chester DePratter

1985   Coosa: A chiefdom in the sixteenth-century southeastern United States. *American Antiquity* 50:723–37.

Jones, B. Calvin

1982   Southern cult manifestations at the Lake Jackson site, Leon County, Florida: Salvage excavation of Mound 3. *Midcontinental Journal of Archaeology* 7:3–44.

Laudonnière, René

1975   *Three Voyages.* Translated by Charles Bennett. Gainesville: University of Florida Press.

Lawson, Sarah, trans.

1992   The Notable History of Florida . . . . In *A Foothold in Florida: The Eye-Witness Account of Four Voyages made by the French to that Region . . .,* by Sarah Lawson and W. John Faupel, 1–148. East Grinstead, West Sussex, England: Antique Atlas Publications.

Lewis, Clifford M.

1978   The Calusa. In *Tacachale: Essays on the Indians of Florida and Southeast Georgia during the Historic Period,* edited by J. T. Milanich and S. Proctor, 19–49. Gainesville: University of Florida Press.

Marquardt, William H.

1987   The Calusa social formation in protohistoric South Florida. In *Power Relations and State Formations,* edited by T. C. Patterson and C. W. Gailey, 98–116. Washington, D.C.: Archaeology Section, American Anthropological Association.

1988   Politics and production among the Calusa of south Florida. In *Hunters and Gatherers,* vol. 1: *History, Environment, and Social Change among Hunting and Gathering Societies,* edited by D. Richies, T. Ingold, and J. Woodburn, 161–88. London: Berg Publishers.

Marquardt, William H., ed.

1992   *Culture and Environment in the Domain of the Calusa.* Institute of Archaeology and Paleoenvironmental Studies, Monograph 1. Gainesville: Florida Museum of Natural History, Department of Anthropology, University of Florida.

Milanich, Jerald T.

1972   Excavations at the Richardson site, Alachua County, Florida: An early 17th century Potano Indian village (with notes on Potano culture change). *Bureau of Historic Sites and Properties Bulletin* 2:35–61. Tallahassee.

1978   The western Timucua: Patterns of acculturation and change. In *Tacachale: Essays on the Indians of Florida and Southeastern Georgia during the Historic Period*, edited by J. T. Milanich and S. Proctor, 59–88. Gainesville: University of Florida Press.

1994   *Archaeology of Precolumbian Florida*. Gainesville: University Press of Florida.

1995   *Florida Indians and the Invasion from Europe*. Gainesville: University Press of Florida.

1996   *The Timucua*. Oxford: Blackwell Publishers.

Milanich, Jerald T., and Charles Hudson

1993   *Hernando de Soto and the Florida Indians*. Gainesville: University Press of Florida.

Scarry, John F.

1981   Fort Walton culture: A redefinition. *Southeastern Archaeological Conference Bulletin* 24:18–21.

1984   Fort Walton Development: Mississippian Chiefdoms in the Lower Southeast. Ph.D. dissertation, Case Western Reserve University.

1990a   Mississippian emergence in the Fort Walton area: The evolution of the Cayson and Lake Jackson phases. In *Mississippian Emergence: The Evolution of Ranked Agricultural Societies in Eastern North America*, edited by B. D. Smith, 227–50. Washington, D.C.: Smithsonian Institution Press.

1990b   The rise, transformation, and fall of Apalachee: A case study of political change in a chiefly society. In *Lamar Archaeology: Mississippian Chiefdoms in the Deep South*, edited by M. Williams and G. Shapiro, 175–86. Tuscaloosa: University of Alabama Press.

Smith, Bruce D., ed.

1990   *Mississippian Emergence: The Evolution of Ranked Agricultural Societies in Eastern North America*. Washington, D.C.: Smithsonian Institution Press.

True, David O., ed.

1945   *Memoir of D. d'Escalante Fontaneda Respecting Florida, Written in Spain, about the Year 1575*. Coral Gables, Fla.: Glade House.

Widmer, Randolph

1988   *The Evolution of the Calusa, a Nonagricultural Chiefdom on the Southwest Florida Coast*. Tuscaloosa: University of Alabama Press.

Williams, Mark, and Gary Shapiro, eds.

1990   *Lamar Archaeology: Mississippian Chiefdoms in the Deep South*. Tuscaloosa: University of Alabama Press.

Worth, John E.

1998a   *The Timucuan Chiefdoms of Spanish Florida*, vol. 1: *Assimilation*. Gainesville: University Press of Florida.

1998b   *The Timucuan Chiefdoms of Spanish Florida*, vol. 2: *Resistance and Destruction*. Gainesville: University Press of Florida.

CHAPTER 11

The Evolution of the Powhatan
Paramount Chiefdom in Virginia

Helen C. Rountree and E. Randolph Turner III

Chiefdoms have become a major focus of anthropological concern in recent times, as shown in the comparative analyses by scholars such as Carneiro (1981), Earle (1987b, 1991), Feinman and Neitzel (1984), and Spencer (1987). The term *chiefdom* is used to cover a tremendous variety of middle-range political organizations, from simple aggregations of villages to near-states, with leaders who vary from first-among-equals to demigods.

For valid historical reasons, the study of chiefdoms has been skewed in certain directions. Most of the cases studied by cultural anthropologists are or were in the tropics, and because of the thoroughness and availability of early studies such as Sahlins's (1958), there has been an overreliance upon Polynesia in the description of chiefdoms in general (Feinman and Neitzel 1984, 43, 45).[1] On the other hand, chiefdoms located in the temperate latitudes tended to have been superseded by states before anthropologists ever came on the scene; consequently our knowledge of such polities comes mainly from archaeology. A case in point is the chiefdoms of the southeastern United States, the destruction of which chiefdoms was accelerated, if not directly caused, by the Europeans who invaded their territories (Hudson and Tesser 1994). Though there are sketchy Spanish records of these polities, it is through archaeology that we know that some of them achieved the paramount chiefdom level.

Examining the Powhatan Indians may correct some of this skewing. They constituted a temperate-zone society that remained on the paramount chiefdom level well into the contact period, so that they are accessible through eyewitness accounts as well as archaeology. And those eyewitnesses, notably John Smith and William Strachey, took more trouble to describe the Indian culture per se than did any other European visitors to the east coast of North America.

The Powhatan paramountcy in 1607–10 was unusual among Eastern Woodland chiefdoms for reasons other than its time of existence. More complex chiefdom organizations usually have larger populations and larger settlements than simpler chiefdoms (Feinman and Neitzel 1984, 60, 64–65, 70, 72–73). The Powhatans differed. They had a three-level administration that ruled some thirty districts (fig. 11.1; Smith 1986b, 146–48, 150, 173; Strachey 1953, 63–69, 77), with leaders who had even more functions and status markers than Feinman and Neitzel show (Strachey 1953, 50–59).[2] And yet their population was only middling—13,000 to 22,000 persons in 1607–8 over an area of slightly less than 16,500 square kilometers (Turner 1982; Feest 1973)—and the vast majority of their towns were mere hamlets and small villages (Potter 1982; Rountree 1989, 60; Turner 1992, 110; Turner and Opperman 1993, 72–77). Not only that, but the Powhatan paramountcy had spread to those thirty districts in only one human lifetime, for the paramountcy during the man Powhatan's childhood had covered only six districts. That is a very rapid and far-flung development.

The Powhatans are unusual from an archaeological standpoint, too. It is hard enough to identify chiefdoms archaeologically (Carneiro 1981, 52–54; Feinman and Neitzel 1984, 75–76, Turner 1986), for the main difference between them and more egalitarian societies is social, not technological (Service 1971, 134–35). Even when we do find status indicators archaeologically, we may not be seeing them as the people themselves saw them (Earle 1987b, 290–91). But the Powhatans left practically no material evidence of having had a complex polity. If it were not for the historical accounts, we might not know that in Virginia the coastal plain people, who lacked mounds, were in fact more sophisticated politically than the piedmont people, who did build mounds (Hantman 1990, 683–84; 1993). Altogether, the Powhatan paramount chiefdom is a phenomenon that needs explaining. It is also a phenomenon that can enlighten us considerably about the nature of chiefdoms in general.

The Powhatans first appear in the European records as simple chiefdoms. The Spanish records of the 1570s, which are sketchy about Virginia too, show that chiefs existed but indicate little about links between them (Lewis and Loomie 1953). Three decades later, various English observers mentioned not only the paramount chief, in whom they were mainly inter-

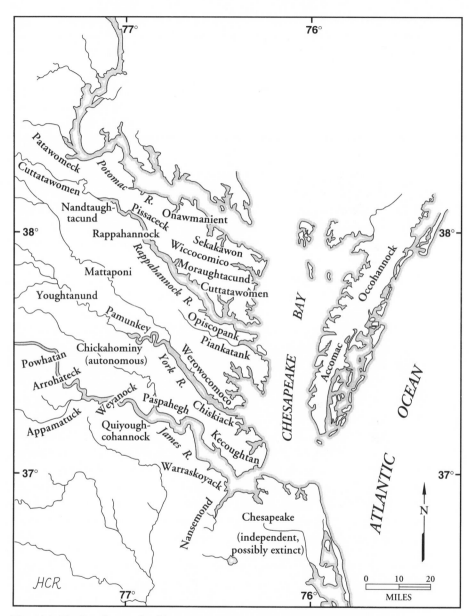

Fig. 11.1. The Powhatan chiefdom in 1607. Copyright Helen C. Rountree.

ested, but also the district and even village chiefs in Powhatan's organization. Since the data are adequate, let us take these lesser chiefs to represent the earlier, independent village chiefs, and reconstruct what an eastern Virginia chiefdom was basically like. In doing this, we will also begin to fathom why that chiefdom would not leave many archaeological traces.

Eastern Virginia chiefs lived in larger, more elaborate houses than other people (Smith 1986a, 51; Smith 1986b, 173; Spelman 1910, cvi; Strachey 1953, 59). Larger houses are a major marker of chiefdoms both archaeologically (Carneiro 1981, 53) and ethnographically (Earle 1978b, 291). But Powhatan chiefs' houses were aboveground structures and were made entirely of biodegradable materials—a sapling framework covered with bark; commoners used reed mats (Strachey 1953, 78). In fact, much of Powhatan technology was based upon wood, for stone is scarce in the coastal plain. Powhatan houses of whatever elaboration would leave only postmolds and hearths behind. And since most Powhatan groups had a dispersed settlement pattern and shifted as new fields were cleared (Rountree 1989, 46, 58; Potter 1982; Turner and Opperman 1993, 72–77), it is hard for an archaeologist to know exactly where to look for the postmolds of a chief's house. Finding one is a matter of luck, except in the rare palisaded towns.

Chiefs had more elaborate clothing, using more deerskins, than commoners did. They also wore more ornaments, the preferred materials being copper, shell beads, and pearls from freshwater mussels (Archer 1969a, 92; Smith 1986a, 53; Smith 1986b, 161, 173; Smith 1986c, 150, 155, 157; Strachey 1953, 65, 75). These items would show up mainly in high-status burials, if we found any in Virginia (see later discussion). We do have the good fortune to retain two heavily decorated chief's garments, both of which found their way into an English "cabinet" at an early date. The famous "Powhatan's Mantle" and the pouch called the "Virginia Purse" are both in the Ashmolean Museum and are embroidered with shells and shell beads respectively (Feest 1983). The shells of the mantle, all 17,000-plus of them, have recently been reidentified as *Prunum* (formerly *Marginella*) *limatulum*, a fossil species available in cliffs along the rivers in the coastal plain (Coovert and Rountree n.d.).

Virginia chiefs collected tribute from their people. Some of it was in foodstuffs, which chiefs everywhere need to support their elite lifestyle (Earle 1978, 15, 181; Kirch 1984, 134; Schwerin 1973, 10). This kind of "staple finance" (Johnson and Earle 1987, 208) does not constitute redistribution in the strict sense elsewhere in the world; collections are often irregular (Earle 1978, 188–90; Schwerin 1973, 11) and the proceeds are usually not extensively shared with commoners later (Brumfiel and Earle 1987, 2; Earle 1977;

Kirch 1984, 166–67; Steponaitis 1978, 420). Powhatan chiefs' staple finance, limited as it was, shows the same characteristics: irregular collections (Spelman 1910, cxiii) and little sharing (Rountree 1989, 14–15). But much of the tribute collected was not food. For one thing, chiefs had fields planted and harvested for them (Spelman 1910, cxii), so they did not need much more from commoners' own fields. For another thing, there is little evidence of places where much food could have been stored. Archaeologists in the region have not found granaries or large storage pits; that may have meant, as Potter suggests (1993, 172–73), that much of the Indians' corn was paid over to chiefs who then stored it aboveground. But English colonial writers mention only temples as chiefly storage places (see later discussion), while William Strachey (1953, 87) recorded that tribute was collected in little baskets. Nonetheless, chiefs in Virginia did have enough corn in the crib and venison on the hoof that they could and did feast English visitors at all times of the year—Powhatan in various months and district chiefs in the late spring (Hamor 1957, 39–40, 43–44; Smith 1986a, 53, 65ff; Smith 1986c, 150, 155, 194; Archer 1969a, 84, 92; Archer 1969b, 103; Percy 1969, 135–37). Whether or not they feasted one another as lavishly (the only account is Archer 1969a, 84) is another question, one we cannot answer.

Much of the tribute collected by Virginia chiefs, at least in the time of Powhatan's paramountcy, took the form of luxury goods, that is, copper, pearls, shell beads, and deerskins (Archer 1969a, 93; Magnel 1969, 153; Smith 1986a, 69; Smith 1986b, 174; Spelman 1910, cxiii; Strachey 1953, 53, 56–57).[3] This sort of wealth finance, in preference to staple finance, is common in chiefdoms worldwide (Brumfiel and Earle 1987, 4, 7–8; Schwerin 1973, 10), for luxury items are usually reasonably small for their value and therefore easier to control and transport. Earle (1987a, 69) sees a greater reliance on wealth finance as a marker of more complex chiefdoms. The paramountcy in Virginia qualifies, certainly; it is a pity that the Spaniards did not tell us whether the simple chiefdoms of their time collected more luxury goods than foodstuffs.

Most of the high-status goods that Virginia district chiefs took in, they kept. They threw a few beads to the people cultivating their fields (Spelman 1910, cxii), and their relatives threw out more beads at their funerals (Spelman 1910, cx). They "hired" warriors for payments in copper and rewarded them for valor in the same medium (Strachey 1953, 107, 114). But they kept most of the goods for themselves and their families.

Powhatan chiefs were treated differently from commoners when they died. We may expect this, since high-status burials are a standard marker of chiefly status both archaeologically (Carneiro 1981, 53) and ethnographically (Earle 1978, 7; Earle 1987b, 290–91; Little 1967b, 192–93; Richards 1940, 99; Schwerin 1973, 10). The grave goods buried with them can also inform us about what elements of their duties were considered the most important (Earle 1987b, 300). However, Powhatan status burials were carried out in such a way as to leave at best only minimal archaeological evidence (Turner 1992, 117), and we have to trust English accounts about them. Chiefs' bodies received secondary burial; accounts conflict, but they were either exposed on scaffolds or defleshed in some other way before being wrapped up in mats, along with their luxury goods, and deposited on a bier in the local temple (Percy 1921–22, 263, 272; Smith 1986a, 59; Smith 1986b, 169; Spelman 1910, cv, cx; Strachey 1953, 88–89, 94–95). Temples were constructed in the same sapling-and-bark or mat fashion that dwelling houses were. This means that chiefs' bodies were disposed of in an entirely aboveground manner. Moreover, temples were often located away from town sites (Rountree 1989, 133) and were eventually abandoned and left to fall down (Spelman 1910, cx). It becomes clear that the chances of finding a chief's body anywhere in the Powhatan area are practically nil. Commoners, on the other hand, we do find. They were buried in the ground, either in primary inhumations or in ossuaries (Turner 1992, 117–19). The grave goods with them, when present, are usually scanty.

Virginia chiefs, at least the male ones, could have multiple spouses. Polygyny is recorded for both district chiefs (Archer 1969b, 104; Hamor 1957, 39) and village chiefs (Spelman 1910, cvii–cviii). The paramount chief, and possibly the others, did not have to endure negotiations about bridewealth; he simply called for a "line-up" of girls, picked one, and paid what he felt like paying (Strachey 1953, 116). His wives, who came from all over his dominions and were said to number over 100,[4] were ranked, but their rank depended entirely upon his favor (Strachey 1953, 61). Their family background seems to have been irrelevant; the Powhatans, unlike the Polynesians, apparently did not have conical clans (Rountree 1989, 92–94; for dissenting views see Binford 1964, 90–92, Turner 1976, 126, and Turner 1985, 199). Powhatan women had considerable sexual freedom (Strachey 1953, 112–13), but the wife of a chief was off limits to any other man (Archer 1969b, 104; Spelman 1910, cviii).

Powhatan chiefs, even village ones, had servitors who looked after them on official occasions and possibly at other times as well. The paramount chief had an established bodyguard of 50 men, some of whom acted as sentinels watching the house where he slept at night (Smith 1986b, 173; Strachey 1953, 59). In 1615 Hamor (1957, 39) described "an hundred" bowmen guarding him. His brother, a district chief, is recorded as having a similar bodyguard during an English visit (Smith 1986a, 65), but he may not have retained that many men at other times. Chiefs and their guests were served their food during feasts (Spelman 1910, cxiii); the paramount could and did employ a district chief's wife in that capacity on one especially grand occasion (Smith 1986a, 65). Even village chiefs had retainers to accompany them when they met guests (Archer 1969a, 92), and one village chief's wife got away with insisting on being carried ashore while her husband was willing to disembark from the canoe under his own power (Strachey 1953, 65). However, that is the only record we have of any Powhatan chiefly person being physically carried anywhere.

Chiefs are normally closely connected with religious matters, and the Powhatans were no exception. Chiefs' valuables—luxury goods, surplus weapons, and medicinal specimens—were kept in temples, and the chiefs themselves were eventually buried there (Clayton 1965, 22; Smith 1986a, 67; Smith 1986b, 169, 173; Spelman 1910, cv). Chiefs and priests alike were considered semidivine by the common folk, and only they were supposed to have any afterlife at all (Smith 1986b, 149, 172; Strachey 1953, 77, 100; White 1969, 149–50; possibly contradicted by Archer 1969b, 104). The holiest of Powhatan temples was off limits to all but priests and chiefs (Smith 1986b, 169–70; Strachey 1953, 95). Chiefs competed among themselves for the priests who seemed most influential with the gods, and it was the priests who had the most influence over chiefs in council sessions (Strachey 1953, 88–89). One priest, Uttamatomakkin, even married a daughter of the paramount chief (Purchas 1617, 954).

Powhatan chiefs, like other chiefs in societies not approaching the state level, had limited judicial power with which to control the behavior of their subjects (Rountree 1993a). The English recorded that they had full life-and-death power (Smith 1986b, 174–75; Strachey 1953, 59–60, 62, 77), although another English account of Powhatan actions shows that blood revenge on the part of a commoner was possible even when the culprit was the guest of a district chief (Smith 1986a, 49). The paramount chief either could not or did not interfere in feuding that went on between some of his districts: the Weyanokes and Paspaheghs in 1607 (Archer 1969a, 82) and the Rappahannocks and Moraughtacunds in 1608 (Smith 1986c, 173ff). And on the same day that Powhatan had feasted an English diplomatic mission, trying to win them as allies, a neighboring and thoroughly loyal district chief had still felt free to show hostility to the English as they headed downriver (Smith 1986a, 79). Yet the paramount and his district chiefs could and did summon men to go to war, whether the men wanted to go or not (Smith 1986b, 165; Strachey 1953, 104). The paramount could even get men to attack the supposedly loyal Piankatanks in 1608, in spite of the fact that they may well have been related by blood and marriage to the victims (Strachey 1953, 44).

The paramount Powhatan chiefdom in Virginia was inherited matrilineally; that was very likely the means of succession in the six district chiefdoms from which it sprang and also in other districts. Inheritance patterns among the commoners are much less clear. The immediate successors of Powhatan were his brothers, then his sisters, then the children of his eldest sister (Smith 1986a, 59, 61; Smith 1986b, 174; Smith 1986c, 196; Strachey 1953, 77). These siblings and heirs were often made chiefs of lesser administrative units, so that Powhatan's brothers ruled districts. That pattern was practiced on the lower levels of the regional administrative hierarchy as well. For example, we know of four districts, Appamattuck and Quiyoughcohannock (in the Powhatan heartland) and Occohannock and Patawomeck (on the Powhatan fringes), in which a sister and brothers, respectively, of the district chief each ruled over a village. Moreover, the paramount chief, and perhaps others, could make his noninheriting sons into chiefs. Clearly a chief's high status extended to his immediate relatives, at least those he favored. In many ways Powhatan chiefly kinship resembled that of other southeastern peoples (cf. Knight 1990), though the lack of clear historical evidence of conical clans in Virginia makes further comparison difficult.

Though the elaboration and heritability of chieftainship in Virginia shows that at least simple chiefdoms had been established there for some time, there were other ways in which the Powhatan paramountcy showed its shallow time-depth. In spite of the deference shown to chiefs upon arrival at a town, they were difficult to distinguish from ordinary people on nonceremonial occasions (Spelman 1910, cxiii). Even the paramount chief was never addressed by anything other than his personal name (Strachey 1953, 56). He also could and did perform any tasks appropriate to his sex (e.g., making his own hunting gear)—and he took pride in so doing (Smith 1986b, 173; Smith 1986c, 151).

The Powhatan paramountcy differed from other complex chiefdoms in another way. Usually organizations in which leaders have many powers and status markers also show a considerable difference in size between the largest and the smallest settlements, with the largest ones being where important chiefs reside (Feinman and Neitzel 1984, 65–66; Carneiro 1981, 53–54). But Powhatan's capital in 1607 was Werowocomoco, a sparsely populated district with only 40 warriors (Smith 1986b, 147). Its main advantages seem to have been its centrality in the coastal plain, as Powhatan rapidly expanded his paramount chiefdom (Turner 1985, 204), and its access to less populated territory that may have been a hunting preserve (Rountree 1989, 15). Some other chiefdoms, notably Gonja in Ghana (Goody 1967, 196), show the same anomaly. For both the Powhatans and the Gonja, the reason probably relates to the practice of appointing relatives to serve as district chiefs and village chiefs. This practice resulted in fewer important people (and their entourages) residing "at court."

Chieftaincies, if not full-fledged chiefdoms, were well established in coastal Virginia by the sixteenth century, but why the move to a paramount chiefdom? And why just then? There are several views of why chiefdoms, and presumably also larger, more complex paramount chiefdoms, arise. As we shall see, only one of them really fits the Powhatan case.

It was formerly thought that in regions with diverse natural resources, occupational specialization would arise and would in turn encourage, if not cause, the emergence of chiefs who would control such specialization (Fried 1967, 183; Johnson and Earle 1987, 210–11; Service 1971, 135–38; Service 1975, 75–78). However, many chiefdoms are now known to have had little specialization (Brumfiel and Earle 1987, 6–7; Earle 1977, 223; Earle 1978, 10, 184–85, 195; Earle 1987a, 65–66; Kirch 1984, 32–33; Steponaitis 1978, 420). Muller (1987, 17) believes that specialization is a late development in the growth of chiefdoms. As it happens, the Powhatans had practically no occupational specialization, even at the height of their paramountcy. Their territory was crossed by four large rivers and a myriad of tributaries. They divided that territory in such a way that each town had access to a wide variety of local aquatic and terrestrial ecozones (Rountree 1996). Everyone therefore drew subsistence from the full range of resources, with even the paramount chief engaging in hunting and fishing. Only priests are reported to have lived extensively on the labor of others (Whitaker 1936, 26), and that may have happened only while they were on duty in the temples. So the environmental diversity that existed in the Virginia coastal plain did not encourage specialization, and that in turn played no part in the emergence of a paramount chief in the region.

Another hypothesis has it that chiefs originate as entrepreneurs who make themselves useful, not to say powerful, by handling the environmental risks faced by local populations. In some areas the chief's method of dealing with risks may be primarily economic, through collecting and storing food for hard times (Earle 1987b, 293–96; Fried 1967, 183; Johnson and Earle 1987, 209–10; Kirch 1984, 132–35; Muller 1987, 14–15; Service 1971, 140–41). In other parts of the world the method may be a religious one, with the chief appeasing the supernatural and making himself responsible for the welfare of the people and the land (Earle 1987, 168; Packard 1981, 6–8; Richards 1940, 83, 97–99; Rowlands 1987, 56; Schwerin 1973, 11–12; Shorter 1974, 39, 41; Spencer 1987, 367). It is not uncommon in the ethnographic literature to see chiefs whose ceremonial power is a given but whose political power is limited.

The evidence we find for the Powhatans argues against this hypothesis being a *primary* explanation. For one thing, the Powhatans' region is not prone to natural disasters (as both the present authors have observed, being lifelong residents there). Major hurricanes are infrequent and tidal waves unknown. There are occasional droughts, though rarely for as much as two years running, so that only non-native, domesticated plants and animals are affected. The observed Powhatan response to drought was to disperse and live on the better-adapted wild resources (Quiros in Lewis and Loomie 1953, 89).[5] Only when a prolonged drought, like the six-year one recorded in 1570 (Lewis and Loomie 1953, 89–90), made even the wild foods scarce did the Powhatans actually face starvation. And as for control of the weather, that remained in the hands of the priests, who were not chiefs (Percy 1921–22, 277; Smith 1986b, 171). By and large, Powhatan chiefs were not heavily involved in their subjects' subsistence activities.

There may have been one other kind of disaster in late sixteenth-century Virginia: epidemics of European diseases (Barker 1992, 73; Dobyns 1983, 44n). If they occurred among the Powhatans, they would have been "virgin-soil" epidemics that killed many people and caused social disruption. Such disruption would not in itself lead to a paramount chiefdom, but it could well assist the rise of one that was already forming. However, the evidence for them is poor historically (Rountree 1990, 25), with the Spaniards describing the region as early as 1570 as having a higher population than other, more southerly regions with which they were familiar (Rogel in Lewis and Loomie 1953, 111). Consistent with this observation is the absence of archaeological evidence for mass deaths in Virginia during the sixteenth century. Further, the Powhatans of 1607 and after said nothing of their own population having once been larger. All available evidence shows gradual but consistent population increases in coastal Virginia over time, culminating in the Powhatan paramountcy by 1607. Although some loss of life due to European diseases may have occurred during the sixteenth century, there is simply no firm evidence whatever to indicate that it was substantial (Rountree 1990, 25; Turner 1985, 212; Rountree and Turner 1994).

Yet another hypothesis has been put forward by Carneiro (1970, 1987), who postulates that warfare leads to the coercive aggregation of polities, first into chiefdoms and later into states. The warfare is caused by population pressure, which occurs in areas with concentrated food resources. People are attracted to richer regions, and once there, their populations grow until they must either expand territorially or, if environmental or social circumscription makes that difficult, compete with one another. Over time, more people will be gathered into fewer political groupings (Carneiro 1978).

We do find evidence for this scenario having occurred among the Powhatans. Resource concentration is definitely present in the Virginia coastal plain (Rountree 1996; Turner 1976, 16–86; Turner 1992, 116; Turner and Opperman 1993, 86; Potter 1993, 152–54). There are greater amounts of edible wild foods in the coastal plain than in the piedmont—or, for that matter, in the coastal plains of North Carolina or Maryland. The inner coastal plain of Virginia is also richer than the outer coastal plain.

The waterways of the Tidewater, those four close-together rivers and their tributaries, are rich in wild foods even now; in the early seventeenth century their wealth amazed the English. The rivers teemed with fish, especially in the springtime when herring, shad, and alewife migrated up to the fresher waters to spawn (fig. 11.2). Shellfish populations were huge: both freshwater and saltwater mussels, clams, and oysters averaging half again as long as any that can be found today. One of the largest aboriginal Powhatan populations, the Nansemonds (see fig. 11.3 for warrior-counts), lived close to an oystering area that is still one of the richest in the Chesapeake. There were also shallow-water edible plants (fig. 11.2): wild rice (*Zizania aquatica*) and "tuckahoe" which may have been arrowhead (*Sagittaria* sp.), arrow arum (*Peltandra virginica*), and golden club (*Orontium aquaticum*). All of these plants require fresh or nearly fresh waters (Beal 1977, 66–68, 92, 137; Brown and Brown 1984: 59–62, 115, 296, 298; Radford et al. 1968, 52–54, 125, 258, 256). The Virginia piedmont has such waters, in the rivers that cross its moderate gradient. But the inner coastal plain has such fresh waters in abundance, especially where the rivers meander across nearly flat floodplains that allow wide expanses of sun-drenched marshes. Further, the wide floodplains of the James, Chickahominy, Pamunkey, and Rappahannock rivers, above the limits of saltwater inundation from the Chesapeake, contain the region's most fertile land, highly preferred by Indian farmers, who did not fertilize their fields (Rountree 1989, 47; U.S. Dept. of Agriculture soil surveys under various authors—see Rountree 1996). Not only that, but the Virginia coastal plain, unlike the Gulf-Atlantic coastal plain to the south, is well drained and cloaked in a forest that is predominantly hardwoods rather than pines, so that an abundant crop of

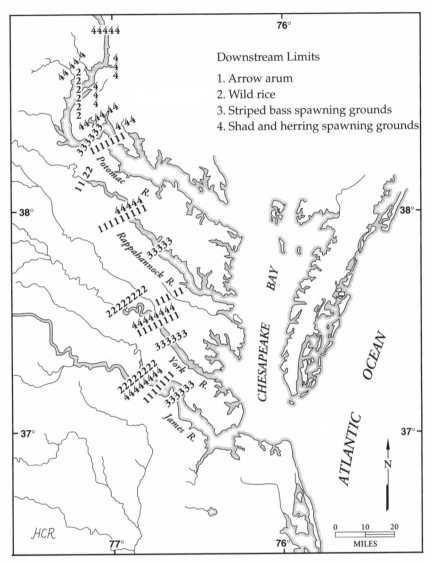

Fig. 11.2. Downstream limits. Copyright Helen C. Rountree.

nuts is readily available in the fall. All of these things add up to a concentration of resources that was rich by any standards in North America. It is
no accident that the majority of Powhatans were located within the inner
coastal plain (fig. 11.3). It is also no accident that two of the largest aboriginal populations, the Chickahominies and the Pamunkeys (the most populous chiefdom in Virginia in 1607), lived along the freshwater rivers that
meander the most extravagantly across wide floodplains.[6]

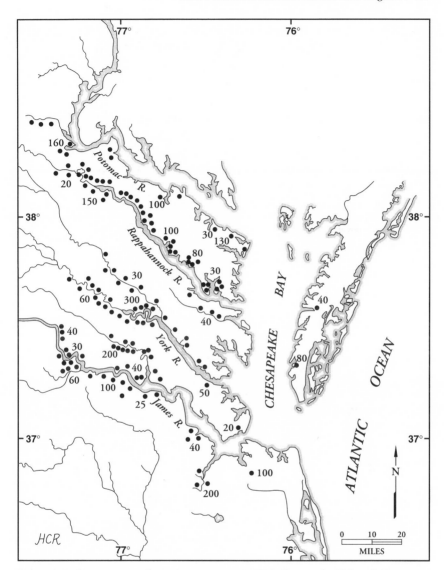

Fig. 11.3. Indian towns and warrior counts in 1607–8. Copyright Helen C. Rountree.

Living in territory rich in wild resources may lead to sufficient population growth to encourage the development at least of chiefdoms without the introduction of agriculture (Carneiro 1987, 250; Widmer 1988). People in such a region may achieve a paramount chiefdom when they merely add part-time agriculture. That was the case with the Powhatans, who— far from using the agricultural intensification methods seen in Polynesia and Amazonia (Earle 1978, 17–18, 182–83; Kirch 1984, 166ff; Schwerin 1973,

10)—supported their paramountcy while living on wild foods from 25 to 50 percent of the year (Rountree 1989, 45; Turner 1976: 179–87).

However, the Powhatans did experience circumscription in their territory, even if they were not having to use it to its very limits. The circumscription in question was not environmental, in the sense of natural barriers hemming them in (Carneiro 1970; 1987, 246; 1988, 498–503). If they had expanded north or south along the coastal plain or west into the piedmont, they could still have practiced their subsistence successfully, if less rewardingly. Instead the circumscription they faced was social (Carneiro 1987, 247), for they were prevented from migrating to new territory by the presence of people—nay, chiefdoms—in the areas around them (Clark and Rountree 1993; Feest 1978a, 1978c; Hantman 1990; Potter 1993, 154–61; Turner 1992, 116). Externally, there were Algonquian-speaking chiefdoms (Piscataways, Chowanocs, and others) to the north and south of them, Iroquoian-speaking tribes or chiefdoms (Nottoways, Meherrins, and Tuscaroras) in the inner coastal plain to the south of them, and Siouan-speaking tribes or chiefdoms (Monacans and Mannahoacs) to the west. Internally, the most populous Powhatan groups, already mentioned, were surrounded by other, smaller Powhatan chiefdoms.[7]

Access to concentrated resources leads to population growth. Circumscription, or limits to territorial expansion for whatever reason, leads to population pressure, or competition for resources which are now becoming less plentiful per capita (Carneiro 1987, 249–50). There is archaeological evidence that the people of Virginia's coastal plain had grown in number for some time; the number of settlements grew steadily from the Early Woodland through the Late Woodland period (Potter 1982; Turner 1976, 1992). There is also both archaeological and historical evidence that in the Late Woodland period the people were competing among themselves more than ever before.

The English who observed the Powhatan men found that they were constantly either at war or making ready for war (Rountree 1989, chap. 4). However, the wars were not always over territory—something that comes later, apparently, when populations are really big and the land shortage is acute. The wars were fought also for revenge and the capture of women and children, who could be put to work in the fields (Smith 1986b, 165). Yet competition for resources was still at the bottom of the fighting: the Powhatans either captured territory or captured personnel to produce more food in the territory they already had.

Even under Powhatan's paramountcy, some district chiefdoms—adjacent ones—still feuded among themselves, as already described. Powhatan's own administrative activities centered mainly around military matters (Rountree 1989, 147–48). It is significant that district chiefs were also war captains (Smith 1986b, 165; Strachey 1953, 104); further, their political importance usually ensured them immunity from maltreatment or death in captivity (Smith 1986b, 166, 175, 253; Strachey 1953, 109).

The archaeological evidence in Virginia for competition over resources takes two forms: territoriality and fortification. Territoriality shows up best in ceramics (Turner 1992, 1993). In the latter half of the Middle Woodland period (A.D. 200–900), the dominant ceramic ware over the entire region and beyond was shell-tempered Mockley ware, especially cord-marked and net-impressed types. But by the Late Woodland period (A.D. 900–1600), Mockley had been replaced by several discrete wares, different ones being dominant in different parts of the region—and identifiable with certain strong district chiefdoms by the late 1500s and early 1600s. At first much of eastern Virginia used shell-tempered Townsend ware, with fabric-impressed, incised, and plain types being most common. However, by the latter half of the Late Woodland period, three additional wares appeared (fig. 11.4). Sand-tempered or crushed quartz–tempered Potomac Creek ware, in plain and cord-marked types, was heavily used by the Patawomecks and their neighbors; simple-stamped shell-tempered Roanoke ware was preferred by the lower James River districts (Chesapeakes, Kecoughtans, and Nansemonds) and their allies southward to Roanoke Island (see Quinn 1955, 244ff); and simple-stamped sand- or crushed quartz–tempered Gaston/Cashie ware was current among the James River districts near the fall line (Appamattucks, Weyanocks, Arrohattocks, and Powhatans [the district][8]) and also in Iroquoian- and Siouan-speaking areas to the south. The implications of Gaston ware's distribution for Powhatan trading relations are taken up later in this chapter.

As for fortification, it took the form of wooden palisades. The palisaded sites found so far in eastern Virginia (Turner 1992, 108–9) all date to the Late Woodland period, perhaps to the terminal Late Woodland, and they occur throughout coastal Virginia. Examples known to archaeologists have been found in the Potomac, Rappahannock, York, and James river drainages, and none of them predates the Late Woodland period.

Another source of population pressure was the limited amount of first-class farmland. Much of eastern Virginia is arable, but Indian people preferred flat, erosion-free soils that were naturally fertile and quick to warm up in the spring (Rountree 1996). Though such soils are more plentiful in coastal Virginia than in surrounding regions, their extent is still limited. Further, their natural fertility could be maintained only through a lengthy

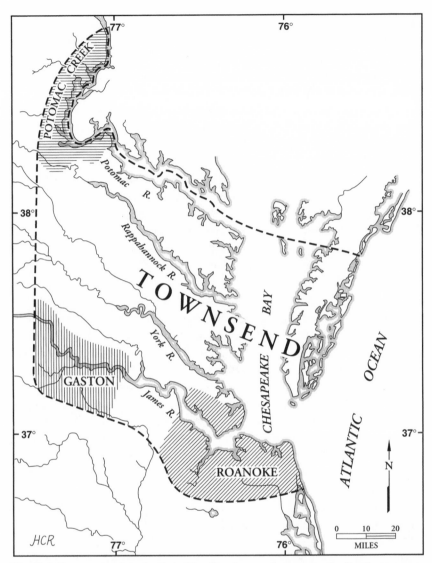

Fig. 11.4. Core areas of major Late Woodland ceramic types in the Powhatan area. Copyright Helen C. Rountree.

fallow period, which for temperate deciduous forests can easily exceed 50 years. And there is evidence that most of them were being utilized as of 1607–8, when the English first explored the coastal plain (Rountree 1996; Turner 1976, 188–98; Turner 1985, 210; Turner and Opperman n.d.).

All these evidences of population pressure are indicative, though they do not show that the pressure was acute. To them, however, must be added the historical fact that in the late sixteenth century the native people of eastern Virginia were being pressured by more distant outsiders.

The people of the coastal plain were in a constant state of war with the Siouan Monacans by 1570 (Martínez in Lewis and Loomie 1953, 161), a war which included the Mannahoacs and was still going strong in 1607 (Archer 1969a, 88; Smith 1986b, 166). The fighting was probably over edible resources: possibly over Powhatans encroaching westward during their communal deer hunts (Turner 1978a), since deer were becoming scarce closer to home (Strachey 1953, 82–83), and possibly over Monacans encroaching eastward to tap the edible tubers that were more abundant on the coastal plain (L. Daniel Mouer, personal communication 1991).

By 1607, and probably for some years before, the Powhatans were warring with invaders from the north and northwest who were probably Iroquoian speakers, called variously Massawomecks and Pocoughtaonacks (their identity is uncertain). Powhatan as paramount chief was known to be their avowed enemy; an English boy observed them attacking a Patawomeck town; and the Kecoughtans far to the southeast were seen to be petrified of them (Smith 1986a, 55, 67; Smith 1986b, 230–31, 229; Spelman 1910, cxiv; Strachey 1953, 35, 132). The advent of Europeans in the region was certainly a source of external pressure on the Powhatans, but the English only compounded a serious external threat that already existed.

In the late sixteenth century, Europeans began visiting the Virginia coastal plain, sometimes in a friendly way and at other times acting hostile (Rountree 1990, chap. 1). In 1570 Spanish Jesuits planted a mission, apparently on the York River; it was destroyed in 1571 and avenged in 1572 (Lewis and Loomie 1953). The missionaries' guide, and later their killer, was a local man who had lived with the Spaniards for a decade, seeing Havana, Mexico City, and Madrid, and getting to know the Spaniards and their colonization policy well (Gradie 1988, 1993). The Spaniards could therefore have influenced directly the development of Powhatan's paramountcy—*if* their presence was sensed strongly enough and if that former dweller with them had enough influence upon the native leadership. The 1580s saw more Spanish reconnaissance and also a wintering-over among the Chesapeake tribe of an English party from the fledgling colony on Roanoke Island. Sometime after that, the Chesapeakes moved their major town inland, from Lynnhaven Bay to the Elizabeth River (cf. Smith n.d.; Hulton 1984, 86). Since they were known to have been enemies of Powhatan's right up until their extermination by him around 1607, their move in his direction could have been made to escape the attentions of more European parties probing in through the Virginia capes. An alternative explanation of the relocation is that the later town was populated by Powhatan loyalists after the Chesapeakes had been disposed of (Egloff and Turner 1984).

The Indians of the Virginia coastal plain therefore had enough population pressure, for internal and external reasons, to encourage the development of a paramount chiefdom through warfare, especially in the late sixteenth century. Their leaders needed to make quick decisions in the face of hostilities, and they had reason to want as many politico-military allies as they could find, even if they had to make them out of Algonquian-speaking former competitors.

The first paramount chief in Virginia used all the mechanisms listed in the introduction to this volume as he consolidated his position. It is significant that he arose on the rich inner coastal plain in the James and York river basins. Powhatan inherited six districts, three in each basin, and then expanded his holdings tremendously. The English colonists heard that he had either conquered or intimidated adjacent polities into submission. The "intimidation" was probably a matter of military threat, but it may also have been a matter of enticement—the lure of access to the full range of luxury goods that had long been the visible hallmark of chiefdomship. Most of the chiefdoms Powhatan collected were on the outer coastal plain. And as we shall see, few kinds of status goods were produced there; most were produced in the inner coastal plain or traded in from beyond. With judicious expenditure of these things, Powhatan could "hire" allies and (except for the Chickahominies) make them subjects. A closer examination of the status goods used by Powhatan chiefs can therefore help us to account for the location of that first six-district paramountcy.

Shell beads, exclusive of those fossil marginellas on the Powhatan Mantle, came mainly from saltwater molluscs and were of several kinds (Beverley 1947, 227–28; Rountree 1989, 71, 73–77). *Roanoke* consisted of rough disks made of mussel shells, apparently either freshwater or saltwater species; it was worth little, being easy to make with the thin shells. *Peak* was hard to make (it still is, even with steel tools; Michael Taylor, personal communication 1990); therefore it was much more valuable. The white variety was made from whelk shells, the purple from clam shells. All the whelks and clams in the region require salty or brackish water to live in (Abbott 1974, 222–23) and are found in the Chesapeake Bay and the saltier reaches of its tributaries (Lippson and Lippson 1984, 210–11). The Indian people said to make the most peak were the Cuskarawaoks, or Nanticokes (Smith 1986c, 168), on the Maryland eastern shore. A bead-making site has been found archaeologically in Virginia Beach—that is, in the area occupied by the Chesapeakes (Turner 1992, 105). Shell beads were used in both jewelry and embroidery throughout the Powhatan area; they had to be traded into the inner coastal plain.

Pearls were common in Virginia and came from mussels (Percy 1969, 137). The mussels may have been the local *Anodonta* species (Clarke 1977, 294) or, if Percy meant that the mussels were really prolific in pearls, the species would be the high-producing *Margaritifera margaritifera*, the eastern river pearl mussel. The last-named now occurs no farther south than the Little Schuykill River in Pennsylvania (Clarke 1977, 248), but during the Little Ice Age, which ended around A.D. 1800, this mussel may have occurred in Virginia waters. More to the point, all these pearl-producing mussels are freshwater species, which would make them local to the inner coastal plain. Pearls would be a status item to trade with downriver chiefdoms; if they came from *Margaritifera*, they would be also useful for trading with peoples farther south.

Animal hides, especially tanned deerskins, were also a luxury item when used in quantity. Elite people wore not only loin coverings but also multihide mantles, with fringes cut into them for conspicuous consumption. Deerskins were a standard item of tribute (Magnel 1969, 153; Smith 1986b, 174; Strachey 1953, 63). As we have seen, deer had become increasingly scarce by 1607 on the coastal plain, and that was especially true on the outer coastal plain where the necks of land are narrower. Deerskins would thus have been more readily available as status goods in the inner coastal plain.

Native copper had to be imported into eastern Virginia. It was found in small quantities in the piedmont (Hantman 1990, 1993; Turner 1992, 105) and in larger quantities in the Great Lakes region. The likely route into Virginia was from the Great Lakes southward and then across the mountains in North Carolina and finally to the North Carolina Siouans or Iroquoians, who were friendly with the Powhatans (see later discussion). Apparently ordinary Powhatan people could trade for copper, but Powhatan demanded most of what they bought in tribute. Powhatan also tried to insist upon a monopoly of English copper goods later (Strachey 1953, 107). Native copper was useful for trade anywhere in the Powhatan area, for all people desired it; none would sell it to the English later on (Archer 1969a, 93). It is specifically mentioned as the medium used to "hire" warriors, whether the employer was the paramount chief or a district chief (Strachey 1953, 107, 114).

When Virginia Indian people dressed up, they painted their faces, necks, and shoulders red. The preferred root for making paint they called puccoon, a name that two species of *Lithospermum* still bear (sources for both species are Brown and Brown 1984, 779; Harvill et al. 1986, 64; Radford et al. 1968, 883). One is hoary puccoon, *L. canescens*, which grows mainly in the mountains and less commonly in the piedmont in the middle Atlantic states and northward. Powhatan's major source of it in 1607 would have been the Siouan speakers who were his enemies, so we may rule that species out. Plain ("true") puccoon, *L. caroliniense*, is a southerly species that prefers sandhills. It occurs in only one county in all the middle Atlantic states (Harvill et al. 1986, 64): Sussex County, Virginia, which in 1607 was in friendly Nottoway territory to the south. The next closest place to find it today is in the southern coastal plain of South Carolina, a place then dominated by the chiefdom of Cofitachequi (Hudson and Tesser 1994). The plant material would have been accessible to Powhatan traders, if it was purchasable at all, through various North Carolina groups, with some of whom the paramount chief was known to be on reasonably friendly terms (Smith 1986a, 49, 53; Smith 1986c, 215; Strachey 1953, 56–57). Powhatan had a great deal of puccoon at his disposal; he needed plenty, for on important occasions he and all his many wives wore it. Puccoon is not mentioned in John Smith's list of tribute items; it apparently had to be imported. Puccoon may therefore have been a major item in the regular trade that Powhatan had with the "Anoegs" (Tuscaroras?). That trade was so frequent that the Weyanock district chief, Powhatan's emissary, had learned the Anoeg language (Strachey 1953, 56–57). The direction, south, correlates with the extent of Gaston ceramics outward from Powhatan's original inheritance of six districts. Such trade may have involved copper, thereby circumventing the hostile Monacans to the west (Turner 1993, 91–92).

The luxury goods observed by English writers (e.g., robes, hides, puccoon)—and used in status burials, which cannot be found archaeologically—indicate an advantage for eastern Virginia chiefs who lived in the inner coastal plain, especially for those living in the more southerly part of it, in the James and York river basins. Not surprisingly, that is where the first paramount chiefdom in Virginia arose.

Warfare leads to the consolidation of polities first into chiefdoms, then into paramount chiefdoms (Carneiro 1978, 207–8), especially in the case of economically self-sufficient towns which would otherwise have no reason to coalesce (Spencer 1987, 367). There are well-documented cases of chiefdoms arising for purely military reasons and whose leaders' power was primarily military (Little 1967a, 1967b, 182; Richards 1959, 37).[9] In other cases the rhetoric of consolidation will have a different ring, akin to the *pax romana* of the Romans and the "white roots of peace" of the Iroquois, but the military element will always be present. The result of population pressure has always been a steady tendency toward fewer autonomous polities, each one of larger size (Carneiro 1978). Stronger villages conquer weaker ones, and larger polities become chiefdoms, which then begin competing with each other, the victors eventually becoming paramount chiefdoms and finally states (Carneiro 1970; 1978, 207–8; 1981, 63–65; Johnson and Earle 1987, 21; Kirch 1984, 201, 206–7).

The Powhatan Indians traveled much of this road—and they did it rapidly. Military necessity, originating in population growth among socially circumscribed people living on concentrated resources, apparently built up and exploded many simple chiefdoms into a far-flung paramount chiefdom that covered most of the Virginia coastal plain—in the space of one human lifetime. Powhatan's own policy of acquiring new wives while visiting his territories from time to time must have helped the process.

In 1570 there were many district chiefs in eastern Virginia, as far as the Spaniards found out (Lewis and Loomie 1953, 108–9, 137, 161). By that time Powhatan's predecessor may have bound together the six districts that we know he inherited: Pamunkey, Mattaponi, and Youghtanund in the York River basin, and Appamattuck, Arrohateck, and Powhatan (the district) in the James River basin. The date of Powhatan's accession is unknown. He began expanding his holdings thereafter, working eastward and northward. We know that he took over the Kecoughtans in 1595 or 1596; he exterminated the Chesapeakes around 1607, though whether before or after the Jamestown colony was founded is uncertain. At unknown dates he brought the Virginia Eastern Shore under his sway, along with the chiefdoms along the Rappahannock River and the south bank of the Potomac. He had taken his "throne" name from the district where he was born; as he expanded his dominions eastward he moved his capital to Werowocomoco ("king's town"), in the lower reaches of the York River, a more central location. However, the highest-ranking religious site remained in Pamunkey territory, already a fairly central location.

The major recorded goals of Powhatan's conquests involved eliminating enemies and dissidents to the east. That meant not only taking over Kecoughtan and Chesapeake but also depopulating Piankatank in 1608 (Strachey 1953, 44, 68, 104–5). One major aspect of creating a paramountcy is forging a supradistrict loyalty, a supradistrict ethnic identity, if you will. That means achieving internal unification in both military and psychological terms. Depopulating places and then repopulating them with loyalists (done in all three districts mentioned) is one method. But Powhatan's most effective way of doing it seems to have been in setting his subjects against "outsiders." Males in the Powhatan world were trained to be aggressive; they proved they were "men" by going through a tough initiation aimed at binding them more to their chiefs than to their families. Powhatan the paramount chief then saw to it that his male subjects had the most to gain—in personal prestige and in rewards in status goods—from channeling their toughness and aggressions outward toward people like the Monacans and Massawomecks (Rountree 1989, 82, 87). Unification was not an easy task to accomplish, and Powhatan was known to have had quarrels in the past with his subordinates (Strachey 1953, 58). But he accomplished a great deal, as shown by the fact that when his paramount chiefdom crumbled, it did so slowly and only at the outer edges (Turner 1985, 213–15; Rountree 1990, chaps. 3–4). His original inheritance and also several downriver subjugated chiefdoms remained loyal to the paramount chief for as long as there was a paramount chief at all (Rountree 1990, chap. 4; 1993c).

Powhatan may in his early years have felt a greater military threat from the Siouans to the west than from the competitive Algonquians—and the visiting Europeans—to the east. This is indicated by his choice of direction of expansion. He could have worked at incorporating into his organization the Siouans, in whose territory were found more deer and some hoary puccoon. But instead he incorporated the Algonquians, slowly, over several decades, while remaining braced to face the Siouans. Similarity of dialects was probably not a major reason for his choice of whom to incorporate; the capturing and keeping of women and children in war had made most Woodland Indian towns into multilingual communities for many years (Rountree 1993b). A better reason for taking over the Algonquians may have been a desire to control more firmly the territories that produced shell for jewelry, the one luxury commodity not easily available through his original trading partners to the southwest.

Had a European threat (from the distant east) been a major factor in the swelling of his holdings, Powhatan would surely have acted more quickly than he did to incorporate the chiefdoms ringing the Chesapeake. The Chesapeakes would have been conquered or eliminated long before they actually were. Interestingly, when Powhatan finally did conclude that the English were inimical to him, a process that took until about 1610 (Rountree 1990, chap. 1), he made allies of his long-standing enemies, the Monacans (Strachey 1953, 106), who themselves were not yet threatened by the English presence. Therefore the part played by Europeans in causing the rise of the paramount chiefdom in the late sixteenth century was apparently small. The paramountcy arose mainly for reasons having to do with Indians (cf. Turner 1985, 209–11, 1993, 92–93).

The foregoing discussion has serious implications for our understanding of the development of chiefdoms, simple or paramount, elsewhere. First, any chiefdom with any amount of elaboration can, given the "right" conditions, flourish and yet leave little or no tangible trace of its passing. Such conditions consist in living in a wet climate, having a technology that uses little metal or stone, and building houses and disposing of dead chiefs entirely aboveground. It also helps to live in a region with such lush wild food resources that no agricultural intensification need be practiced to support the elite. Add a preference in the general populace for living in small hamlets and villages with a dispersed settlement pattern, and you have a nearly perfect recipe for frustrating archaeologists.

Second, any chiefdom and any paramountcy can be—and some probably were—relatively ephemeral, unstable polities. Earle (1987b, 289) has already said it; the Powhatans illustrate it vividly. Chiefdoms, unlike states, lack bureaucracies that give greater continuity when dynasties change (Earle 1987b, 291; Spencer 1987, 374–75). Chiefs are also essentially less powerful leaders, whose interference in their subjects' daily lives may be severely limited. Chiefs often need personal charisma, not only to assume power when the succession entitles them to it but also for the duration of their reign. A chief is, after all, "not a member of an elite class; rather, he is the elite member of his group" (Earle 1978, 11). He—or, occasionally in Virginia, she—must show by his or her comportment and actions that the elite status is deserved. The Powhatan case illustrates this necessity very well. The famous Opechancanough who succeeded Powhatan and led the two great attacks on the English in 1622 and 1644 was the third of the brothers and therefore second-place heir. But when Powhatan showed his age and the second brother proved decrepit as a leader, Opechancanough overshadowed them both and held the paramountcy together. Had there been no Opechancanough, perhaps another district chief would have emerged as paramount—after a period of interregnum. And the Powhatan paramountcy would then have lasted only two generations, the far-flung paramountcy only one. We know now that a paramountcy of considerable size can come and go quickly.

To describe any given chiefdom best, we must see it at its peak, however brief. Most of the chiefdoms in the southeastern United States flourished before the advent of Europeans and their records, so we have only archaeological evidence to tell us about them. The rate of development of chiefdoms varies depending on many factors (Carneiro 1987, 258), and these southeastern chiefdoms probably flourished earlier in part because environmental as well as social circumscription was present. But the Powhatans, living in a lush, northerly temperate coastal plain, so that social circumscription came later and environmental circumscription not at all, reached their peak later. It is our good fortune that they reached it (and may have gone farther if left alone) at the beginning of a colonization effort in Virginia, when some of the colonists were interested in sending home detailed records of the new and exotic things they saw. The Powhatans also were being observed by colonists whose reasons for being there, unlike those of the Spaniards or the English Puritans, were not so much religious ones to make them closed-minded as economic ones to make them interested in what they saw. The result was a richness of accounts of Indian life, at its political peak and before it was badly disturbed, that is unequaled elsewhere in North America. Between the reconstructions of ethnohistorians (Feest 1966, 1978b; Rountree 1989; Rountree and Turner 1994; Turner 1985) and archaeologists (see especially Potter 1982; also Turner 1976 and 1992), we know at least as much about the Powhatan paramount chiefdom—and why it evolved—as about other such chiefdoms in North America.

Notes

1. For example, there is Steponaitis's statement (1978, 419) that conical clans are common in chiefdoms. Yet conical clans are not documented for African chiefdoms, and the evidence for them in eastern North American societies is poor.

2. Powhatan chiefs were definitely involved in warfare; district chiefs were war captains. Chiefs were paid elaborate obeisance when they arrived on a visit. They also enjoyed the services of commoners (other than servants), who planted and harvested special corn fields for them.

3. John Smith, who saw more Powhatan people because he was in Virginia in peacetime, does not list puccoon among the items of tribute. On the other hand, William Strachey, who saw fewer people but had better interpreters for longer interviews, includes "dying roots" among the goods collected. Those roots could be either puccoon (*Lithospermum caroliniense*; Powh. *puccoon*) for painting people, or bloodroot (*Sanguinaria canadense*; Powh. *musquaspenne*) for painting objects.

4. There is nothing in the English sources to indicate whether the 100-plus was Powhatan's tally over a lifetime (a distinct possibility, and perhaps an underestimate) or constituted his holdings at the time John Smith met him (more difficult to accomplish in a paramount chiefdom with only 13,000–22,000 souls in it).

5. John Smith recorded that "Powhatan . . . and some others that are provident, ro[a]st their fish and flesh upon hurdles . . . and keepe it till scarce times" (1986b,

163). No similar practice is recorded for corn, a resource much more subject to periodic shortages than is fish.

6. The concentration of towns on the north side of the Rappahannock River (fig. 11.3) is potentially misleading. Most of them were hamlets, and their concentration was partly the result of the growth of the Powhatan chiefdom, leading them to settle on the far side of the river from Powhatan's capital (Speck 1925, 36; Turner 1982, 56).

7. The Chickahominies were not a chiefdom; instead they were ruled by eight elders.

8. The word *Powhatan* had multiple meanings in the early historical accounts of Virginia, including the "throne" name of the paramount chief in 1607, the term used by the English for his chiefdom, the village of his birth, and the river upon which his birthplace was located.

9. Timothy Earle believes that in the case of Polynesia, neither environmental nor social circumscription accounts for the rise of chiefdoms. Instead he sees the Polynesians' conical clans or ramages as contributing heavily to chiefly development (Earle 1978, 193–96). That may be true in Polynesia, but there is no clearcut evidence that the Powhatans had any clan or ramage system.

References

Abbott, R. Tucker
1974   *American Seashells.* 2nd edition. New York: Van Nostrand.
Archer, Gabriel
1969a   Relayton of the discovery of our river (1607). In *The Jamestown Voyages under the First Charter,* edited by P. L. Barbour, 80–98. Hakluyt Society 2nd series, no. 136. Cambridge: Hakluyt Society.
1969b   Description of the people (1607, authorship uncertain). In *The Jamestown Voyages under the First Charter,* edited by P. L. Barbour, 102–4. Hakluyt Society 2nd series, no. 136. Cambridge: Hakluyt Society.
Barker, Alex W.
1992   Powhatan's pursestrings: On the meaning of surplus in a seventeenth century Algonkian chiefdom. In *Lords of the Southeast: Social Inequality and the Native Elites of Southeastern North America,* edited by A. W. Barker and T. R. Pauketat, 61–80. Archaeological Papers of the American Anthropological Association, no. 3.
Beal, Ernest O.
1977   *A Manual of Marsh and Aquatic Vascular Plants of North Carolina with Habitat Data.* Technical Bulletin 247. Raleigh: North Carolina Agricultural Experiment Station.
Beverley, Robert
1947   *The History and Present State of Virginia* (1705). Edited by L. B. Wright. Chapel Hill: University of North Carolina Press.

Binford, Lewis R.

1964 Archaeological and Ethnohistorical Investigation of Cultural Diversity and Progressive Development among Aboriginal Cultures of Coastal Virginia. Ph.D. dissertation, University of Michigan, Ann Arbor.

Brown, Melvin L., and Russell G. Brown

1984 *Herbaceous Plants of Maryland.* Baltimore: Port City Press.

Brumfiel, Elizabeth M., and Timothy K. Earle

1987 Specialization, exchange, and complex societies: An introduction. In *Specialization, Exchange, and Complex Societies,* edited by E. M. Brumfiel and T. K. Earle, 1–9. Cambridge: Cambridge University Press.

Carneiro, Robert L.

1970 A theory of the origin of the state. *Science* 169:733–38.

1978 Political expansion as an expression of the principle of competitive exclusion. In *Origins of the State: The Anthropology of Political Evolution,* edited by R. Cohen and E. R. Service, 205–23. Philadelphia: Institute for the Study of Human Issues.

1981 The chiefdom: Precursor of the state. In *The Transition to Statehood in the New World,* edited by G. D. Jones and R. R. Kautz, 37–75. Cambridge: Cambridge University Press.

1987 Further reflections on resource concentration and its role in the rise of the state. In *Studies in the Neolithic and Urban Revolutions,* edited by L. Manzanilla, 245–60. BAR International Series 349. Oxford: BAR.

1988 The circumscription theory: Challenge and response. *American Behavioral Scientist* 31:497–511.

Clark, Wayne, and Helen C. Rountree

1993 The Powhatans and the Maryland mainland. In *Powhatan Foreign Relations, 1500–1722,* edited by H. C. Rountree, 112–35. Charlottesville: University Press of Virginia.

Clarke, Arthur H.

1977 *The Freshwater Molluscs of Canada.* Ottawa: National Museums of Canada.

Clayton, John

1965 The aborigines of the country: Letter to Dr. Nehemiah Grew (1687). In *The Reverend John Clayton,* edited by E. Berkeley and D. S. Berkeley, 21–39. Charlottesville: University Press of Virginia.

Coovert, Gary A., and Helen C. Rountree

n.d. The marginellas of Powhatan's mantle. In preparation.

Dobyns, Henry F.

1983 *Their Numbers Became Thinned: Native American Population Dynamics in Eastern North America.* Knoxville: University of Tennessee Press.

Earle, Timothy K.

1977 A reappraisal of redistribution: Complex Hawaiian chiefdoms. In *Exchange Systems in Prehistory,* edited by T. K. Earle and J. E. Ericson, 213–29. New York: Academic Press.

1978   *Economic and Social Organization of a Complex Chiefdom: The Halelea District, Kaua'i, Hawaii.* University of Michigan Museum of Anthropology, Anthropological Papers, no. 63. Ann Arbor.

1987a Specialization and the production of wealth: Hawaiian chiefdoms and the Inka empire. In *Specialization, Exchange, and Complex Societies,* edited by E. M. Brumfiel and T. K. Earle, 64–75. Cambridge: Cambridge University Press.

1987b Chiefdoms in archaeological and ethnohistorical perspective. *Annual Reviews in Anthropology* 16:279–308.

Earle, Timothy, ed.

1991   *Chiefdoms: Power, Economy, and Ideology.* School of American Research. Cambridge: Cambridge University Press.

Egloff, Keith T., and E. Randolph Turner III

1984   The Chesapeake Indians and their predecessors: Recent excavations at Great Neck. *Notes on Virginia* 24: 36–39.

Feest, Christian F.

1966   Powhatan, a study in political organization. *Wiener Völkerkundliche Mitteilungen* 13:69–83.

1973   Seventeenth-century Virginia Algonquian population estimates. *Quarterly Bulletin of the Archeological Society of Virginia* 28:66–79.

1978a Nanticoke and neighboring tribes. In *Handbook of North American Indians,* vol. 15: *Northeast,* edited by B. G. Trigger, 240–52. Washington, D.C.: Smithsonian Institution Press.

1978b Virginia Algonquians. In *Handbook of North American Indians,* vol. 15: *Northeast,* edited by B. G. Trigger, 253–70. Washington, D.C.: Smithsonian Institution Press.

1978c North Carolina Algonquians. In *Handbook of North American Indians,* vol. 15: *Northeast,* edited by B. G. Trigger, 271–81. Washington, D.C.: Smithsonian Institution Press.

1983   "Powhatan's mantle" and "skin pouch" [the "Virginia purse"]. In *Tradescant's Rarities,* edited by A. MacGregor, 130–37. Oxford: Clarendon Press.

Feinman, Gary, and Jill Neitzel

1984   Too many types: An overview of sedentary prestate societies in the Americas. In *Advances in Archaeological Method and Theory 7,* edited by M. B. Schiffer, 39–102. New York: Academic Press.

Fried, Morton H.

1967   *The Evolution of Political Society: An Essay in Political Anthropology.* New York: Random House.

Goody, Jack

1966   Introduction. In *Succession to High Office,* edited by J. Goody, 1–56, Cambridge: Cambridge University Press.

1967   The over-kingdom of Gonja. In *West African Kingdoms in the Nineteenth Century,* edited by D. Forde and P. M. Kaberry, 179–205. Oxford: Oxford University Press.

Gradie, Charlotte M.
1988 Spanish Jesuits in Virginia: The mission that failed. *Virginia Magazine of History and Biography* 96:131–56.
1993 The Powhatans in the context of the Spanish empire. In *Powhatan Foreign Relations, 1500–1722,* edited by H. C. Rountree, 154–72. Charlottesville: University Press of Virginia.

Hamor, Ralph
1957 *A True Discourse of the Present State of Virginia* (1615). Richmond: Virginia State Library.

Hantman, Jeffrey L.
1990 Between Powhatan and Quirank: Reconstructing Monacan culture and history in the context of Jamestown. *American Anthropologist* 92(3):676–90.
1993 Powhatan's relations with the piedmont Monacan. In *Powhatan's Foreign Relations, 1500–1722,* edited by H. C. Rountree, 94–111. Charlottesville: University Press of Virginia.

Harvill, A. M. Jr., Ted R. Bradley, Charles E. Stevens, Thomas F. Wieboldt, Donna M. E. Ware, and Douglas W. Ogle
1986 *Atlas of the Virginia Flora.* 2nd edition. Farmville, Va.: Virginia Botanical Associates.

Hudson, Charles, and Carmen Tesser, eds.
1994 *The Forgotten Centuries: Indians and Europeans in the American South, 1521–1704.* Athens: University of Georgia Press.

Hulton, Paul
1984 *America 1585: The Complete Drawings of John White.* Chapel Hill: University of North Carolina Press.

Johnson, Allen W., and Timothy Earle
1987 *The Evolution of Human Societies.* Stanford: Stanford University Press.

Kirch, Patrick V.
1984 *The Evolution of the Polynesian Chiefdoms.* Cambridge: Cambridge University Press.

Knight, Vernon James Jr.
1990 Social organization and the evolution of hierarchy in southeastern chiefdoms. *Journal of Anthropological Research* 46:1–23.

Lewis, Clifford M., and Albert J. Loomie
1953 *The Spanish Jesuit Mission in Virginia, 1570–1572.* Chapel Hill: University of North Carolina Press.

Lippson, Alice Jane, and Robert L. Lippson
1984 *Life in the Chesapeake Bay.* Baltimore: John Hopkins University Press.

Little, Kenneth
1967a The Mende chiefdoms of Sierra Leone. In *West African Kingdoms in the Nineteenth Century,* edited by D. Forde and P. M. Kaberry, 239–59. Oxford: Oxford University Press.

1967b *The Mende of Sierra Leone: A West African People in Transition*. Rev. edition. New York: Humanities Press.

Magnel, Francis

1969 Relation of what Francis Magnel, an Irishman, learned in the land of Virginia during the eight months he was there, 1 July 1610 (1610). In *The Jamestown Voyages under the First Charter*, edited by P. L. Barbour, 151–57. Hakluyt Society 2nd series, no. 136. Cambridge: Hakluyt Society.

Muller, Jon

1987 Salt, chert, and shell: Mississippian exchange and economy. In *Specialization, Exchange, and Complex Societies*, edited by E. M. Brumfiel and T. K. Earle, 10–21. Cambridge: Cambridge University Press.

Packard, Randall M.

1981 *Chiefship and Cosmology: An Historical Study of Political Competition*. Bloomington: Indiana University Press.

Percy, George

1921–22 A trewe relacyon. *Tyler's Quarterly* 3:259–82.

1969 Observations gathered out of a discourse of the plantation of the southern colonie in Virginia by the English 1606 (1608). In *The Jamestown Voyages under the First Charter*, edited by P. L. Barbour, 129–46. Hakluyt Society 2nd series, no. 136. Cambridge: Hakluyt Society.

Potter, Stephen R.

1982 An Analysis of Chicacoan Settlement Patterns. Ph.D. dissertation, University of North Carolina, Chapel Hill.

1993 *Commoners, Tribute, and Chiefs: The Development of Algonquian Culture in the Potomac Valley*. Charlottesville: University Press of Virginia.

Purchas, Samuel

1617 *Purchas His Piligrimes*. 3rd edition. London.

Quinn, David B., ed.

1955 *The Roanoke Voyages, 1585–1590*. Hakluyt Society 2nd series, no. 104. Cambridge: Hakluyt Society.

Radford, Albert E., Harry E. Ahles, and C. Ritchie Bell

1968 *Manual of the Vascular Flora of the Carolinas*. Chapel Hill: University of North Carolina Press.

Richards, Audrey L.

1940 The political system of the Bemba tribe—north-eastern Rhodesia. In *African Political Systems*, edited by M. Fortes and E. E. Evans-Pritchard, 83–111. London: Oxford University Press.

1959 *East African Chiefs: A Study of Political Development in Some Uganda and Tanganyika Tribes*. New York: Praeger.

Rountree, Helen C.

1989 *The Powhatan Indians of Virginia: Their Traditional Culture*. Norman: University of Oklahoma Press.

1990   *Pocahontas's People: The Powhatan Indians of Virginia through Four Centuries.*
       Norman: University of Oklahoma Press.
1993a Who were the Powhatans and did they have a unified "foreign policy"?
       In *Powhatan Foreign Relations, 1500–1722,* edited by H. C. Rountree, 1–19.
       Charlottesville: University Press of Virginia.
1993b The Powhatans and other Woodland Indians as travelers. In *Powhatan For-
       eign Relations, 1500–1722,* edited by H. C. Rountree, 21–52. Charlottesville:
       University Press of Virginia.
1993c The Powhatans and the English: A case of multiple conflicting agendas. In
       Powhatan Foreign Relations, 1500–1722, edited by H. C. Rountree, 173–205.
       Charlottesville: University Press of Virginia.
1996   A guide to the Late Woodland Indians' use of ecological zones in the Chesa-
       peake region. *The Chesopiean* 34(2–3).

Rountree, Helen C., and E. Randolph Turner III
1994   On the fringe of the southeast: The Powhatan paramount chiefdom in Vir-
       ginia. In *The Forgotten Centuries: Indians and Europeans in the American South,
       1521–1704,* edited by C. Hudson and C. Tesser, 355–72. Athens: University of
       Georgia Press.

Rowlands, Michael
1987   Power and moral order in precolonial west-central Africa. In *Specialization,
       Exchange, and Complex Societies,* edited by E. M. Brumfiel and T. K. Earle, 52–
       63. Cambridge: Cambridge University Press.

Sahlins, Marshall D.
1958   *Social Stratification in Polynesia.* Seattle: University of Washington Press.

Schwerin, Karl H.
1973   The anthropological antecedents: Caciques, cacicazgos, and caciquismo. In
       *The Caciques: Oligarchical Politics and the System of Caciquismo in the Luso-
       Hispanic World,* edited by R. Kern, 5–17. Albuquerque: University of New
       Mexico Press.

Service, Elman R.
1971   *Primitive Social Organization: An Evolutionary Perspective.* 2nd edition. New
       York: Random House.
1975   *Origins of the State and Civilization: The Process of Cultural Evolution.* New York:
       Random House.

Shorter, Aylward
1974   *East African Societies.* Boston: Routledge and Kegan Paul.

Smith, John
n.d.   Virginia Discouered and Described by Captayn John Smith, 1606 (1608, Map
       in various editions). Richmond: Virginia State Library.
1986a A true relation (1608). In *The Complete Works of Captain John Smith (1580–
       1631),* 3 vols., edited by P. L. Barbour, 1:3–118. Chapel Hill: University of
       North Carolina Press.
1986b A map of Virginia (1612, Historical section compiled from various texts by
       William Simmond). In *The Complete Works of Captain John Smith (1580–1631),*

3 vols., edited by P. L. Barbour, 1:119–90. Chapel Hill: University of North Carolina Press.

1986c The general historie of Virginia, New England, and the Summer Isles, 1624 (1624). In *The Complete Works of Captain John Smith (1580–1631)*, 3 vols., edited by P. L. Barbour, 2:25–488. Chapel Hill: University of North Carolina Press.

Speck, Frank G.

1925 The Rappahannock Indians of Virginia. *Indian Notes and Monographs* vol. 5, no. 3. New York: Heye Foundation.

Spelman, Henry

1910 Relation of Virginea (1613?). In *The Travels and Works of Captain John Smith*, edited by E. Arber and A. G. Bradley, ci–cxiv. New York: Burt Franklin.

Spencer, Charles S.

1987 Rethinking the chiefdom. In *Chiefdoms in the Americas*, edited by R. D. Drennan and C. A. Uribe, 369–90. Lanham, Md.: University Press of America.

Steponaitis, Vincas

1978 Location theory and complex chiefdoms: A Mississippian example. In *Mississippian Settlement Patterns*, edited by B. D. Smith and J. B. Griffin, 417–53. New York: Academic Press.

Strachey, William

1953 *The Historie of Travell into Virginia Britania.* Edited by L. B. Wright and V. Freund. Hakluyt Society 2nd series, no. 103. Cambridge: Hakluyt Society.

Taylor, Donna

1975 Some Locational Aspects of Middle-Range Hierarchical Societies. Ph.D. dissertation, City University of New York.

Turner, E. Randolph III

1976 An Archaeological and Ethnohistorical Study on the Evolution of Rank Societies in the Virginia Coastal Plain. Ph.D. dissertation, Pennsylvania State University.

1978a An intertribal deer exploitation buffer zone for the Virginia coastal plain— piedmont regions. *Quarterly Bulletin of the Archaeological Society of Virginia* 32(3):42–48.

1978b Population distribution in the Virginia coastal plain, 8000 B.C. to A.D. 1600. *Archaeology of Eastern North America* 6:60–72.

1982 A re-examination of Powhatan territorial boundaries and population ca. A.D. 1607. *Quarterly Bulletin of the Archaeological Society of Virginia* 37:45–64.

1985 Socio-political organization within the Powhatan chiefdom and the effects of European contact, A.D. 1607–1646. In *Cultures in Contact: The European Impact on Native Cultural Institutions in Eastern North America, A.D. 1000–1800*, edited by W. W. Fitzhugh, 193–224. Washington, D.C.: Smithsonian Institution Press.

1986 Difficulties in the archaeological identification of chiefdoms as seen in the Virginia coastal plain during the Late Woodland and early Historic periods. In *Late Woodland Cultures of the Middle Atlantic Region*, edited by J. F. Custer, 19–28. Newark: University of Delaware Press.

1992   The Virginia coastal plain during the Late Woodland period. In *Middle and Late Woodland Research in Virginia: A Synthesis,* edited by T. R. Reinhart and M. E. Hodges, 97–136. Archeological Society of Virginia, Special Publication no. 29. Richmond: Dietz Press.

1993   Protohistorical Native American interactions in the Powhatan core area. In *Powhatan Foreign Relations, 1500–1722,* edited by H. C. Rountree, 76–93. Charlottesville: University Press of Virginia.

Turner, E. Randolph III, and Anthony F. Opperman

1993   Archaeological manifestations of the Virginia Company period: A summary of surviving Powhatan and English settlements in tidewater Virginia, circa 1607–1624. In *The Archaeology of 17th Century Virginia,* edited by T. R. Reinhart and D. J. Pogue, 67–104. Archeological Society of Virginia, Special Publication no. 30. Richmond: Dietz Press.

n.d.   Searching for Virginia Company period sites: An assessment of surviving archaeological manifestations of Powhatan-English interactions, A.D. 1607–1624. Virginia Department of Historic Resources, Survey and Planning Report Series, in preparation.

Whitaker, Alexander

1936   *Good Newes from Virginia* (1613). New York: Scholars' Facsimiles & Reprints.

White, William

1969   Fragments published before 1614 (1608?). In *The Jamestown Voyages under the First Charter,* edited by P. L. Barbour, 147–50. Hakluyt Society 2nd series, no. 136. Cambridge: Hakluyt Society.

Widmer, Randolph J.

1988   *The Evolution of the Calusa: A Nonagricultural Chiefdom on the Southwest Florida Coast.* Tuscaloosa: University of Alabama Press.

CONTRIBUTORS

Robert L. Carneiro is curator of South American ethnology at the American Museum of Natural History.

Winifred Creamer is associate professor of anthropology at Northern Illinois University.

Jonathan Haas is MacArthur Curator of North American anthropology at The Field Museum.

Elsa M. Redmond is a research associate of anthropology at the American Museum of Natural History.

Charles S. Spencer is curator of Mexican and Central American anthropology at the American Museum of Natural History.

William C. Sturtevant is curator of North American ethnology at the National Museum of Natural History of the Smithsonian Institution.

Neil L. Whitehead is associate professor of anthropology at the University of Wisconsin, Madison.

Pita Kelekna received her Ph.D. in anthropology from the University of New Mexico in 1981 and resides in New York City.

Doris Kurella is curator of Latin American anthropology at the Linden-Museum, Staatliches Museum für Völkerkunde, Stuttgart.

William F. Keegan is curator of anthropology at the Florida Museum of Natural History, University of Florida, Gainesville.

Morgan D. Maclachlan is professor of anthropology at the University of South Carolina, Columbia.

Bryan Byrne is staff ethnographer at GVO, Inc., Palo Alto, California.

Jerald T. Milanich is curator of archaeology at the Florida Museum of Natural History, University of Florida, Gainesville.

Helen C. Rountree is professor of anthropology at Old Dominion University.

E. Randolph Turner III is senior prehistoric archaeologist in the Virginia Department of Historic Resources, Richmond.

Index

Numbers in italics indicate an
illustration.

Acosta, José de, 139
adumasis, 158
Ais Indians, 251, 252–53
Akwẽ-Shavante, 4
Apalachee Indians, 245–49, 251, 253–
  56, 260–61
Appamattucks, 267, 272, 279, 285
Arrohattocks, 267, 279, 285
Aruacas, 155, 157–59
arutam power, 9, 29, 75, 166–68
audiencia, 205, 209n.22

behetrías, 139
biased transmission, 48, 60n.1

Calusa Indians, 146, 159, 225, 246–49,
  251, 255, 259–60
Caquetío, 108–10
Caribs, 25–28, 155, 160, 207–8n.6;
  chieftain, 157–58; of Guiana, 25, 33–
  34; paramount chief, 2; selection of
  chiefs, 33–34; of Venezuelan coast,
  26, 33; wartime powers of chiefs, 23,
  26
Carneiro, Robert, 1, 13, 20, 58, 78, 129,
  138, 141, 154–55, 165, 169, 274–75
Casimiroids, 228

Castañeda, Pedro de, 50, 53, 54, 56–57
Castellanos, Juan de, 196, 201
Catío, 23
Cauca Valley: chiefdoms, 19, 37n.1,
  38n.3, 38n.7, 170, 172, 174–75;
  warfare, 169, 181
centralized leadership: archaeological
  evidence of, 7, 106–8, 115–21, 247–
  48; among autonomous village
  societies, 5–6, 70–71, 89–90, 94, 96–
  97, 169; conditions favoring, 5, 7, 10,
  12–13, 31, 47, 78, 80, 99, 129, 223,
  228, 235–36, 248; hereditary
  succession of, 10–11, 34–35, 78, 80,
  96–97, 129, 195, 221, 236–37, 272,
  285, 287; ritual sanctification of, 9–
  12, 96–97, 174, 196, 232, 235, 271
Chamuscado, Francisco Sánchez, 53–
  54
Chesapeakes, 267, 279, 281–82, 285–86
Chickahominies, 267, 276, 282, 289n.7
chiefdoms: administrative hierarchy
  of, 106–7, 231–33, 266, 273; archaeological evidence of, 44, 106–7, 110,
  112–28, 118, 120, 151–52, 154, 218,
  233, 247–48, 252–54, 257–59, 261–62,
  266, 268–70, 274, 279–80, 282, 287;

chiefdoms—*continued*
  avunculocal, 156, 217–18, 222–25,
    224, 228, 230, 232–33, 235–38;
  collapse of, 155, 157–58, 259;
  complex, 2, 12, 46, 218, 232–33, 246–
    50, 253–55, 257–62, 266, 269, 272;
  definition of, 1, 19–20, 44, 69, 105,
    141, 151, 159, 207n.3, 208n.9, 218;
  emergence of, 2, 10, 13, 19, 25, 34,
    36–37, 45, 69, 99, 128–29, 220, 236–
    37, 282, 285–86; historical documen-
    tation of, 1–3, 18, 26–28, 32, 108–10,
    138–41, 146, 150, 152, 155, 159, 169,
    205, 217, 235–36, 246–48, 250, 252–
    58, 266, 268–74, 278–79, 281–86, 288;
  political economy of, 107–8, 125–26,
    126, 198–200, 205, 209n.20, 220–22,
    232, 268–69; as response to histori-
    cal factors, 249–50, 252, 257, 259;
  theocratic vs. militaristic, 164;
  theory of development, 19, 21, 24,
    36, 128–29, 154, 220, 233, 273–75
chieftain: definition of, 3, 158, 160; in
    northern Rio Grande, 58; as ritual
    leader, 9, 11; Robb Roy as, 13n.2;
    social rank of, 12; training of, 11,
    34–35, 79–80, 96–97
chieftaincy: Chaco Canyon as, 7, 43–
    44; definition of, 3, 151, 160;
    duration of, 71–73, 75, 77, 228; Early
    Gaván phase as, 116, 117; as
    emergent simultaneous hierarchy, 4,
    9; geographical extent of, 70–74, 76–
    77, 80; hierarchical structure, 3–4, 6,
    69, 91–94, 93, 99; Hohokam as, 43;
    inherited leadership positions, 10–
    11, 34–35, 78, 221; permanent
    institutionalization of, 6, 10, 13, 78,
    221; Pueblos as, 44, 59; as response
    to historical factors, 8, 156–60
circumscription, environmental and
    social, 5, 8, 31–32, 128–29, 154–55,

160, 165, 183, 192, 225, 275, 278, 285,
    287–88, 289n.9
Colón, Bartolomé, 232
Colón, Cristóbal, 217, 229, 232, 235,
    238n.1
Colón, Diego, 238n.1
Colón, Hernando, 217
Cooper, Father John, 68
Coronado, Francisco Vázquez de, 53,
    56
curaca, 38n.10, 70–78

decision making: centralized, 47;
    consensual, 3–4, 58–59, 68, 139–40

Espejo, Antonio de, 53–54, 56

Fernández de Oviedo y Valdés,
    Gonzalo, 26, 39n.13, 217
Fort Walton culture, 245, 247–48, 254–
    56, 260–61
Fried, Morton, 20, 44, 141

Gaston ware, 279, 280, 284
Geertz, Clifford, 165, 181
Guane, 193, 201–2, 203

Hamor, Ralph, 270
Hobe Indians, 251, 252–53
Huitzilopochtli, 175–84

International Congress of
    Americanists, ix, xi

Jeaga Indians, 251, 252
Jiménez de Quesada, Gonzalo, 192
Jivaroan: acquiring shamanic power,
    77, 89–94; alliances,
    30, 71–72, 165; ecological factors, 32;
    myths, 166–67, 172, 174–75;
    shamans (uwíshin), 72, 75, 80, 90–
    94, 93, 99, 167, 171, 181–82, 184;

trading partners (amikri), 87–89, 88, 91; training of warriors, 29, 34–35, 74, 79–80, 166–67; tsantsa, 73, 168, 180, 184; uunt status, 72–73, 79, 90; war leaders (kakáram), 29–30, 34, 69–80, 168–69, 182
Johnson, Gregory, 1, 3–4, 6, 48

Kallinago, 26
Kecoughtans, 267, 279, 281, 285
Kuma, 4, 8–9

Las Casas, Bartolomé de, 217, 229, 232–33, 238n.2
llanos, 108, 113–18, 114, 126–29, 155–56, 209n.19

maikiua (Datura arborea), 75, 79, 166–67
Massim, 10–12
mechanisms of sociopolitical transformation, 2, 8, 10, 21, 34, 48
Melanesian big man, 8–10, 30–31, 84–85; synonymous with
chieftain, 3, 9, 218
middle-range societies, 2, 105, 154, 265
Miranha, 23
Mártir de Anglería, Pedro, 217
Menéndez de Avilés, Pedro, 254, 259
Mockley ware, 279, 280
Mocoso, 251, 258–59
Morales, Andrés, 217, 232
Moraughtacunds, 267, 271
Muisca, 207n.5; administrative hierarchy, 194–96, 195, 209; archaeological representation, 2, 197, 207n.2, 207–8n.6, 208n.14; emeralds, 201–2, 208n.16; gold, 200–204, 208n.15; historical documentation, 3, 156, 190, 192, 193, 205, 207n.4; long-distance exchange, 156, 191, 199–205, 203, 208n.11, 209n.19;

microverticality, 198–99, 208n.10; professional warriors (guechas), 198, 209; zipa and zaque chiefs, 193, 194, 196, 198

Nansemonds, 267, 275, 279
Nárvaez, Pánfilo de, 249, 260
natém (Banisteriopsis caapi), 75, 80, 90–92, 94, 166
northern Utina, 251, 255–56, 261
Northwest Coast tribes: as autonomous village societies, 20–21, 139; as chiefdoms, 20, 225

Oberg, Kalervo, 19–20, 141
Occohannocks, 267, 272
Oñate, Juan de, 53
Orinoco River: chiefdoms of, 108–10, 151, 153, 155–58; chieftains of, 154–56, 158–59; Parmana region, 110–12, 111–13, 127–28
Ostionoids, 228–29
Outina, 250, 251, 257

Pamunkeys, 267, 276, 285
Pané, Ramón, 217, 235
paramount chiefs, 28, 34–35, 58, 97, 142–44, 155–56, 194–96, 198, 201, 204, 209, 232–33, 235–36, 247, 265–66, 270–73, 281–82, 284–86
Paspaheghs, 267, 271
Patawomecks, 267, 272, 279, 281
peak, 282
Piankatanks, 267, 271, 285
Potano Indians, 250–52, 251, 254, 257, 259
Potomac Creek ware, 279, 280
Powhatan paramountcy, 2, 265–66, 267, 272–74, 277–78, 281–82, 285–88, 289nn.6, 8
puccoon (Lithospermum sp.), 283–84, 286, 288n.3

Puget Sound tribes, 20–21

Quijos, 23
Quiyoughcohannocks, 272

Rappahanocks, 267, 271
reciprocal altruism, 221
research designs, 106–8, 116
Rio Grande pueblos, 44, 49; archaeo-
    logical record, 50, 58; ceramic
    production, 52; historical documen-
    tation, 50, 53, 58; political organiza-
    tion, 53–54, 58; religious leaders, 59;
    trade, 51–52, 55, 58–59; warfare, 52,
    55–59
roanoke, 282
Roanoke ware, 279, 280

Safety Harbor culture, 258
Sahlins, Marshall, 5, 30, 68, 265
Saladoids, 227–28
Saturiwa, 251, 257–58
sequential hierarchy, 3–4, 48
Service, Elman, 1, 19–20, 35, 141, 157
shipwreck salvage, 248–49, 252–53
simultaneous hierarchy, 1, 4
Smith, John, 284, 288n.3, 288–89n.5
social ranking, 20, 35, 45, 107, 114,
    123–25, 123–24, 142–44, 196, 197
social status: achieved, 20, 59;
    ascribed, 20, 35, 143, 248, 254–55
Sosa, Gaspar Castaño de, 48–49, 53–57
Soto, Hernando de, 248–50, 254–56,
    258–59
Strachey, William, 269, 288n.3

Taino: complex chiefdoms, 12, 229,
    232–33, 234; historical
documentation, 146, 217, 228–29, 235–
    36; social order, 12, 230–33
Tapuya, 32

Tequesta Indians, 246, 251
Timucua, 140, 245, 247–50, 252, 254–58
Tocobaga, 251, 259
Townsend ware, 279, 280
trade: and chiefdom development,
    45–46, 85–86, 89–90, 95;
intervillage, 81–82, 85, 89, 202; long-
    distance, 108, 126–27, 144, 155–56,
    158, 169, 171, 199–205, 229, 235, 282–
    84; slave, 153, 156
Tupinambá: aldeia, 142–46;
    chiefdoms, 27, 32; chiefs, 23–24, 27,
    143, 145; ecological factors, 32;
    historical documentation, 3, 27, 32,
    140–41, 146; maloca, 141–43;
    peacetime powers of chiefs, 28;
    shaman (pajé), 145; wartime powers
    of chiefs, 23, 27, 144

Urriparacoxi, 251, 258–59
Uzachile Indians, 255–56, 261
Uzita, 251, 258–59

Waiwai administrative hierarchy, 97–
    99, 98
warfare: archaeological evidence of,
    108, 120, 122–23, 122, 125, 127, 129,
    279; among autonomous villages,
    22, 27, 81, 84, 94, 168–69; and
    ballgame, 172–74, 236; among
    chiefdoms, 108, 144, 155, 169–70,
    194, 198, 209, 235, 236, 255, 271–72,
    278–79, 281; and intervillage
    alliances, 22, 24, 27, 81, 84, 95; role
    in chiefdom emergence, 21, 24–25,
    31, 34, 36, 129, 154, 223, 233, 235–37,
    248–50, 255, 257, 261, 274–75, 282,
    284–85; and war captives, 25, 35,
    109, 125, 129, 142, 144–45, 169–71,
    177–79, 182, 198, 231, 286; and war
    leaders, 13n.3, 22–27, 69–80, 94–95,
    99n.1, 129, 279

Werowocomoco ("king's town"), 267, 272, 285
Weyanocks, 267, 271, 279, 284

Yanomamö: alliances, 22, 29, 81–82; ceremonial dialogue (wayamou), 82–84; ecological factors, 32; shamans, 95–97, 100n.1; trade, 81–82, 86; trade partnerships, 87; waiteri, 70; warfare, 68, 85, war leaders, 28–29, 69–70, 99n.1